Technology as Human Social Tradition

ORIGINS OF HUMAN BEHAVIOR AND CULTURE

Edited by Monique Borgerhoff Mulder and Joe Henrich

Technology as Human Social Tradition

Cultural Transmission among Hunter-Gatherers

Peter Jordan

UNIVERSITY OF CALIFORNIA PRESS

University of California Press, one of the most
distinguished university presses in the United States,
enriches lives around the world by advancing scholarship
in the humanities, social sciences, and natural sciences. Its
activities are supported by the UC Press Foundation and
by philanthropic contributions from individuals and
institutions. For more information, visit www.ucpress.edu.

Origins of Human Behavior and Culture, No. 7

University of California Press
Oakland, California

CIP data for this title is on file at the Library of Congress.

ISBN 978-0-520-27692-5 (cloth)
ISBN 978-0-520-27693-2 (pbk.)

Manufactured in the United States of America
23 22 21 20 19 18 17 16 15 14
10 9 8 7 6 5 4 3 2 1

The paper used in this publication meets the minimum
requirements of ANSI/NISO Z39.48–1992 (R 2002)
(*Permanence of Paper*).

Contents

Preface

This book examines three interlocking topics that are central to all archaeological and anthropological inquiry: the role of technology in human existence, the reproduction of social traditions, and the factors that generate cultural diversity and change. The overall aim is to outline a new kind of approach for researching variability and transformation in human material culture; the main argument is that these technological traditions exhibit heritable continuity: they consist of information stored in human brains and then passed on to others through social learning. Technological traditions can therefore be understood as manifestations of a complex transmission system; applying this new perspective to human material culture builds on, but also largely transcends, much of the earlier work conducted by archaeologists and anthropologists into the significance, function, and social meanings associated with tools, objects, and vernacular architecture.

In this new study, the main focus is on exploring how multiple material culture traditions are propagated through social learning, the factors that promote coherent lineages of tradition to form, and the extent to which these lineages have historical congruence with one another and with language. Chapters work through hunter-gatherer case studies set in Northwest Siberia, the Pacific Northwest Coast, and Northern California, generating cross-cultural and comparative insights on how and why different kinds of material culture traditions evolve and change. Overall, the analyses and approaches presented in this book promise new ways of exploring human cultural diversity, both in the deeper past and through to the present.

Acknowledgments

The research presented in this book has taken shape slowly, over a number of years. The work spans academic appointments in London, Sheffield, Aberdeen, and Groningen, as well as sabbaticals in Oslo and in Kyoto, and ethnoarchaeological fieldwork in Northwest Siberia. All this means that I have many friends, academic colleagues, and local communities to thank for all their encouragement, advice, practical assistance, hospitality, and general support along the way.

It all started with a postdoctoral research fellowship at the new Centre for the Evolutionary Analysis of Cultural Behavior (CEACB), Institute of Archaeology, University College London (UCL), which was funded by the UK Arts and Humanities Research Council (AHRC) and directed by Stephen Shennan. This period at UCL provided an enormously stimulating and yet also highly supportive intellectual environment in which to start exploring the general theme of cultural transmission, particularly in relation to Californian hunter-gatherer ethnography and the Western North America Databases.

I am very grateful for having had the chance to exchange ideas and establish contacts with many UCL staff, especially Andy Bevan, Mark Collard, James Connolly, Fiona Jordan, Stephen Shennan, James Steele, and Jamie Tehrani. Further funding from the AHRC led to the CEACB becoming the Centre for the Evolution of Cultural Diversity (CECD). This was a more extended research network led by James Steele, and it provided further context, direction, and practical support for the research that has eventually become this book.

The Siberian chapter draws on materials collected during a two-year Leverhulme Trust Special Research Fellowship (SRF/2002/0218), which was hosted at UCL and later at the Department of Archaeology, University of Sheffield. I am grateful to Peter Ucko, John Barrett, and the UK Leverhulme Trust for supporting this fellowship. In Siberia, I thank N.V Lukina, Konstantin Karacharov, and Andrei Filtchenko for their input, and I am also deeply grateful to all the Eastern Khanty communities I visited during ethnoarchaeological fieldwork, especially the families at Achimovy 1 and Achimovy 2, and also V.S. Kogonchin and Aleks Riskin for their logistical support in the remote field settings.

Many of the deeper insights into the importance of kinship and social institutions, and the contrasting ways in which they structure cultural inheritance, started to emerge only after sustained immersion in the Californian, Pacific Northwest Coast, and Siberian ethnography during a wonderful year spent at the Centre for Advanced Study (CAS) in Olso; these understandings functioned as comparative insights in the collaborative project on Early Networking in Northern Fennoscandia, led by Charlotte Damm.

Over the years that this book has taken shape, I recall fondly many insightful conversations with Marek Zvelebil (1952–2011) about the general theme of intergenerational cultural inheritance and its deeper relevance to the archaeology and anthropology of hunter-gatherers. I am also thankful to Sean O'Neill, CECD PhD candidate, for pointing out many novel features of Northwest Coast architecture, such as the modular design of the Coast Salish longhouses. The research was also presented in various conferences, symposia, and lectures, and the core ideas and conclusions were enriched, clarified, and strengthened thanks to many comments and questions received along the way. Specific conversations with Bob Bettinger, Olivier Gosselain, Brian Hayden, and Mike O'Brien all helped crystalize important ideas and questions during this period. I'm also grateful to Junzo Uchiyama for arranging stimulating research visits to the Research Institute of Humanity and Nature (RIHN) in Kyoto, where further progress was made.

As ideas for a more extended comparative analysis of hunter-gatherers, technology, and cultural transmission started to take clearer shape, Joe Henrich and Monique Borgerhoff Mulder encouraged me to publish this book in their new series with the University of California Press.

For that I am grateful. Blake Edgar has provided encouragement and support throughout the extended writing process, as well as timely reminders as the original (and rather optimistic!) writing schedule started to lapse.

External peer reviews of the first full manuscript led to substantive revisions. These changes were eventually completed, approved, and then further improved, thanks to a second round of external reviews and a final internal review at University of California Press. I thank Monique Borgerhoff Mulder, Aubrey Cannon, and the five anonymous reviewers for all their detailed comments and constructive suggestions throughout this process. Amazingly, Monique and Aubrey also took the time from their busy schedules to provide additional comments and valuable intellectual "steerage" on an intermediate draft. This provided an important psychological boost at a time when I felt I that the whole project was starting to founder.

With the book manuscript approved by University of California Press, the final stages have felt much more like plain sailing. Merrik Bush-Pirkle at University of California Press has provided close support and technical advice while compiling the final text and figures. In Groningen, Frits Steenhuisen of the Arctic Centre worked hard to produce all the base maps; all the other artwork was completed at short notice by Erwin Bolhuis, Siebe Boersma, Miriam Los-Weijns, and Sander Tiebackx in the Drawing Office at the Groningen Institute of Archaeology.

Beyond the realms of academia, I have benefited greatly from valuable friendships with Jörg Bröskamp, Rob McGowan, and Bob Hawley. In Aberdeen, many happy weekends were spent scaling remote Scottish peaks with Nick Spedding and Rob Bingham. During the final phases of writing, Nick also shared two memorable adventures in the Stubai and Ötztal Alps.

And as ever, my deepest personal thanks is reserved for the "home team" who provided their own kind of special encouragement and support, and in the end, made all this possible: Christine, Dave, Andrew, Susan, Lauren, Ben, Sarah, Cristian, Pablo, Manolo, Clarisa, and Paloma.

Note on Archiving of Data Sets

This book follows an "integrated publication" model.

All the original data sets from this book will be lodged with the *Archaeology Data Service* (see Jordan 2014a): http://archaeologydataservice.ac.uk/.

In addition, the author will publish an *Internet Archaeology Data Paper*: http://intarch.ac.uk/authors/data-papers.html (see Jordan 2014b).

This paper will complement and contextualize the data sets, describing their basic content and the methods used to create them. It also provides some suggestions for their likely reuse potential.

CHAPTER I

Introduction

UNDERSTANDING TECHNOLOGY AS A HUMAN SOCIAL TRADITION

One definitive feature of the human condition is reliance on highly sophisticated *technological* solutions. These physical objects are termed *material culture* and include elaborate tools for capturing, processing, and storing resources, technologies for travel, vernacular architecture, as well as all the other objects used by people in all spheres of social life. In general, however, people tend not to invent such objects and technologies for themselves through personal trial-and-error learning but predominantly acquire existing designs and cultural ideas from other people. Nor is this a relatively new phenomenon, linked only to the rise of modern urban and industrial life. Even in small-scale hunting and gathering societies, people primarily learn how to make useful things from other individuals during childhood and adolescence. And, of course, they may also add their innovations and improvements to these designs later on in life, passing these changes on to later generations. People actively participate in the reproduction of such cultural knowledge, and most technologies used by humans form long-term historical tradition that are passed on to others through exactly this kind of social learning.

As anthropologists and archaeologists frequently document, these enduring lineages of cultural tradition can extend in recognizable formats over many, many generations, in some cases persisting for millennia. But if these material culture traditions are reproduced through social learning, then whom people learn from, what they learn, why, and when can all have major cumulative effects on larger patterns of cultural diversity and change. In one way or another, exactly *how* such material culture lineages are reproduced, and *why* they are subject to continuity or transformation, have been the focus of debate for well over a century.

This book therefore examines three interlocking topics that are central to all archaeological and anthropological inquiry: the role of technology and material culture in social life; the reproduction of social traditions; the factors that generate and sustain cultural diversity. In fact, the overall aim of this book is to outline a new kind of approach for researching variability and change in material culture. This can be summarized as "Technology as human social tradition." The main argument is that human technological traditions exhibit heritable continuity: they consist of information stored in human brains that is then passed on to other individuals through social learning; people born into specific cultural settings acquire, participate in, and thereby reproduce these material culture traditions, transmitting them down to future generations. This system of inheritance involves both the reproduction and modification of cultural information, but also the expression of these ideas and skills in production of material objects over time. Such technological traditions can therefore be understood as *material* manifestations of a complex transmission system in which cultural information is inherited, reproduced, and cumulatively transformed by the actions of individuals and their communities.

Applying this perspective to human technology builds on, but also largely transcends, much of the earlier work conducted by archaeologists and anthropologists into the significance, function, and social meanings associated with patterns of continuity and change in material culture. In the nineteenth and early twentieth centuries anthropologists collected objects and artifacts from various cultures either to assess the cultures' relative levels of progress or to simply catalogue global cultural diversity in terms of the artifacts and objects used by different tribes and ethnic groups. But for most of the twentieth century, anthropological interest shifted to other themes such as kinship and religion, with material culture largely overlooked. More recently, there has been renewed interest in material culture research (Tilley et al. 2006) and in the anthropology of technology, that is, how individuals acquire and practice embodied craft skills within the daily routines of specific sociocultural settings (Ingold 2000; Leroi-Gourhan 1993; Mauss 1979; Stark et al. 2008a).

Archaeologists have also built most of their discipline on the recovery and documentation of human technology, but they have done so in a range of different ways, generating contrasting and at times contradictory insights into material culture variability and change. Until the early twentieth century, major changes in material culture were also used to map either general stages of human progress, and in the days before radiocarbon dating was developed, artifact lineages were used to construct relative chronologies and to trace the traditions and histories of different archaeological "cultures" as well as the prehistoric origins of modern ethnic groups and nation-states (Lyman et al. 1997; Shennan 1989; 2002a:67; 2009a:2; Trigger 2006:211–313). By the mid-twentieth century, archaeological interests had shifted toward investigating the functional roles played by artifacts, objects, and toolkits, especially among prehistoric hunter-gatherers. In this period, interests in the archaeology of cultural traditions was largely eclipsed by an overarching concern with studying the adaptive dynamics of human cultural systems, which required identification of cross-cultural regularities in technology across different environmental settings (Lyman et al. 1997:217, 230; Shennan 2002a:72, 184; Trigger 2006:480).

By the end of twentieth century, however, theoretical fashions were beginning to swing in the opposite direction, deliberately highlighting the local, idiosyncratic, and historically contingent nature of cultural phenomena, as well as the social and symbolic dimensions to material culture, the active role that objects play in social life, and their significance in expressions of identity, religion, and ideology (Hodder 1982, 1986). Some general interest in researching cultural traditions returned, but it was generally limited to examination of small-scale social settings and the description of the microroutines of daily practice. Less effort was directed to linking these small-scale processes to the deeper mechanisms of long-term culture change (Trigger 2006:444–78).

Most current anthropological and archaeological work on technology now tends to be united by a shared interpretive interest in the contextual significance of material culture (or "materiality') and its general historical contingency. The broad consensus is that creation of material culture through day-to-day practice forms part of the wider process of cultural and social reproduction and that this involves creativity and subjective cultural choices, and hence the agency and history of individuals and their social collectives (Apel 2001; Dobres 2000; Gosselain

1998; Ingold 2000; Killick 1994; Leroi-Gourhan 1993; Lomonnier 1993; Mauss 1979; McEachern 1998:246; Sillar 2000; Sillar and Tite 2000; and see Tilley et al. 2006).

This book takes a different tack. It draws on the substance, content, and focus of many of these earlier debates about the relative functional versus symbolic roles performed by material culture but takes research into new directions by employing some of these older concepts as useful points of departure. The main starting point is the absolutely central and now consensus idea that the practice of craft traditions form part of general cultural reproduction. However, the book argues that this renewed emphasis on understanding technology as a fundamentally *social* tradition—that is, as cultural information reproduced through social learning—generates some broad analogies with the ways in which evolutionary biologists have investigated the transmission of genetic information. Both genetic and cultural inheritance systems can therefore be argued to exhibit evolutionary properties of "descent with modification" (Boyd and Richerson 1985; Cavalli Sforza and Feldman 1981; Ellen et al. 2013; Lycett 2011; Mesoudi 2011; Mesoudi et al. 2006; O'Brien et al. 2013; Shennan 2002a, 2009b; Richerson and Boyd 2005).

On one level, exploring these analogies between cultural and genetic inheritance systems is important for archaeologists and anthropologists because, on a *heuristic* level, they generate new frameworks within which to think about the social reproduction of material culture traditions, especially the links between individual actions and long-term outcomes, including the broader patterns of variability and long-term culture change that result. On another, and perhaps more important *empirical* level, these analogies also provide a bridge for applying some of the powerful analytical methods developed in the biological sciences to material culture data sets, thereby tackling long-standing questions about the factors that generate continuity, diversity, and change in material culture traditions across an interlocking range of different social, spatial, and temporal scales.

One of the most important challenges is generating suitable data for implementing this kind of approach. Building on key arguments in the anthropology of technology, it is argued in this book that the composition of particular material culture traditions can be defined and documented in terms of distinctive sets of "cultural traits." This is because all craft traditions can be studied in terms of their unique production sequences, or "design grammars," which consist of different stages of production and the associated choices by human practitioners as to what materials or methods to deploy within the different production stages. Each of these choices can be defined as traits, and specific combinations of these design traits can then be argued to make up particular kinds of artifacts and their associated craft traditions. Defining and documenting these traits is therefore about understanding the inherent creativity and historical agency central to the practice of craft production. Moreover, large data sets recording variability in material culture can be generated by the same trait-based approach and then subjected to further analysis, hypothesis testing, and contextual interpretation in order to understand how specific technological traditions have diversified and changed over time.

If this general approach holds fast—and if material culture variability and change can be productively approached in terms of dynamic social traditions—then three overarching research themes emerge:

1. *Propagation of Cultural Traditions.* How are material culture traditions reproduced through social learning; how do individuals acquire knowledge of specific design traits and how best to combine them; what factors promote them to maintain or adjust these traditions; what patterns of cumulative change are generated?

2. *Coherence in Cultural Traditions.* To what extent do material culture traditions consist of particular combinations of design traits; is there just a rapid and relentless mixing of traits, or do specific combinations form coherent designs endure in recognizable formats over generations? At what social scales do such coherent lineages of tradition emerge? To what extent can the deeper history of these coherent lineages be reconstructed, and what forms do these histories take? Do they undergo repeated splitting processes, with the branching away of new descendent traditions, all of whose genealogies can be traced back to a common ancestor?

3. *Congruence among Cultural Traditions.* Does each lineage of tradition have its own independent history, or are technological traditions propagated in ways that ensure that a number of different traditions eventually become bundled together?

This book systematically addresses these three themes, applying a descent-with-modification perspective to the study of material culture traditions across a range of concrete empirical case studies. These are united by a shared focus on understanding the technologies of different hunting and gathering societies across a range of different cultural settings.

This research is neither limited to anthropology nor directed just at an archaeology readership—its themes and approaches span both disciplines: the case studies employ anthropological information and ethnographic data, but many of the questions addressed, and the insights that are produced, are of equal relevance to archaeologists seeking to understand the significance of spatio-temporal patterning in prehistoric material culture. In this sense, the book can best be understood as an interdisciplinary exercise in hunter-gatherer *ethnoarchaeology* (David and Kramer 2001; Lane 2014), one that undertakes a sustained contextual and comparative analysis of material culture evolution, integrating it to the newly emerging science of cultural diversification and change that now spans archaeology, anthropology, biology, evolutionary psychology, and historical linguistics (Ellen et al. 2013; Henrich and McElreath 2003; Lycett 2011; Mesoudi 2011; O'Brien et al. 2013; Rogers and Ehrlich 2008:3416; Shennan 2009b; Steele et al. 2010).

This introductory chapter aims to contextualize the aims of the research, its general approach, and the debates and questions it addresses. It starts from first principles by examining the unique sophistication of human social learning and the ways in which it underpins the maintenance of cumulative cultural traditions. It then examines how cultural transmission theory, which was inspired by exploring some of the broad analogies between cultural and genetic inheritance, can be used to provide a general framework for examining the reproduction of cultural traditions within different populations, and also how some of these specific processes of cultural *propagation* link directly into long-standing anthropological and archaeological debates about large-scale patterning in the *coherence* and historical *congruence* of different material culture traditions. Chapter 2 outlines the central methodology, chapters 3, 4, and 5 contain the main case studies, and chapter 6 undertakes a cross-cultural comparative analysis of the overall results, linking these insights back to general debates about variability and change in material culture.

WHAT MAKES HUMAN CULTURE UNIQUE?

The human species is unique. What makes it so special is the highly developed capacity for maintaining cumulative cultural traditions through the practice of teaching, imitation, and other forms of social learning. But biologists are quick to point out that the enormous species gulf between humans and other even closely related animals is only a *relative* one. Understanding some of these relative similarities and differences forms a useful starting point for examining what is so distinctive about human social learning and the elaborate cultural traditions that it can sustain.

A broad distinction can be made between *individual trial-and-error* learning and *social* learning. According to the former, individuals learn directly from their own experiences of the surrounding world. However, when this individual dies, these accumulated understandings are lost, and each new offspring must embark anew on his or her own process of environmental learning (Shennan 2002a:38, 2002b:185–86). In contrast, social learning involves acquiring information from *other* members of the same species, which can lead to replication of that information over time. This distinction rests on the *source* of the information learned and is not about the specific information content (Shennan 2002b:186). Thus, "social learning is learning that is facilitated by observation of, or interaction with, another individual" (Hoppit and Laland 2013:4).

Although learning from other individuals is central to the reproduction of human culture, for example, in language or in craft traditions, social learning in itself is not unique to humans, and transmission of this kind of nongenetic information between individuals is surprisingly common among a wide range of organisms (see Bentley et al. 2008; Danchin et al. 2010; Humle and Newton-Fisher 2013; Krützen et al. 2005; Laland et al. 2013; Lycett 2010, 2011; McGrew, 2004; Van Schaik et al. 2003; Whiten, 2007, 2010; Whiten et al. 1999; Whiten et al. 2005; and see Hoppit and Laland 2013 for a general overview

However, the mechanisms by which such traditions are maintained are very variable and span a wide range of cognitive complexity (Shennan 2002b:188). An insightful way to examine the central features of human cultural transmission systems is to run through a short comparative analysis of social learning among humans and chimpanzees, their closely related sister genus (see general summary by Whiten 2011; table 1.1). The goal here is to distinguish which features of social learning and cultural transmission can be ascribed to common ancestry, and which features reflect changes since the ancestral divergence around 6–7 million years ago (Whiten 2011:998). Exploring exactly what makes human social learning capable of sustaining the intergenerational transmission of so many rich and diverse forms of cultural information quickly becomes central to understanding the deeper evolutionary dynamics of their technology and material culture.

Understanding cultural transmission involves studying social traditions. Thus, it is important to define exactly what constitutes a

TABLE 1.1 FEATURES OF CULTURE SHARED BETWEEN HUMANS AND
CHIMPANZEES VERSUS FEATURES OF CULTURE THAT ARE DISTINCTIVE TO HUMANS

	Shared Features (chimpanzees and humans, and, by inference, their last common ancestor)	Distinctive in Humans (evolved since ancestral divergence 6-7 million years ago)
1. *Social Learning Process*		
a. Copying sophistication	Includes emulation and imitation, with adequate copying fidelity	Imitation can be very high fidelity
b. Selective and rational copying	Sensitivity to features both causal and psychological	Rational imitation can be more selective
c. Conformity	Limited evidence of conformity to majority	Strong conformity common: essential for communicative conventions
d. Ratcheting	Existence inferred in technology, yet minimal	Repeated upgrading of repertoire by invention and social learning
e. Teaching	Minimal, limited to "scaffolding"	Elaborate and verbal in some contexts
2 *Cultural Content*		
a. Social	Social customs, tool use, dialects	Includes language and symbolic conventions
b. Physical	Extensive tool-kits and foraging techniques	Vast repertoire of material culture traditions
3. *Population Level Patterning*		
a. Multiple diverse traditions	More than forty traditions in each species	Numerous traditions ("countless")
b. Communities have unique traditions	Distinct local cultures, includes suites of traditions	Local cultures differ in *vast* numbers of ways
c. Cumulative cultural evolution	Existence inferred in technology, yet minimal	Extensive, elaborate, potentially progressive and continuing

SOURCE: Adapted from Whiten 2011:998.

social tradition; following Fragaszy and Perry (2003:xiii), this can be defined as a "distinctive behaviour pattern shared by two or more individuals in a social unit, which persists over time and that new practitioners acquire in part through socially aided learning." This definition is important because it renders culture as a community-level phenomenon, minimally defined by a tradition shared by at least two individuals, but typically many more (Whiten 2011:999). It also includes the requirement for *persistence,* which has two implications: (1) traditions can become more substantial as they spread from a minimum of two individuals, and then potentially across larger communities and populations; (2) these traditions are enduring and can potentially persist over multiple generations (Whiten 2011:997). It is these features of culture that enable each new generation to build on the innovations of the previous one, meaning that human traditions involve transmission, but also the more selective capacity for accumulation and editing of this cultural information. It is these combined features of human cumulative culture that make it possible to argue that their cultural traditions can evolve according to principles of descent with modification.

Working through the details summarized in table 1.1, it is clear that *three* broad themes make the attributes and capacities associated with human cultural traditions quite different than those of even closely related primate species: (1) specific social learning processes, (2) unique cultural content, (3) distinctive population-level patterning.

In particular, it is the sophisticated social learning processes that appear to underpin the distinctive features of human cultural traditions (table 1.1: 1 a–e). Human copying includes both emulation (reproducing end results) and imitation (reproducing actions); in fact, the highly developed capacity for imitation among humans may be key to the phenomenon of cumulative culture, and it certainly seems to be important in the emergence and long-term stability in cognitively opaque and often essentially arbitrary human technological traditions such as stone-tool making, basketry, and pottery (Tehrani and Riede 2008; Want and Harris 2002; but see Caldwell and Millen 2009).

This highly developed human capacity for social learning is important, because it underpins (1a) "copying sophistication and fidelity" (Whiten 2011:1001)—there has to be fidelity, otherwise traditions cannot persist in recognizable format. In fact, this kind of high-fidelity transmission appears to be one of the key drivers of human cumulative culture (Lewis and Laland 2012) and is underpinned by a package of other sociocognitive processes—including teaching through verbal instruction, imitation, and also prosociality (Dean et al. 2012), such that teaching, language, and cumulative culture can all work together to reinforce one another.

Humans also engage in (1b) "rational" copying" (Whiten 2011:1002)—this means that humans' imitation mechanisms include a substantial element of selectivity. There is also (1c) a striking degree of "conformity" in human cultural traditions (Whiten 2011:1002–3)—the apparently deep and enduring human motivation to be like others in a small-scale social group has long been a phenomenon studied by social psychologists (and see Pagel and Mace 2004). Another important feature of human social learning is (1d), "ratcheting versus conservatism"—in human culture, progressive accumulation and improvement plays important roles, probably because humans tend to imitate, whereas chimpanzees rely to a greater extent on emulation (Whiten 2011:1003; and see Tomasello et al. 1993; but also Caldwell and Millen 2009).

Humans also engage in (1e), explicit "teaching" (Whiten 2011:1003). The subject of teaching is now, in fact, a major interdisciplinary research field spanning cognitive psychology, comparative biology, anthropology, and archaeology (Csibra and Gergely 2006, 2011; Richerson and Boyd 2005; Tehrani and Riede 2008; Tomasello et al. 1993; Want and Harris 2002). Many human cultural traditions pose enormous learnability problems, and simple imitation alone cannot account for high-fidelity human copying; it must be reinforced through other mechanisms (Tehrani and Riede 2008:318). These range from direct teaching and explicit linguistic interaction (e.g., Tomasello et al. 1993) through to the broader concept of "natural pedagogy," which is "a particular kind of social learning in which knowledge or skill transfer between individuals is accomplished by communication" (Whiten 2011:1150).

At a general level, this involves experienced individuals modifying their behavior in ways that include implicit communicative gestures in order to facilitate the learning of a novice. Such gestures might include simple expressions of approval or disapproval, which help replicate arbitrary traditions (Castro and Toro 2004); a pedagogical instinct that expresses itself in "motherese," for example, when distinctive tone, vocal modulations, eye contact, and infant-directed speech are used when parents address children (Csibra and Gergely 2011:1150), as well as in a range of other cues that enable parents and tutors to increase the efficiency of social learning. These forms of communication are important in focusing attention on functionally important aspects of behavior, skill, or sets of tasks, and this kind of relevance-guided instruction is particularly essential for transmission of difficult-to-master skills (Csibra and Gergely 2006, 2011).

The acquisition of complex cultural traditions—such as crafting and tool-making skills—is generally based on acquiring combinations of different kinds of information, including routinized motor patterns that are eventually enacted automatically without much conscious thought. These skills are not so much taught as discovered anew via "progressive teaching" or "scaffolding" (Tehrani and Riede 2008:320). This often includes repeated cycles of demonstration of the complex motor tasks and then self-practice for cumulative reinforcement and correction, all of which make human cultural learning an extended and very complex cognitive process (Shennan 2002b). In general, there is huge global diversity in child-rearing practices, but all these practices appear to be united by at least some form of communication, either explicit, or implicit, or a mix of the two, all of which enable more experienced practitioners to transmit to novices a wide variety of cultural knowledge, ranging from how to make artifacts, conventional norms and behaviors, arbitrary referential symbols, and a range of other cognitively opaque skills and know-how (Whiten 2011:1152–54). In fact, it exactly this kind of communication-aided teaching, broadly defined, that marks out human cultural transmission as being so different (Csibra and Gergely 2011; Whiten 2011:1150).

The next important theme is to examine how these uniquely human social learning mechanisms make the "cultural content" of their traditions so distinctive (Whiten 2011:1004; table 1.1, part 2 a, b). First, human social culture also has symbolic reinforcement of systems of rules and institutions that regulate actions, including language itself, through to ceremonial traditions, dance, music, and religion (2a). Second, human technological traditions embrace an enormous range of complex subsistence-related tools and equipment that are used even by highly mobile hunter-gatherers (2b), including hafted and multicomponent weaponry and tools, leather clothing, knots, lashings, mats, basketry, and other woven fabrics (Whiten 2011:1004).

Third, what are the broader outcomes of these unique human capacities for maintaining cultural traditions? (See table 1.1, part 3 a, b, c.) Many of the cultural traditions passed on by social learning in fish, bird, and other mammal populations concern only *single* patterns of behavior. In contrast, (3a) human culture differs profoundly in encompassing countless traditions that span a huge range of behaviors. No species even comes close to this breadth and diversity. Interestingly (3b), social learning in chimpanzees also sustains "local cultures incorporating, and differentiated by, multiple traditions," such that chimpanzees also live in communities able to display unique cultural profiles for a defined subset of such traditions (Whiten 2011:999–1000). However, this does not really compare to the ways in which distinctive cultures are expressed by humans in vast numbers of ways. Finally, and perhaps most crucially, humans also exhibit (3c) "cumulative cultural evolution" (2011:1001). This capacity enables cultural achievements developed in one generation to be retained by the next one and further refined, a phenomenon reflected in the vast complexity and variety of human cultures today, for example, in relation to technology, language, and social institutions. In other species, cumulative culture is at best rudimentary, though the reasons for this remain poorly understood, but it must be linked to the evolved human capacity for sophisticated, high-fidelity, and selective social learning.

Implications for Human Culture: "History Matters—Pass It On"

Thus, humans are strikingly different from even closely related primate species in requiring social learning mechanisms to become such an enormous and essential part of their behavioral repertoire. For example, the oldest form of human subsistence adaptation is hunting and gathering, and yet even the daily practice of foraging requires skills, strategies, and bodies of knowledge that have accumulated and been refined over many, many generations. In addition, the wide range of ethnographically documented forager societies would not be able to inhabit such utterly diverse ecological settings as Arctic sea ice and tropical rainforests without complex multicomponent tools such as toggling harpoons, blow guns, poison-tipped arrows, sleds, kayaks, warm winter clothing, snow knives, and knowledge of how to build basic shelters, as well as baskets, pottery, and other containers for transporting, processing, and storing foods and fuels.

Each of these items of technology embodies stocks of knowledge and skill that couldn't be learned in an entire human lifetime of simple, individualized trial-and-error experimentation. Instead, the objects represent bodies of cultural knowledge that are reproduced, refined, and adjusted over many generations in the form of enduring lineages of tradition. These diverse material culture traditions are complemented by other forms of nonmaterial culture, such as deeper understandings of how to hunt seal through the winter ice or to detoxify seeds and obtain medicinal plants from a tropical rainforest. These bodies of cultural knowledge are also passed on in the form of socially learned rules, heuristics, and techniques, often with little or no understanding of how or why they work in practice (Henrich and McElreath 2003).

To summarize, human existence has several strikingly different features. One is the maintenance of large numbers of *cultural traditions*. The second is the widespread use of *complex technologies*—these are the elaborate multicomponent tools, artifacts, built structures, and other items of material culture that people learn to construct and use as part of their daily engagements with the world. Since earliest prehistory, material culture traditions like stone-tool making, basket weaving, and pottery manufacture have all been developed and maintained through the evolved human capacities for sophisticated social learning. This capacity for high-fidelity replication and selective improvement appears to underwrite the human capacity for cumulative culture, which is as much an evolved characteristic of human biology as being able to walk upright (Henrich and McElreath 2003:1, 27).

WHAT GETS PASSED ON?

These general insights into the cumulative nature of human culture are important, but they immediately generate some deeper questions: What exactly gets passed on during human social learning? Earlier work on this theme had sought to identify discrete "units" or "memes" of cultural inheritance that were able to replicate themselves (Dawkins 1976). However, this simple "meme-as-replicator" model is problematic because the process of cultural inheritance is far more complex (Shennan 2002a:47). Similarly, social and cultural anthropologists are quick to emphasize that cultural knowledge is not passed on in a ready-made formats via a simple process of information transmission, akin to a kind of telegraphic transfer system, but that knowledge undergoes a process of continual regeneration through the social contexts of interaction that link novices and instructors (Ingold 2007:17).

More recent work on cultural inheritance has therefore shifted toward broader and more fluid concepts such as the generic term *cultural information* (Boyd and Richerson 1985; Richerson and Boyd 2005; Shennan 2000, 2002a; Smith 2001:96), which can be defined as skills, beliefs, values, and attitudes that are stored in human brains and acquired from others by teaching, imitation, and other forms of social learning (Richerson and Boyd 2005:61). In fact, there are many reasons to believe that what is transmitted is neither discrete nor faithfully transmitted, so the flexible and more general term of *cultural variant* is probably more appropriate (2005:63), at least when discussing human cultural inheritance in more generic terms.

There is also growing interest in understanding how these cultural variants are reproduced as social traditions. Noting that Kroeber and Kluckholm (1952) once listed 168 different definitions of culture, Whiten et al. have argued that the term *tradition* is less controversial (e.g., Whiten et al. 2011:940). In this sense, a tradition can be defined as "a distinctive behaviour pattern shared . . . and acquired by social aided learning." They key point here is that new traditions can emerge and and persist over multiple generations, so the importance of social learning is embedded within the concept. In other words, it is the enactment of the enduring tradition that is social, rather than the constituent cultural variants that they reproduce.

Luckily, more precise definitions of "cultural information" or "cultural variant" have long been deployed in the study of material culture traditions (see chapter 2). Here, the choices made at different stages in the production of complex technologies like basketry, skis, or tailored clothing can be defined as "cultural traits," with the presence and absence of such traits documented across different artifacts. Of course, the knowledge, insights, and skills associated with the reproduction of these traits are acquired through observation, imitation, and other forms of social learning, are stored as information in human brains, and are then deployed strategically and creatively in further craft production activities—this creates heritable continuity. Variability in such traits, and the ways in which they are combined across different traditions and social groups, can then be recorded through systematic ethnographic survey. Importantly then, the defining, recording, and studying of distribution of such traits involve understanding human decision-making processes and the ways in which this creativity and historical agency generates broader patterns of cultural diversity and longer-term transformation (see Ingold 2007:16) Together, these combined features of heritable continuity on the one hand, and the cumulative addition of novelties and change on the other, also mean that these human cultural traditions can also be argued to exhibit evolutionary properties of descent with modification (e.g., Lycett 2011; and see following).

RESEARCHING CULTURAL EVOLUTION

If the propagation of human cultural traditions can be examined from this kind of ' social learning' perspective, then what is the best theoretical framework for investigating the deeper, cumulative dynamics of this historical process? Specifically, what creates different spatial and temporal patterns of variability and change in different cultural traditions?

Exploration of this kind of descent-with-modification perspective on the history of human cultural traditions builds on the foundations of dual inheritance theory (or cultural transmission theory) associated with the work of Boyd and Richerson (1985) and Cavalli Sforza and Feldman (1981). Its main argument is that humans possesses *two* distinct systems of information transfer, one *genetic* and the other *cultural* (see also Mesoudi et al. 2006; Mesoudi 2011; O'Brien et al. 2013; Richerson and Boyd 2005; Shennan 2002a, all with references). The biological inheritance system involves replication of genetic information via sexual reproduction and is shared by humans and other animal species. Simply put, human parents pass their genes on to their biological offspring, but to no one else.

In contrast, the inheritance system involved in the replication of cultural traditions is purely cultural; it involves the transfer of cultural information between individuals via social learning, as examined previously. And although people can and do acquire substantial information through their own trial-and-error experimentation, they most often tap into the enormous bodies of accumulated cultural information by learning socially from others. Having acquired this information, they replicate and modify it through their own actions and practices before passing it on to others, all of which can generate a kind of dynamic heritability in long-term cultural traditions. This means that these cultural traditions, just like genes, can also be understood as a complex system of information transmission that exhibits evolutionary properties (Lycett 2011; Mesoudi et al. 2006:329).

Before examining this relatively new perspective in some greater detail, it is important to define what is meant by an *evolutionary* approach to culture in order to clarify how it relates to other kinds of evolutionary thinking. This also serves to situate the current descent-with-modification approach within earlier streams of research.

Defining Cultural Evolution

The concept of evolution has had a long history, and many of the central ideas have changed significantly during the past hundred or so years, with some undergoing fundamental revisions in the past fifty years. In archaeology and anthropology, by far the most influential strand of evolutionary thinking has been the idea of "progressive" social evolution. This emerged in the later nineteenth century and was associated initially with Herbert Spencer and Lewis Henry Morgan, charting general cultural developments from the stages of "savagery" through to "barbarism" and eventually to "civilization" (see Pluciennik 2005). In the mid-twentieth century, a more multilinear understanding of cultural evolution emerged through the work of V. Gordon Childe and Julian Steward; others, like Leslie White, continued to focus on understanding more general patterns of cultural evolution (Childe 1951; Steward 1955; White 1949, 1959). These perspectives had emerged in the 1930s and 1940s and influenced archaeology and anthropology in the 1950s and 1960s. These by now neoevolutionary approaches were eventually combined with ecological neofunctionalist thinking in the work of Elman Service, Marshall Sahlins, and Marvin Harris (Shennan 2009a:1–2; Trigger 2006:386–444). However, just as these two general strands of evolutionary thinking (social evolution and neoevolutionism) came under sustained critique within each discipline throughout the 1970s and 1980s (Trigger 2006:444–78), the evolutionary branch of anthropology began a process of intellectual renewal, largely because of integration of earlier developments that had taken place outside the discipline some decades earlier (Shennan 2009a: 2).

These previous developments were all associated with the early to mid-twentieth century neo-Darwinian "modern evolutionary synthesis" in biology, which successfully integrated Mendelian theories of genetic inheritance with Darwinian processes of natural selection (see Huxley 1940, 1942). This provides a widely accepted view of biological evolution in which transmission, mutation, selection, and drift combine within in the general process of descent with modification. This process works at different scales, generating changing frequencies of genetic traits *within* populations (microscale evolution) but is also linked to evolution of traits across populations, where phylogeny (a branching tree diagram) reconstructs the general tendency for new evolutionary lineages, such as species, to split away from ancestral forms (macroscale evolution).

Central concepts of the modern evolutionary synthesis were slowly incorporated into anthropology, initially spawning the controversial field of human sociobiology, which explored links between patterns of human social behavior and the process of natural selection (Dawkins 1976; Shennan 2009a:2, 11–12; Wilson 1975), or how different human cultural and social institutions affect individuals' survival and reproductive success (Chagnon and Irons 1979). This field eventually fragmented into two new branches, the first being evolutionary psychology (Bentley et al. 2008:120–22; Fuentes 2009:44–52; Shennan 2002a:15–16, 2009:3; Smith 2000), and the second being human behavioral ecology (Bentley et al. 2008:117–20; Fuentes 2009:38–44: Shennan 2002a:15–16; 2009:3–4; Smith and Winterhalder 1992; Winterhalder and Smith 2000).

Meanwhile, a *third* neo-Darwinian approach was emerging: dual inheritance theory (or cultural transmission theory). This was developed through the work of Cavalli Sforza and Feldman (1981), and initially involved experimentation with modified mathematical models developed in population genetics to understand how cultural attributes (as opposed to genes) were passed on from one person to the next by social learning, and how these processes could eventually have larger-scale outcomes by affecting the frequencies of cultural attributes carried within human populations over time. A first full statement of the dual inheritance approach was eventually set out in their *Cultural Transmission and Evolution: A Quantitative Approach* (1981) and established a basis for modeling cultural changes within a modern evolutionary framework (Shennan 2009a:3). This was followed by publication of Boyd and Richerson's *Culture and the Evolutionary Process* (1985) and later by Durham's *Coevolution: Genes, Culture and Human Diversity* (1991).

Elements from this broader evolutionary approach to cultural transmission provide the main theoretical framework for the book. Genes and culture are approached as two analytically distinct systems of inheritance, each of which creates historically contingent patterns of cultural and genetic diversity (Boyd and Richerson 1985; Cavalli Sforza and Feldman 1981; Durham 1979, 1982, 1990, 1991; Richerson and Boyd 2005; and see Collard et al. 2008). Therefore, cultural evolution, in this very specific sense, refers to change over time in the *non*genetic information possessed by human societies as it is affected by transmission and innovation processes.

On the one hand, dual inheritance theory drew analogies between the parallel mechanisms for inheritance, mutation, selection, and drift as they operated on both cultural information and on genes. For example, the genetic system is based on biological reproduction, while the cultural one involves transmission of cultural information via teaching, imitation, and other forms of social learning.

But on the other hand, dual inheritance theory also served to highlight a range of powerful forces in cultural evolution that have no real analogue in genetic inheritance systems—these features make cultural evolution unique. For example, people cannot *decide* on their own genetic parentage—they are literally born with it, but over the course of their lives, they can—and generally do—choose what kinds of cultural information to copy, when, and from whom. These sources of cultural information can range from biological parents and close kin through to friends, strangers, or influential leaders; moreover, people can modify, adjust, or even discard the kinds of cultural information they acquire, basing these judgments on a wide range of factors (see following).

These distinctive aspects of cultural transmission mean that new ideas can spread rapidly through populations within a single generation, ensuring that cultural evolution can potentially be much faster than genetic evolution; in addition, the routes of cultural transmission may not always be in step with the parent-to-offspring routes of genetic transmission. Together, these two unique features of cultural transmission systems can enable rapid adoption of adaptively useful traits among biologically unrelated individuals, but can also lead to the widespread dispersal of nonadaptive or even maladaptive traits. In fact, "culture is interesting and important because its evolutionary behaviour is distinctly different from that of genes" (Richerson and Boyd 2005:7).

More generally then, dual inheritance theory involves analysis of social learning and intergenerational cultural inheritance, but it is also a theory about history; and for humans, it is about the unique histories of specific social traditions and how the cultural content of these traditions evolves through time (Bentley et al. 2008:112–13; Boyd and Richerson 1985; Cavalli Sforza and Feldman 1981; Collard et al. 2008:204–5; Durham 1990, 1991; Fuentes 2009:52–57; Richerson and Boyd 2005). Thus, the three key implications of this descent-with-modification approach to cultural evolution are worth highlighting:

1. Cultural evolution has broad similarities with biological evolution, and thinking about culture within a descent-with-modification framework can generate new perspectives and questions about how best to explain patterns and processes of historical change in human cultural traditions, such as language and complex technologies, as well as a range of other behaviors (Richerson and Boyd 2005:58–98). Cultural evolution is cast as a *historical* process that involves the cumulative decision-making processes of human agency, which affect consciously and unconsciously how social traditions are replicated, as well as the specific cultural content of those traditions. How these cultural attributes evolve *within* populations (microscale

cultural evolution)—and also across *different* populations, societies, or cultures (macroscale cultural evolution)—then becomes a question for empirical research. This serves to ground the approach within long-standing debates in archaeology, anthropology, and related disciplines about what factors generate continuity, diversity, and change in human cultural traditions.

2. The analogy between genetic and cultural transmission also has important methodological implications. Despite some key differences, the two inheritance systems share enough general similarities that some of the powerful analytical tools developed to study biological evolution and genetic transmission can be adapted to undertake empirical study of cultural evolution (Collard and Shennan 2008; Collard et al. 2008; Mesoudi et al. 2006). Creative exploration of both the positive and negative analogies between these genetic and cultural inheritance systems then provides a useful starting framework for the wider cross-disciplinary application of models, methods, and theory developed in the biological sciences to analysis of cultural data (Collard and Shennan 2008; Lipo et al. 2006; Lycett 2011; Mace et al. 2005; Mesoudi et al. 2006; Mesoudi 2011; O'Brien and Lyman 2003a, b, O'Brien et al. 2013; Steele et al. 2010).

3. Finally, genes and culture can be argued to form separate components of a wider "coevolutionary" system. This means that independence can be maintained between the study of cultural and biological evolution (Bentley et al. 2008:112). However, humans clearly inherit both genes and cultural information, generating a "swirling dance" of genetic information and cultural traditions that are reproduced among individuals and across generations (Boyd and Richerson 1985; Durham 1990, 1991. 1992; Richerson and Boyd 2005:191–95; and see chapter 6). In other words, biological histories of people and the histories of cultural traditions are linked to one another, but they are certainly not the same thing (Shennan 2004:25).

The next sections of this chapter examine some of the productive conceptual issues that arise from identifying these general parallels between genetic and cultural inheritance systems. These can be explored under three main headings: (1) How is cultural information reproduced by social learning within specific populations? This relates to the theme of "cultural propagation." (2) Do coherent cultural lineages form, and what kind of historical patterns emerge? This relates to the theme of "cultural coherence." (3) Humans simultaneously maintain large numbers of enduring cultural traditions, but to what extent does the history of these cultural lineages become bundled together? This relates to the theme of "historical congruence." At this stage, the focus is on understanding the general process of cultural evolution. The more specific ways in which technology and material culture traditions might start to evolve are examined toward the end of the chapter.

In contrast, methodological implications arising from the positive and negative analogies drawn between genetic and cultural transmission are considered more fully in chapter 2 and are applied to empirical data sets in chapters 3, 4, and 5. The third implication—genes–culture coevolution—also of great importance, remains beyond the scope of the book but is considered briefly in the conclusion in chapter 6.

PROPAGATION OF CULTURAL TRADITIONS

The main argument here is that the propagation of information in cultural traditions has some broad similarities, but also some important differences to genetic inheritance. This creates a useful framework for exploring how cultural information (attributes, variants, or traits) evolve *within or between* different human populations.

Genetic Inheritance

Biological organisms reproduce after their own kind, and they are fundamentally genetic systems that carry information. Each organism contains a distinctive genome, a collection of nucleic acid molecules that contain genes. Genes carry information; they also replicate. When an organism reproduces it makes copies of itself, passing on this information to another generation of similar creatures. In this way, organisms are self-reproducing structures that operate on the instructions of a genome—this encodes a genetic program that specifies the basic structures of the organism and its general mode of operation. The genome also specifies the structure of a new replica of itself, so that each offspring will have its own copy of a genome. Changes are inevitable in a heredity system, and during the processes of replication, new organisms sometimes inherit genomes that contain either errors (mutations) or novel combinations of genes. These changes make offspring different from their parents in a stable, heritable way.

Evolution emerges naturally from this picture. The process is played out in local ecosystems because reproduction is generally so successful that each new generation tends to produce more offspring than can possibly survive. In local ecosystems every new generation of organisms has to find a way of making a living for itself within a specific ecological niche, but because of minor variations in their genomes, some of these organisms tend to be marginally better at this than others. These better-adapted individuals will be better nourished and tend to have more offspring, and they will thereby be selected as the parents of the next generation of offspring, which will inherit the features that made their parents better adapted. Through this general process, organisms will acquire new characteristics generation by generation.

Biological evolution has four essential features: (1) *transmission*: the inheritance of genetic information via sexual reproduction that links parents and their direct offspring; (2) *mutation*: this is the ultimate source of all variation and the key to evolution. Genetic mutation and recombination is a random, low-frequency, and nondirectional process that creates new variants and injects novelty into the inheritance system; (3) *selection*: these processes change the frequencies of the genetic information being passed on; selection on different variants is directional, that is, certain variants within the wider pool of variants will have characteristics that enable them to adapt, survive, and reproduce better in particular environmental conditions; (4) *drift*: this relates to random changes in the frequency of genetic traits over time, which is not a result of selection. In small populations these random patterns of change can have major impacts on what gets passed on to future generations. The dynamic interplay of these four factors feeds into an evolutionary processes of descent with modification that affects the frequency of genetic traits over time.

Biological evolution is a historical process, and changes injected at every new generation are cumulative. However, new features must be designed by slowly modifying what is already present, and each new pattern depends on what has gone before. This means that each organism has a unique combination of genes and is a unique historical object that carries with it genetic information derived from its ancestors. The implication is that diverse sets of creatures will have acquired their structures through evolution from common ancestors that were then shaped, generation after generation, by the evolutionary forces of descent with modification.

Every unique organism becomes what it is through a long evolutionary process, but this process can be studied at two different scales:

(1) *microevolution* focuses on the smaller-scale changes that occur in genetic trait frequencies within a single species or population, but it can also be studied in terms of (2) *macroevolution,* which operates at the scale of separated gene pools and focuses on change that occurs at or above the level of species, including the process of speciation, which refers to the splitting away of different evolutionary lineages through a process of "cladogenesis" or "phylogenesis" (see following).

Cultural Inheritance

Cultural inheritance systems share some general similarities: (1) information (cultural) is passed on between individuals via social learning, generating heritable continuity (transmission); (2) change is also introduced into the system, potentially through simple copying error (mutation); (3) at any one point in time, people are able to choose from a pool of cultural variants, and this affects what gets passed on to the next generation (selection); (4) small-scale statistical anomalies in populations can lead to the disappearance of traits (drift) (see Richerson and Boyd 2005:69; Shennan 2002a:55; and see following). Viewed in these terms, cultural evolution can also can be viewed as a complex set of sampling and modifying process that affect what cultural information is passed on to subsequent generations.

"Population thinking" is also central to cultural evolution (Richerson and Boyd 2005:5, 59). For example, biological species are populations of individuals that carry a pool of genetically acquired information through time; some genetic variants are able spread through time, others diminish. In similar ways, human populations can be argued to carry a pool of socially acquired cultural information that they reproduce through imitation and other forms of social learning. Decisions made by individuals will work to increase or decrease the frequency of particular cultural attributes within that population, and over time, this affects the cultural attributes carried by future generations within the population. The classic exploration of this kind of population-scale phenomenon relates is Everett Rogers's work on the dispersal of innovations (1962). Some of the main features of a successful adoption cycle can be summarized in figure 1.1, where the bell curve records the *rate* of adoption. At first, no one in the population has the new attribute, but as it starts to catch on, more and more people in the population decide to take it up, and the rate of adoption rises sharply, but eventually peaks. Later in the adoption cycle, few people have yet to take up the innova-

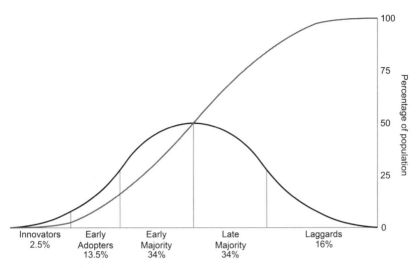

FIGURE 1.1 Bell and S-curve diagram.

Schematic depiction of how successful innovations tend to spread in a population over time. The black line depicts the *rate* of adoption: initially, just a very few individuals possess the new cultural trait, followed by an acceleration in the rate of adoption over time, and then a gradual slowdown during the middle phases, as the early and late majority take up the innovation, and ending with the entire population eventually possessing the new trait. The grey line plots the *cumulative* adoption of the same trait by the population over time: again, this process of conversion builds slowly over time, accelerates during the middle phases, and then slows toward the end as the entire population eventually comes to possess the trait. The key point made here is that these dramatic population-scale outcomes are driven by single decisions made by *specific* individuals.

tion, and the rate drops until everyone in the population eventually has it.

This kind of adoption dynamic can also be represented as an S-curve, which charts the *cumulative* uptake of a new attribute, starting in the early stages when only innovators, early adopters, and then the early majority have it, followed by the late majority and, finally, the laggards, who are the last group to adopt it (figure 1.1). This is a fundamentally *historical* process because what has gone before directly affects what can happen next: at first no one in the population possesses the new cultural attribute, but gradually, more and more people choose to adopt it, until eventually, everyone in the population possesses it. Yet the elegant simplicity of these graphs can be deceptive: these changes are not an automatic process; they came about only through the decision-making processes of specific individuals (human agency). Over time, each of these individual decision-making events feeds into cumulative, and sometimes dramatic, population-scale outcomes, involving radical shifts in the range of cultural attributes maintained by human communities. Understanding persistence and change in the traits carried by populations is therefore about understanding the intersections between historical processes and human agency.

So much for the general similarities between genetic and cultural inheritance. But what are the major differences? The rest of this section examines some of the important forces that are present only within cultural evolution, the most important being: (1) people can potentially have very many cultural "parents," not just their biological mothers or fathers; (2) humans have agency and are to a great extent able to make their own decisions about what kinds of information to adopt, when they adopt it, and also from whom.

Unique Modes of Cultural Transmission

In human populations, genetic information can only be passed "vertically" between parents and their biological offspring. Transmission of cultural information can also follow this vertical route but often does not, opening out other possible routes for cultural attributes to spread in populations. For example, "oblique" transmission involves learning members of the older generation who are not biological parents; "horizontal" transmission is furthest from the genetic route and involves individual learning members of the same generation. Cultural transmission may also be "one to many" (for example, a teacher instructing a class) or "many to one" or "concerted" transmission (for example, members of a conservative older generation insist on respectful practices during interactions with children). This might also tend to ensure uniformity in cultural practices, but also perhaps slower rates of change.

Shennan (2002a:50) provides a useful summary of these diverse modes of cultural transmission and also explores some the potentially different ways in which they might affect the acceptance of innovation, generate variation between individuals within populations, create general cultural differences between groups, and eventually affect the overall rate of cultural evolution (table 1.2). Cultural information transmitted from parents to offspring may be slower to change, whereas novel traits picked up from peers may lead to faster changes. Teachers instructing a school class can quickly pass on new information to a large group,

TABLE 1.2   DIFFERENT MODES CULTURAL TRANSMISSION AND IMPACTS ON
CULTURAL UNIFORMITY AND CHANGE

	Vertical (parent to child)	Horizontal (or contagious)	One to Many	Many to One (or concerted)
Transmitter	Parent(s)	Unrelated	Teacher /leader/media	Older members of social group
Transmittee	Child	Unrelated	Pupils/citizens /audience	Younger members of social group
Acceptance of innovation	Intermediate difficulty	Easy	Easy	Very difficult
Variations between individuals within population	High	Can be high	Low	Lowest
Variations between groups	High	Can be high	Can be high	Probably smallest
Rates of cultural evolution	Slow	Can be rapid	Most rapid	Most conservative

SOURCE: Adapted from Shennan 2002:50.

and this may result in relative cultural homogeneity within that particular group because the new information stems from a single source. In contrast, a powerful generation of conservative elders may reduce capacity for new information to spread easily. Of course, these are simple predictions, and their veracity would need to be examined in specific ethnographic settings, but they are useful here in sketching out some of the potential links between contrasting modes of transmission and resulting patterns of general cultural diversity and change.

Distinctions between these different modes of transmission (vertical, oblique, horizontal, etc.) are useful in mapping out some of the divergent different routes along which cultural information can be transmitted. But in order for culture to evolve, there also has to be a mechanism that injects novelty in to the system. This is where some of the unique and potentially very powerful features of cultural inheritance really start to emerge, and a important distinction can be made between "random forces," which have some analogues in genetic inheritance; and "decision-making forces" which do not (Richerson and Boyd 2005:69; and see table 1.2).

Random Forces in Cultural Evolution

These forces range from a kind of "cultural mutation" through to "cultural drift," both already noted. Mutations emerge through simple copying error or misremembering aspects of cultural information (Eerkens 2000; Eerkens and Lipo 2005). These kinds of novelties are nondirectional, and they may die out quickly if corrected by group consensus or peer group pressure, but in some cases they may catch on and eventually have substantial cumulative effects in the wider population.

Demographic factors are also important because these can affect patterns of cultural variation and change over time. The phenomenon of cultural "drift" is directly linked to such parameters (e.g., population size, density, and interconnectedness; see Henrich 2004). For example, when populations are relatively small, chance (i.e., stochastic) factors can play a much greater role in determining which cultural elements will be retained and transmitted to future generations (see Neiman 1995; Shennan 2000). This is because smaller populations are more likely to experience statistical anomalies that mean, for example, that information replicated by only a few specialists can disappear for chance reasons. For example, if an elderly master carver living in a small and isolated community on a very remote island happens to have no biological offspring and cannot find any apprentices in the local population, then his entire repertoire of carving skills will die out when he passes away.

In much larger populations, these kinds of specialized cultural attributes are generally maintained by a greater number of individuals, such that chance effects like this are less likely to have such dramatic outcomes—there are simply more master carvers, most have offspring, and many other youngsters may also be willing to learn the skills and then share them with others. This means that in a larger and better connected population the carving skills and attributes simply have more opportunities for longer-term persistence. In general then, sustained population growth combined with expanded social transmission networks will result in more effective instances of cultural transmission, serving to "buffer" against the loss of useful cultural traits via this kind of cultural drift process (Henrich, 2004; Kline and Boyd 2010; Lycett and Norton 2010; Powell et al. 2009; Shennan, 2000, 2001, 2002:55).

Decision-Making Forces in Cultural Evolution

These forces are more numerous and include both guided variation and biased transmission. The term *guided variation* refers to *deliberate* changes made by an individual to an existing cultural variant, generating changes that are subsequently transmitted to others. This would equate, in essence, to purposive innovation whereby an individual learned one way of doing something from a parent or other source and then modified the cultural variant they'd learned through practical experiences and trial-and-error experimentation. For example, a hunter might initially learn from his father how to haft knives with bone, which he initially followed for a few years, but after trying many different materials, eventually realized that willow was better because it had a superior grip and was easier to work into the required handle form. He then started to use willow-handled knives and eventually taught his sons to haft knives in the same way.

In many potential settings, and with much cultural information inherited from others, this kind of systematic experimentation among a range of different cultural variants may simply not be possible: it may just take too long to generate enough comparative information for a proper evaluation (because a hunter only hafts a new knife every ten or twenty years), or require too much effort (blades are costly and each hunter can afford to have only one knife at one time), or just generate "noisy" performance data that are hard to interpret (it doesn't seem to make much difference whether the handle is willow, beech, or bone—they all seem to do the job equally well). As a result, it may be easier to just stick with what's been learned during childhood and get on with other more important matters in life.

But another important alternative is to watch others, see what they do, observe the decisions they make, and then copy some of these alternative ways of doing things. This is termed "biased" cultural transmission and occurs when people *preferentially* adopt some preexisting cultural variants rather than others (Richerson and Boyd 2005: 68). This can have a very powerful cumulative effect on the distribution of cultural attributes within populations, for example, in the spread of new innovations (see figure 1.1). Richerson and Boyd liken this process to a process of cultural "shopping," whereby people are continually exposed to alternative ideas and values and can then evaluate and choose among them about which one to adopt—people are generally not stuck with what they have initially been taught, for example, by their parents (2005:68–69).

There are several different forms of biased cultural transmission, and each is distinguished by key differences in the way that the decision about whether to adopt new a variant is reached. For example, content-based (or direct) bias involves careful comparison and evaluation of an initial cultural variant against an alternative variant, based on some kind of objective performance criteria. For example, the hunter's son described previously had initially learned from his father to haft knives with bone, but later in life he may then have seen his neighbor using a leather binding. After trying out both variants the son may have eventually switched to leather because it provided a better grip in the cold conditions of the winter hunting season. In this way, directly biased transmission arises from some kind of generalized cost-benefit calculation (Richerson and Boyd 2005:69).

In contrast, indirectly biased transmission occurs when the choice to adopt a new variant as part of the wider "cultural shopping" process is based on other contextual factors rather than the intrinsic features of the rival variants. In fact, this forms part of a number of unique forces in cultural evolution that can be grouped under the more general heading of "context biases." These biases arise due to some aspect of the particular social context that influences what is transmitted. This is because in many fast-moving social situations, there is limited time and opportunity for careful evaluation of alternative variants, and so judgments are based solely on the source of the copying—that is, on what other people are already doing within the population.

The category of context bias can further be divided into "model-based bias"—here the choice to adopt a new cultural attribute is based on the observable characteristics of individuals who already exhibit the new trait. For example, plausible model-based biases might include a predisposition to imitate the general attributes (clothing, manners, habits, etc.) of important leaders (prestige bias) even though none of these traits may have actually made them successful in the first place, or perhaps a desire to imitate individuals similar to oneself. However, a better indication of how good a new attribute performs can be derived from just watching how many other people have it already; the more people who have it, the greater the odds that it might be more suitable. This tendency generates "frequency-based bias"—the most advantageous variant is thought likely to be the one already in most common usage, so copying this variant is likely to be a simple fast-track route to the correct attribute, or the variant that tends to perform best.

In complex cultural worlds, often defined by limitless opportunities for acquiring or inventing new kinds of cultural attributes, these context biases provide cheap and potentially useful heuristics or cultural "rules of thumb" that allow individuals to reach decisions quickly, and in ways that often require less investment in costly evaluation or time-consuming experimentation.

As a result of these uniquely cultural transmission mechanisms, useful or potentially adaptive technologies and behaviors can spread rapidly within a single generation. In fact, this is one of the key evolutionary advantages of culture: behavioral responses can be much quicker than adjustments brought about by natural selection working only on genetic variation. But while allowing rapid culture change, neither frequency-based bias nor model-based bias includes any kind of objective reality check—the decision to adopt a trait is based purely on *who* already has it and also on what *other* people in the population are doing rather than the features of the trait itself. These features mean that cultural transmission mechanisms can exhibit runaway properties that lead to the rapid spread of nonadaptive or even maladaptive traits (Richerson and Boyd 2005:148–90).

Selection Mechanisms in Cultural Evolution

Building on these insights, the cultural attributes carried by individuals and their wider populations will also be subject to different forms of selection, but in contrast to genetic inheritance, this operates on several different levels due to variability in the range of transmission modes (e.g., contrast vertical, oblique, and horizontal transmission), as well as the other random and decision-making forces that affect cultural evolution (see, e.g., Shennan 2008, 2011). To summarize: (1) selection operates directly on the people replicating these cultural traditions via their genetically inherited dispositions, for example, via their susceptibility to specific diseases such as virulent new strains of an influenza virus (this is akin to natural selection in the narrow biological sense)—this might kill off some, most or even all, members of a specific population; if some cultural traits are carried exclusively by this population, these will also disappear when that population dies out (e.g., a particular language or way of making pots); (2) selection can also operate on populations via their cultural traditions—for example, farming communities may enjoy better general nutrition than foragers, leading to more offspring who live longer; in time, the cultural traits propagated by the expanding farming population will spread, and perhaps even replace those carried by the foragers; (3) complex processes of purely cultural selection that also affect the frequencies of cultural attributes in populations (table 1.3; Shennan 2002a:53; 2004:22–22; 2008; 2011:1070–71). It is these latter, purely cultural forces of selection that are the primary manifestations of human agency, that is, they directly reflect the conscious and

TABLE 1.3   SUMMARY OF DIFFERENT FORCES IN CULTURAL EVOLUTION

Force	General Type	Subtype	Illustrative Example
1. Random Forces			
Cultural mutation			Misremembering or simple copying-error
Cultural drift			Random effects in different populations (e.g., disappearance of a tradition in a small island population due to chance factors)
2. Decision-Making Forces			
Guided variation			Deliberate invention of a new trait (or modification of an older variant) and then transmission of this version to others
Biased transmission			
	i. *Content-based (or direct) bias*		Comparison of cultural variant currently being used with an alternative variant, and using objective performance criteria when deciding to switch
	ii. *Context-based (or indirect) bias*		
		Frequency-based bias	Observe the population and copy what the majority do
		Model-based-bias	Copy traits from prestigious individuals or leaders (e.g., the fashions worn by famous sportsmen)
3. Selection Forces			
Natural selection	Operates on individuals		New strain of influenza causes high mortality rates
Natural selection	Operates on individuals via their cultural traditions		Farmers much better nourished than hunter-gatherers and have more offspring causing traits carried by farmers to spread
Cultural selection	*See* **Decision-Making Forces** (above)		*See* **Decision-Making Forces** (above)

NOTE: Terminology drawn from Richerson and Boyd 2005; Shennan 2002a, 2004, 2009.

unconscious decision-making processes that people employ throughout their lives when choosing *whom* to copy and *what* cultural attributes to retain, discard, adopt, or modify, as reviewed previously.

If microscale *biological* evolution is about studying the changing frequencies of genes in populations through time as a result of such processes as natural selection, then microscale *cultural* evolution refers to the changing distributions of cultural attributes in populations. This can also be seen as a kind of steady but cumulative copying and editing process, but one that involves social learning and human decision-making processes. Thus, distributions of cultural traits are likewise affected by certain processes such as natural selection, but also by a range of others forces that have no analogue in genetic evolution, all of which make the outcomes of cultural transmission much harder to predict (Shennan 2002a:65).

Parental Investments and Psychological Biases in Learning and Copying

The acquisition of cultural information through social learning does not necessarily come for free. In fact, it can be very costly for everyone involved. Passing on many complex cultural traditions can require sustained investment of time, concentration, and energy, both by the experienced practitioner and by the novice, especially in the acquisition of the many sophisticated but essentially arbitrary practices that humans devote so much time to maintaining. For example, many inherited cultural attributes are very hard to acquire, such as the complex motor skills required in basket weaving or flint knapping, or the the ability to play a musical instrument well, or to speak and write in a language with deep fluency. The same goes for all the skills and knowledge that humans have relied on over many millennia to undertake their routine subsistence activities like hunting, fishing, gathering, or the ability to process animal skins and make tailored clothing or store up resources for the lean season. In fact, becoming an accomplished practitioner of the many cultural traditions that individuals rely on in every sphere of their daily existence can require literally years of close pedagogic interaction, and during this time, infants must also be fed and sheltered until they can make their own active contributions to subsistence activities; only later will they become both independent members of the population. Perhaps for this reason, it often appears to be parents who invest most heavily in rearing their direct biological offspring, equipping them with the essential skills and cultural attributes that they need. For example, there is compelling ethnographic evidence that children's acquisition of crafting and subsistence skills generally involves vertical or oblique rather than horizontal transmission—novices are generally more likely to learn from parents or other members of the older generation than horizontally from members of the same generation (Shennan 2002a:40, 49; Shennan and Steele 1999; and see Hosfield 2009 for a broader discussion).

However, the general interest in studying children's acquisition of cultural attributes may have overemphasized the role of vertical transmission at the expense of other modes of transmission that become more important later in the life cycle (Tehrani and Collard 2009b:289): understanding how social learning over the entire human life history feeds into the evolution of specific craft traditions therefore remains an important topic for future research (chapter 3). Archaeologists, with their interest in longer-term histories of human cultural tradition, are particularly interested in the dynamics of social learning in the smaller-scale band societies that are typical of some modern foraging groups. However, ethnographic research on hunter-gatherer cultural transmission has been limited, though Hewlett et al. (2011), for example, have studied cultural inheritance in African forager communities. They concluded that cultural transmission is initially very rapid and predominantly vertical, but then switches to oblique routes between the ages of six and twelve and tends to involve broader general observation and wider imitation. Thus, it may be more useful to think of cultural transmission as a more extended process, whereby (1) infants initially acquire a repertoire of cultural skills and attributes vertically from their biological parents (and perhaps also obliquely from related members of the older generation), but then (2) older children, adolescents, and young adults eventually become much more selective in choosing from the range of other available cultural models, updating their cultural repertoire by innovating and imitating, thereby generating some of the wide range of cultural transmission biases explored previously (Whiten et al. 2011:944).

That said, many inherited cultural traditions may, in fact, require so much sustained social and material investment in teaching and learning that it may be difficult or even impossible to find the time and resources later in life to dedicate to such an endeavor. In contrast, other traits, like a catchy tune, fashionable new words, or expressions, small technical improvements, or even novel decorative motifs can easily be picked up at any stage of life from any range of sources and then built into existing traditions. Overall, this may mean that certain elements of a single cultural tradition like pottery making may be more stable, such as its basic method of coiling and shaping, which may have been acquired early in life and are harder to adjust, while other more ephemeral features like its surface decorations may be much more dynamic and variable over time, especially if they can diffuse easily and quickly among different groups of potters. These factors make it important to be specific about the kinds of cultural information being acquired and modified at different life stages.

A number of psychological factors also play an important role in cultural inheritance (see: Henrich and McElreath 2007). For example, even during their early phases of learning, children do appear cognitively able to make informed choices about whom to copy. Harris and Corriveau (2011) have argued that children tend to be less discerning about the *kinds* of information they learn but very aware of *whom* they learn from, including increased receptivity to information from familiar and reliable caregivers (with a tendency to reinforce vertical transmission from parents to offspring), and greater receptivity to informants from within the same cultural group. In general then, children may be less likely to endorse, imitate, and trust information from deviants from their own groups or from informants from a different group. Overall, this cognitive disposition may promote vertical transmission between parents and offspring, and where oblique or horizontal transmission does occur, it tends to be of a relatively conservative nature, primarily involving conformist members of their own cultural group (2011:1185).

In a similar way, general copying decisions may at all life stages relate not just to the specific cost or difficulty associated with acquiring new traits or attributes but may be affected by psychological biases. These may include a psychological tendency to preferentially imitate individuals perceived to be successful (Richerson and Boyd 2005:124–26), or a strong cognitive desire to conform to behaviors of the majority (Richerson and Boyd 2005:120–24; Henrich and McElreath 2007; McElreath and Henrich 2007, with references). In the latter case, such conformity bias would then serve to reduce general cultural variation *within* a population but tend to increase it *between* populations. Overall then, many of the ways in which people acquire and maintain cultural traditions through imitation and general social interaction appear to promote cumulative patterns of cultural diversification that can eventually become self-reinforcing (Boyd and Richerson 2005:379–96; Pagel and Mace 2004).

How Do Social Institutions Structure Propagation of
Cultural Traditions?

Clearly, these microscale transmission dynamics are "agent centred" (Shennan 2011:1071); they focus on specific people and the ways in which their individual decisions lead to the propagation of cultural attributes and the cumulative effects of these processes at the scale of populations. In this sense, the analytical focus is on shorter time scales: from day to day, year to year and also along human biographic time scales. The interactions among all these factors are highly complex, and cultural traditions can potentially evolve along many different kinds of trajectories. However, simply highlighting complexity and potential variability does not address the more challenging question of what range of outcomes is more or less likely in any given historical setting and why? At this stage in the argument, it therefore becomes important to consider how other kinds of factors might start to structure opportunities for interaction, social learning, and skilled practice, and thereby, influence the deeper evolutionary patterns manifested by specific cultural traditions.

If a focus on the role of human agency within microscale cultural evolution highlights the role of individual decision making and personal choices, then it should also be tempered by an examination of other contextual factors that can structure opportunities for social interaction and cultural imitation. For example, one potentially important factor is the ways in which human populations organize themselves into kin groups and communities and how they move and interact within and between these groups over during different stages of their life. Borrowing from agency/practice theory, these enduring structures can be termed "social institutions" because they extend beyond the life spans of individuals and often persist over many generations (Giddens 1984:35–36; Pred 1990:123). For example, in many of the smaller-scale societies documented by ethnographers, these social institutions include settlement and subsistence patterns, territoriality and property rights, but perhaps most important, gender roles, kinship relations, and in particular, postmarital residence and resocialization patterns (Herbich and Dietler 2008). In fact, the structuring role played by these kinds of social institutions—and especially postmarital residence rules—starts to emerge as one of the primary factors that mediates between microscale propagation of cultural traditions and larger-scale patterns of cultural diversity (see chapters 3–6).

COHERENCE IN CULTURAL TRADITIONS

The previous section examined some of the enormously variable ways in which cultural attributes can be propagated. The interplay of these factors mean that cultural traditions can potentially, evolve in any number of different ways, which in turn affects larger-scale patterns of cultural diversity. Building on these insights, this next section asks an important follow-up question: To what extent are human cultural traditions *coherent?* This is a more controversial topic and raises some deeper questions about the likely patterns of human cultural evolution.

What is meant by *cultural coherence?* As attributes are propagated within specific social traditions, certain sets of traits may become integrated together and subject to strong heritable continuity within a given population, whereas other traits have a more individualistic history as a result of being borrowed from others or recombined in different ways.

A good example is the social tradition of having regular meals with family, friends, or members of the wider community. On a more abstract and theoretical level, it might be possible to speculate that this meal could just involve collective consumption of foodstuffs—during different meals, there could be any number of different foodstuffs and drinks, all from different sources, and in any order or combination, in any location, and using an infinite and perhaps even random range of serving vessels. In this scenario, the social tradition of having a daily, weekly, or monthly meal together endures, but it has little internal *cultural coherence* in terms of the way in which internal cultural elements of the tradition are being combined. The social tradition of having the meal has a history, but there is little coherence in its specific cultural content, which is more or less random, just a churning turnover of endless variability.

In contrast, and on a more realistic level, the social traditions associated with eating meals across most human cultures appear to have at least some structure and internal coherence, although the specific content is often arbitrary and subject to enormous cross-cultural variation: usually only certain foodstuffs are sourced and used; dishes are usually served in a particular order and combination, and often with certain kinds of vessels, specific seating arrangements, and even with formalized opening, serving, and closing ceremonies. In some cultural and ritual settings, these kinds of repeated events might have a highly structured and precisely defined internal cultural grammar. In this way, these general dining activities persist as a social tradition, but as an integral part of the reproduction of this tradition, a tightly integrated combination of specific cultural traits and attributes are also propagated. In these kinds of setting, the social tradition of dining together persists over time, but so too does this *coherent* combination of specific cultural traits and attributes, which together make up a distinctive lineage of cultural tradition, which will have its own history and genealogy. Theoretically, the deeper history of these coherent cultural lineages can also be reconstructed with the right kinds of concepts, methods, and approaches.

Social Scales of Cultural Coherence?

Specific combinations of cultural traits can therefore persist over time, but at what kinds of social scale might such coherent cultural entities emerge? Theoretically, distinctive cultural traditions can emerge within individual friendships or household units via their defining routines and microrituals, but they can also be shared by larger kin groups, settlements, communities, and small religious sects, as well as by large-scale political units or centrally organized religions. Perhaps one of the clearest examples of a coherent cultural tradition is what linguistics call a "speech community"—this a unique communication system propagated by a specific population, and consists of essentially arbitrary sets of traits, attributes, and collective rules (i.e., the words, syntax, and grammar that make up a particular linguistic tradition). Together, these cultural conventions and established combinations provide an effective means for communicating with others who are also participating in the same linguistic tradition. These acts of participation within a particular linguistic tradition reproduce its distinctive cultural content within the community over time. Different groups tend to speak different languages; each language forms a distinctive and relatively coherent lineage of tradition that outlives the lives of particular individuals and persists in recognizable format over many human generations.

History and Genealogy of Cultural Lineages?

Coherent cultural entities such as language clearly endure within populations over time; other cultural lineages may evolve in similar ways. But to what extent can the deeper history and genealogy of particular cultural lineages be reconstructed? What kinds of descent relationships emerge? Can different cultural lineages be traced back over time to to a single common ancestral entity, or do other kinds of historical patterns emerge?

These questions can also be examined by exploring some of the interesting parallels between cultural and genetic inheritance. If human culture is an inheritance system, defined by heritable continuity, then the argument can be made that cumulative process of social learning and cultural inheritance over generations might lead to the formation of phylogenetic descent relationships among different cultural entities, just as genetic transmission does at the scale of biological macroevolution (Foley 1987; Grancolas and Pellens 2005; Lycett 2011; Mace et al. 2005; Mace and Holden 2005; Lipo et al. 2006; O'Brien and Lyman 2003a, b; Mesoudi et al. 2007; O'Brien et al. 2001; O'Brien et al. 2013). In exploring how cultural traditions evolve at the scale of different populations, societies, cultures, or language communities, the most useful analogies here are with biological processes of *macro*evolution, which operate at the scale of separated gene pools and focus on change that occurs at or above the level of species (Ridley 2004). This change includes the process of "speciation," which refers to the splitting away of different biological lineages through an evolutionary process of cladogenesis or phylogenesis. This occurs when individuals in one population slowly become separated from others, and then remain apart long enough for the two new populations to evolve genetic differences. These genetic differences can emerge from, and are often sustained by, a wide range of factors, such as increasing habitat isolation (physical separation), temporal isolation (breeding at different times), sexual isolation (due to incompatible behavior or conduct, e.g., via different mating rituals), mechanical isolation (incompatible genitalia), together broadly termed as "hybridization barriers" or reproductive isolating mechanisms (RIMs).

The biological study of phylogeny involves reconstructing the history of a species and how it has changed into others; this pattern is usually represented by a branching tree diagram. Just as real-world trees grow from a single base, then steadily diverge into smaller branches, and then twigs and the final tips that spread out widely, so a phylogenetic tree is used by biologists to depict how descendants from one kind of ancestral organism have branched out and evolved into an array of diverse but historically related forms. Each line on the phylogenetic tree divides from an ancestral species into two or more descendant species, mapping out the process of speciation, which usually involves a pattern of cumulative divergence.

Each new evolutionary lineage will be characterized by shared set of mutations, and branches that divided earlier in evolutionary time will be differentiated by the large numbers of mutations that have occurred on independent branches since they split. In contrast, closer to the tips of the tree, the species that diverged much more recently are more closely related; they will share many more common mutations and be differentiated only by a few recent ones.

This treelike branching pattern is therefore a foundational model in evolutionary biology. The concept of *homology* is an essential tool for reconstructing phylogeny. A good example is the similarity in the fore-limbs of mammals, for example, a human hand, a seal's flipper, or a bear's paw, all of which can be defined as homologous traits because they are all derived from a common ancestor somewhat further back in evolutionary history. Homologous traits can be at the morphological and also molecular level, and biologists can reconstruct phylogenies on the basis of the fossil paleontological record, through comparative anatomy, or increasingly, through analysis of DNA sequences.

Is the branching tree model applicable to the evolution of cultural traditions? Since the pioneering arguments of Sir William Jones in 1786, analysis of descent relationships between different cultural entities has also played an important role in historical and comparative linguistics, enabling the classification of languages into a structured taxonomy, made up of phyla, stocks, families, and subfamilies. Similar parallels were also drawn by Charles Darwin in *Origin* and also in *Descent* when he speculated that language evolution consisted of tree-like patterns of homologies due to shared communities of descent (Shennan 2011; Whiten et al. 2011). Like phylogenetic analysis in biology, rigorous comparative analysis has enabled linguistics to reconstruct how the ties of descent have created a hierarchy of differential similarity among particular sets of languages (Durham 1992:335; see, e.g., Lee and Hasegawa 2011 for examples; and see Heggarty et al. 2010; Mc Mahon and McMahon 2005 for a broader discussion).

But of the many different cultural traditions that are propagated by humans, linguistic evolution may represent a very special kind of cultural evolution (Gray et al. 2010:3928). This may be due to the distinctive ways in which languages are propagated and the unique social roles that they perform, all of which may ensure that language traditions tend to be more coherent and potentially evolve in more treelike ways. First, children mainly learn language vertically from their parents, and this enforced vertical parent-to-offspring transmission tends to maintain some degree of intergenerational consistency. Second, after acquiring initial knowledge of language from parents, most children, adolescents, and even adults then go on to acquire other linguistic traits and attributes from a vast range of other sources, often horizontally from peers in the same generation. But despite this, overall language change remains strongly constrained by the need to communicate effectively with others, injecting a strong "conformity bias." Languages can and do change, but they cannot change completely overnight; there is an inevitable conformist bias reinforcing fidelity of transmission because usage must be coordinated and errors corrected if mutual intelligibility is to be maintained. As a result, languages exhibit heritable continuity—they are passed on between generations, and in the process modified; but with enough time, one linguistic community may eventually start to diverge into two related languages, and this cumulative splitting process may eventually produce genealogies that can be depicted as branching trees mapping ties of historical relatedness (Gray et al. 2010; Steele et al. 2011:3783).

But what of other *nonlinguistic* cultural traditions propagated by humans? Do they share similar kinds of interindividual and intergenerational transmission routes and community-scale stabilizing mechanisms? Some anthropologists argue not. Kroeber (1948), for example, famously accepted a branching tree models for genetic descent and the evolution of species but argued that cultural evolution was characterized by a more reticulate pattern, with cultural lineages branching away but also rejoining again, producing a different kind of cultural tree that had a complex tangle of both splitting but also interconnecting branches (figure 1.2). More recently, other anthropologists have again argued that historical branching patterns in cultural traditions are nearly impossible to reconstruct because of the inherent nature of cultural evolution and the ways in which different cultural traits and attributes tend to be propagated (Dewar 1995; Hornborg, 2005; Moore, 1994a, b, 2001; Terrell, 1988, 2001, 2004; Terrell et al., 1997, 2001; Welsch et al. 1992; Welsch and Terrell, 1994).

According to this perspective, cultural evolution is argued to be a fundamentally different kind of process than macroscale biological evolution. It has a much faster tempo due to very high rates of cultural innovation, and it also has a fundamentally different mode—horizontal transmission—that creates reticulation. These features prevent deeper branching histories from forming and reduce the cultural landscape to little more than a blur of interrelated forms. This general process is often referred to as *ethnogenesis*, defined broadly as cultural evolutionary patterns that are produced by the borrowing and blending of ideas and practices among contemporary populations (Borgerhoff Mulder et al., 2006:54).

FIGURE 1.2 Kroeber's tree of life and tree of culture.

The "tree of life" (left) and the "tree of culture" (right) (after Kroeber 1948:138): "The course of organic evolution can be portrayed properly as a tree of life, as Darwin has called it, with trunk, limbs, branches, and twigs. The course of development of human culture in history cannot be so described, even metaphorically. There is a continual branching-out, but the branches also grow together again, wholly or partially, all the time. A branch on the tree of life may approach another branch; it will not normally coalesce with it. The tree of culture, on the contrary, is a ramification of such coalescences, assimilations, or acculturations" (Kroeber 1948:138).

According to this argument, mixing forces dominate cultural evolution: coherent cultural entities tend not to form, and even if they briefly do, any coherence is rapidly swamped by the combined effects of borrowing and rapid innovation. This makes it virtually impossible to reconstruct deeper historical or genealogical relationships between cultural entities using phylogenetic approaches employed by biologists and historical linguists. Thus, if analogies between cultural and genetic inheritance have any validity at all, it is at the biological *micro*evolutionary scale (see previous), that is, involving the ebb and flow of genetic information within a *single* interacting population, and not the process of branching *macro*scale diversification that involves largely separate gene pools.

More recent work is starting to move away from these rather polarized debates about the extent to which cultural traditions evolve *either* by branching processes (phylogenesis) *or* according to a more reticulate or hybridized model characterized by rapid cultural mixing (ethnogenesis). In fact, rather than arguing for the absolute dominance

of either branching versus mixing processes within overall cultural evolution, a more subtle and interesting set of questions can explored if the
history of one particular cultural tradition is examined in relation to
number of intersecting axes (Gray et al. 2010:3924).

Gray et al. (2010) therefore argue that when investigating the transmission of traits and the descent history of a single cultural tradition
like language, it is more productive to ask where particular aspects of
tradition are positioned along a three-dimensional continuum rather
than to argue a priori for the exclusive validity of splitting processes
(that can be mapped by trees) or mixing processes (that cannot). This
culture-evolutionary continuum consists of three axes: Rv, Rh, and C.
Rv indicates the rate of change in traits or attributes transmitted from
generation to generation within each of the populations. If this rate is
too slow relative to the time period studied, then there will be little
character change to allow for the reconstruction of phylogenies. If it is
too fast, then all historical signals will be erased, making phylogenetic
reconstruction redundant. Rh is rate of horizontal mixing of traits and
attributes between the different populations. At low rates of horizontal
mixing, the estimated phylogenies will be good estimates of history, but
at higher rates, the estimated phylogenies will be increasingly inaccurate
and serve as poor summaries of the overall history. C forms the third
dimension and measures cultural cohesion—the extent to which the different cultural traits are tightly coupled together as coherent entities.
For example, in the case of languages, morphosyntactical traits will tend
to evolve more slowly and are often tightly bound together, so that
instances of horizontal borrowing tend to be rare. In contrast, a random
sampling of the total lexicon would demonstrate that these traits tend
to evolve more rapidly, often have lots of horizontal borrowing (e.g.,
loan words), with each trait (or loan word) exhibiting its own independent descent cultural history. The content of core vocabularies will tend
to occupy a more intermediate position, with a slower rate of evolution
and possibly a limited degree of horizontal borrowing.

This is an important conceptual development because it transcends
the simple branching versus mixing debates examined previously, and
argues that in fact, different elements of a single tradition like language
or canoe making might evolve in different ways, some elements retaining a deeper historical signal, others influenced to a greater extent by
rapid innovation, or by the horizontal mixing of traits between populations. This can be illustrated by further simple linguistic example:
Swedish, English, Frisian, Dutch, German, Czech, Polish, Russian, and

Japanese are all different languages, and all have features that define them as internally coherent and individually distinct cultural entities, such that each of these different cultural entities has a separate history. Some of these histories also exhibit higher levels of genealogical relatedness; Swedish, English, Frisian, Dutch, and German fall within the Germanic language family, and Czech and Russian fall into the Slavic language family, though Japanese falls outside these groupings and has a very different history. However, at another level, all these languages also *share* large numbers of loan words as a result of long histories of cultural contacts, interactions, mixing, and exchange among all the different linguistic communities groups. In this sense, different evolutionary patterns fit different sets of cultural traits and attributes even within a single and relatively easily defined cultural tradition like language. This is because the history of single traits (e.g., loan words) can be studied, as well as the history of the more coherent entity (e.g., the language).

Differential patterns of evolution have also been noted for other cultural traditions, for example, among functional and symbolic traits within ethnographic canoe designs in the Pacific (see Gray et al. 2010:29–31; Rogers and Ehrlich 2008; Rogers et al. 2009); in other words: "different aspects of culture can have quite different evolutionary histories" (Gray et al. 2010:3931).

These emerging insights into the complex evolutionary dynamics of particular cultural traditions therefore take future debates beyond the more divisive arguments about whether human culture evolves exclusively *either* by phylogenesis *or* by ethnogenesis. In fact, the key challenge in future research is to identify the extent to which all traits within a single cultural or linguistic tradition fit one overall pattern, or whether different sets of traits follow a range of different evolutionary histories. The same kind of reasoning applies to identifying contrasting evolutionary patterns among a range of *different* cultural traditions, a theme examined next.

HISTORICAL CONGRUENCE AMONG MULTIPLE CULTURAL TRADITIONS

These discussions of cultural coherence in *single* cultural traditions are important and useful, but it should also be remembered that the evolved human capacity for high-fidelity social learning enables populations to simultaneously propagate *multiple* cultural traditions, ranging from language through to subsistence strategies, ritual practices, and crafting traditions (table 1.1, part 3a). As a result, each of these individual traditions may in turn have its own degree of coherence and unique evolutionary history. Understanding this aspect of cultural evolution is particularly important because human groups tend to differ from one another in vast numbers of ways, with each group maintaining many unique sets of cultural traditions (table 1.1, part 3b). In fact, humanity appears to be extremely adept at organizing itself into distinct cultural groups and then signaling membership of, and loyalty to, these defined social units through a wide range of cultural media ranging from language, clothing, and adornment through to cuisine and religious cults (Mace and Pagel 2004). It has therefore become customary in anthropology to describe these units as "cultures," or "ethnolinguistic groups," with the implication that each of these groups has a distinct set of cultural attributes and internal features that serve to distinguish it from others.

How then do these entire human cultures evolve? Following early formulations of dual inheritance theory in the 1980s, there were renewed reconsiderations of the extent to which entire *sets* of cultural traditions might evolve through treelike branching processes similar to those observed in macroscale biological evolution biology (Durham 1991, 1992; and see Boyd et al. 1997; Foley 1987; Mesoudi et al. 2006:332–36; O'Brien and Lyman 2003b; O'Brien et al. 2001, 2013). For example, Durham (1991, 1992) presented the general argument that (1) socially transmitted information systems constitute entire "cultures," and that these provide human populations, in addition to the genetic information they carry, with a second important source of heritable variation; (2) these human cultural systems are historically interrelated by hierarchical patterns of descent; and (3) splitting was the dominant process in cultural macroevolution, generating cultural phylogenesis—this involves one entire culture branching away into two or more descendant cultures. This cultural splitting process was followed by cumulative cultural "transformation" within each of the descendant cultural lineages. In general then, the principle argument was that new cultures tend to originate from preexisting "parental cultures" via a branching process termed "diversification" or "culture birth," generally a result of "uniparental fissioning" Durham (1992:333).

Although acknowledging that there may be occasional instances of horizontal borrowing and hybridization of limited numbers of cultural traits and attributes between cultures, Durham (1992) argued that strong and pervasive barriers served to lock out the potential for horizontal cultural exchange between cultures. These barriers were termed TRIMS (transmission isolating mechanisms) and were linked to a range of ecological, psychological, linguistic, or cultural factors that would effectively dampen cultural exchanges between populations and served an analogous role to RIMs (reproductive isolating mechanisms—see previous) in biological speciation theory (and see Tehrani and Collard 2013).

More generally, TRIMs might also be linked to the effects of different kinds of social institutions such as strictly endogamous kinship systems, highly developed and strictly defended property rights, that tie particular groups to exclusive territories. TRIMs may also arise through enforced resocialization of individuals moving into a new community after marriage; this would lead them to abandon cultural attributes acquired from their original culture, and adopt the practices and behaviors of the new group. Durham argued that TRIMs are important because they serve to canalize cultural inheritance within discrete populations; where these forces were strong and diversification was consistently uniparental, that is, one culture split into a series of daughter cultures, then there would be no mixed ancestries in a group of related cultures. Arguments for this kind of cultural phylogenetic process are supported by the observation that languages of genuinely mixed origin are relatively rare and that the same characteristics probably also apply to entire cultures (Durham 1992:334). Cultural phylogeny was therefore argued to underlay most patterns of cultural diversity—a distinct pattern of historical relationships that was generated by process of culture birth that led to the formation of a "systematic hierarchy of successive splits." Cultural phylogenies could then describe ancestor-descent relationships between these cultures, the family tree specifying a unique and unambiguous phylogeny like cladistic classification in biology.

More recently, a similar argument has been made by Foley and Larr (2011), who conclude that cultural phylogeny played a dominant role in much of human prehistory. This is expressed by an accelerating trend toward treelike growth in regional cultural diversity, as lineage-based communities fissioned over time, resulting in cultural divergence and the formation of new groups and cultural boundaries. They note that local ecosystems served to structure general patterns of cultural diversification. For example, the general global diversity in human cultures is striking, but it is most pronounced in areas of high ecological productivity, which tended to encourage the dense bunching of populations around predictable and locally abundant resources that could be easily be owned and defended (e.g., in regions like California and the Pacific Northwest Coast; see chapters 4 and 5). However, the expansion and cumulative fissioning of groups into new generations of descendant cultures was also intermixed with frequent population extinctions and assimilations, followed by renewed expansions. Consequently, most regional patterns of cultural diversity consist of a series of historically related cultures interspaced with a few cultural isolates. Overall, these distinctive patterns are generated by the specific ways in which human populations have expanded and dispersed since the origin of the species, with the processes of phylogenesis ultimately driving cultural diversification (Foley and Lahr 2011:1086–87).

Given these arguments, the main research mission of archaeologists and anthropologists was to "elucidate the patterns and processes of descent with modification in cultures" (Durham 1992:332), with the "family tree hypothesis" serving as the default hypothesis for all incidences of human macroscale cultural evolution (1992:333).

The key differences between competing phylogenetic and ethnogenetic models of human cultural macroevolution should now be clear. However, what tends to get lost in these debates is that all human populations simultaneously maintain a large number of *different* cultural traditions, ranging from language through to religion and cuisine, and that each *individual* lineage of tradition may be characterized by different degrees of coherence and entirely different historical patterns. In this sense, it is an oversimplification to seek to examine how *entire* cultures evolve; a more productive approach is to start by looking first at *individual* cultural traditions, trace how these evolve across populations, and only then examine the extent to which there is deeper historical congruence among a range of different cultural traditions. For example, do culinary traditions or religious practices form coherent lineages, and is the branching history of each of these lineages closely related to language history? If yes, this would suggest that multiple cultural lineages are evolving in tandem with one another. If not, this would suggest that each lineage has its own unique history.

Boyd et al. (1997) undertook an insightful exploration of the kinds of broader-scale cultural patterning that might emerge through the evolution of multiple cultural traditions, which in turn affect the manner in which entire human cultures might evolve. These four models have played a central role in subsequent debates about macroscale cultural evolution.

Model 1: Cultures as Species. This is where entire human cultures are either entirely isolated from one another (due to TRIMS—see previous discussion) or have a high degree of internal integration, or a combination of both (Boyd et al. 1997:365; see figure 1.3). As a result, they evolve in the same overall manner as vertebrae species do—each entire culture forms a coherent and tightly integrated system in which cultural information is only propagated internally within the culture. Horizontal exchange of cultural information between the different groups is minimal. Each culture is, however, made up of distinct cultural traditions. In this kind of setting, the full suite of the cultural traditions carried by each local population is therefore isolated from all outside influences, and the only pathways of information flow are *within* each local culture. Inheritance of all cultural information within each population therefore involves members of the older generation passing on traits to younger generations without any external cultural influences. If these essentially insulated populations then diverge and split, a new generation of descendant "daughter" cultures will then be formed, each of which may then split further into a new generation of related cultures. Hierarchical patterns of cultural descent with modification among these historically related daughter cultures can then be mapped as branching tree diagrams. According to this model of cultural diversification, phylogenetic methods of historical reconstruction should perform well for all the individual cultural traditions maintained by each population (e.g., for language, basketry, pottery, clothing), and the branching history of each of these cultural lineages will also be highly congruent with all the other cultural traditions.

Model 2: Cultures with Hierarchically Integrated Systems. Here, cultures consist of a core set of closely integrated traditions that are inherited from older to younger generations within each population, and perhaps canalized by the effects of TRIMS, which reduce overall cultural borrowings between populations (Boyd et al. 1997:365; figure 1.3). Beyond these core traditions, a greater degree of horizontal cultural mixing does take place between populations, but this only affects some of the more peripheral traditions, and not the cultural traditions that form the core elements of the system. In this scenario, phylogenetic methods will work well for all the integrated core traditions, but not for the traits that make up the more peripheral traditions, which tend to evolve via mixing and rapid innovation.

Model 3:'Cultures as Assemblages of Many Coherent Units". Here, cultures still consist of many single coherent traditions, but each tradition

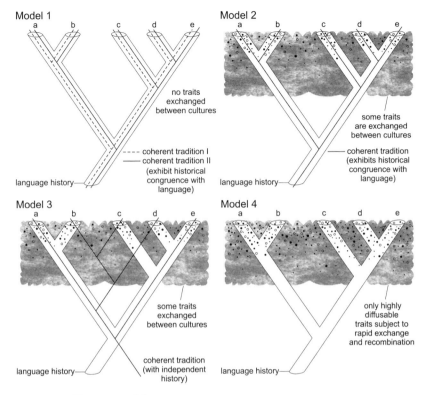

Model 1

a b   c   d   e

no traits
exchanged
between cultures

- - - - coherent tradition I
——— coherent tradition II
(exhibit historical
congruence with
language)

language history

Model 2

a   b   c   d   e

some traits
are exchanged
between cultures

——— coherent tradition
(exhibits historical
congruence with
language)

language history

Model 3

a   b   c   d   e

some traits
exchanged
between cultures

coherent tradition
(with independent
history)

language history

Model 4

a   b   c   d   e

only highly
diffusable
traits subject to
rapid exchange
and recombination

language history

FIGURE 1.3 Four tree models.

Schematic depiction of Boyd et al.'s (1997) four macroscale culture-evolutionary models;
for further explanation see main text. In this schematic figure, the main focus is on
exploring how a series of different material culture traditions might evolve across
different populations in relation to language history. Language history is held constant
and assumed to follow a treelike, branching pattern, with a, b, c, d, and e representing
different linguistically defined "cultures" or "ethnolinguistic groups." In Model 1 (cultures
as species), there is no exchange of information between populations because of the
effects of TRIMS, and highly coherent material culture traditions like basketry, housing,
or clothing may form and then evolve via branching processes. Phylogenetic methods will
work well on reconstructing the histories of all these traditions, and these branching
histories will map very closely onto language history. In Model 2 (cultures with
hierarchically integrated systems), there is exchange of some traits between populations
(depicted by the dots in the grey cloud), though one (or more) coherent material culture
traditions may still be present. The history of these coherent traditions will map closely
onto language history, together forming an integrated set of "core" traditions that can
successfully be studied with phylogenetic methods. In Model 3 (cultures as assemblages
of many coherent units) there is also exchange of traits across populations, though one
(or more) coherent material culture traditions may still form. However, the origin and
history of the coherent tradition(s) is very different from language history. Phylogenetic
methods will still work well on the coherent individual tradition(s), but not on other
cultural traditions strongly affected by the mixing and recombination of traits between
populations. In Model 4 (cultures as collections of ephemeral entities) material culture
traditions are affected by a relentless mixing of traits between populations (depicted by
the clouds of drifting dots). Coherent traditions will not be able to form and so
phylogenetic methods will not work well because no historical signals are retained.

is essentially independent and has its own independent branching history (Boyd et al. 1997:365–66). This may result from the fact that the specific packages of traits propagated within a highly coherent tradition—for example, a new religion, a novel way of preparing and serving food, knowledge of how to make iron—can sometimes "jump" horizontally between different populations, undergoing a process of descent with modification along the way. According to this model, cultures are made up of several of these distinct traditions, but each tradition will have its own independent source and descent history, each of which can be reconstructed with phylogenetic methods, but only on an individualistic case-by-case basis. For example, in a given world region, iron working and pottery traditions each have separate origins and independent branching histories, but neither of these histories maps onto the other or onto local language history. Each single tradition is therefore coherent, but there is no historical congruence *between* these separate traditions.

Model 4: Cultures as Collections of Ephemeral Entities. Finally, if rapid innovation and relentless horizontal mixing of information between populations dominates the propagation of cultural traditions, then there are no coherent cultural entities (Boyd et al. 1997: 366; figure 1.3). Instead, cultures will consist of little more than unstructured sets of highly diffusible traits subject to rapid exchange and recombination. According to this model, little historical signal is retained, and phylogenetic methods simply won't work, either at the scale of individual traditions, or at scale of the entire culture: all that can be detected is a blur of hybrid forms.

Boyd et al.'s (1997) four models succeed in sketching out positions along a potential continuum of evolutionary scenarios. Although models 1 and 4—cultures as species and cultures as collections of ephemeral entities plot opposing ends of this continuum, they appear unlikely to exist in reality. First, in one way or another, human groups have always interacted with one another despite speaking different languages or possessing different senses of identity. As a result, cultures have rarely, if ever, been hermetically sealed, and the widely documented range of contacts and exchanges between human groups suggest that it is highly unlikely that cultures could have evolved in ways analogous to biological species. Second, there is also little evidence to support the assertion that cultures are merely made up of a blur of hybridized traits and that their traditions have little or no historical continuity—archaeologists, for example, regularly identify artifact lineages that exhibit both internal coherence and long-term multigenerational continuity (Tehrani and Riede 2006).

A key research question therefore arises (Boyd et al. 1997: 386): In what kinds of historical settings are models 2 and 3 most likely to emerge? What is the highest scale of cultural coherence—is it possible to identify the existence of coherent traditions that are tightly bundled together and form enduring cultural cores (model 2), or is the highest scale of cultural coherence a series of distinctive but essentially independent traditions, each with its own unique history of decent (model 3)? Understanding which of these particular models fits a specific historical scenario requires first understanding how each of the individual cultural traditions has evolved. Only then does it become possible to examine the extent of historical relationships (congruence) between the different lineages of tradition that make up overall cultural history.

STUDYING DESCENT WITH MODIFICATION IN TECHNOLOGY AND MATERIAL CULTURE

The preceding section has examined three overarching themes: the ways in which general cultural information is *propagated* through social learning, the extent to which these processes form cultural traditions that are *coherent,* and the degree to which there is *historical* congruence between different lineages of cultural tradition. Clearly, the conceptual parallels between genetic inheritance and the inheritance of cultural information have been a useful framework for understanding these themes, as has exploration of the ways in which micro- and macroscale processes of biological and cultural evolution can productively be compared and also contrasted.

Beyond these more heuristic frameworks, the analogy between genetic and cultural inheritance has also had important methodological implications, paving the way for analytical tools developed by biologists in the study of genetic inheritance to be applied to cultural data sets. (Collard and Shennan 2008; Collard et al. 2008; Lipo et al. 2006; Lycett 2011; Mace et al. 2005; Mesoudi et al. 2006; Steele et al. 2010). As a result, an extensive body of empirical research has arisen from the early formulations of dual inheritance theory (Cavalli Sforza and Feldman 1981; Boyd and Richerson 1985; Durham 1991, 1992), generating the foundations for a rigorous science of cultural diversity and change that spans biology, evolutionary psychology, archaeology, and anthropology (Rogers and Ehrlich 2008:3416).

To one degree or another, all of this is premised on the recognition and exploitation of these central analogies and conceptual parallels between cultural and biological inheritance systems examined previously (see Mesoudi et al. 2006 and Mesoudi 2011; Whiten et al. 2011). Across this new interdisciplinary research field, there has been particularly rapid progress in the development of theoretical models and simulation studies. However, empirical research has developed at a much slower pace; one major obstacle continues to be the lack of large-scale high-resolution cultural data sets of the kind that are typical in evolutionary biology and population genetics (Shennan 2008:3176). Building suitable new data sets therefore emerges as a major challenge (chapter 2).

How Do Material Culture Traditions Evolve?

So far, much of this discussion has revolved around the theme of generalized cultural evolution, often citing examples of the evolution of linguistic traditions. But language evolution may form a very unique kind of cultural evolution. As examined previously, it is heavily structured by particular modes of transmission, and though innovations and borrowing may occur, it still needs to solve the basic collaborative problem of effective group-scale communication, which injects a strong conformity bias. This, in turn, appears to encourage strong heritable continuity, the formation of coherent lineages of tradition, which seem to evolve via branching processes of diversification, making deeper linguistic histories amenable to phylogenetic reconstruction.

What about the evolutionary dynamics of other kinds of cultural tradition? This book aims to improve understandings of one relatively underdeveloped area of research: the evolution of technology and material culture. Understanding spatio-temporal patterning in tools, artifacts, and other surviving objects is absolutely central to archaeology and also important for anthropology, yet the exact range of processes that can characterize *material* culture evolution remain somewhat unclear. For example, do material culture traditions exhibit strong heritable continuity, and if yes, what patterns of diversity are produced? On the one hand, there are many reasons to suspect that macroscale material culture evolution may also exhibit tree-like properties. Active participation in many craft traditions often requires years of long-term investment by both experienced practitioners and novices, typically ensuring formation of distinctive artifact lineages; community-scale propagation of these crafts may also be subject to strong conformity biases within a population, while TRIMs can insulate the craft from external influences, both of which would contribute to strong heritable continuity of distinct traditions within the population, and dampen the influence of external borrowings. In fact, humanity does appear to be highly adept at forming high levels of cultural diversity (Pagel and Mace 2004), and material culture may—in some cases—play an important role in actively signaling different kinds of group-based identities (but see Shennan 1989; Trigger 2006:3009–10, 452–53).

On the other hand, other roles played by technology and material culture may result in very different evolutionary patterns. Humans make tools and equipment to perform specific tasks, and some designs or entire technologies simply work better in certain functional and environments contexts than others. Thus, the set of traits combined in certain technologies can make them more efficient than other technologies, for example, if they can capture more energy or resources in relation to the time invested (a key insight to emerge from ecological and adaptive approaches in archaeology and anthropology). The deep attractions and functional advantages offered by some technological traits—or trait combinations—may simply override TRIMS, enabling knowledge of these to spread rapidly, effectively jumping horizontally between different populations (Dunnell 1978).

This book argues that a descent-with-modification perspective provides a productive approach for investigating exactly these kinds of historical dynamics in technology and material culture traditions. At the *micro*scale, a focus on cultural propagation highlights the roles of social learning, cultural context, and individual choice—this broadly aligns with current research being conducted within the anthropology of technology, with its focus on apprenticeship, intergenerational learning, and the embedded nature of different material culture traditions (see Stark et al. 2008b). The descent-with-modification approach, however, also raises important questions about how lineages of material culture tradition evolve at the *macro*scale, that is, between populations and societies. In part, this requires understanding better how *micro*scale processes of propagation actively feed into these *macro*scale patterns of material culture diversity. However, only limited attention is being directed at this central issue because of current interpretive interests in exploring routine practice and day-to-day reproduction of cultural traditions. In fact, this exclusive focus on the local and the particularistic tends to characterize most of the material culture research currently underway in both archaeology and anthropology.

At this point, it is worth reflecting back on the fact that descent-with-modification approaches to material culture traditions have a deeper history, especially in archaeology. Early ideas about cultural transmission—and reconstructing artifact lineages—can be traced back to North American cultural history, but this work was primarily directed at the challenge of developing relative chronologies prior to the development of radiocarbon dating (Lyman et al. 1997:231). A more explicitly evolutionary theory of artifact studies later arrived into archaeology from another direction, triggered by developments in palaeontology, the science of long-term evolutionary processes. Here, the development of phylogenetic methods gave palaeobiology new meaning: this was no longer about just cataloguing the diversity of life forms; it now represented a means of reconstructing macroscale evolutionary processes. It was not long before scholars interested in material culture began to take interest (Prentiss 2011), generating the unique offshoot branch of evolutionary archaeology (Dunnell 1978, 1980) within the new archaeology movement and its processual offspring (Trigger 2006:428–29). The central argument was that artifact variation through time and space should be approached in the same way that palaeobiologists explain patterning in the bony morphology of the organisms that make up the fossil record in terms of natural selection and drift processes (Collard and Shennan 2008: 18–19; Trigger 2006:428–29). At a deeper level then, Dunnell's (1978, 1980) general approach was an important conceptual breakthrough because it attempted to reconstruct the process of cultural evolution by studying the characteristics and attributes of the surviving artifacts that made up the archaeological record, that is, from the perspective of the material culture itself (Shennan 2008a:3176; 2008b:78; 2011). This stands in contrast to the more agent-centered approach developed by early formulations of dual inheritance theory (e.g., Cavalli Sforza and Feldman 1981; Boyd and Richerson 1985).

The current intellectual descendants of this unique Dunnellian form of evolutionary archaeology can now be grouped into two main strands of research, both united by a shared commitment to viewing the archaeological record in terms of the descent with modification of cultural information propagated by social learning (Lycett 2011). Some of the first attempts at using contemporary biological methods in archaeology built on the argument that the use of population genetic models of transmission and selection might be useful in trying to explain variability and change in artifacts making up the archaeological record (Boyd and Richerson, 1985; Cavalli Sforza and Feldman 1981). The suggestion here was that these models could provide useful means of testing hypotheses about patterns of cultural variability and change. This stemmed from the growing recognition that at a statistical level, many of the factors known to structure variation in genetic data (e.g., population size, drift, dispersal, etc.) should also be considered when trying to explain variation in material culture (e.g., Bentley et al. 2004; Bettinger and Eerkens 1999; Eerkens 2000; Eerkens and Lipo 2005; Kohler et al. 2004; Lipo et al. 1997; Lycett 2008, 2011; Mesoudi and Lycett 2009; Neiman, 1995; O'Brien and Lyman 2000, 2003; O'Brien et al. 2008; Shennan 2000, 2001, 2006; Shennan and Wilkinson 2001).

A second stream of research has explored other implications of a descent-with-modification approach to artifact lineages, and builds on earlier arguments that modern phylogenetic concepts might also have utility in the study of human cultural evolution (Foley 1987; Lycett 2011: 153). There is now a growing archaeological literature on the application of cladistic and related methods of phylogenetic reconstruction developed in biology to study variability and change in artifact lineages. Here, the general principles of applying these methods to archaeological data sets are now clear (e.g., O'Brien and Lyman 2000, 2003; O'Brien et al. 2001), and involves detailed characterization of artifact lineages linked by cultural transmission through time, with the appearance of new variants representing new branches on an evolutionary tree, whose history can be reconstructed through cladistic analysis (e.g., Buchanon and Collard 2007, 2008; Cochrane 2009; Cochrane and Lipo 2010; Lipo et al. 2006; Lycett 2007, 2009a, b, 2011; O'Brien et al. 2001; O'Brien et al. 2013; Prentiss et al. 2014). These methods have been argued to offer archaeologists a set of highly rigorous procedures for measuring artifact variability and change, and for identifying the critical variables that impact on their evolutionary history (Prentiss 2011; and see Mesoudi et al. 2006:334; Mesoudi 2011).

In sum, archaeologists and anthropologists continue to study material culture in a range of very different ways and from contrasting theoretical perspectives. Application of an explicitly descent-with-modification approach to material culture has some deeper intellectual roots that stretch back into culture historical archaeology as practiced in North America and Europe, but its current and more concerted theoretical and methodological fluorescence is still a relatively recent development within archaeology (Prentiss 2011). It is clear, however, that this specialist and now self-sustaining research literature is growing apace.

More generally, however, phylogenetic studies of material culture evolution are still not that common (Gray et al. 2010:3929) One of the main challenges to all archaeological studies is having to infer social learning, cultural transmission, and other evolutionary processes such as drift directly from the documentation and analysis of continuity and change in artifact lineages. Although the studies cited previously illustrate that that this kind of approach is now logistically and empirically feasible, other, more detailed contextual insights into other aspects of human social behavior linked with the propagation of these cultural lineages tend to be lacking, or at very best, must be inferred from other archaeological evidence, which brings its own additional challenges. In contrast, studying material culture evolution in more recent, ethnographically documented or contemporary fieldwork settings can draw on independent information on many other related aspects of human behavior. Despite these obvious attractions, exploration of this more resolutely "ethnoarchaeological" branch of culture-evolutionary research has been rather limited to date.

Renewed Scope for Ethnoarchaeological Studies of Material Culture Evolution?

Ethnographic research generates rich opportunities for undertaking detailed recording and and analysis of variability in craft traditions in relation to social learning, pedagogic patterns and cultural practices, in combination with detailed contextual information pertaining to the the life histories, and social identities of the individuals or groups that produced the artifacts (Tehrani 2006). Also usually available is information on the social institutions and settlement systems within which of the craft traditions are being propagated. Examination of the former is important for understanding the intentionality and general agency of people involved in making the objects and sharing the traditions with others; insights into the latter can clarify how local factors such as kinship, interaction patterns, politics, and territoriality can lead to the formation of diversity in material culture traditions. For example, increasing hostility between groups may reduce contacts and exchange, resulting in the emergence of cultural boundaries and growing stylistic differences between local craft traditions.

In contrast to the substantial archaeological literature on cultural transmission cited previously, a much smaller body of empirical research has emerged to address this potentially rich vein of inquiry. Generally, the main goal is to work with cultural trait lists to document geographic variability in material culture, and then use a range of cladistic and related methods of phylogenetic reconstruction to investigate the evolutionary histories of material culture traditions within relatively well-known ethnographic and historical settings (see chapter 2). Recent studies have examined Turkmen textiles (Tehrani and Collard 2002; Collard and Tehrani 2005, 2009a, b, 2013; Tehrani et al. 2010), indigenous clothing traditions in Northwest Siberia (Jordan 2009), various craft and architectural traditions in California (Jordan 2007; Jordan and Shennan 2003, 2005, 2009), and on the Pacific Northwest Coast (Jordan and Mace 2006, 2008; Jordan and O'Neill 2010); Polynesian bark-cloth traditions (Larsson 2011), European table cutlery (Riede 2009), Polynesian canoe designs (Rogers and Ehrlich 2008; Rogers et al. 2009; and see Gray et al. 2010: 3929–31), and musical instruments (Tëmkin and Eldridge 2007).

While all these studies have generated important contextual and historical insights into the contingent ways in which material culture traditions can potentially evolve, their focus has remained on understanding the evolutionary dynamics of a *single* craft tradition within *one* specific cultural or geographic setting. Some have attempted to compare evolution of craft traditions to language, but only a handful have attempted to examine more complex scenarios in which *multiple* material culture traditions potentially coevolve and the extent to which they exhibit deeper historical congruence (see Jordan and Mace 2006, 2008; Jordan and Shennan 2009; Riede 2009). This leaves an important gap in the current research literature, because the capacity to maintain multiple traditions is one of the defining features of human culture (table 1.1). Investigating how a range of different cultural traditions evolve is also central to the evaluation of all four of Boyd et al.'s (1997) models (figure 1.3). Likewise, the general focus on single-craft traditions within each ethnographic case studies also leaves it unclear as to the kinds of cross-cultural commonalities and divergences that might characterize overall material culture evolution at a more general comparative level (but see Collard et al. 2006a, b). Clearly, substantial progress has been made on many fronts, but much more empirical research remains to be done: the current research literature remains rather fragmented, with somewhat disconnected insights into the evolution of material culture traditions dispersed across multiple case studies; no studies to date have attempted to undertake a strategic and more explicitly comparative and contextual analysis of how multiple material culture traditions might evolve across a more targeted range of ethnographic settings.

To conclude, it is clear that there is now scope for making substantive progress on some of the most important themes, topics, and debates surrounding the broader evolutionary analysis of material culture traditions. In particular, there are exciting opportunities for a more explicitly coordinated cross-cultural study of how *multiple* material culture traditions evolve across a range of analogous—or at least broadly comparable—culture-historical settings. Conducting this research project within an ethnoarchaeological framework, linking social action to histories of artifact production, would also mean that the main insights would have a much deeper relevance to general debates spanning anthropology and archaeology about the main factors that generate variability and change in material culture traditions. In fact, undertaking exactly this kind of integrated and interdisciplinary research project now emerges as the central goal of this book.

DESIGNING AN EMPIRICAL STUDY: HOW DO MULTIPLE MATERIAL CULTURE TRADITIONS EVOLVE?

With so little empirical investigation into how multiple material culture traditions evolve, it is important to embed a new collection of case studies within a well-structured framework that enables sets of mutually reinforcing insights and understandings to feed into one another.

Northern Hunter-Gatherers

At a starting level, the book develops an explicit focus on evolution of *hunter-gatherer* technological traditions, which provides a basic sense of ethnographic unity to what otherwise might be a disparate collection of case studies. First, the technology of hunter-gatherers tends to consist of relatively *simpler* data sets, and their relationships with immediate environments tend to be more localized and direct, reducing the number and complexity of potentially confounding variables. While a descent-with-modification approach could, of course, be applied to cultural traditions within a wide range of different settings, such as modern nation-states and complex urban societies, progress on the basic arguments and issues is probably best achieved via a sustained focus on understanding technological evolution in smaller scale societies.

Second, the central focus on foragers also provides a useful framework for comparative integration of the results and insights. This is because hunter-gather populations have been the focus of systematic cross-cultural documentation and analysis (Jordan and Cummings 2014), generating a common vocabulary and shared terminology for describing different aspects of behavioral variability and major social institutions such as mobility regimes, kinship, and postmarital residence rules, settlement systems, and land-holding regimes (Kelly 1995, 2013). Moreover, all three case studies are also set in higher-latitude environments, where hunter-gatherer populations face broadly similar ecological challenges consisting primarily of the uneven distributions of resources over the landscape at different times of the year (figure 1.4). Populations in all three areas have responded to these opportunities and challenges via similar strategies of seasonal storage, complex mobility regimes, and distinctive social institutions that allocate people in highly structured ways to specific social groups, resources, and territories. These general contextual behaviors are important in studies of cultural transmission because these kinds of common institutions may also serve as TRIMS that structure how particular traits evolve across populations and cultures.

Third, to strengthen the framework for cross-cultural analysis of results, broadly similar sets of hunter-gatherer container and transport technologies, clothing, and built structures are examined across all the case studies, adding further conceptual linkages. Many of these craft traditions have an explicit gender association, enabling some interesting contrasts to be traced out between the histories of "male" and "female" technologies within and between the different case studies, as well as contrasting evolutionary patterns in more collective social traditions like house building versus more individualized crafts such as basketry.

Fourth, the entire phenomenon of cumulative culture emerged in first in prehistoric forager societies, so studying propagation of cultural traditions in these kinds of modern yet broadly analogous societies can also shed light on some of the basic mechanisms and factors that structure social learning and general cultural propagation within mobile small-scale communities who derive much of their primary subsistence from hunting, fishing, and gathering (Whiten 2011). Moreover, many early technological traditions also emerged first in forager settings, ranging from lithic tools through to the world's first pottery containers, and the surviving material residues of these crafts now form an extensive component of the earlier archaeological record for many world regions. Of course, by drawing such parallels between ethnography and archaeology—basically adopting an *ethno*archaeological approach to

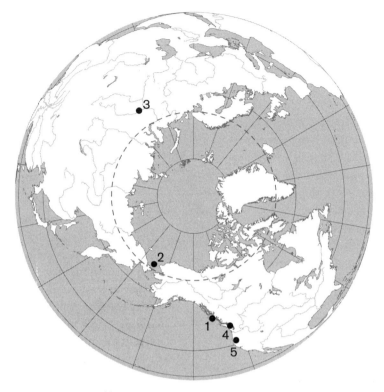

FIGURE 1.4 General location map: northern hunter-gatherers.

Geographic locations of book's main case-studies. Locations: (1) Pacific Northwest Coast (general) and (2) North Pacific Rim are discussed in chapter 2; Northwest Siberia (3) is examined in chapter 3; the Pacific Northwest Coast (Gulf of Georgia) (4); and Northern California (5), are examined in chapters 4 and 5 respectively.

analysis of material culture evolution—is not to argue that modern or ethnographically documented hunter-gatherers are somehow devoid of historical dynamism and are trapped in an earlier social evolutionary stage or that they have been unaffected by the effects of culture contact and colonialism. For example, the Siberian case study (chapter 3) examines cotemporary communities of "commercialised hunter-fisher-gatherers" with long histories of colonial contact (Jordan 2003, 2011a, b), while the Western North American case studies (chapters 4 and 5) examine the relatively high-density populations who occupied rich ecological niches, and whose societies and technological traditions were the outcome of many millennia of localized cultural developments. Ethnoarchaeologists have long been aware of the limitations to their approach but believe that important insights into the complex links between material culture and social action can still be produced (Lane 2014).

Social Scales

The interlocking themes of propagation, coherence, and historical congruence unite all the case studies, but these topics are deliberately examined across a range of intersecting social scales. The case studies employ linguistic diversity as a general measure of social scale, and in many cases, also use language or dialect speech communities to define specific ethnolinguistic populations. These scales range from single-dialect communities, a chain of related dialect communities, through to regions with high levels of linguistic diversity, where populations speak languages with very different histories. Organized in such a way, the insights generated at one scale of analysis can also feed into interpretations and understandings at other scales, generating better comparative understandings of how different kinds of material culture tradition tend to evolve.

Organization of the Book

This opening chapter has outlined the main research themes and identified the key questions to addressed (see table 1.4), starting with a clear definition of the problem to be solved (Richerson and Boyd 2005: 65).

Chapter 2 aims to provide a bridge between current debates about best to understand and explain the evolution of craft traditions and the conduct of empirical research. It examines how comprehensive material culture data sets can be collected in ethnographic settings, and explains how the main research questions can be addressed by applying a single methodological framework. This approach is based on the use of a range of relatively straightforward techniques drawn from evolutionary biology. Choice to use these specific methods was guided by the book's more general anthropological and archaeological readership and represents a relatively simple and easily accessible approach to the kinds of material culture and linguistic data sets that other regional specialists should also be able to reproduce and start to analyze. Emphasis is also placed on the importance of integrating wider ethnographic insights so that observed patterns of cultural evolution can be contextualized within specific historical settings.

Chapter 3 is set in Northwest Siberia and focuses primarily on understanding the microscale propagation of a range of material culture traditions, examining the different scales of coherence that tend to emerge. Here, the emphasis is very much on the agency of individuals as they practice different craft and architectural traditions, but these propagation processes are also examined from the perspective of the artifacts that are produced. Data are derived from the author's own ethnoarchaeological surveys (1997–2005) illustrating how active field research is an ideal method for generating new data and studying cultural propagation within complex living settings. Here, the methods are used as part of a "pattern recognition" approach to understanding the extent to which more coherent material culture traditions are likely to emerge.

Chapter 4 picks up on these Siberian insights but expands the social scale to examine the inheritance of three material culture traditions across communities of Pacific Northwest Coast hunter-fisher-gatherers who speak a chain of related Coast Salishan dialects. The main concern here is exploring coherence at the macro-scale of cultural evolution; in particular, it examines whether local community traditions have evolved via branching or blending processes, and the degree to which language and craft traditions exhibit historical congruence. As such, the chapter looks first at the general ethnographic context and then examines the process of evolution from the perspective of the artifacts being reproduced, attempting at the end to link these patterns to the agency of individuals responsible for the propagation of the traditions. This approach highlights the important role played by local social institutions, which appear, in *some* cases, to play the role of TRIMS, playing a major structuring role in the propagation of these different cultural traditions and producing distinctive macroscale patterns of material culture diversity.

Chapter 5 casts the widest net and focuses on macroscale cultural inheritance among populations inhabiting Northern California, an area of very high linguistic diversity. The main goal is to examine how variability in social institutions affects the coherence and historical congruence of different craft traditions. This approach also examines the general ethnographic context and focuses on reconstructing evolutionary patterns from the perspective of the artifact lineages, linking these patterns back to the role of the agents who propagate these traditions. Again, some social institutions appear to serve as TRIMS, but only for certain traditions, and only in certain geographic areas.

Chapter 6 concludes the book with a cross-cultural analysis of results derived from each case study, and is structured by detailed discussions of

TABLE 1.4   THE BOOK'S THREE MAIN RESEARCH THEMES MAPPED ONTO THE
STRUCTURE OF CHAPTERS

Main Research Themes	Main Questions	Relevant Social Scale	Chapters
1. *Propagation* General reproduction of cultural traits across a range of traditions	How are different material culture traditions maintained and transformed?	Mainly microscale evolution of material culture traits *within* defined populations	Chapter 3 (primarily); also general insights in 4 and 5
2. *Coherence* In *single* material culture traditions	To what extent do material culture traits form coherent entities; do these cultural lineages evolve through splitting or mixing processes?	Macroscale evolution of material culture traits *across* ethnolinguistic populations	Chapters 3, 4, and 5
3. *Historical Congruence* Across *multiple* material culture traditions	Which of Boyd et al.'s (1997) models best characterize general material culture evolution (figure 1.3)?	Macroscale evolution of material culture traits *across* ethnolinguistic populations	Chapters 4 and 5

the three main themes of propagation, coherence, and historical congruence. Finally, the chapter aims to explore the general relevance of a descent-with-modification approach to the broader analysis of cultural traditions and highlights themes and questions requiring further research.

CONCLUSION

This book argues that the vast range of material culture and technology made and used by humans forms a unique form of social tradition. In fact, all cultural habits can be understood as collections of information that are passed on to others by social learning. It is argued that this process of cultural transmission has some general analogies with the ways in which genetic information is inherited and cumulatively adjusted within and between populations: in short, cultural traditions can also be argued to evolve via a broadly similar process of descent with modification.

Drawing on a wide range of methodological and disciplinary sources, this book aims to apply such a descent-with-modification perspective to the study of variability and change in material culture traditions. Recent work using a similar framework has generally been limited to broader theoretical syntheses and position statements, single empirical case studies, edited collections, or general summary overviews of the evolved human capacities for cumulative culture and social learning. In particular, ethnographic research into the evolution of material culture traditions has also been rather limited and reflects a general challenge generated by a shortage of appropriate high-resolution data sets suitable for this kind of approach. In contrast, *Technology as Human Social Tradition* undertakes the first book-length *empirical* analysis of cultural transmission and the evolution of complex technological traditions, presenting some new data sets and focusing on detailed case studies, so that the propagation, coherence, and congruence of specific material culture traditions can be linked to other behavioral factors, such as the role of social institutions, all within an explicitly comparative framework.

This latter goal is supported by a sustained focus on northern hunter-gatherers, their material culture and social institutions, and by the application of the same methods and approaches across these different historical and cultural settings. This central focus on material culture also means that the results and insights from these essentially ethnographic case studies have central relevance to some central archaeological debates. As such, the book can also be defined as a comparative, cross-cultural exercise in hunter-gatherer ethnoarchaeology, and, with a central focus on the role of social traditions and material culture—and not adaptation and ecology—also aims to take this specialist field into some productive new research directions (David and Kramer 2001; Lane 2014).

Therefore, the book is primarily aimed also at a more *general* anthropological and archaeological readership as much as at existing culture-evolutionary researchers, and the methods deployed also represent a range of widely available and also readily accessible approaches to researching material culture traditions for those without an advanced training in computational biology. In fact, it is hoped that by reading this book, which consists of a series of worked empirical examples of how a descent-with-modification approach can be applied to the study of different material culture data sets at an interlocking range of social and spatial scales, other regional specialists will start to explore some these ideas and approaches, and by drawing on their in-depth regional knowledge and period-specific expertise, will generate and analyze a new generation of archaeological and ethnographic data sets that are, frustratingly to date, such a rarity (Whiten 2011: 945).

Finally, and more generally, the three recurring themes of themes of propagation, coherence, and historical congruence in material culture traditions that stretch through this book clearly emerge from a dual inheritance perspective on culture that has its roots in (modern) evolutionary biology. Other intellectual lineages also play a role: highlighting human material culture and technology as an embodied and embedded social tradition means that human decision-making processes, cumulative history, and local contingency all become central to the research, intersecting in a novel and productive way with long-running archaeological and anthropological debates about enculturation and enskillment, the operation of human agency, the performance of culture, and, at larger and more enduring scales, with long-standing questions about how best to understand the origins and social significance of specific distributions of material styles over time and space, still generally described as "archaeological cultures."

Therefore, rather than an abstract position statement or theoretical overview, the book aims to empirically demonstrate several points of intellectual convergence between some of the new and emerging strands of culture-evolutionary research and a range of more established interpretive, historical, and particularistic approaches, the most important being that a shared focus on the study of inheritance—both cultural and biological—can serve to unite future studies of human diversity, both in the more distant archaeological past and also in the present.

CHAPTER 2

Methodology

This chapter aims to build a bridge between the theoretical perspectives on human technological traditions outlined in the previous chapter and the application of these ideas and approaches to empirical research. In short, this chapter provides a methodological framework for assembling appropriate information, and then analyzing these data sets in ways that address the book's three main themes of propagation, coherence, and historical congruence in material culture traditions. Given that the book also aims to produce a series of higher-level and comparative cross-cultural insights into the general processes generating variability and change in material culture, this methodology has also been designed so that it can be applied across different case studies, thereby generating results that can be integrated into a final concluding discussion (note 1).

The chapter starts by looking at the basic elements of material culture traditions. For analytical purposes, the production of particular items of material culture can be broken down into an operational sequence that consists of a series of stages. At each of these stages, there are usually choices about the raw materials that can be employed, the appropriate methods, skills, and techniques used to integrate and combine them, as well as a whole host of other design-, function-, and performance-related considerations. For analytical purposes, these specific choices can be described as *cultural traits,* and in enduring technological traditions, these sets of traits are propagated through social learning, with novel traits appearing constantly through the process of general

cultural improvisation, either as a result of deliberate creativity and pur-
poseful innovation, but also via copying error.

When researching the evolution of specific material culture traditions,
it is useful to understand how particular collections of traits are propagated through social learning both *within* and also *between* populations.
It then becomes important to understand the degree to which individual
traits form only rather ephemeral collections or the extent to which they
become more tightly integrated together into more coherent cultural entities that endure in recognizable formats over time. To what extent can the
deeper history of these coherent cultural entities be reconstructed—do
they form distinct cultural lineages that appear to evolve via cumulative
branching processes from a common ancestor, or does the ready mixing
of traits between groups erode these deeper historical signals? Finally, is
it possible to identify any deeper historical congruence between different
lineages of material culture tradition and language history?

As examined in chapter 1, the ways in which cultural traits are propagated within and between human social groups has broad conceptual
analogies with the ways in which genetic information is transmitted
between individuals and across generations. The current chapter builds
on these parallels and outlines how a range of relatively straightforward
analytical methods developed and widely used by evolutionary biologists can be used to address analogous questions about the contingent
histories of the traits that make up cultural traditions.

In order to make the approach more accessible to general archaeological and anthropological researchers, each method is illustrated with
a worked example, and a summary table outlines how specific research
questions can be addressed by the different methods. Finally, a hypothetical case study is presented to explain how the general approach can
be applied to the study of material culture evolution in a specific culture-historical setting. In conclusion, this integrated methodology provides the backbone of the three sets of case studies presented in chapters
3, 4, and 5, and the application of the same methods across this chapters
generates local insights that can be readily integrated into the cross-
cultural discussion and synthesis that forms chapter 6.

INVESTIGATING VARIABILITY IN MATERIAL CULTURE TRADITIONS

What is culture and what exactly gets passed on through social learning? Are there discrete units of cultural inheritance? As examined in

chapter 1, these questions link back to a long-standing debate in culture-evolutionary research, but one that has shifted significantly over recent years. Early formulations focused on the role of more particulate forms of cultural information, such as memes, which were thought to be able to replicate themselves. According to this formulation, memes were easy-to-remember units of culture that competed with each other and were argued to have the capacity to spread rapidly throughout the minds of individuals in a population, akin to viral marketing (Dawkins 1976). However, the simple "meme-as-replicator" model is now viewed as problematic, because the process of cultural inheritance is acknowledged to be far more complex (Shennan 2002a:46–47).

In more recent debates, there has been a steady shift toward more fluid concepts such as "cultural information," which can broadly be defined as skills, beliefs, values, and attitudes stored in human brains and acquired from others by teaching, imitation, and other forms of social learning (Richerson and Boyd 2005:61). In fact, there are many reasons to believe that what is transmitted is neither discrete nor always transmitted faithfully, and the term *cultural variant* has been proposed as a more appropriate alternative (2005:63). Consensus is also shifting toward analysis of how these cultural variants are actually propagated within the context of more enduring social traditions (e.g., Whiten et al. 2011:940). In other words, it is the enduring traditions that are social rather than the cultural attributes or particular information they reproduce. This is important, because recent research into cultural inheritance is now focusing on the importance of "scaffolding," whereby the experienced practitioner guides an initiate over a longer-term learning process, which often involves substantial investment of time and effort from both sides. These new developments are also important because they potentially provide greater scope for productive engagement with social and cultural anthropology around exploration of the broader themes of social traditions, enculturation, and enskillment; here, knowledge is not passed on ready-made; it undergoes continual regeneration through a guided process of rediscovery that takes place in the social contexts of interaction between instructors and novices (see Ingold 2000; 2007:16).

Defining Cultural Traits within Technological Traditions

The concept of cultural variants is useful in general discussion of how culture evolves, but a more precise set of terminology can be developed for the study of technological traditions. Anthropologists and archaeologists have now examined variability and change in material culture using a range of different theoretical and methodological approaches, but all tend to emphasize the contingent nature of much technology, and thereby, the considerable scope for individual creativity and choice during its manufacture. For example, Stark has argued that most everyday objects and artifacts are made through *repetitive* and *mundane* activities that tend to reflect *the ways things are done* in a local tradition, and that "in most media used to manufacture traditional technology, technical problems have alternative solutions" (Stark 1998:6).The particular choice of materials, forms, and combination of elements generally reflects an internalized cognitive understanding of the manufacturing tradition—as such, these "choices" reflect conscious and unconscious ways in which individuals actively participate in the reproduction of specific technological traditions.

Here again, the emphasis is on the importance of *social tradition*—having acquired mastery of specific "ways of doing," practitioners of particular crafts then tend to "pass this knowledge from one generation to the next," with some aspects of the tradition often more stable than others (Stark 1998:6, with references). The basic point here then is that the passing on of the traditions is an inherently *social* process, forming part of the broader regeneration of cultural knowledge between instructors and novices that takes place within contexts of social and environmental interaction (Ingold 2007:16), but it is also a social process that can result in deeper historical *continuity* in many material culture traditions. In this latter aspect, an understanding of the long-term material *outcomes* (or physical residues) of this enskillment process is as important as insights into the daily regeneration of cultural knowledge through creative social action (Ingold 2000). In fact, archaeologists invest much of their research effort into the documentation and analysis of these enduring material cultural lineages, noting the striking human capacity for the relatively faithful replication of highly complex, but essentially arbitrary, material culture traditions over many, many human generations. And it is this focus on understanding the long-term *persistence* of tradition that tends to distinguish archaeology from anthropology. But in turn, identification of these long-term material traditions also highlights the importance of understanding the role played by social learning, guided rediscovery, and the continual process of knowledge regeneration (Ingold 2000, 2007:16), all of which impact upon the contingent choices that are central to the long-term propagation of such cultural lineages (Riede and Tehrani 2006).

One other important insight that emerges from the extensive literature on the anthropology of technology is that most crafts involve an extended production process, or "operational sequence" *(chaîne opéra-toire)*. The internal elements and logic of this sequence—or "way of doing"—are, of course, generally learned through explicit teaching, observation, and other forms of social learning, such natural pedagogy, but are then stored as cultural information in the brains of individuals, who then drawn on this information when habitually practicing the craft within particular social and environmental settings. In most situations, then, this cultural inheritance process tends to create at least *some* heritable continuity in technological traditions rather than an endless blur of entirely new variants.

Although designs can and do change, they cannot change overnight, and they usually tend to involve modification of existing trait combinations or "design grammars." Moreover, the designs of many items of technology consist of different subcomponents, such as the skin-working and stitching techniques used in a kayak hull, in combination with the wood-carving and joinery skills deployed for the kayak frame (see book cover). The persistence of one set of cultural traits depends on its relationship to other cultural variants used in the overall design. Most human technologies have multiple interacting parts and components, and studying their evolution requires understanding change in each of the individual parts, but also about how these different parts fit together.

The key insight here is that if technological traditions are made up of extended operational sequences, then the specific constitution of particular socially propagated traditions can be carefully studied to first identify different *stages* in the artifact production process, and second, the range of *choices* at each of these stages. For example, the Siberian ski-making traditions examined in chapter 3 can be broken down into their constituent parts, with each stage involving strategic choice. Production stages range from acquiring timber, shaping the main wooden baseboard, making the foot binding, and fitting the furs underneath to aid forward traction in snow. The ski maker has choices at each stage: should the wood be pine, birch, or aspen; should the fur be reindeer skin or moose; should the bindings consist of wood and leather, or just leather straps; how should the bindings fasten up, and so on? In this way, a number of stages can be identified (e.g., sourcing the wood) and the choices available at each of these stages defined (e.g., pine *versus* birch *versus* aspen). In fact, such material culture traditions are ideal for systematic documentation because their constituent cultural traits can be readily defined, measured, and recorded according to formal and design criteria. If variability in ski-making traditions are carefully documented across a region, it generally becomes clear that different individuals and communities living in that region propagate a wider general "pool" of ski-making traits in slightly different ways, raising interesting questions about the factors that promote continuity, change, and diversity in the vast array of specific traits that make up such local technological traditions. Using the term "cultural trait" within this analytical framework enables both detailed empirical recording of variability in technological designs and also opens the way for the study of historical agency in relation to the propagation and distribution of those traits, that is, how the active and cumulative choices made by generations of human persons have produced variability in those designs.

Assembling this kind of trait-based information across a range of social groupings is also analogous to data sets commonly used by biologists to reconstruct the evolutionary histories of different biological lineages. This generally consists of comparative information (e.g., on morphology or genetic data) across a range of taxa, with each taxon often ascribed a discrete character state for a number of different characters. Similarly, in studies of material culture variability, these taxa would equate to specific "populations" within which the particular traits are being propagated as a social tradition, for example, a kin group, speech community, or defined ethnic or social grouping. Researchers can then examine the propagation of these traits within each population (microscale cultural evolution) and also how the traits evolve across different populations (macroscale cultural evolution).

Defining Populations in Material Culture Surveys

The concept of "population" is defined by biologists as a group of individuals of the same species who have a high probability of interacting with one another, and by population geneticists as a group of interbreeding organisms of the same species—in short, a population can be understood as a "defined collection" (Kelly 2002:249). The concept of populations can also be used to structure the recording of cultural traits, but in designing a research project, it is important to clarify exactly how these populations are being defined (Kelly 2002:251). For example, in material culture surveys, Hosfield (2009:46–48) defines populations along an ascending range of "social units," from lodges to compounds through to villages and valleys.

This book also employs an ascending range of social scales to define the populations that structure the case studies, employing kinship, geographic, and also ethnolinguistic criteria. For example, in chapter 3, the main concern is understanding the *microscale* propagation of traits across different material culture traditions within populations. Variability in traits is therefore recorded at the scale of individual examples of technology (e.g., examples of skis made by a particular person), through to examples of artifacts made by specific kinship groups (patrilineages), as well as different sections or branches of the large rivers upon which communities live, and through to the various major river basins whose inhabitants speak distinctive dialects. Chapters 4 and 5 focus more on *macroscale* evolution of material culture traditions across different populations and employ the concept of "linguistically defined populations"—these speech communities are termed "ethnolinguistic communities" (and see Durham 1990; Jordan and Shennan 2003, 2009). Having defined the scale and type of population under investigation, the distribution of traits across these different groups can then be recorded.

Generating Trait-Based Material Culture Data Sets

Although comprehensive and open access data sets are widely available in the biological sciences and have now become standard research practice, this is still not the case in culture evolutionary research. In fact, the lack of suitable, high-resolution cultural data sets remains a major challenge in taking research beyond theory and simulation studies and into more empirical directions (Shennan 2011). However, suitable cultural data sets can be generated in three main ways: (1) *primary ethnographic fieldwork:* this is the model followed in chapter 3, and it provides scope for integrating trait-based material culture surveys with targeted interviews and participant observation, using the wider ethnographic and historical literature for additional contextual details and the addition of further temporal depth to study how traditions change over time; (2) *reworking data from older ethnographic surveys:* systematic culture element surveys were conducted across Western North America (see Jorgensen 1980, with references) and many other world regions, including Siberia (e.g., Levin and Potapov 1961). However, since the *Kulturkreis* school became unpopular, there has been remarkably little systematic recording of cross-cultural similarities and differences in material culture (McEachern 1998:111; Shennan 2011), although many of these older ethnographic data sets can now be adapted for quantitative analysis (see following; case studies in chapters 4 and 5); (3) *analysis of collections:* many museums contain remarkably complete material culture

collections, and with good provenance and contextual data, these artifacts can be used to conduct large-scale retrospective surveys of trait-
based material culture variability over substantial geographic areas (see,
e.g., Jordan and Shennan 2003, which used Elsasser's 1978a tabulations
of California basketry variability, primarily based on work with older
museum collections).

Assembling and screening such primary information can often
require major investments of effort, but large, high-resolution data sets
can usually be produced. Most data sets of this kind quickly become too
large and unwieldy to answer particular questions about cultural transmission through only visual inspection alone (Stark et al. 2008b:9). In
fact, one of the key general arguments made in this book is that a quantitative approach to the study of material culture traditions eventually
becomes essential if specific predictions about coherence and historical
congruence are to be properly tested (Boyd et al. 1997; Gray et al. 2010)
and the distributions of specific technological traits across populations
explained (Holden and Shennan 2005:14). The next section illustrates a
simple step-by-step example of how a suitable data set can be generated,
and then moves on to look at how a range of analytical methods can be
used to test specific culture-evolutionary hypotheses.

A Worked Example: Ethnolinguistic Populations and Recording
Trait-Based Variability in Material Culture Traditions

The general approach to trait-based data collection can be illustrated by
Jordan and O'Neill's (2010) recent analysis of the macroscale evolution
of long-house designs on the Pacific Northwest Coast. Using older data
from Drucker's 1950 *Culture Element Distributions* and Thompson
and Kincade's (1990) work on local language history, they were able to
identify seventeen distinct ethnolinguistic populations resident along
the coastline (figure 2.1). These populations and their linguistic affinities
are listed in table 2.1.

Drucker's (1950) original surveys were conducted in the 1930s and
involved detailed interviews with elders, aiming to record the main features of "traditional" (pre-European contact) housing styles in a trait-
based presence/absence format (see some of the general examples of
Northwest Coast housing traditions in figure 2.2). Such surveys generated remarkably detailed and comprehensive records, although some
sections contain missing information. Jordan and O'Neill (2010) edited
this ethnographic data set to remove any rows with missing data and

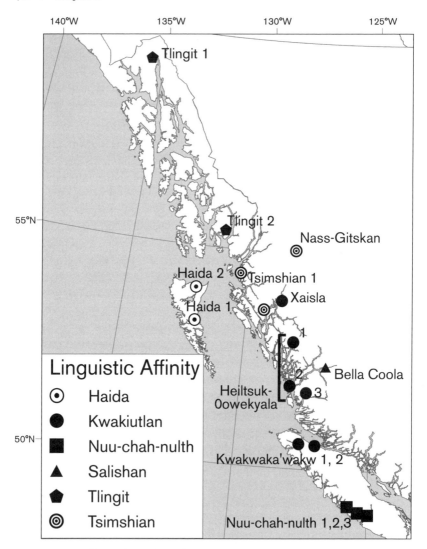

FIGURE 2.1 Pacific Northwest Coast location map.

Geographic locations and linguistic affinities of seventeen ethnolinguistic populations on the Pacific Northwest Coast (after Jordan and O'Neill 2010).

then worked closely with the remaining list to define general aspects of local house design, such as "house pits." This category was then used to define constituent traits, for example, whether there was an "excavated central pit" (trait number 1), or "series of steps into pit" (trait number 2), or "pit walls plank lined" (trait number 3), and so on (see table 2.2).

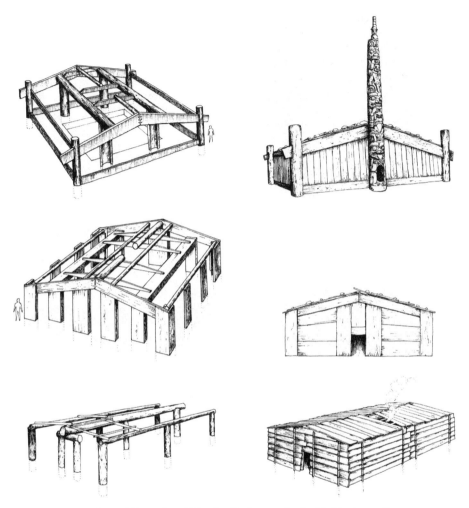

FIGURE 2.2 General Examples of Housing Designs on the Pacific Northwest Coast.
Examples of housing designs along different sections of the Pacific Northwest Coast.
Interiors views on the left; exteriors views on the right. *Top row:* Haida; *middle:*
Tsimshian; *bottom:* Wakashan (possibly Nuu-chah-nulth). SOURCE: Stewart 1984:66,
68–69. *Cedar: Tree of Life to the Northwest Coast Indians* by Hilary Stewart, 1995,
Douglas and McIntyre. Reprinted with permission from the publisher.

If the trait was definitely *present*, it scored 1, and if definitely *absent*,
it scored a 0. This approach was applied systematically to the housing
styles recorded for each of the seventeen ethnolinguistic populations.
For example, a house with no "excavated central pit" (and hence no
steps or plank lining either) would be recorded as 000 for traits 1–3. In

TABLE 2.1 NORTHWEST COAST ETHNOLINGUISTIC POPULATIONS (NAMES, CODES, AND LINGUISTIC AFFINITIES). *(For geographic locations, see figure 2.3.)*

No.	Ethnolinguistic Community[a]	Code (Figure 2.1)	Language (local)[b]	Language (branch)[b]	Language (family)[b]
1	Chilkat	Tlingit 1	Tlingit	Tlingit	Tlingit
2	Sanyakwan	Tlingit 2	Tlingit	Tlingit	Tlingit
3	Skidegate	Haida 1	Haida	Haida	Haida
4	Massett	Haida 2	Haida	Haida	Haida
5	Gitskan (Kispiyox division)	Nass-Gitskan	Nass-Gitskan	Tsimshian	Tsimshian
6	Tsimshian Proper (Gilutsa division)	Tsimishian 1	Coast Tsimshian	Tsimshian	Tsimshian
7	Southern Tsimshian (Kitqata division)	Tsimishian 2	Coast Tsimshian	Tsimshian	Tsimshian
8	Xaisla (Kitimat)	Xaisla	Xaisla	Kwakwaka'wakw	Wakashan
9	Xaihais (China Hat)	Heiltsuk-Oowekyala 1	Heiltsuk-Oowekyala	Kwakwaka'wakw	Wakashan
10	Bella Bella (Oyalit division)	Heiltsuk-Oowekyala 2	Heiltsuk-Oowekyala	Kwakwaka'wakw	Wakashan
11	Bella Coola	Bella Coola	Bella Coola	Bella Coola	Salishan
12	Wikeno	Heiltsuk-Oowekyala 3	Heiltsuk-Oowekyala	Kwakwaka'wakw	Wakashan
13	Kwexa	Kwakwaka'wakw 1	Kwakwaka'wakw	Kwakwaka'wakw	Wakashan
14	Koskimo	Kwakwaka'wakw 2	Kwakwaka'wakw	Kwakwaka'wakw	Wakashan
15	Clayoquot	Nuu-chah-nulth 1	Nuu-chah-nulth	Nuu-chah-nulth	Wakashan
16	Tsishaat	Nuu-chah-nulth 2	Nuu-chah-nulth	Nuu-chah-nulth	Wakashan
17	Hupachisat	Nuu-chah-nulth 3	Nuu-chah-nulth	Nuu-chah-nulth	Wakashan

[a]After Drucker 1950.
[b]After Thompson and Kincade 1990.

contrast, a house with a pit, a series of steps down into it, but no plank lining, would score 110 for the same set of traits. Finally, a house with a pit that had no steps, but was plank lined, would be documented as 101, and so on.

This approach was extended across the wider pool of traits that made up each local architectural tradition, generating fifty-seven specific housing traits that were documented as being definitely present or

TABLE 2.2 NORTHWEST COAST HOUSING TRADITIONS

Trait Number	General Category	Trait Description
1	House pits	Excavated central pit
2		Series of steps into the pit
3		Pit walls plank-lined
4	Pilings	House built on pilings
5	Wall planks	Wall planks detachable for move to summer houses
6		Framework and wall planks inseparable
7	Posts	Round posts
8		Squared posts
9		Zoomorphic relief carvings on posts
10	Roof construction	Two-pitch roof
11		One-pitch roof ("shed roof")
12		Single ridgepole
13		Ridgepole as lintel directly on posts
14		Ridgepole on cross-lintel
15		Double ridgepole
16		Intermediate beams
17		Roof plates and sills
18	Wall support	Slots for wall sheathing
19		Wall sheathing horizontal
20		Supported between vertical stakes
21		Overlapping clapboard
22		Wall sheathing vertical
23	Roof boards	Roof of boards
24		Roof of bark
25		Overlapping peak
26		Ridge cover: dug-out pole
27		Ridge cover: horizontal boards

NOTE: Only traits 1–27 out of a total of 57 traits are shown. For full data set, see Jordan and O'Neill 2010, and for original data set, see Drucker 1950.

definitely absent across each of the seventeen ethnolinguistic populations. An illustrative selection of twenty-seven of these trait descriptions is outlined in table 2.2 (for full descriptions of all traits, see Jordan and O'Neill 2010). These strings of binary data generated for each of the seventeen populations are presented in table 2.3.

In conclusion, this section has argued that the variable ways in which material culture traditions are propagated across a region can be broken down into sets of cultural traits, and the presence or absence of these traits recorded across a range of defined populations, in this case study, ethnolinguistic populations. These binary data sets, consisting of

TABLE 2.3 CHARACTER MATRIX OF PACIFIC NORTHWEST COAST HOUSING
TRADITIONS FOR SEVENTEEN ETHNOLINGUISTIC POPULATIONS

Tlingit 1	11100101010000101110011001001001010110001101100101000000
Tlingit 2	11100101110000101100011110001001010111101111111110110000
Haida 1	11100111010000101100010100001001010111111101011101111101
Haida 2	11100111110000111100011100001001010111111111111110111101
Nass-Gitskan	00000110110000111100010100010001100110001001101100111111
Tsimishian 1	11110110110000111100011100110001100111001011101011111111
Tsimishian 2	00010110110000101100011010010001100111001011111001111101
Xaisla	11110110110000101100011010010001100111100011101110111101
Heiltsuk-Oowekyala 1	11100110110000101100011010010001100111101011110111011101
Heiltsuk-Oowekyala 2	11100110110000101100011010010001100111011011101011011101
Bella Coola	11110110111000101111010100010001100111101111011101111101
Heiltsuk-Oowekyala 3	11110110110000101111110001101101001111011110111011011101
Kwakwaka'wakw 1	11111010110111100011101010010110101001001101100101111100
Kwakwaka'wakw 2	11101010110111100011101010010110101001011011111011011100
Nuu-chah-nulth 1	00001010110110000111010001101100110011010101110000010000
Nuu-chah-nulth 2	00001010111000000011101010010110101001111100010011010000
Nuu-chah-nulth 3	00001010101000000011101000010110101001111100010010010000

NOTE: See Jordan and O'Neill 2010.

strings of 1s and 0s, are analogous to the basic "character matrix" used
by evolutionary biologists to reconstruct the deeper evolutionary histories of organisms. This next section argues that the broad analogies
between cultural and genetic inheritance mean that the powerful, computational methods developed by evolutionary biologists can be
deployed to analyze these kinds of material culture data sets and to
study propagation, coherence, and historical congruence across different human technological traditions.

INVESTIGATING MATERIAL CULTURE AS A
SOCIAL TRADITION: AN INTEGRATED
ANALYTICAL FRAMEWORK

There is now growing appreciation among anthropologists and archaeologists that the phylogenetic approaches biologists have developed to
reconstruct the evolutionary relationships of biological entities can also
serve as useful tools for identifying and explaining different kinds of
patterning in human cultural diversity (and see Buchanon and Collard
2008; Collard et al. 2006a, b; Collard et al. 2008; Collard and Shennan
2008; Lycett 2011; O'Brien and Lyman 2000, 2003b; O'Brien et al.

2001, 2008, 2013 for wider discussions). Specifically, these computational phylogenetic methods offer a useful means of creating testable propositions about heritable continuity—how one thing is related to another in terms of descent, and also to what extent different cultural lineages are congruent with one another and with language history (see O'Brien et al. 2013).

One major criticism of earlier attempts to apply phylogenetic methods to cultural data was the assertion that reticulation would always tend to dominate in cultural evolution, thereby destroying the maintenance of deeper historical signals (Bateman et al. 1990:310; Dewar 1995; Hornborg 2005; Moore 1994a, b, 2001; Terrell 1988, 2001, 2004; Terrell and Stewart 1996; Terrell et al. 1997, 2001; Welsch et al. 1992; Welsch and Terrell 1994). According to this view, cultural evolution is a fundamentally different kind of process than is biological evolution, with a much faster tempo and a different mode—horizontal transmission—that quickly eradicates any signals for phylogenetic history, reducing the landscape of cultural variants to little more than a blur of interrelated forms (O'Brien et al. 2013). This general process is often defined as *ethnogenesis* (Borgerhoff Mulder et al. 2006:54).

It is worth returning here to the book's main research theme: What factors generate variability and change in material culture traditions? Thus, the overarching goal of this book is to reconstruct historically contingent patterns of technological continuity and change across a comparative range of settings and social scales, and then seek to explain, on a case-by-case basis, why particular patterns have emerged (see Boyd et al. 1997). In this sense, the book is not seeking to make a general position statement about whether phylogenesis or ethnogenesis will always predominate in material culture evolution, but aims to assemble appropriate methods and data sets to test contrasting models of cultural evolution across a series of empirical case studies (Boyd et al. 1997). In other words, the most important question about material culture evolution is testing *what particular model best fits the data* (O'Brien et al. 2013).

As a result, this task requires building a methodology that does not assume or prioritize any one process or model over another a priori but that enables a range of very different evolutionary scenarios to be tested within a more cautious step-by-step approach. As discussed previously, this approach starts with systematic trait-based recording of the material culture traditions being propagated across a region, with variability in these traits recorded at the scale of a predefined set of populations. This next section examines how these binary data sets can then be analyzed with the suite of analytical methods. These methods, and the way in which they map onto the book's main research questions, are summarized in table 2.4. This same general approach is applied throughout chapters 3–5, providing scope for an integration of results in chapter 6.

Computational Phylogenetic Methods

Charles Darwin (1859) produced one of the first illustrations of, and crucially popularized, the notion of an evolutionary "tree" in his seminal book *On the Origin of Species*. More than a century and a half later, evolutionary biologists still use tree diagrams to depict evolution because such diagrams effectively convey the concept that speciation occurs through the splitting away of new lineages (Ridley 2004). A phylogenetic or evolutionary tree is therefore a branching tree diagram that attempts to depict the implied evolutionary relationships among various biological species or other entities based upon similarities and differences in their physical and/or genetic characteristics. Phylogenetic reconstruction is based on a model of "descent with modification" (Darwin 1859:459), in which new taxa arise from the bifurcation of existing ones. Phylogenetic analysis was developed by evolutionary biologists to reconstruct the genealogies of organisms and rests on the axiom that their evolutionary relationships can be represented in the form of a branching tree diagram (Forey et al. 1992; Hennig 1966; Kitching et al. 1998; Smith 1994; and see Lycett 2011; O'Brien et al. 2013; Ridley 2004).

In phylogenetic reconstruction, these ancestor–descendant *relationships* are defined in terms of relative recency of common ancestry: two taxa are deemed to be more closely related to one another than either is to a third taxon if they share a common ancestor that is not also shared by the third taxon (O'Brien et al 2013:45–46. The empirical evidence for exclusive common ancestry is the presence of evolutionarily novel, or *derived*, character states. Two taxa are inferred to share a common ancestor to the exclusion of a third taxon if they exhibit derived character states that are *not* also exhibited by the third taxon. This is because of the powerful but simple idea that as different species arise during the course of evolution they acquire novel features at different times. It then becomes possible to use these features to infer the historical sequence of changes that has led to a particular species, and the changes can be classified more rationally.

The main challenge is therefore to distinguish primitive characteristics that are present earlier in evolutionary time from the derived char-

TABLE 2.4 SUMMARY OF MAIN QUESTIONS AND RESEARCH METHODS *(for further explanation, see text)*

Main Research Questions	Method	Approach	Results
Have coherent traditions formed; have they evolved via phylogenesis or ethnogenesis?	Phylogenetic networks (NeighborNet)	Preliminary evaluation of data set to generate broad brush visualization of main patterns	Splits graphs map extent of conflicting signals in data sets
Have coherent traditions formed; have they evolved via phylogenesis or ethnogenesis?	Phylogenetic trees (PAUP*4.0)	Attempts to reconstruct the branching history of cultural lineages as a tree diagram; measures how well the data fit this branching tree model	Generates tree diagram and statistical measures of how well the data fit this phylogenetic model
Is there evidence for significant historical congruence between different cultural traditions?	Co-phylogenetic analyses (a) (COMPONENT)	Compares the structure of different trees (e.g., of material culture lineages and language history)	Measures whether the trees are statistically more similar than would be expected by chance alone
Is there evidence for perfect historical congruence between different cultural traditions?	Co-phylogenetic analyses (b) (Kishino-Hasegawa tests)	Attempts to constrain the evolution of one set of cultural traits (e.g., for technology) with the structure of an independent tree (e.g., for language history)	Identifies whether different cultural lineages exhibit perfect historical congruence (has the propagation of technological traits been sharply canalised by language history)
To what extent does variability in material culture across populations correlate with linguistic affinity or geographic distance?	Matrix-based correlations (Mantel tests)	Performs pairwise and partial correlations among material culture of different populations, their linguistic affinity, and geographic proximity	Generates simple statistical measures of correlations between material culture variability, language and geography.

acteristics that emerge later: every lineage starts with some ancient species that exhibits certain primitive characteristics that all its descendants retain. Thus, the taxa joined together in the tree are implied to have descended from a common ancestor. In a rooted phylogenetic tree, each node with descendants represents the implied most recent common ancestor of the descendants. The key principle involves defining character states and then identifying the presence or absence of these traits across a range of taxa; deeper evolutionary relationships among these taxa can be reconstructed by determining that similarities are derived from a shared common ancestry *(homologies)*, and those that are a result of other processes, including lateral borrowing and hybridization *(homoplasies)* (Forey et al. 1992; Hennig 1966). Given these goals, biologists have tended to regard homologies as the most important signal for discovering branching evolutionary relationships among lineages (Forey et al. 1992:3).

Computational phylogenetics arose to meet the substantial empirical challenges of conducting phylogenetic analyses of large data sets. Traditional phylogenetics relies on morphological data obtained by measuring and quantifying the phenotypic properties of representative organisms, while the more recent field of molecular phylogenetics uses genetic data as the basis for classification. Phylogenetic approaches are now being increasingly applied to cultural data sets (see Collard et al. 2008; Lycett 2011; O'Brien et al. 2013 for broader discussions), though it is worth examining in more detail which particular phylogenetic methods are most suitable for this book's core methodology and approach.

Phylogenetic Networks

Given the importance of ongoing debates about the relative importance of phylogenesis versus ethnogenesis in macroscale cultural evolution (see previous), it is useful to start any new empirical analysis by deploying "exploratory" tools that are designed to examine the general kinds of signal contained within a data set. For example, are only more reticulate signals present, as predicted by the ethnogenesis model, or is there evidence of evolution via branching processes, as predicted by the phylogenesis model? In fact, biologists have faced broadly similar challenges, because between-species hybridization is now known to play an important role in biological evolution and may be as high as 15–25 percent in plants and around 10 percent in animals (see O'Brien et al. 2013:15).

Phylogenetic networks have been developed by biologists to explore exactly these kinds of more complex evolutionary relationships that are characterized by potentially higher levels of lateral transfer between lineages (Bryant et al. 2005:80). Thus, a phylogenetic network is a graph used to visualize a potentially wide range of evolutionary relationships, and they tend to be employed when reticulate events such as hybridization, horizontal transfer, recombination, and other processes are thought likely to be involved. In such cases, phylogenetic trees may have trouble depicting specific events, especially when there is no existing species boundary to prevent gene flow between populations, and so a *phylogenetic network* is often a more appropriate analytical tool.

These attributes of phylogenetic networks also make them very useful tools for the preliminary "screening" of material culture data sets (Jordan 2009), when it is generally far from clear from the outset which particular culture evolutionary processes may have predominated (and see also Bowern 2010; Grey et al. 2010; Heggarty et al. 2010; Lee and Hasegawa 2011 for some recent examples of phylogenetic networks for reconstruction of language histories). For example, there may have been intense horizontal transfer of cultural traits *between* different populations; conversely there may have been strong heritable continuity in cultural traits *within* these populations, leading to the formation of coherent cultural lineages that have evolved via a phylogenetic branching process.

The basic approach has been described by Gray et al. (2011; and for additional applications to analysis of material culture evolution, see Jordan 2007, 2009; Jordan and O'Neill 2010; Jordan and Shennan 2009; and for some examples of applications to language, see also Bowern 2010; Bryant et al. 2005; Gray et al. 2010; McMahon and McMahon 2005, etc.). The approach starts by positing a biological (or cultural) data set that consists of comparative information on a range of taxa (and/or ethnolinguistic populations). Each taxon (or population) has been assigned a discrete character state for a number of characters, for example, nucleotide present at a specific point on a DNA sequence (or the presence or absence of a cognate word across different languages, or the presence or absence of a particular kind of architectural trait, using the Northwest Coast housing data set described previously). For each character, the taxa (or ethnolinguistic populations) can be partitioned into a group that shares a specific character state and those that do not. In phylogenetic terminology this is called a "split." The more characters that group the taxa in the same way, the stronger the support for that split. When all the splits are compatible (none of the splits group the taxa/ethnolinguistic populations in contradictory ways), it is possible to represent the set of splits derived from the whole data set in a neat branching tree format. However, in some cases, these individual splits may be incompatible with one another, and this can be represented in a splits graph.

There are now a number of methods for obtaining the set of splits that can be represented in a split graph. One popular method is the NeighborNet algorithm (see note 2) (Bryant and Moulton 2002, 2004; Bryant et al. 2005 68–69, 74–79; Kennedy et al. 2005; (see Huson and Bryant 2004, 2006). NeighborNet closely resembles agglomerative clustering algorithms like the single and average linking methods. It constructs splits by progressively combining clusters in a way that allows overlap, and the resulting graphs provide quick visualization of the extent to which the data contain a general treelike signal. In other words, "these graphs can be useful in providing a 'broad brushstroke' depiction of any conflicting signal within a given dataset" (Gray et al. 2010:3925).

Each NeighborNet splits graph therefore contains *two* kinds of information: "the splits, which represent the groupings in the data; and the branch lengths, which indicate the degree of separation for each split" (Bryant et al. 2005:77). For example, where phylogenesis has entirely dominated the process of cultural evolution, the splits graph will closely resemble a branching tree diagram. Conversely, if there has been widespread hybridization, then the diagram will be much more complex, with conflicting signals represented as "boxlike" sections in the center of the graph. Simply put: phylogenetic networks that are more "twiggy" in appearance are more likely to reflect significant branching; those that are more "boxy" mean that the data set is more likely to have been affected by greater degrees of horizontal mixing (Prentiss et al. 2014:32).

Jordan and O'Neill (2010) employed NeighborNet splits graphs in their preliminary analysis of Northwest Coast housing styles, using the binary data sets discussed previously (table 2.2). The graph (figure 2.3) is characterized by extended lengths in some of the individual branches, which appear to indicate considerable underlying differences in the housing styles propagated by the different ethnolinguistic populations living along the coast (figure 2.2). The most southerly of these groups are pulled out to the bottom right, and the more northerly groups to the left and upper right. This extent to which the individual housing styles are pulled apart suggests some hierarchical structuring in the data set, which is consistent with evolution of coherent local lineages through phylogenetic branching processes. At the same time, the boxed sections

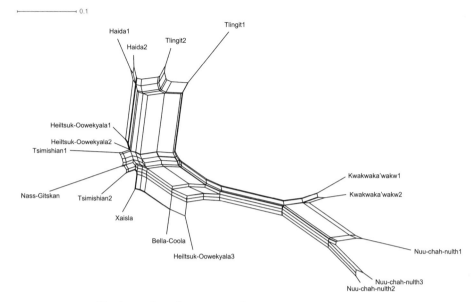

FIGURE 2.3 Northwest Coast houses network.

Splitstree NeighborNet network illustrating potential branching and blending relationships among the housing traditions of different ethnolinguistic populations living along the Pacific Northwest Coast (for geographic locations, see figure 2.1). Replotted from the data set originally published in Jordan and O'Neill (2010). For further discussion, see text.

indicate a degree of conflict in the data because of horizontal mixing in traits between the different ethnolinguistic populations.

In sum, NeighborNet splits graphs provide one useful method for undertaking a preliminary screening of both biological and cultural data sets because they do not assume a priori that any particular evolutionary process has dominated. This makes them ideal for the kind of "prospective" approach being developed here. In this Northwest Coast case study, there are some general indications that a phylogenetic signal is present, justifying the application of other phylogenetic methods that can measure the strength of this signal.

Phylogenetic Trees

In contrast to phylogenetic networks, tree-based phylogenetic analyses begin with the assumption that evolution has treelike properties, and then generate quantitative measures for how well a particular data set actually fits a tree model generated from those data. As seen previously, a phylogenetic tree or evolutionary tree is a branching diagram that shows implied relationships among various biological species or other entities based upon similarities and differences in their physical and/or genetic characteristics. The implication is that the taxa joined together in the tree have descended from a common ancestor. Various computational methods have been developed for this kind of phylogenetic reconstruction, each based on different models and each having its own strengths and weaknesses. It is important to emphasize from the outset that the tree diagrams produced by all these methods represent hypothetical statements of historical relatedness, not irrefutable statements of precise phylogenetic relationships (see O'Brien et al. 2013:46).

One relatively straightforward tree-building method is *maximum parsimony,* which is based on a model that seeks to identify the least number of evolutionary events required to arrange the taxonomic units under study and explain the observed patterning in the data. Parsimony trees are evaluated on the basis of the minimum number of character-state changes required to create them, without assuming in advance that there has been a specific distribution of trait changes (ibid. 2013:46). A number of heuristic search methods have been developed to locate a highly parsimonious tree, if not the most parsimonious tree, in a given set (see Felsenstein 2004).

When constructing tree diagrams, it is important to identify the direction of evolutionary change, and to do this, the outgroup method is commonly applied. In a rooted phylogenetic tree, each node with descendants represents the *implied* most recent common ancestor of the descendants. Each node is called a "taxonomic unit." Internal nodes are generally called "hypothetical taxonomic units," because they cannot be directly observed. The most common method for rooting trees is the use of an uncontroversial outgroup—this is usually close enough to allow inference from sequence or trait data, but far enough to be a clear outgroup (Clark and Curran 1986; Farris 1982; Kitching et al. 1998; Smith 1994:55–58; Watrous and Wheeler 1981).

Two other methods now commonly used by biologists are probabilistically based (see O'Brien et al. 2013, with references): *maximum likelihood* and *Bayesian inference,* where the criterion for constructing trees is calculated with reference to an explicit evolutionary model from which the data are assumed to be distributed identically. The maximum likelihood method deploys standard statistical techniques for inferring probability distributions in order to assign probabilities to particular possible phylogenetic trees (Felsenstein 2004:248-74). Bayesian inference can be used to produce phylogenetic trees in a manner closely related to the maximum likelihood methods. Bayesian methods assume a prior probability distribution of the possible trees, which may simply be the probability of any one tree among all the possible trees that could be generated from the data, or may be a more sophisticated estimate derived from the assumption that divergence events such as speciation occur as stochastic processes. Implementations of Bayesian methods generally use Markov chain Monte Carlo sampling algorithms (Felsenstein 2004:280-306).

Cultural phylogenetic studies based on language evolution tend to rely on probabilistic methods (Greenhill and Gray 2009; O'Brien et al 2013:46). Those not based on language evolution—material culture phylogenies, for example—tend to use maximum parsimony approaches and are used in a more prospective sense, in order to identify basic patterning in the data (see Lycett 2011:153–56, with references; O'Brien et al. 2013: 46). This more prospective kind of approach is also followed in this book—all case studies employ the tree-building program PAUP*4.0b10 (Swofford 1998) to find the set of trees that required the fewest evolutionary events to explain the ordering of the data (i.e., a maximum parsimony approach). This choice of method is also guided by the fact that the book is aimed at a broader anthropological and archaeological readership; the approach is more readily accessible than the two probabilistically based methods, which can be daunting to new users who lack advanced training in computational biology.

Having built a tree diagram, it is important to identify which specific sections are well supported by the underlying signals in the character matrix (Smith 1994:48). This is because computer algorithms will attempt to construct branching tree diagrams even from randomly generated data (see discussion about the utility of comparing trees built directly from material culture traits to independent language trees, following), and it is so important to have a means of measuring how much phylogenetic signal resides in the data (Smith 1994:47). Bootstrap analysis (Smith 1994:50) is a random sampling program that calculates percentage levels of support for each branch in the tree (e.g., Forey et al. 1992:76). Bootstrap supports are calculated using multiple replications, and only tree branches with a certain percentage threshold of support are retained in the final tree. For example, levels of support over 50 percent should be interpreted as highly conservative measures of the accuracy of a postulated tree structure (Smith 1994:51).

Other descriptive statistics can be calculated to test for relative degrees of branching and blending in the data set. The "retention index"

(RI) (Farris 1989a, b; Kitching et al. 1998) calculates the amount of homoplasy as a fraction of the maximum possible homoplasy (Forey et al. 1992:75). The RI ranges in principal from 0.0 to 1.0, with a higher RI taken as being consistent with a stronger signal for differences evolving through the branching process (see Collard et al 2006a, b). Recent simulation work by Nunn et al. (2010) has also tested the robustness of these RI measures, concluding that higher RI values (greater than 0.60) are indicative of low levels of horizontal transfer between populations, and therefore indicate that the distribution of cultural variation is a result of branching, phylogenetic processes. However, low values were not consistently associated with high levels of horizontal transfer between populations because the RI is heavily influenced by a range of other factors. In other words, RI values above 0.60 do appear to indicate evolution by phylogenesis, but low RI values appear to be largely uninformative and remain difficult to interpret (Nunn et al. 2010:3817).

Despite these challenges, the RI values are useful for comparative analysis of the overall strength of branching signals across a range of different data sets. This is because the RI statistic, unlike other possible measures like the "consistency index" (CI), is not affected by either the number of taxa or the number of characters under analysis (Smith 1994:48–49), enabling results to be compared across a range of diverse case studies. For example, Collard et al. (2006a, b) tested the assertions that (a) branching signals are always stronger in biological data sets than in cultural data sets, and that (b) cultural data sets have higher degrees of reticulation due to the high likelihood of horizontal borrowing between populations. Their study assembled twenty-one biological data sets and twenty-one cultural data sets including basketry, prehistoric pottery, projectile points, textiles, and other kinds of cultural attributes. Collard et al. (2006a, b) systematically compared the RI across all these data sets and concluded that these results did *not* support the hypothesis that blending is always more important than branching in cultural evolution, but rather that it varies substantially on a case-by-case basis (2006b:177). More generally, this study made an important move toward explicit comparative analysis of the range of evolutionary signals contained within both biological and also cultural data sets, and it remains an important empirical benchmark against which the results of new research can be assessed (see chapter 6).

Tree-based phylogenetic analysis of material culture traditions can also illustrated by a short review of Jordan and O'Neill's (2010) case study of the evolution of long-house architecture on the

Pacific Northwest Coast. Here, the housing data recorded from ethno-linguistic populations living across the region (figure 2.1) were converted into the character matrix outlined in table 2.3. The PAUP* 4.0b10 tree-building software (Swofford 1998) was used to perform a general heuristic search on this character matrix using the following settings: optimality criterion as parsimony; starting trees obtained via stepwise addition and the branch swapping algorithm set as tree-bisection-reconnection. The trees generated by this search were routed using the outgroup method (Clark and Curran 1986; Farris 1982; Kitching et al. 1998; Smith 1994:55–58; Watrous and Wheeler 1981), with the Salish-speaking Bella Coola as the selected outgroup, on the basis that they are a linguistic isolate in the region, whereas all other communities are aligned with the coast's larger language families (i.e., Tlingit, Haida, Tsimshian, and Wakashan; see Thompson and Kincade 1990; table 2.1), as depicted in the general language tree shown in figure 2.4.

Bootstrapping of this new tree built directly from the trait-based housing data was also performed (Forey et al. 1992:76; Smith 1994:50–51), and in this case study, only branches with more than 70 percent support were retained. The final tree diagram (figure 2.4) indicated a branching tree model for the evolution of long-house styles. The RI score for the final tree was 0.64, confirming the presence of a phylogenetic signal in the housing. Interestingly, this RI value of 0.64 falls *above* the mean for both the biological and cultural data sets included in Collard et al.'s (2006a, b) comparative study. On the basis of these results, Jordan and O'Neill were able to conclude that local housing traditions on the Northwest Coast had been largely evolved via a process of phylogenesis (2010:3885). An identical series of phylogenetic analyses are performed in chapters 3–5 using the same software, settings, and general methods as described here (see note 3).

Measuring Historical Congruence between Cultural Traditions: Co-phylogenetic Analyses

In culture evolutionary research, the theme of historical congruence focuses on the extent to which separate lineages of coherent material culture tradition have tracked each other—or language history—through time. In fact, identifying potential historical congruence is central to many of Boyd et al.'s models (1997; and see Gray et al. 2010; figure 1.3). The key empirical issue is to identify the extent to which separate cultural traditions have become bundled together, exhibiting a closely shared history of descent, or the extent to which they have

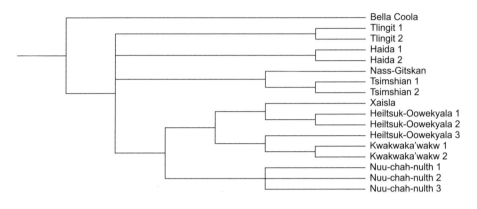

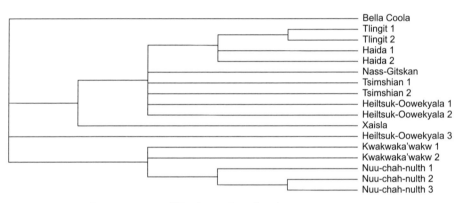

FIGURE 2.4 Language tree and Northwest Coast housing tree.

Top: Language tree for seventeen ethnolinguistic populations living along the Pacific Northwest Coast (after Jordan and O'Neill 2010). *Bottom:* Phylogenetic tree (created by maximum parsimony) of housing traditions among seventeen ethnolinguistic populations living along the Pacific Northwest Coast (after Jordan and O'Neill 2010). For further discussion, see text.

entirely independent histories (Jordan and Mace 2006). Analogous problems have also been faced by evolutionary biologists, once again providing scope for cross-disciplinary application of methods and approaches. Some of these methods are now being applied to study the potential coevolution of cultural traditions and language histories (e.g., Jordan and Mace 2006:161–65; Jordan and O'Neill 2010; Jordan and Shennan 2009; Riede 2008; Tehrani et al. 2010).

In biology, the study of "co-phylogeny" spans several research areas, including co-speciation in host and parasite organisms, and the reconciliation of species trees and gene trees (e.g., Brooks and McLennan 1991; Page 2003). The main empirical challenge in analysis of both biological and culture evolutionary patterns is to identify how far the history of one group of entities (e.g., the parasites, genes, organisms, cultural traditions) is determined by the history of another group of entities (i.e. the hosts, the species, language histories) (see Tehrani et al. 2010). In biology, these questions are addressed by attempting to map a dependent phylogeny (i.e., the parasite, gene, or organism tree) onto an independent phylogeny (the host, or the species tree).

A similar approach can be applied to the study of evolution in cultural traditions. Here, it is important to identify the extent to which different cultural and linguistic traditions have either become bundled together and exhibit *congruent* histories, or the extent to which each has its own independent and thereby *incongruent* descent history with the other traditions (Jordan and Mace 2006). For example, Boyd et al.'s (1997) model 1, cultures as species (figure 1.3), predicts that all cultural traditions and languages will evolve via similar branching processes, with all these different lineages becoming closely bundled together, together forming a single and highly integrated set of core, cultural traditions that together exhibit the same general branching history. Model 2, cultures with hierarchically integrated systems, also predicts that *some*—but not *all* cultural traditions—will tend to share a congruent descent history, such that the trees mapping languages and the history of at least *some* cultural traditions will tend to have a very similar branching structure.

Investigating co-phylogeny between different cultural lineages (i.e., identifying the extent of their historical congruence) requires first the ability to build accurate phylogenetic trees from the relevant data sets, as examined previously. Where such branching signals can be identified in particular cultural data sets (i.e., bootstrapping indicates that branches are well supported, the RI scores are found to be over 0.60), then several further hypotheses can be tested. Primarily, this involves comparing the structure of independent trees, each built from built from entirely different data sets, in order to identify the potential degree of historical congruence between these different lineages (see Jordan and Mace 2006; Jordan and Shennan 2009; Riede 2009; Tehrani et al. 2010).

The structure of tree models generated by phylogenetic reconstruction of material culture history are sometimes compared with tree diagrams depicting language history. Language represents an interesting parallel tradition, whose evolutionary dynamics can be compared to those of technical traditions, but language trees can also be used in some cases as useful, independent estimates of population history (Gray et al. 2010:3929; O'Brien et al. 2013:6). As examined in chapter 1, languages tend to evolve via the branching process of phylogenesis (Cameron 1987; Platnick and Cameron 1977; Rexová et al. 2003) because many core elements of language appear to be less prone to horizontal movement (Gray et al. 2010; O'Brien et al. 2013:7; Steele et al. 2010).

Ideally, the independent language trees employed in co-phylogenetic studies should be well resolved, that is, with a clear branching structure, and the progressive splitting away of descendant lineages. If language and material culture traditions *have* been co-transmitted, then the structure of this language tree, and the tree built from the material culture data should be at least broadly similar, if not identical. There are different ways of testing for this kind of historical congruence between different cultural lineages, of which two are reviewed here and applied to case studies in chapters 4 and 5. At this point, it is also worth noting that rigorously comparing trees built directly from cultural traits with well-resolved language trees can provide some deeper reassurance about phylogenetic analysis of material culture evolution. This is because some critics have argued that computational phylogenetic tree-building software like PAUP* 4.0b10 has been designed to tackle biological research questions and will seek to create trees from even randomly generated data. Although bootstrapping tree models to test for the degree of support for individual branches, and using the RI values to gauge the overall strength of a phylogenetic signal, can to some degree address these concerns (see previous), there are many basic aspects of macroscale material cultural evolution that have received extensive theoretical treatment but await sustained programs of empirical research. In contrast, basic processes of linguistic evolution are much better understood, and identifying close historical congruence between a tree built directly from material culture traits and an independent language trees can generate yet further reassurance that the branching histories reconstructed by this approach have a deeper empirical validity.

One relatively straightforward approach to testing general historical congruence between material cultural traditions and language history is to undertake a direct comparison of the structure of the trees using COMPONENT 2.0 (Page 1993). This software measures how similar or different a range of trees are, but unlike PAUP* 4.0b10, the software does not infer trees from the original data but rather requires that preexisting trees are entered into the program. COMPONENT 2.0 then proceeds by calculating an overall measure of similarity between the sets of trees, for example, between a tree recording the branching history of material culture traditions and a tree mapping language history. The level of similarity between these two trees can be estimated by breaking each tree down into sets of simpler structures. One useful measure is the "triplet," which is the smallest possible informative subtree on a rooted tree. If the structure of the two trees is very similar, then only a low number of these subtrees will be resolved differently between the two trees. In contrast, if the structure of two trees is very different, then a large number of these triplets will be resolved differently, generating a higher score. Comparison of two or more trees then becomes a relatively straightforward exercise: COMPONENT 2.0 calculates the "number of triplets resolved differently," providing a numerical score of relative degrees of similarity and difference among the range of different trees under examination.

However, the triplets scores calculated in COMPONENT 2.0 generate only an overall measure of relative similarity between trees. It is therefore important to identify the point at which the apparent similarity between two trees becomes *statistically* significant, that is, whether two trees are more similar than would be expected by chance alone. The software can also randomly generate large numbers of additional trees as the basis for these statistical tests. For example, a tree of material culture traditions and an independent tree for language history can be compared using the triplets measure. If this comparison reveals that the number of triplets resolved differently between the cultural and the language tree falls *below* the range of measures for a randomly generated set of additional trees, then it can be concluded that apparent similarity between the language tree and the cultural tree is *greater* than would be expected as a result of chance alone, and that a substantial degree of historical congruence probably does exist between the two traditions.

Conversely, if the number of triplets resolved differently between the language tree and the material culture tree fall *within* the range of triplets scores generated through comparison of the large number of randomly generated trees, then it could be concluded that the apparent similarities between the language tree and the cultural tree were no stronger than would have been generated by chance alone. In other words, each of these traditions has an independent branching history, but there is no deeper historical congruence between these histories. In fact, this result would confirm Boyd et al.'s (1997) model 3 (see chapter 1), that is, cultures as assemblages of many coherent units, which is defined by the presence of a number of different coherent traditions, each exhibiting strong heritable continuity, such that the *independent* branching history of each single tradition can be reconstructed on a case-by-case basis by phylogenetic methods, although there is no historical congruence between these lineages of tradition.

Like the phylogenetic network analyses described here (which provide a quick visualization of signals within in a data set), the triplets scores calculated by COMPONENT 2.0 generate only a preliminary set of insights into overall historical congruence between different cultural lineages. Where there results are positive, that is, where the two trees are more similar in structure than would be expected by chance alone, then a further set of analyses can test for perfect historical congruence between the two trees. The Kishino-Hasegawa test (Kishino and Hasegawa 1989), modified to fit PAUP* 4.0b10 phylogenetic software (Swofford 1998), calculates the difference between (1) a best-fit material culture tree that has been built directly from the traits recorded in the character matrix, and (2), a second tree built from the same data set, but this time with the search for a new best-fit tree artificially constrained by the structure of an "independent tree" that has been selected to test a specific hypotheses. For example, it is often useful to test whether the evolution of material culture traits across a number of populations has been closely "canalized" by branching language history (see also Jordan and Mace 2006; Jordan and Shennan 2003, 2009). In this case, a new search for a best-fit cultural tree would be deliberately constrained by the branching structure of an independent language tree imported into the program. If there was no statistically significant difference between the original best-fit tree for the material culture traits, and the new best-fit material culture tree constrained by language history, then the hypothesis of *perfect* historical congruence would be correct. In contrast, if the two trees were significantly different, then the hypothesis of perfect congruence between material culture history and language history could be rejected.

To summarize, application of both sets of tests makes it possible to identify different degrees of potential historical congruence between traditions: the triplets tests of COMPONENT 2.0 can be deployed to identify whether there is *significant* historical congruence; the Kishino-Hasegawa tests identify whether there has been *perfect* congruence between trees mapping the branching histories of different cultural traditions.

This general approach to studying historical congruence between material culture traditions and language history can again be illustrated using Jordan and O'Neill's (2010) recent case study of Northwest Coast housing styles (and see Jordan and Mace 2006; Jordan and Shennan 2003, 2009 for additional applications to the study of material culture traditions). This case study employed the same binary data sets described previously (table 2.1) and also employed the tree generated by phylogenetic analysis of these data (figure 2.5). In addition, it also employed an independent language tree (figure 2.4) that was based on Thompson and Kincade's (1990:30, 34–35) analysis of regional linguistic history. Jordan and O'Neill (2010) then used the tree-building software Mac-Clade 4.05 (Maddison and Maddison 2000) to manually convert this language history into a branching tree model that could be imported into both COMPONENT 2.0 for the triplets tests and into PAUP* 4.0b10 for the Kishino-Hasegawa (1989) tests for co-phylogen.

Jordan and O'Neill (2010) were interested in examining the extent to which the apparent branching history of Northwest Coast housing traditions that they had reconstructed through phylogenetic analysis of the material culture traits was congruent with local language history (see trees in figure 2.4), or whether these housing traditions had entirely independent history from that of language. These two alternative hypotheses equated to testing which of Boyd et al.'s (1997) models (figure 1.3) better describe the evolution of cultural traditions in the region—either model 2 (close historical congruence between housing traditions and language history, which together may have formed an tightly integrated and enduring set of core traditions) or model 3 (coherent housing traditions at the scale of the ethnolinguistic populations, and evolving through phylogenesis, though independently of language history). They started by testing for general historical congruence between the housing tree and language trees in COMPONENT 2.0. The initial results indicated that 164 triplets had been resolved differently in the language tree and housing trees.

A further set of 1,000 trees was randomly generated in order to test whether the structure of the housing tree and language tree was more similar than would have been expected by chance alone. The numbers of triplets resolved differently among these 1,000 randomly generated trees ranged between 186 and 504, with a mean of 372.7 (SD = 42.7). Clearly, the 164 triplets resolved differently in the housing tree and language trees was *lower* than range of triplets resolved differently across the 1,000 randomly generated trees (186–504). This enabled them to conclude that the structure of housing tree and the language tree were *more similar* than would have been expected by chance alone, and that the histories of the two sets of traditions exhibited significant historical congruence in the region.

The authors next performed a Kishino-Hasegawa test in PAUP* 4.0b10, using the independent language tree (figure 2.4) to constrain the search for a new best-fit housing tree. The tests indicated that the new tree, which was also built directly from the housing traits (table 2.3), but this time with the search constrained by language history, was significantly *different* from the original best-fit housing tree ($p < 0.05$) (see figure 2.4). This indicated that there had not been *perfect* historical congruence between housing traditions and the region's language history.

On the basis of these combined results, Jordan and O'Neill (2010) concluded that the branching history of housing traditions had tracked language history with *some* fidelity through time, suggesting that there was at least some general historical congruence between these two traditions along this part of the Pacific Northwest Coast. To some extent then, house-building and language traditions did appear to have become loosely bundled together, perhaps with the language boundaries serving to constrain the mixing of housing traits among the different ethnolinguistic groups. However, there was no evidence of perfect historical congruence between language history and local housing traditions.

Additional Methods: Matrix-Based Correlations

Finally, more general geographic and linguistic influences on material culture diversity can be examined with Mantel tests (Mantel 1967; for similar applications, see Barbujani 1995:776; Jordan and Shennan 2003, 2005, 2009; Rogers and Ehrlich 2008; and see Welsch et al. 1992), which provide a useful set of complementary analyses to those already described. These tests involve two steps. The first is the calculation of matrices recording numerical values for material culture similarity, linguistic affinity, and geographic distance between different populations, for example, among a set of defined ethnolinguistic groups. Mantel tests then perform pairwise correlations on these matrices to test, for example, the strength of general correlations between material culture similarity and language affinity, or between material culture similarity and geographic proximity. As geography and language frequently co-vary (populations closer to one another often tend to speak similar languages and may also have similar material culture), Mantel tests can also perform partial correlations, for example, to examine the effects of language affinity on material culture similarity, while controlling for the effects of geographic distance.

Although these Mantel correlations provide useful insights into general correlations between material culture and other variables, they can also be combined with some of the other methods outlined here. For example, if (1) the phylogenetic network graphs indicate high levels of conflict in a data set, (2) phylogenetic analyses also indicate little evidence for branching patterns of evolution, but (3) there also is a *strong* correlation between material culture diversity and geographic proximity, then it can be concluded that there have probably been high levels of horizontal exchange in traits between populations living in close proximity. In contrast, if these latter correlations with geography are weak, then this probably signals very high levels of local innovation: each group possesses a rather ephemeral collection of traits subject to rapid turnover—historical signals are not preserved within these traditions and traits are also changing too fast for similarities between adjacent groups to develop through sustained horizontal exchange of traits between adjacent groups. Finally, if (1) the network- and tree-based methods do identify a strong signal for branching histories in the material culture traditions, as well as (2) strong correlations between material culture variability and geographic distance, this can cautiously be interpreted as evidence for strong heritable continuity of coherent traditions within each local population, but only limited mixing of traits between them.

A recent case study of the macroscale evolution of basketry technology in Northern California by Jordan and Shennan (2009) can be used to illustrate how Mantel (1967) tests can be integrated with other methods reviewed earlier (and see chapters 4 and 5). They recorded eighty-seven basketry traits across fourteen ethnolinguistic populations. Phylogenetic analysis of the data had already demonstrated a strong branching signal (the RI score was 0.74), and there was evidence for significant—but not perfect—historical congruence between these material culture traditions and language, using the triplets measures described. Pairwise Mantel tests indicated that geography accounted for 62 percent of basketry variability and that language accounted for 36 percent. In this region, groups speaking related languages also tended to group together in adjacent areas. Partial correlations indicated that 30 percent of variability in basketry appeared to be due to geography alone, and that 32 percent was due to the combined effects of language and geography; 4 percent was accounted for by language alone. On the basis of these combined results, they concluded that (1) local basketry assemblages had formed coherent local traditions; these had evolved via branching processes into a series of distinct local lineages; these lineages also had broader historical congruence with language; and finally that (2) these material culture lineages tended to be more similar among geographically adjacent groups (Jordan and Shennan 2009; see also results in chapter 5).

INTERPRETING CULTURE EVOLUTIONARY PATTERNS IN CONTINGENT HISTORICAL SETTINGS

All these methods—deployed individually, or in combination—are useful ways of generating insights into particular *patterns* of cultural evolution that have predominated in a specific culture-historical setting. When applied to synchronic ethnographic data sets, they represent useful ways of tackling the "inverse problem" of reconstructing how these particular patterns of material culture diversity have emerged over time (Steele et al. 2010: 3783). In assessing the fit between a model and a set of data, forward approaches to modeling use the known dynamics of the empirical system to predict outcomes for a given parameter constellation. In inverse problems, the outcomes are known to some degree (e.g., patterns of cultural diversity), but the dynamics of the empirical system and the parameter constellation are less well known and must be reconstructed by reverse engineering.

One important advantage of studying material culture evolution in ethnographic settings is that there is usually independent information on a range of other behavioral factors that may have structured cultural propagation and generated particular patterns of variability. For example, in contrast to archaeological data sets, there is usually some information on which genders in the ethnolinguistic populations practice the craft, and how these traditions are acquired, adjusted, and replicated through childhood, adolescence, and beyond, as well as the roles and values of these technologies have in wider social life. Broader social institutions, including social structure, kinship, and postmarital residence rules, subsistence, and mobility strategies, and general interaction patterns, are all classic themes in anthropological research and tend to be relatively well researched and documented. When these independent contextual insights are carefully integrated with analysis of the material culture traditions, the combined results can provide scope for building more detailed interpretations of not just *how* particular material culture traditions have evolved, but also *why*.

One of the book's primary aims is to integrate the study of cultural propagation, coherence, and historical congruence with a broader comparative analysis of the role played by social institutions in material culture evolution. To improve the scope for developing such cross-cultural insights through systematic integration of ethnographic information with a quantitative model-based analytical approach, all case studies in the book focus on material culture evolution within small-scale *hunter-gatherer* societies. The advantages presented by this focus include the ready access to an extensive cross-cultural literature on hunter-gatherers, which provides a shared analytical vocabulary for describing all the key dimensions of variability in the "spectrum" of forager economies, kinship practices, settlement systems, and mobility patterns (Kelly 1995; Kelly 2013). As a result, when discussing how and why specific patterns of material culture diversity have emerged across a range of different hunter-gatherer societies, broadly similar sets of behavioral factors can be compared and contrasted across different historical settings.

A HYPOTHETICAL CASE STUDY: INVESTIGATING THE EVOLUTION OF TWO ARCTIC TECHNOLOGIES

The chapter has so far examined how variability in material culture traditions can be recorded as cultural traits, and how such data sets can be assembled and structured in ways that make them amenable to a quantitative, model-based analytical approach. A range of complementary and relatively straightforward methods have been introduced, each illustrated with an example drawn from the published literature (Jordan and O'Neill 2010). None of these methods assumes a priori that any particular evolutionary process has predominated, and they enable a range of different questions and models to be addressed empirically on a case-by-case basis.

Because this book also aims to engage with broader streams of anthropological and archaeological research, this next section runs through a simple worked example to illustrate how the entire methodology can be applied to a specific case study. The region, data sets, and culture-historical setting are all *hypothetical,* but are useful in explaining how and why the case studies in chapters 3–5 were selected, designed, and structured, using the questions, methods, and general analytical approaches outlined here.

General Culture-Historical Setting

This illustrative example examines some communities of hunter-fisher-gatherers living along an Arctic coastline. The physical geography is very distinctive, with high interior mountains descending to a shoreline of cliffs and steep, rocky outcrops extending over long stretches, affording only a few sheltered but widely scattered beach landing areas where human habitation is possible. This topography appears to have encouraged the settlement of highly clustered communities within each of the sheltered bay areas. Each small bay forms the end of a steep valley that drains fresh water down to the sea and is occupied by a dense cluster of permanent villages strung out along the beach ridge, together forming a discrete population. Members of each of these local populations tend to operate primarily within a given travel radius of each bay, concentrating on intercepting large marine mammals as they pass along the coast on their seasonal migrations. This area therefore includes the open sea around their settlement, the rocky shorelines, and the middle and upper reaches of each locale, all of which generally provide all the primary subsistence resources. Given these factors, there tends to be intense social interaction within each population, but only more occasional marital and trade contacts with other populations living at other landing areas along the coast (figure 2.5).

This coastline also has a very distinctive linguistic geography, with a discrete language spoken by each of the local populations. One language is an isolate (Kachik), and perhaps it originated from the earliest populations to settle the region. A second group of languages (Chorok) appears to have spread intrusively into the coastline from the continental interior at a somewhat later date, so that historically related languages from this larger family are also spoken at different points along the coast (Okvin, Torok 1, Torok 2, Kinik 1, and Kinik 2). More recently, languages from a third family (Iptak) appear to have arrived at different points along the coastline (Untak 1, Untak 2, Kipak, and Yipik). In all these cases, the rich coastal resources appear to have been the major attraction for groups moving into the area through the narrow network of mountainous valleys that link these coastal access points to the continental interior. Currently, then, a series of related and unrelated languages are spoken by the different populations living along the coast, and the general historical relationships between these languages can be neatly depicted in the form of a branching tree diagram (figure 2.6).

Designing a Hypothetical Case Study

Starting with a general interest in Arctic hunter-gatherers, and a specific interest in the factors that affect macroscale evolution of material culture traditions, this stretch of coast forms an interesting setting about which to ask how the traits associated with local technologies were

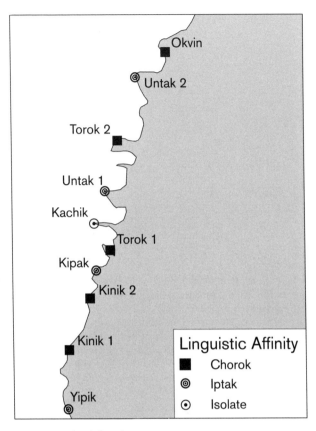

FIGURE 2.5 Arctic location map.
Location map and linguistic affinities of ten (hypothetical)
ethnolinguistic populations living along a stretch of Arctic
coastline in the North Pacific Rim. These languages fall into three
main groupings: (1) Kachik (linguistic isolate), (2) Chorok
language family, (3) Iptak language family.

being propagated, and what patterns of coherence and historical congruence had been produced. The region's distinctive cultural and linguistic geography make it relatively straightforward to define ten ethnolinguistic populations, each settled in one of the sheltered bays along the
otherwise inhospitable coast (figure 2.6). Each population speaks a distinct language (figure 2.7).

Looking it at the items of material culture being propagated among
these populations, it is interesting to examine the extent to which local
traditions have formed coherent cultural entities or been affected by

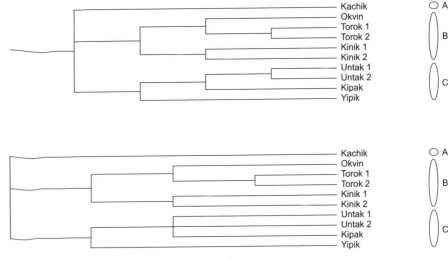

FIGURE 2.6 Arctic language tree and Arctic housing tree.

Top: Language tree for ten (hypothetical) ethnolinguistic populations living along a stretch of Arctic coastline in the North Pacific (see figure 2.5). This tree plots the history of the three main language groupings: (A) Kachik (linguistic isolate); (B) Chorok family (Okvin, Torok 1, Torok 2, Kinik 1, and Kinik 2); (C) Iptak family (Untak 1, Untak 2, Kipak, and Yipik). *Bottom:* Phylogenetic tree of housing traditions among the same ten (hypothetical) ethnolinguistic populations. The branching history of these housing traditions appears to map closely onto the language tree, with the same major groupings detected (A = Kachik (linguistic isolate); B = Chorok languages; C = Iptak languages). For further discussion, see main text.

rapid innovation and the mixing of traits between populations. If coherent entities have formed, is there evidence that they have evolved via branching processes, and to what extent are these material culture histories congruent with local language history? More generally, which of Boyd et al.'s (1997) four models best characterizes cultural evolution along the coast (figure 1.3)?

To address these questions, two material culture traditions can be selected for a preliminary analysis. These exhibit some interesting contrasts in relation to their close associations with different genders, and the extent to which they form socially coordinated or more individualistic crafts:

- *Arctic Basketry.* This is an exclusively female tradition, with women learning the craft through long apprenticeship with their mothers. However, because of local kinship and postmarital residence rules, women move into other households and local villages within the same bay after marriage; occasionally brides sometimes move into more distant populations where they acquire new languages. Basketry is a personal craft, and having learned a series of basic coiling and twining techniques through direct instruction, women can readily invent, adopt, and exchange different construction and decorative traits with other women throughout their adult lives. In fact, demonstrating a capacity for personal creativity within this craft is a highly valued attribute. Women will makes scores of baskets throughout their life spans, because baskets are subjected to hard sustained usage in transport, processing, and storage activities. The basic range of raw materials used in the baskets are identical along the coast because of the similar ecology and vegetation, and a large selection of different basketry forms, designs, and decorations can be recorded across the local populations, but these complex distributions are hard to understand.

· *Arctic Housing.* The different populations live in local settlements that are clustered into each sheltered bay. These villages consist of large, communally built multifamily houses that are constructed on an occasional basis by teams of local men under the close supervision of the village elders. Within each of the local ethnolinguistic populations, extremely similar kinds of structures are built, but there appear to be major differences between the housing styles of different populations. For example, the group speaking the linguistic isolate occupy large plank-built long houses, with single entrances facing the sea; some of the other populations used the abundant driftwood to build broadly similar variants of a hexagonal, semi-subterranean structure with access through the smoke hole in the roof. The remaining populations build a very different kind of surface structure that resembles a conical, log-built tepee covered with earth and sods, and generally accessed by tunnels facing both inland and also toward the sea. Although each population appears to have a distinctive local type of housing, these complex patterns of variability, and their possible links to language history, are difficult to interpret.

Defining and Documenting Material Culture Traits

Having defined the ten ethnolinguistic populations, the operational sequence of the two different material culture traditions can then be studied and recorded. Production of basketry involves making choices at each operational stage, providing scope for a wide range of forms, methods, and decorations to be combined. Each production step can be defined for analytical purposes as a cultural trait, with a different combinations of traits making up the specific local tradition. The definite presence or absence of these different traits can then be recorded across the basketry assemblages made by all the local population. This generates a binary character matrix of 128 different traits across the ten populations. Housing construction is also a complex process involving a large number of steps, with choices at each of these stages. The construction choices made at each of these different steps can also be defined as cultural traits and can be systematically recorded across the groups' vernacular architecture. This generates a second binary character matrix of 110 traits over the ten populations. These two data sets are now amenable for quantitative analysis in order to address the research questions identified earlier.

Culture-Evolutionary Analysis

In this hypothetical example, variability in basketry traditions is analyzed first. With no a priori understanding of how basketry traits have evolved across the populations, the data set is subjected to a preliminary broad-brush "pattern recognition" analysis in NeighborNet. The resulting plot (not shown) has very short branch lengths and substantial boxing at the center, which suggests weak coherence in the local traditions and probably a substantial horizontal exchange of traits between populations. Analysis in PAUP*4.0b10 phylogenetic software, using the language isolate as the outgroup, generates a preliminary branching tree model, but when bootstrapped, only very few branches are retained, indicating little coherence in traits when mapped on the tree diagram and suggesting that branching processes have not generated the observed variability in the basketry assemblages (final tree not shown). These insights are reinforced by an RI statistic of 0.12, which also suggests that processes other than branching phylogenesis have been operative.

Finally, Mantel tests are used to investigate general correlations among basketry variability, the geographic proximity of the populations, and similarities in language. Language distances are calculated by point-to-point map distances, and the language distances are calculated from the language tree classifications. For example, groups speaking completely unrelated languages are given scores of 5 percent similarity, groups speaking languages from the same phyla 50 percent, and from the same family, an 80 percent level of similarity. The pairwise Mantel results indicate that 65 percent of basketry similarity is accounted for by geographic proximity and only 10 percent by language. However, when partial correlations are conducted, the results indicate that 56 percent of basketry variability is accounted for by geography alone, and 9 percent by the combined effects of geography and language, but only 1 percent to language alone. Overall, these results suggest that basketry traditions have evolved via a substantial mixing of traits among populations in the greatest geographic proximity.

The results for the housing traditions are very different. The NeighborNet plot reveals very long branch lengths, with populations pulled out in different directions, and also little boxing at the center of the plot, all of which suggests a high degree of coherence in traits associated with each local housing tradition (not shown). Analysis in PAUP*4.0b10 phylogenetic software confirms these results. Again, using the language isolate as an outgroup, a branching tree structure is generated, with all branches very well supported by the bootstrapping (figure 2.6). The RI statistic is also 0.89, which confirms a strong branching signal in the data set. Local housing traits appear to have formed coherent cultural entities at the scale of the ethnolinguistic groups, and the deeper history of these entities appears to map closely to a branching tree model.

With this strong branching signal identified in the housing data set, further tests investigated the extent of historical congruence between housing traditions and language history. These compared the structure of the housing tree, which was built from the cultural traits (figure 2.7) with the structure of the language tree (figure 2.8). Analysis in COMPONENT 2.0 revealed that only three triplets were resolved differently in these two trees, well outside the range of triplets for 1,000 randomly generated trees (126–357). Finally, a Kishino-Hasegawa test revealed that there was no significant statistical difference between the original housing tree that had been built from the traits alone and a second housing tree that had been constrained by the hypothesis that the branching language tree had *constrained* the evolution of the housing traits. In other words, the history of local housing traits appeared to be highly congruent with the different languages spoken across the region: housing traits had formed coherent entities, and these entities had tracked language history with great fidelity. Mantel tests also highlighted the important associations between variability in housing traits and language history. Partial correlations indicated that 68 percent of variability was linked to language alone, 10 percent was due to the combined effects of language and geography, and geography alone accounted alone for only 3 percent of variability. Overall, these results suggest extremely limited exchange of housing traits *between* adjacent populations, and strong heritable continuity of traits *within* each of the populations.

General Interpretations and Explanations

Which of Boyd et al.'s (1997) models best summarizes the evolution of material culture traditions among these Arctic populations (figure 1.3)? Basketry traditions are clearly a collections of ephemeral traits, with rapid recombination of traits between adjacent populations, rendering it impossible to reconstruct any form of deeper phylogenetic history. In contrast, housing traits exhibit greater coherence, and these local cultural "lineages" of tradition appear to have evolved via branching processes.

There is also evidence for substantial historical congruence between these housing traditions and regional language history, which together appear to have formed an integrated set of core cultural traditions to the extent that the deeper branching histories of housing and language appear to map very closely onto one another. On the basis of these results, the best model for regional-scale cultural evolution appears to be model 2, cultures as hierarchically integrated systems. As examined previously, according to this model, several independent cultural lineages are being propagated—in this case distinct local housing and language traditions—but over time they have become closely integrated to the extent that they form a durable cultural core whose deeper history can be reconstructed using phylogenetic methods. This cultural core is surrounded by traits associated with other traditions that are evolving via rapid innovation and frequent horizontal borrowing and blending between populations, in this case the more hybridized basketry traditions.

Having successfully identified these basic patterns of coherence and congruence in contrasting basketry, housing, and language traditions, the next task is to try to explain *why* these local cultures are evolving as hierarchically integrated systems (Boyd et al. 1997). This demands understanding how traits associated with each tradition are being propagated within and between the different populations, and why there appears to be such a tight coupling between the coherent housing trait lineages and language history. Here, insights drawn ethnography and history can be productively combined with the quantitative analytical approaches to develop deeper interpretations of variability and long-term change in local material culture traditions.

In the case of housing styles, for example, it is clear that these long-lasting domestic structures form important social spaces that are central to local community life, especially over the long dark winters when they are shared by large groups of related families, forming the epicenter of cultural and also biological reproduction for many months. Kinship and postmarital residence rules also appear to play important roles in the evolution of these material culture traits—houses are built by adult men, but in these patrilineal, patrilocal communities, all these male individuals will tend to have lived in the same local settlements for their entire lives, with virtually minimal movement of adult males among the different populations. Construction of new houses is a large undertaking, and rather infrequent, with construction directed by the elders; these are also social coordinated spaces, such that scope for personal innovation beyond the collective norms may be severely curtailed. Local housing traits therefore appear to have been propagated in ways that ensure strong, long-term heritable continuity in distinct lineages of coherent tradition. The striking historical congruence between housing history and language is particularly interesting; it may indicate that the three distinct housing traditions have been brought into the region by waves of migrants, each moving into the coast along the mountain valleys, also bringing new languages from the interior as they settled on the coastlines to exploit the rich and locally abundant marine resources. The plank housing traditions appear to form the oldest style in the region, followed by the pit houses, and then by the conical tepee structures. Archaeological excavations across the region could further test this hypothesis.

In contrast, basketry traits are clearly being propagated in very different ways. This is essentially a highly personalized craft, and the tradition is not coordinated across larger social groups; once the basic skills have been mastered in childhood, new traits can easily be observed and imitated later in life, and there are also few constraints on personal innovation of new traits or in making novel recombinations of traits acquired from different sources. Women will also make vast numbers of baskets in their lifetimes, so that there are multiple opportunities to experiment with new variants.

These inherent features of the craft are amplified by strikingly different patterns in female mobility—individual practitioners of the craft are moving regularly between households and settlements after marriage, and occasionally between populations that speak related or unrelated languages, no doubt carrying knowledge of older traits with them into these new communities. Annual month-long trade fairs held at different points on the coast also draw in populations from both the entire coastline and the interior and provide a temporary lull in the hostility and suspicion that generally characterizes interpopulation interaction along the coast for the rest of the year. These events provide a locus for the exchange of marriage partners, and many families travel with woven containers to bring provisions for trade and local subsistence, all of which provides further opportunity for observing and exchanging traits among populations. In this way, basketry traits are transmitted vertically between parents and offspring, but it is the activities conducted later in the life cycle that produce this characteristic mixing of traits between adjacent communities, which over time produce highly reticulate histories.

In conclusion, this hypothetical case study started with some general questions about the factors that affect variability and change in the material culture of Arctic coastal communities. It has drawn on data systematically collected from populations living on different parts of the coast and used a range of methods to reconstruct primary patterns of coherence and congruence in two contrasting traditions. Drawing on contextual ethnographic data, these patterns can be linked to the differential ways in which the traditions are propagated along the coast, which in turn is linked to a range of geographic and social factors, including the highly localized settlement patterns and the differential mobility of men and women during different stages of their life cycles. The inherent nature of each tradition also plays a role, with some crafts being more personal and indeed experimental, and others being reproduced on a more occasional and socially coordinated manner.

Of course, this is a purely hypothetical case study and is designed to simply illustrate how the general data collection and analytical approach outlined in this chapter can be applied to a specific culture historical setting in ways that generate original empirical insights into material culture evolution and all its historical contingencies. Looking forward, then, one major goal for future research is to try to characterize the range of factors that promote the tight coupling of cultural lineages versus those that lead to lineages following separate historical pathways (Gray et al. 2010:3931; O'Brien et al. 2013). This challenge is taken up in the remaining chapters of this book.

CONCLUSION

The chapter has outlined a methodological framework for the rest of the book. It has aimed to provide a means by which the theoretical perspectives outlined in chapter 1 can now be applied to a series of empirical case studies. This starts by defining the basic problem to be solved: individuals carry cultural information in their brains and pass this information to others via processes of imitation and other forms of social learning. The dynamics of this cultural inheritance system are highly complex, but they can usefully be understood in terms of a careful and cumulative "editing" process that affects what information gets passed on to the next generation.

Humans also propagate their numerous material culture traditions through social learning, and the specific content of these technological traditions can be documented in terms of cultural traits. These consist of specific choices made by individuals during the craft production sequence, such that each object, built structure, or artifact will be defined by a different combination of traits. Following this approach, craft traditions can be defined, recorded, and studied from first principles, breaking them down into operational sequences and emphasizing the role of choice at each stage in their production sequences (Note 4).

Variability in specific material culture traditions can therefore be documented by the presence and absence of particular traits, and at different scales, ranging from individual material objects to the traits used by specific social units such as households, kin groups, or linguistically defined communities. Explaining the variability in traits within and between these populations becomes a classic "inverse problem" akin to analogous problems in evolutionary biology and population genetics. In a similar vein, this chapter has also demonstrated that variability in material culture can actually be studied with models and methods drawn from the biological sciences in order to address overarching questions about the factors that affect propagation of cultural traits, the deeper patterns of coherence in technological traditions that tend to emerge, and the potential historical congruence between different craft traditions and language. However, the approach outlined here does not assume that any particular process will have dominated, but seeks instead to test different models of cultural evolution empirically on a case-by-case basis (Boyd et al. 2010; figure 1.3) and then explain these patterns through detailed integration of contextual ethnographic data on kinship, territoriality, and other contingent factors.

In conclusion, then, this chapter forms the methodological backbone for the three extended case studies presented in chapters 3–5: these examine propagation, coherence, and historical congruence in material culture traditions over an ascending range of social scales; the application of a single methodological framework allows the results of each local case study to be integrated into a cross-cultural analysis in chapter 6.

NOTES

Note 1

This methodological framework has been developed and refined over a number of earlier publications, starting with Jordan and Shennan (2003, 2005), which used tree-based methods (PAUP* 4.0b10 (Swofford 1998), Mantel (1967) tests, correspondence analysis and Kishino-Hasegawa (1989) tests. Host-parasite co-speciation tests (e.g., COMPONENT 2.0; (Page 1993) were first employed in Jordan (2007) and Jordan and Mace (2006) and the use of network-based methods was also explored in Jordan (2007, 2009). The full methodology for testing Boyd et al.'s (1997) models (figure 1.3) was first piloted in Jordan and Mace (2006) and again in Jordan and Shennan (2009) and Jordan and O'Neill (2010). The editing of data sets has also been refined and improved over these publications. For example, in the binary data matrices in these earlier studies missing data were recorded as a zero (i.e., a definite absence); in later studies—and in all case-studies presented in this book rows with missing data were removed. In addition, earlier pilot-studies including Jordan and Mace (2006, 2008) tended to analyse large general datasets like built structures or textiles while later work has focused on analysis of narrower and more tightly defined material traditions like ceremonial dress or earth lodges (Jordan and Shennan 2009) or long-houses (Jordan and O'Neill 2010).

Note 2

A program that calculates NeighborNets and displays split graphs, SPLIT-STREE4, can be downloaded from http://www.ab.informatik.uni-tuebingen.de/software/splitstree4.

In the case-studies (Chapters 3–5) NeighborNet (Bryant and Moulton 2004) incorporated into Splits Tree 4beta10 (Huson and Bryant 2006) was employed.

Note 3

The data sets in Chapters 3-5 were all analyzed in the same way. The character matrices of primary presence/absence data were converted into NEXUS files and subjected to a range of analyses. The character matrices of primary presence/absence data were converted into NEXUS files and then subjected to similar tree-based phylogenetic analyses. A general heuristic search was performed using the PAUP 4.0b10 phylogenetic software (Swofford 1998), with the following settings: optimality criterion as parsimony; starting trees obtained via stepwise addition and the branch swapping algorithm set as tree-bisection-reconnection. The results were interpreted using the outgroup method, which is commonly used to root the tree (see main text). In the different case-studies various taxa (i.e., artifacts through to ethno-linguistic communities) are selected as the relevant outgroup, and justifications for these choices provided on a case-by-case basis. RI statistics and bootstrapping were also performed in PAUP*4.ob10, and tree branches with over 50 percent support were retained.

Note 4

The original data sets from Siberia, Gulf of Georgia, and California (Chapters 3-5) will all be made open access (see Jordan forthcoming a, b).

CHAPTER 3

Northwest Siberia

This chapter focuses on processes of microscale evolution in material culture traditions in Northwest Siberia. It primarily aims to examine how technological traditions are propagated *within* populations, exploring how individuals acquire knowledge of cultural traits through social learning, which persons they copy during their different life phases, and what factors promote them to then reproduce, adjust, or reject the traits they have acquired. It also explores how all these factors work together to generate continuity and change in material culture traditions, and then examines the extent to which more coherent cultural traditions are likely to form and the likely social scales at which these cultural entities might emerge.

The extended case study opens with a general ethnographic sketch of the local culture-historical setting, focusing on subsistence routines, interaction patterns, and kinship structures. Propagation of a range of contrasting woodworking crafts are examined: storage platforms, shrines, and skis are subjected to quantitative analysis, and more descriptive, qualitative insights into the propagation of canoe- and sledge-making traditions are also included, because they add to general understandings of how microscale evolutionary dynamics affect material culture traditions.

Two broadly different sets of insights are produced, the first in relation to evolution of material culture traditions, the second in relation to social learning dynamics. First, when focusing on general variability and change in different technologies, it is clear that the individual traits that make up each tradition can have broadly shared—but also very different—origins and transmission histories. In some cases, large numbers of traits appear to be integrated into highly standardized design "recipes," but in other cases, diverse sets of traits are combined on a much more pragmatic case-by-case basis, resulting in little overall coherence in the general tradition. Traits making up each material culture tradition are therefore propagated in a very different ways, and each trait can have its own unique microevolutionary dynamics. Strongly contrasting patterns of coherence, continuity, and change therefore emerge in each of the different technological traditions that are investigated.

Second, when viewed in terms of social learning, the case studies indicate that knowledge of many traits is acquired early in life through substantial investment in teaching, primarily between parents and their own children and is then adjusted throughout a person's later life by simple observation, imitation, and personal innovation, though very rarely does this involve *sustained* investment in explicit teaching between adults. The interplay between these two factors within human cultural transmission systems can, at times, result in the persistence of coherent, long-term craft traditions, and also generate rapid shifts in the use of individual traits, eventually triggering major shifts in entire material culture traditions. Clearly, new traits can potentially spread rapidly throughout expanded social networks, but many of the decisions about whether to actually adopt new traits, or reject existing ones, appear to relate to their perceived functional benefits, especially in local transport technologies like skis and sledges. Parent-to-offspring social learning remains important but is frequently subject to payoff-based updates, allowing biased transmission to outcompete vertical transmission in many instances; this process appears to explain the emergence of coherent and highly adaptive technologies over large geographic areas.

These kinds of contextualized investigations are fundamentally important for understanding how *macroscale* patterns of coherence and historical congruence eventually might start to emerge and persist over more extended time scales. Therefore, the main goal of this chapter is to provide a set of foundational insights for the two following chapters, which focus primarily on examining *macroscale* cultural evolution among populations speaking different dialects and languages.

ETHNOGRAPHIC CONTEXT: KHANTY OF NORTHWESTERN SIBERIA

The vast lowlands of Western Siberia are drained by the River Ob' (figure 3.1). For millennia the boreal forests *(taiga)* and tundra of this region have been home to numerous indigenous communities who spoke a range of different languages. These groups subsisted primarily by hunting and fishing, and more recently, especially in northern areas, by reindeer herding (Forsyth 1992; Jordan 2011a). This chapter focuses on one of these groups—the Khanty, who numbered 15,611 in 1897 and 22,283 in 1989 (Glavatskaia 2002:103).

Ethnographers have traditionally divided the Khanty into three major groupings: (1) the Northern Khanty, who live around the Lower Ob' and practice a mixture of hunting, fishing, and large-scale reindeer husbandry (Jordan 2009; Martynova 1998:80–137; Perevalova 2004); (2) the Southern Khanty—now largely assimilated—who lived along the Irtysh River and combined hunting and fishing with agriculture and cattle breeding, which they adopted from the South Siberian Tatars and later Russians (Fedorova 2000; Martynova 1998:12–79); and (3) the Eastern Khanty who live in the taiga forests and extensive wetlands of the Middle Ob' region (figure 3.1) and practice hunting, fishing, and gathering, along with some local small-scale reindeer herding, which was more common north of the Ob' River (Fedorova 2000, Golovnev 1993, Jordan 2003, Martynova 1995, 1998:138–202; Wiget 2002a, b; Wiget and Balalaeva 2011).

Eastern Khanty

This chapter investigates the material culture traditions of several Eastern Khanty communities. These communities live on the Pim, Agan, Trom"egan, Vakh, Iugan, and Vasiugan Rivers, all of which are tributaries to the main River Ob'. Each of these local Khanty groups is named after one of these tributary rivers (figure 3.1). There is large body of historical information on all these Eastern Khanty communities, starting with Russian fur tax records in the seventeenth century and including comprehensive government surveys of subsistence and demography in the nineteenth and twentieth centuries (Jordan 2011a). There is also an expansive ethnographic literature generated by both Russian/Soviet and international scholars starting from the late nineteenth century and running through to the present day (see Jordan 2011a, b:28–29; Wiget and Balalaeva 2011, with references).

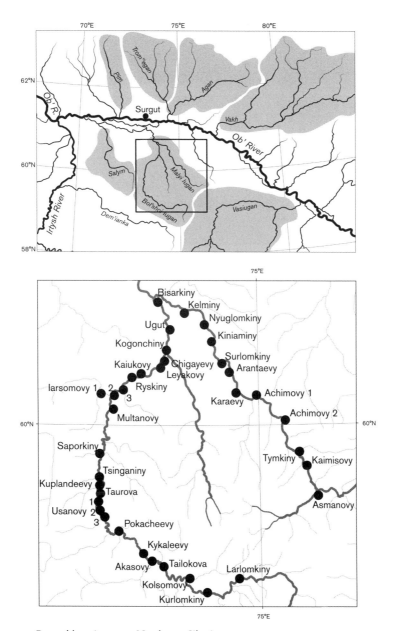

FIGURE 3.1 General location map: Northwest Siberia.

Top: Location map of the main tributary rivers along the middle reaches of the River Ob',
Northwestern Siberia, and the modern city of Surgut. Traditionally, each major tributary river was
occupied by a different Eastern Khanty population. These (starting from the northwest and moving
in a clockwise direction) included the Pim, Trom"egan, Agan, Vakh, Vasiugan, Iugan, and Salym
Khanty (grey shading). Other Khanty communities lived along the main Ob' River. *Bottom:*
Location map of the main Iugan Khanty base camp settlements along the Bolshoi (Great) and
Malyi (Small) branches of the Iugan River. Traditionally, each base camp was inhabited by a
different patrilineage, consisting of two to six households, which together inherited land-use rights
to the surrounding hunting and fishing territories. Each base camp is generally named after the
local patrilineage, and men living in the settlement inherit this as their family name. In contrast, the
kinship system requires that women marry into a different patrilineage, and most females tend to
relocate to a new base camp during the course of their adult lives. For further details, see text.

The approximately 6,000 Eastern Khanty (Lukina 1985:16) are perhaps best understood as "commercialized" hunter–fisher–gatherers who have been in long-term culture contact. Contemporary Khanty populations form the direct descendants of the indigenous communities encountered by Russians in the late sixteenth century as they started to expand their control eastward into Siberia as part of the growing fur trade (Forsyth 1992; Glavatskaia 2002; Jordan 2010; Wiget and Balalaeva 2011). This colonial encounter led to a complex process of mutual accommodation and cultural transformation: the Eastern Khanty were obliged to pay an annual fur tax to the government but also had their land rights protected so that local hunting activities—and the flow of valuable pelts—would not be disrupted (Jordan 2001). The importance of fur hunting meant that contacts and intermarriage with the garrisons of tax collectors and Cossacks were extremely infrequent (Lukina 1985:16); local Eastern Khanty communities were largely left to maintain their own lifeways as long as the annual fur tax obligations were met (Glavatakaia 2002; Jordan 2003, 2011a; Martynova 1995, 1998).

These extensive taiga wetlands remained sparsely populated, and distinctive interaction patterns emerged. In general, there were infrequent contacts between Eastern Khanty groups living on different tributary river basins, but more intensive interaction *within* each of these drainage basins. For example, historical records over the past few centuries indicate that marriages were concentrated *within* the same basins, no doubt linked to the fact that each river basin population went on to develop a sense of its own distinctive group-based identity (Martynova 1998: 209) (note 1). Different dialects of Eastern Khanty language are also spoken on each of the main tributary rivers (e.g., on the Iugan, Salym, Pim, Agan, Vakh, and Vasiugan; see Tereshkin 1981 for further details). Ethnographers have also identified general differences in subsistence economy, religious beliefs, and material culture across the different river basin groups (Shatilov 1931). On this basis, each river basin community can be defined as a different ethnolinguistic population (see figure 3.1).

Several basic subsistence patterns were also found in the region, and in many areas, they persist through to the present day (Dunin-Gorkavitch 1996; Golovnev 1993; Jordan 2011a, 2003; Martynova 1995; Wiget 2002a, b):

- *Sedentary Fisher-Hunters.* Eastern Khanty communities living on the banks of the main Ob' River and the lower reaches of the tributaries lived in larger, permanently occupied settlements and were heavily dependent on aquatic resources. Increasing commercialization of the fishing trade in the nineteenth century attracted large numbers of Russian settlers, who sometimes intermarried with these Khanty communities, generating multi-ethnic settlements. Extensive flood meadows provided pasture and winter fodder for cattle and horses, which were readily adopted from Russian incomers, along with cottage gardening (Golovnev 1993: 202; Glavatskaia 2002: 115–16).

· *Mobile Hunter-Fisher-Herders.* Eastern Khanty communities living on the upper tributary rivers were much more mobile and combined winter hunting in the remote forest hinterlands with summer fishing on the lower tributaries and also the main Ob' River. Very small numbers of domesticated transport reindeer were kept on the Iugan River, with larger herds maintained on the tributaries located on the north side of the Ob' River (Jordan 2011a; Wiget 2002b; Wiget and Balalaeva 2011).

In the Soviet period there were some general attempts at collectivization into hunting, fishing, and herding brigades, although these mainly tended to replicate the subsistence strategies and interaction patterns of earlier centuries, ensuring broad continuity in native traditions, language, and religion (Glavatskaia 2002). Since the 1960s, however, many Eastern Khanty communities have been struggling to balance these traditional lifeways with the pressures of rapid oil and gas development (Wiget 2002b). Some basins like the Pim have been heavily affected, while others, like the Iugan River basin, have seen relatively little development, ensuring remarkable long-term continuity in traditional lifeways (Jordan, 2011a, 2003; Jordan and Filtchenko 2005; Wiget 2002b; Wiget and Balalaeva 2011). For this reason, most of the ethnoarchaeological fieldwork for this chapter was concentrated within the Iugan River's ethnolinguistic population (figure 3.1), with other river basins providing comparative data on material culture traditions (note 2).

Iugan River Khanty

The Iugan River basin is located between 59 and 61 degrees north (Dunin-Gorkavich 1995: 138), with a strongly seasonal climate marked by long dry summers and long, bitterly cold winters. The basin includes four distinct ecosystems (Wiget 2002b: 189): extensive boglands occupy the poorly drained areas between watersheds; pine forests cover sandy hills and ridges; cedar forests (Siberian stone pine) run along the better-drained river margins; and a unique water-edge ecosystem of ivy and taller grasses is on the river banks. The spring snow-melt leads to widespread flooding because there are only a few areas with higher elevation.

The river has two main branches: the "Great-" (Bolshoi) Iugan River, more than 1,000 kilometers (km) in length, and the "Small" (Malyi) Iugan River, which runs for 550 km. These rivers converge and flow into the Iuganskaia Ob' and then the main Ob' River. To the west of the Iugan drainage are the Balyk and Salym Rivers; to the east is the Kul'egan with the Dem'ianka River to the southwest and the Vasiugan River to the southeast (figure 3.1).

Historical records detail local demography and indicate that although most marriages involved partners drawn from within the Iugan basin, there were also some marriages with populations from other basins (note 1). Despite these wider exchanges, the population of the Iugan developed a strong localized sense of group identity and termed themselves *Iagun Iakh* (Khanty: "People of the River'); the frequent interactions and marriages within the basin also ensured that the Iugan Khanty formed a rather uniform ethnic group (Martynova 1998:140), a pattern replicated on other Eastern Khanty rivers (figure 3.1; Martynova 1998:209; Shatilov 1931).

Subsistence, Settlement, and Social Institutions

Intensification of the lucrative Iugan fur trade took hold after the Russian conquest (Lukina 1985:17), producing a general switch from emphasis on meat to fur hunting in the seventeenth century (Glavatskaia 2002:115); it formed one aspect of a series of profound regional economic transformations that affected native subsistence complexes across Western Siberia between the sixteenth and nineteenth centuries (Golovnev 1993:160 for a wider discussion). On the upper reaches of the Iugan basin, distinct patterns of seasonal mobility and settlement emerged; they are documented in great detail by nineteenth-century geographic surveys (Dunin-Gorkavich 1995; Jordan 2003; Wiget 2002b) and also in the Soviet Polar Census, which was conducted in 1926–27 (Jordan 2011a). For example, in the 1920s the entire basin was settled by Khanty, with only a small Russian population living in the administrative village of South Iuganskoe. By far the most Khanty lived in remote base camps strung out along the banks of the upper rivers (figure 3.1).

In general, each base camp was occupied by an exogamous patrilineage consisting of two or three generations of closely related males, all of whom bore the same family name, with this name also forming the name of the base camp. Women generally married into these settlements from other patrilineages located within the Iugan basin, or sometimes from patrilineages on other river basins. In some cases, patrilineages grew in size until they "fissioned" into new base camps, often as a solution to growing social tensions, and were located close by. Each patrilineage was linked at a higher social level into exogamous clans or "sir," though these larger groupings did not cluster into sharply defined geographic areas (see Jordan 2003:69–71). The main social units examined in this chapter therefore include individual households, the local patrilineages, and the larger ethnolinguistic populations living on each tributary river basin and speaking a different Khanty dialect (figure 3.1).

Traditionally, each Iugan Khanty base camp consisted of a few houses, normally between two and six, though some lower river settlements were somewhat larger. The camps faced out onto the river and consisted of log-built cabins, storage platforms, outside ovens, and other sheds and racks, as well as a landing area for boats. Most base camps also had a small cemetery, which was located either inland or downstream from the settlement, as well as a sacred shrine, which housed the local protector spirit and was usually a few hundred meters away, often located inland or upstream from the settlement. These shrines consisted of built structures that housed carved wooden idols, sometimes metal figurines, as well as accumulated gifts and offerings, and were surrounded by the remains of ritual visits—these idols were generally the patrilineage's main protector spirits, as well as other important deities (see Jordan 2003, 2011a, c).

Surrounding the base camp were the remoter hunting, trapping, and fishing territories owned by the patrilineage (see schematic model in figure 3.2). In the early winter, individual households skied out from the base camp into these hinterlands for hunting but returned to the base camp during the darkest and coldest periods of December and January. In the later winter, they went back out into the forests and returned in the spring. In early summer, almost all households from the upper rivers traveled down the Iuganskaia Ob' in large convoys, where large groups would gather on the sandbanks for rich seasonal fishing, providing additional winter food supplies as well as an extra source of income to buy flour, sugar, tea, and other supplies and equipment that facilitated specialization in fur hunting over the winters (Glavatskaia 2002:116; Jordan 2003, 2011a, b; Wiget 2002b; Wiget and Balalaeva 2011).

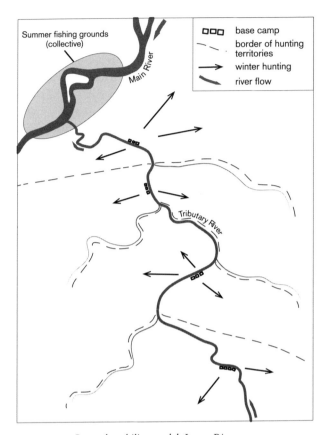

FIGURE 3.2 General mobility model: Iugan River.

Schematic diagram of how kinship traditions intersect with
settlement patterns, social interaction, and seasonal mobility
strategies on the Iugan River. From the patrilineage base camps,
individual households would disperse alone into the surrounding
hunting territories at the start of the winter, regroup back at the
base camp during the darkest period of mid-winter, travel out
again in the late winter, and then regroup back at the base camp
at the end of the winter. After the breakup of the river ice,
virtually all the households living in the base camps along the
entire Iugan river would make the long downstream migration by
boat to collective fishing grounds located in and around the
confluence of the lower Iugan River and main River Ob.' Here,
households drawn from different parts of the Iugan River were
able to interact with each other over several weeks, sometimes
also meeting Khanty groups migrating in for seasonal fishing
from other river basins. Households returned to their home base
camps as the winter approached again.

Throughout the annual round (figure 3.2), the mobility of almost all upriver households was very high, with some families traveling more than 200 km to hunt in the adjacent basins of the Salym, Balyk, Dem'ianka, Vasiugan, and Kul'egan" basins (figure 3.1). Households in the base camp at the very top of the Bolshoi Iugan undertook annual round trips of 2,000 km for summer fishing as well as 400 km out into their winter hunting territories. This latter figure does not take account of the fact that hunters also skied 20–30 km every day to hunt game and check traps, nor does it include the frequent small-scale residential moves by the household around the local hunting territory (Jordan 2011a).

In this way, seasonal mobility routines (figure 3.2) meant that Iugan households alternated between a very isolated existence in the remote taiga during winter hunting season and a more collective existence with other patrilineage households at the base camp during the spring, autumn, and the darkest part of winter. In contrast, the middle of the summer formed an intense period of large-scale socializing with people from right across the rest of the wider basin as all migrated to primary fishing spots on the lower river. The annual migrations to and from these summer fishing sites also required boat travel along the full length of each branch of the Iugan River, with opportunities for visiting all the base camps along the way. The return journey could take several weeks of hard paddling and required numerous overnight stays. It was also common for each local sacred place to be visited during these long return journeys, each visit providing further opportunities for social interaction.

Broadly similar interaction patterns have been documented within other river basins inhabited by the Eastern Khanty (figure 3.1), such as the Pim, Agan, Trom"egan, and Vasiugan (Martynova 1998), although these areas have now been substantially affected by oil development (Wiget 2002b; Wiget and Balalaeva 2011).

Within the Iugan River basin, these general routines of mobility and social interaction continued right through the Soviet period, which also included a failed attempt to resettle the entire population into one larger village at Ugut and to some extent also persist through to the present, although the summer expeditionary fishing no longer takes place because of the closure of the local fish canning plant in the early 1990s (Jordan 2003; Wiget and Balalaeva 2011). Boarding school education was also introduced during the Soviet period, and it remains in place, although children always spent long breaks out in the forest with their parents where they learned traditional skills and lifeways, and many children continue to drop out of formal schooling to spend more time on the land hunting and fishing (Wiget and Balalaeva 2011:68–70). Overall—and despite the enormous political and social changes that have affected indigenous peoples in many parts of Siberia—there is remarkable continuity in Khanty kinship and settlement patterns within the Iugan basin, with many base camps and patrilineages first recorded in the nineteenth century existing in the same locations to the present day (e.g., Bakhlykov 1996:164; Dunin-Gorkavitch 1996; Jordan 2003:8: Jordan 2011a). Family names first recorded in the seventeenth century also remain common along the Iugan to this day (Martynova 1998; Wiget and Balalaeva 2011).

Within the past twenty years, these traditional patterns have largely persisted along the Iugan River. Base camps are still inhabited primarily by patrilineages, with each household living a more isolated existence out in the remoter forests of the hinterlands during the winter hunting seasons. However, in the early 1990s, the summer migrations to the fishing grounds ended, and households tended to stay at their base camps throughout the summer months. However, with greater use of snowmobiles and motor boats other mobility patterns have also changed. More generally, there are many more frequent short-term trips by boat or snowmobile into the main administrative village of Ugut, which generally involve short overnight stays at other base camps along the river. Many river basin dwellers also make occasional visits to the larger cities like Surgut and Khanty-Mansiisk that lie beyond the river. Formal education at boarding schools in Ugut has been the norm for decades, although long holidays are spent back in the bush; many Khanty children continue to drop out of formal education at an early age, or are removed by their parents, who prefer that they live back out on the ancestral hunting lands (Wiget and Balalaeva 2011:68–71).

In conclusion, traditional patterns of Iugan Khanty mobility, social interaction, intermarriage and postmarital relocation remain highly structured by a shared set of common social institutions (figure 3.2). In particular, these relate to the patrilineage, which owns specific tracts of territory and occupies a base camp at the center of this area. Men still tend to stay locally within their own patrilineage, base camp, and ancestral hunting territory, while women move into other patrilineages and base camps after marriage (figure 3.3). Beyond the immediate household, these patrilineage base camps provide the primary locus of social interaction, perhaps even more so today, as many households now remain here throughout the summer. The annual seasonal round remains highly mobile, and although the older practice of summer expeditionary

FIGURE 3.3 General people.
Khanty from the middle and lower reaches of the Bolshoi Iugan River. PHOTOGRAPHS: Peter Jordan, *left:* August 2003; *right:* July 2004.

fishing provided sustained opportunities of intense short-term interactions with individuals and households from across the wider basin, these opportunities have been replaced more recently by general trips into the main village of Ugut. In contrast, contacts with Khanty from other basins remains minimal, but still includes participation in long-range pilgrimages to sacred sites located across the wider region.

SOCIAL LEARNING AND MATERIAL CULTURE TRADITIONS AMONG THE IUGAN KHANTY

How do these common social institutions affect the propagation of cultural traditions among the Iugan Khanty (figure 3.4)? This section of the chapter starts with a general review of intergenerational social learning within these communities. A high premium is placed on raising children to be knowledgeable bearers of native culture and skilled practitioners of skills related to living on the land, including hunting, fishing, and running households (Wiget and Balalaeva 2011:71); all practical subsistence skills and traditional craft technologies are learned from other Khanty living out in the bush; in other words, all these traditions are propagated by social learning within the scope of the local river basin population.

General Social Learning

The patrilineage community forms the primary nexus of social learning, and when assembled together at the riverside base camps, several generations are often present: these consist of related males, as well as their wives, who have married into the local patrilineage from other base camps along the river (figure 3.4). In addition, there are the cohorts of younger unmarried adults, adolescents, children, and babies, all from within the patrilineage. Other individuals and families may also be present for a shorter periods, either guesting on their way up or down river, or as visiting in-laws.

Within this local patrilineage community, the closest interaction is between parents and children from within the immediate household unit, but grandparents who have "retired" from more strenuous activities like hunting also give their grandchildren much attention as they grow up. Younger children also interact continually with older children and with relatives like uncles, aunts, and their families, as well as more distant relatives or visitors who may be present in the base camp for shorter periods.

During their early years, children spend lots of time outdoors playing with homemade toys like sleds and boats, and as they grow older, children engage in elaborate role-playing games with parents, other children, and other relatives. As the children mature to between nine and twelve years of age, practical education in traditional skills becomes more explicit, and they start to engage in guided participation in adult activities, joining their parents on winter stays in the forest and also on hunting and fishing trips. Here, they actively assist their parents who serve as gender role models (Wiget and Balalaeva 2011:68).

Throughout their upbringing, there is very little shouting, spanking, or physical discipline; correction normally consists of harshly whispered sentences, with the last syllable or two barked for emphasis (Wiget and Balalaeva 2011:68). Through these means, children of both sexes learn how to check traps, paddle a canoe, set fishing nets, cook and preserve meat and fish by smoking, drying, and salting, as well as adopt the gendered norms of social decorum (and see Lapina 1998). Boys primarily learn from their fathers how to hunt and handle firearms, and they also practice how to make timber buildings, boats, skis, and sledges, often

FIGURE 3.4 Three generations.

Three generations of Khanty from the middle reaches of the Malyi Iugan River.
PHOTOGRAPH: Peter Jordan, July 2004.

making models before moving onto making larger "adult" versions. Girls learn from their mothers how to make clothing, bake bread, and generally run the household.

Social Learning and Material Culture Traditions

Eastern Khanty communities make widespread use of the local taiga to provide raw materials like timber, bark, and roots for making built structures, shelters and storage facilities, containers and transport technologies. Local animal furs, leather, and sinews are also integrated into these technologies, with imported cloth, beads, roofing materials, and paint and glue also used widely when available.

Boys are skilled practitioners of several interrelated crafts by their early teens, and by their late teens or early twenties—the usual marriage age—they are easily able to construct houses and storage platforms, and produce their own sledges and fur-covered skis, both for personal use and also for commercial sale and exchange. Some also become master dug-out canoe makers. Similarly, girls also become accomplished skin workers and are able to bead and sew, build baskets, and make traditional boots and clothing (Wiget and Balalaeva 2011:68–69). Kinship institutions also intervene in this process: most adult men continue to practice these crafts within their ancestral patrilineages, base camps, and associated hunting lands; in contrast, local women generally marry out into different patrilineages, living much of their adult life in the base camps of their new husbands, where they then tend to interact with, and practice their crafts among, a wider community of women drawn from many different parts of the Iugan River (figure 3.1).

Among the Iugan Khanty, propagation of these material culture traditions involves a mix of observation, imitation, explicit teaching, and supervised practice of children by their parents akin to the system of "natural pedagogy" discussed in chapter 1 (Wiget and Balalaeva 2011: 68–69; and see case studies following). The generic skills and practices required to reproduce a wide range of different technological traits are mastered prior to adolescence, but other traits may be invented or acquired during adulthood. In fact, this equates to a two-stage process of cultural transmission, the different stages of which map broadly onto the biography of individuals, and consists of:

1. General observation and structured role playing in earlier childhood, using toys and sometimes the making of models, then

primarily *vertical transmission* (parent to offspring) of general craft skills and a range of more specific cultural traits between approximately nine and twelve years of age (see chapter 1). This is backed up by a transitional period of increasingly autonomous individual practice during early adolescence, often involving interaction with other children and adult relatives from within the local base camp.

2. This is followed by an extended phase of fully *independent* practice, starting in early adulthood and extending throughout the individual life span. This second stage provides scope for monitoring the performance of traits acquired from parents and experimenting with alternatives acquired through personal experimentation. It also correlates with the rapid expansion of social worlds that marks adulthood, such that new traits and behaviors can be observed among others and then potentially copied, evaluated against existing traits, adopted or rejected as unsuitable—these factors add further transmission biases into the general propagation of different material culture traditions (see chapter 1).

In general, then, initial transmission of craft skills and practices involves vertical transmission between parents and offspring within the immediate household, backed up by a wider processes of observation, imitation, and public practice within the slightly larger social world of the local patrilineage. This is followed by an extended period of independent practice in the expanding interaction networks of adulthood, all of which increase exposure to a wider range of traits than those acquired in childhood and adolescence. This is the same for both men and women, although men tend to stay in their local patrilineage base camps, while women move into other base camps after marriage.

INVESTIGATING PROPAGATION OF TECHNOLOGICAL TRADITIONS: MAIN RESEARCH QUESTIONS

As explored chapter 1, humans are unique as species in having such a developed capacity for maintaining the high-fidelity replication of an enormous range of different cultural traditions. This chapter examines how a contrasting set of technological traditions are propagated by the Iugan Khanty (figure 3.3). This is an ideal setting for this kind of contextualized ethnoarchaeological field research: the community still lives on the land, maintaining many native religious practices, and continues to rely heavily of hunting, fishing, and gathering for its basic subsistence; they maintain numerous craft traditions; and importantly, these objects and structures and produced primarily for local usage. In addition, basic kinship, settlement and interaction patterns exhibit deep historical continuity (note 2), and in addition to the new data sets gathered through fieldwork, there is also an extensive ethnographic and historic literature on Khanty lifeways and material culture, adding further contextual and temporal depth to the research (note 3).

With the main focus on understanding the *propagation* of cultural traditions, several overarching themes are addressed: How are different material culture traditions reproduced through social learning; how do local individuals acquire knowledge of the traits that make up the different craft traditions; whom do they copy from during different life phases; what factors promote them to adjust, innovate, and change this information; how do all these factors work together to generate cumulative variability and change in material culture?

At a more theoretical level, it also aims to examine the extent to which more *coherent* material culture traditions might start to emerge, that is, artifacts, items of technology and material culture that express specific combinations of cultural traits that persist in the form of social traditions over time. Can such standardized design recipes be identified, or is there just a rapid and relentless mixing and recombination of traits as new objects are produced? If more coherent traditions do start to form, then at what social or spatial scale, and why?

A full analysis of all Khanty craft traditions is beyond the scope of a single chapter. For brevity, the themes of propagation and coherence are addressed by more detailed quantitative analysis of three different material culture traditions—storage platforms, shrines, and skis—each of which exhibits strikingly different patterns of microscale evolution. These employ some of the network- and tree-based analytical methods presented in chapter 2 in order to identify general patterning in the data; the application of the same methods across this and the following two chapters facilitates integration and discussion of data from different cultural and geographic settings (note 4).

In order to develop deeper insights into propagation and coherence, the three quantitative case studies are followed by a more qualitative and contextual examination of two other Khanty craft traditions; these add further insights into the ways in which contrasting traditions are propagated, and the likely scales of cultural coherence that can emerge.

STORAGE PLATFORMS

Storage is a key strategy in the delayed-return hunter-fisher-gatherer adaptations that are typical of many higher latitude regions (Rowley-Conwy and Zvelebil 1989). In northern environments like Siberia, storage helps reduce seasonal shortfalls, and the strategy is linked to the organization of wider settlement systems and the use of "collector strategies" that involve logistic mobility patterns (Binford 1980). Among commercialized hunter-fisher-gatherers like the Eastern Khanty, seasonal supplies of supplementary foodstuffs like flour can be transported in and cached at strategic locations, enabling attention to be focused on trapping and fur hunting activities, rather than on other general subsistence tasks. In fact, broadly similar kinds of raised storehouses are found across northern Eurasia, for example among various Evenki groups in Eastern Siberia (Anderson 2006; Sirina 2002; Turov 2008)—through to the Sami in the West (Klement'ev and Shlygina 2003:81–83).

Raised storage platforms are present along all the Eastern Khanty rivers. Each Iugan Khanty household owns up to three or four, which are generally located behind the main log cabin house, and sometimes extend in long, elegant rows running along the back of the base camp (Jordan 2003:201; Wiget 2002b:195; Wiget and Balalaeva 2011:208–9, 248). Here they form part of the primary built infrastructure of the main base camp activity area, which encompasses houses, sheds, clay bread ovens, and boat landing places; around this central zone is a more distant area of forest, which is used for the latrines, fuel dumps, and for the discard of clothing and other refuse (Jordan 2003:201–4; Glavatskaia 2006; Wiget and Balalaeva 2011:204–10).

These distinctive pieces of vernacular architecture (figure 3.5) basically consist of stilts that support horizontal decking, upon which is built a small roofed cabin that is windowless and accessed via a small door. They are primarily used to store food (either locally produced resources like frozen or bottled meat, dried fish, jams made from berries and roasted pine nuts, as well as shop-bought supplies like flour, tea, sugar, and canned provisions), processed furs accumulated over the winter season, as well as spare clothing, tools and equipment. In performing these roles, the main function of the cache houses is simply to protect the contents from sun, snow, and rain; the raised platform keeps supplies and equipment dry, cool in the summer, and also safe from rodents.

New storage platforms are built on a fairly routine basis. Younger male members of the patrilineage will tend to use the storage facilities of

FIGURE 3.5 Winter loading of storage platform.

Loading up cuts of frozen moose meat into a raised storage platform at Achimovy 1 base camp on the Malyi Iugan River (see figure 3.1), with a further example located in the background. The former employs logs to construct the main house walls, but the latter uses planks, illustrating just some of great variability in construction methods noted within many base camps. PHOTOGRAPH: Peter Jordan, March 1999, reproduced with permission from AltaMira Press.

their fathers until they establish their own households. This step is marked by marriage and the resettlement of an "outside" woman into the local patrilineage community, the birth of children, and the building of a new house and associated fixed technologies of bread ovens, garages, and storage platforms. As the household grows, additional storage platforms may be added. As older members of the patrilineage die off, their cache houses may be taken into use by younger households, with inheritance of these facilities usually passing from father to son. As a result, nearly all established base camp communities have a series of storage platforms located around the main cabins, each platform built by generations of related men from the same local patrilineage.

In some Iugan Khanty base camps, the older storage platforms had been built by great grandfathers (born in the late nineteenth century) of the current youngest male generation, with new platforms added through to 2005. In one base camp, one informant reported confidently that some cache houses had been constructed "three hundred years ago," that is, beyond collective memory of when it had been built and by whom. Once built, the cache houses are generally left to stand until the wood rots and they eventually collapse. Occasionally, a roof covering or supports might be replaced, but in general, once built the construction project is completed, and no major modifications are made. If more storage space is required, new platforms are built.

Cultural Significance of Storage Platforms

In one sense, these platforms serve as functional storage solutions, but in others, they serve as a metaphor of the hunter's own household economy. This involves the negotiated harvesting of resources from the forest world of spirits and their processing and transformation in the domain of the human settlement (Jordan 2003). For this reason, bears' skulls are displayed on the top of the storage platform roofs after a lengthy festival; here they exert a symbolic and protective presence over the hunter and his household economy. Occasionally, wooden deities are removed from the local shrines and hosted in the local storage platforms as a gesture of hospitality by the hunter and his family. In his way, these constructions are much more than simple platforms—they reflect individual household autonomy; each platform has its own household owner, and they also reflect the ways in which hunting and gathering are embedded into a wider ideology of reciprocity and exchange with the spirit guardians of the rivers, lakes, and forests (Jordan 2003, 2011a, c).

General Production Sequence

All platforms follow the same generalized basic design, both within the Iugan basin and in the Khanty river basins beyond. The basic structure consists of stilts, the supporting flooring joists, walling to "box in" the stores and supplies, a locked doorway, plus a pitched roof. Building a new storage platform is a considerable undertaking, requiring forward planning and several weeks' labor in the earlier times, when only saws and axes were available, but is still a major task even with the help of petrol-driven chainsaws now widely available. As young adults, Khanty men are already adept at cutting and stripping logs, splitting off boards, working with birch bark sheets, wooden laths and poles, as well as other imported materials like roofing felt, tarpaulin, and asbestos sheets.

There is no specific training for making a storage platform because the production steps that make up the operational sequence (chapter 2) resemble many other component-based cutting, shaping, fitting, and general assembly tasks: trees are felled in the surrounding forests, often in the very early spring when snowmobiles can still be used on the melting snow patches to drag the heavy lengths of timber back to the base camp. As the weather gets warmer, the timbers are usually laid out in the open work area running in front of the houses and along the river bank (figure 3.6). Here breezes from the rivers provide some respite from the swarms of biting insects that appear as soon as the snows melt, and wood shavings are often burned in smudge fires to provide additional relief. The bark is stripped off with spades, and the logs are then cut to length. Boards were formerly split off from cut logs with wooden wedges, but now a petrol chain saw is generally used, with axes used to clean up the final timber surface. The main posts and the component parts of the main box structure and roof are usually cut and assembled at ground level first, and then dismantled and reassembled again on top of the structure, after the main supporting stilts have been sunk into the ground and the main supporting joists and decking have been fitted to them (figure 3.6).

Variability in Core Design Features

Building a storage platform therefore represents a long a complex operational sequence, with multiple choices at every stage in the construction process. Systematic trait-based documentation of variability in storage platforms was conducted within base camps, between different base camps

FIGURE 3.6 Storage platforms being built.

Building a new storage platform requires sustained investment of labor and raw materials. *Top:* Stripping and shaping the sturdy support legs (middle Bolshoi Iugan). *Bottom:* The notched support legs and foundations are being erected to the right; to the left of this, the main house structure and decking is being assembled on the ground, and will later be rebuilt on top of the supporting platform (upper Bolshoi Iugan). PHOTOGRAPHS: Peter Jordan, July 2004.

FIGURE 3.7 Platform: Three examples.

Some general examples of the enormous variability in storage platform construction methods. *Top:* Two adjacent storage platforms from the lower Malyi Iugan. These are unusual because the vertical support legs are set closer together than the width of the store houses they support. The one on the left is plank-built with square rafters in the roof, but the one on the left is log-built with round rafters. *Bottom:* Three storage platforms built at a base camp on the upper Malyi Iugan—these are all built from round logs, and the supporting frameworks are broadly similar, but there are major differences in the roofing designs. *Opposite:* An unusual platform from the Middle Bolshoi Iugan, with square beams used for the floor supports rather than round logs. PHOTOGRAPHS: Peter Jordan; *top:* July 2004; *bottom:* June 1998; *opposite:* August 2003.

FIGURE 3.7. *(Continued)*

along the Iugan River, and also at different base camps on adjacent river basins. This exercise revealed enormous local diversity in specific construction features (figure 3.7). It is worth exploring some of these primary construction choices and the potential range of traits that can be deployed:

- *Vertical Posts and Foundations.* Most platforms are supported by four substantial timber posts sunk vertically into the ground. In some areas the base camps are subject to seasonal flooding, which can weaken the posts and cause collapse. As a result, some men have started to sit these posts into "rafts," consisting of a framework of four horizontal beams laid out in a square plan on the ground, with the posts then sunk into these wooden foundations. However, this practice is also present in camps not subject to seasonal flooding because it forms a more substantial foundation, especially for larger storage houses. Other methods are also appearing—the wooden support posts can eventually rot and weaken, and in earlier times, additional support beams were sometimes sunk in and inserted under the structure or were propped alongside to prevent the structure from slumping. More recently, however, oil drums have become increasingly available and are sometimes now being used instead of wooden posts to support the platforms.

- *Rodent Protection.* Rodents form the major threat to the stores, so most support posts have a deep horizontal lip cut into the wood near the top, above which the mice cannot climb. Some builders have replaced these with a sheet of black plastic nailed around the beam that mice cannot climb beyond. Others have combined both a cut wooden lip and a plastic rim. Oil drum supports are also very good—rodents cannot scale them, and also, the drums don't rot.

- *Main Horizontal Support Beams.* The next basic technological challenge is the construction of the underlying horizontal supports that hold up the decking and the main cabin and roof structure. Again, several choices are open. Some builders run two main beams from front to back, each supported by the support posts located to the left and right. The cabin and floor then rest directly on these. Others run a further support beam from front to back underneath the center of the floor, inserting a further support post at the front and back, making a total of six rather than four posts. Others run a horizontal beam between the two front posts and a second beam between the two rear posts. Further support beams then rest on these, running from front to back, generally just at the sides, though sometimes a third beam runs under the center of the floor, and so on. In most platforms, the support beams project out to the front of the platform, enabling a small open "deck" to be extend out in front of the door. A ladder usually runs up to this external deck, enabling a person to climb up and stand outside the door before entering the main cabin structure.

- *Flooring.* The flooring can either be round poles or flat boards, and these can either rest directly onto the support beams so that they project out to the sides of the building, or be slotted into grooves running down their main length of the support beam.

- *Design of Cache House.* Several choices are open for the construction of the main box and its doorway. A basic distinction can be drawn between *log*-built storage houses and *plank*-built versions. Informants reported that log-built houses were much quicker to make but tended to rot faster, whereas plank-built versions required more skill but lasted much longer because the wood was less likely to rot. With log-built houses the timbers were slotted into each other at the corners, and the ends generally cut to the same length, though rough-cut versions were also present. Planks were usually slatted together at the corners, but in some cases they could be nailed flush. Doors were usually cut with a small step over the threshold, but others had a more substantial step. Doorways were lined both inside and around the opening, adding strength to the doorway and front wall. Because the front wall extended up onto the apex of the roof, with pitches falling to left and right, the gap could be closed by either logs or boards. Plank-built houses generally had planks running to the top, whereas long-built versions sometimes had final planks inserted into the triangle under the roof's apex.

· *Roofing.* Various roofing solutions were also present in a wide array of different combinations. A basic distinction can be drawn between those employing forest resources of planks, beams, laths, and bark and those employing externally acquired roofing felt, asbestos, or plastic or tarpaulin sheets. Most roofs had a number of support beams running from front to back, over which the main roofing materials were laid. Where bark was used, laths underlay the sheets, with further laths and then poles holding down the roof surface. Where only boards were used, these ran from the apex down to the eaves—boards were stacked in overlapping ways that prevented water from leaking in. The hole at the apex was covered by carved beams, angled planks, or strips of bark or roofing felt, and further planks or poles were sometimes laid over the top to prevent damage from winds. Other strategies included nailing a few spaced planks from the apex to the eaves, and then nailing felt over this, with further spaced planks nailed over the top. Asbestos could be deployed in similar ways. Most roofs project out over the front of the main "box," sheltering the open deck that projects out from the front of the building. In some cases, and especially in base camps on the Upper Bolshoi Iugan, this open front deck had been enclosed by planks on two and sometimes three sides, forming a small closed "porch" over the deck.

An enormous range of contextual factors appear to have influenced the choice of which traits to combine in any one storage platform. Local interviews indicated that different combinations of materials and techniques had a wide range of relative advantages and disadvantages, and that the factors guiding these choices was highly variable. For example, using only local forest resources such as timber and bark required substantial inputs of time and effort but were essentially "free". Using imported materials enabled faster construction but also required the manipulation of social networks and personal contacts to acquire felt, asbestos sheets, plastic sheeting, or oil drums via cash or barter. These materials also needed to be brought into the base camp by the occasional motorized barges that plied the upper rivers bringing in fuel and provisions, or in winter via sledges and snowmobiles.

The performance of these different construction materials varied, with black or grey roofing felt being widely criticized for making the interior of the cache house too hot in summer; use of plank or bark roofs provided cooler conditions, though birch bark especially was more prone to rotting and insect infestation. In the end, each new storage platform appears to have been a pragmatic combination of traits—the inherent flexibility in design choice meant that the same basic kind of storage platform could be built in any number of variations and combining very different sets of methods and materials.

Construction, Task Groups, and Cultural Traits

In a society marked by a strong ethos of autonomy each male householder generally built their own platform, often alone. However, with members of the base camp patrilineage community present at broadly similar times of the year, it was not uncommon for local males to form a natural pool of labour to assist with heavy lifting, basic preparation of materials or other jobs, adding words of advice and possible alternative solutions.

At the same time, with the collapse of summer fishing after the early 1990s, it is not unusual for parts of the summer to be spent "guesting" for short periods at other base camps, where sharing of general activities including fishing, repair of motors or skidoos, construction and other tasks forms a usual forum for social interaction between males. Those travelling from upper rivers downstream to the main administrative center will also stop off for nights on the way, joining in any ongoing construction activities on an ad hoc basis. All this interaction creates scope for the exchange of ideas and methods, though there was no explicit social coordination involved in building these cache houses (see Coast Salish houses in chapter 4).

In addition, there appears to be no particular prestige attached to the platforms in terms of the number built or used by a household, or the size or particular ways in which they are constructed; fine quality workmanship is universally admired though not necessarily imitated. For example, the term "artist" was awarded to one particular style of raised cache house on the Bolshoi Iugan, which resembled a kind of kitsch Russian fairy story house. Therefore, within the general tradition of making these stilted storage houses—there appears to be no motivation to copy particular traits or combinations of traits thought to be functionally superior, or culturally or morally more appropriate or even more "prestigious." In other words, there was no evidence for either conformity bias or prestige bias (see chapter 1).

In conclusion, there is a clearly a very generalized design template for a raised cache house—and this general construction recipe is clearly being reproduced over many generations as it fulfils many core functions and solves basic requirements for protected storage facilities. However, very different sets of traits appeared to be combined in different ways to meet these requirements. Given these apparent trends in the propagation of building traits, was there any evidence for construction of storage platforms to form coherent traditions? And if yes, at what social scales might this coherence emerge: at the scale of the individual householder, at the scale of the patrilineage, the different branches of the Iugan River, or at the scale of the different river basins and their associated Khanty dialects?

Analysis of Variability and Coherence in Storage Platform Design Traits

In order to test these hypotheses, a systematic trait-based survey of platforms was conducted along the full length of the Iugan River (1998–2005), with additional fieldwork data from Agan, Trom"egan, and Pim rivers (2003–5), and with additional ethnographic sources also used for the Agan and Vasiugan rivers (figure 3.8).

Tree- and network-based analyses (see chapter 2; note 5) generated some striking results (note 6; figure 3.9): there appeared to be no evidence for coherence in building techniques, either at the scale of the individual patrilineage or along either of the two main (Malyi and Iugan) sections of the Iugan River (figures 3.2, 3.9), or within the different Eastern Khanty river basins (figure 3.1). In addition, the RI score of 0.16 indicated a very poor fit of the data to a branching tree model (not shown). Also interesting was the apparent lack of any pronounced geographic clustering in either the network or tree plots. Overall, these results suggested that there was enormous innovation and variability in designs right across the region, and that each storage platform appeared to consist of a rather pragmatic collection of individual traits.

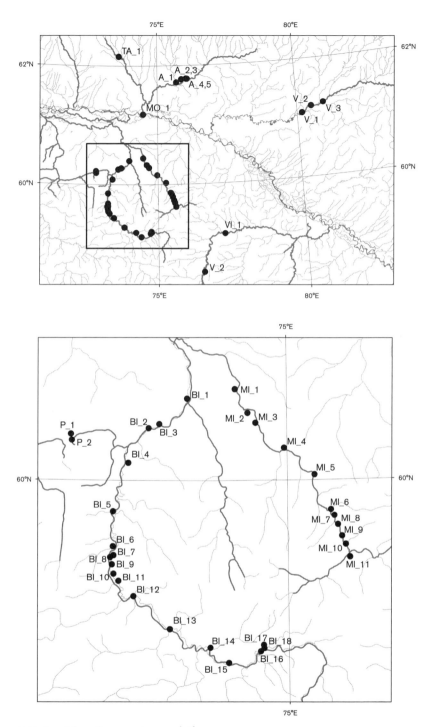

FIGURE 3.8 Location map storage platforms.

Location map of storage platforms surveyed during ethnoarchaeological fieldwork on the Iugan, Agan, and Trom"egan Rivers (1998, 1999, 2003, 2004, 2005). Additional examples from the Vakh, Vasiugan, Punsi (the borderlands between the Iugan and Salym Rivers), and Middle Ob' River are drawn from the ethnographic literature (these locations are more approximate).

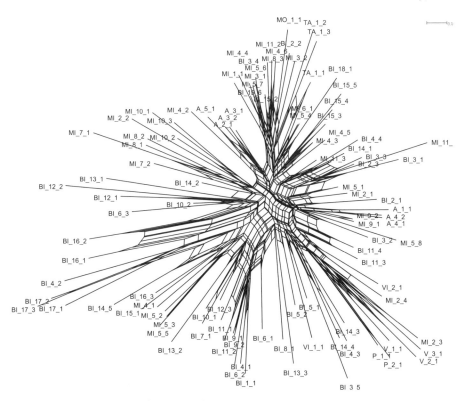

FIGURE 3.9 Storage platform network.

Splitstree NeighborNet network illustrating potential branching and blending
relationships among storage platform–building traditions. Examples are drawn from the
Bolshoi- and Malyi Iugan River (codes starting BI_ and MI_) and from other Khanty
Rivers (codes starting: A_, TA_, V_ and VI_ equate to the Agan, Trom"egan, Vakh, and
Vasiugan Rivers, with one example from Khanty on the Middle Ob' (code: MO_) and
two from the Punsi (P_), and see figure 3.8.

These results were closely checked against the ethnographic field
data and photographic archive. In some base camps, certain small combination of traits—for example, the ordering and orientation of the
floor support beams—did seem to be practiced more in that particular
base camp than elsewhere. However, these platforms also shared many
other combinations of traits—for example, in roof design—with others
located elsewhere. Overall, this relentless mixing and recombination of
different traits in the individual buildings effectively prevented any
coherent styles from forming at any social scale.

Looking again at individual examples (compare some of the structures
in the top and middle rows of figure 3.7), what is striking is minute and

highly localized manner in which different traits are subject of novel recombinations. Some men had even built completely different platforms alongside one another in close chronological succession, for example, one with log wall construction one year, and then an adjacent platform built with planks a year later. Most informants could give no real explanation as to why their design choices had varied; most reported that they had just made platforms as they had seen fit at that particular time, and according to the tools, materials, and ideas they had at their disposal during that season. Pragmatic trade-offs were also reported, between, for example, the attractive speed and simplicity with which a new cache house could be roofed with felt, balanced alongside the fact that this kind of roofing was very hot in summer. Nor, as noted previously, was any style perceived to be more or less prestigious, generating deliberate copying by others. The one kind described as being artistic was regarded as an exception, a definition of personality and worthy of comment and even admiration, though not to an extent that was actually deserving of actual imitation.

Conclusion

Khanty raised cache houses appear to be highly improvised solutions to some of the basic adaptive challenges associated with seasonal storage. Coherent traditions appear not to form at any social scale, and even individual householders build their own cache houses in strikingly different ways (see figure 3.7). Importantly, these storage platforms are constructed and used autonomously by individual householders, and as such none of the strong social coordination or sanction that might lead to conformity bias can be detected in their manner of construction or subsequent usage. Also apparently lacking is any kind of prestige bias or functional selection in the way that construction traits are propagated. What clearly emerges from this case study, is that the raised cache houses are simply being propagated as a blur of hybrid forms.

EASTERN KHANTY SHRINES

Social Significance of Sacred Places

Eastern Khanty communities also construct shrines to house their local protector spirits, and analysis of these "sacred" architectural traditions forms a useful contrast to the study of "routine" storage platforms. The shrines form the focus of some of the most important and materially visible features of the local sacred landscape geography, expressing the deep spiritual connections between people, spirits, and the land (Jordan 2003: 135–81; 2011a, c; Wiget and Balalaeva 2011:101–43). The buildings house the idols of local protector spirits, hunting gods, river basin masters, and other deities. Some idols take the form of carved wooden figurines, others are metal images and castings. They are often surrounded accumulations of gifts and offerings left by each local community during ritual visits to the shrines.

Historical analysis of land use and lineage territoriality along the Iugan River (Jordan 2011a) indicates that use of the remoter and outlying hunting areas is much more flexible and open for negotiation. In contrast, the broad tracts of land along the river banks are where there is the clearest expression of long-term land tenure by specific patrilineages—this is where there is greatest investment and ownership of fixed places and built infrastructure, including the base camps. It is also within these riverine "corridor" zones that most shrines places are found, generally a few hundred or so meters from each patrilineage's base camp (figure 3.2).

Nearly all base camps have their own guardian spirit which is housed in one of these local shrine buildings. In some cases, regionally significant deities are also housed at such holy sites and are looked after by a local patrilineage community, with groups from other camps or rivers traveling in to pay their respects and leave offerings. In others, several deities are housed in one structure, and more rarely, several structures are found in the same location. In one case, the deity—an important river patron—travels between several sacred places, each with its own built structure. In nearly all these cases it is the local patrilineage that has the core obligation to house, dress, and provide the deity with regular gifts and hospitality during the ritualized visits that take place at key breaks in the seasonal round. Usually, each site has a defined human guardian, and where several eligible males are present, this job may rotate every few years to different males in the local community. In one case there is a female sacred site, and here it is women, drawn from both the local base camp and also other stretches of the river, who provide the gifts and other offerings, though build the actual wooden shelter (Jordan 2003:207–16; 2011c).

Visits to these special places are regular but infrequent, usually no more than three or four times a year (figure 3.10). Some of the more regionally important sites are visited by larger crowds, sometimes by Khanty from other rivers, but many of the smaller local sites are known

FIGURE 3.10 Group visiting shrine.

Mixed group of men, women, and children at the start of a visit
to a local protector spirit on the middle reaches of the Malyi
Iugan, with the raised shrine located in the background. This
structure houses the carved wooden idols, ritual equipment, and
earlier gifts of cloths, furs, and valuables. As this deity is male, the
women are not allowed to approach too close to the structure. At
sacred sites with a female deity, this principle is reversed.
PHOTOGRAPH: Peter Jordan, July 2004.

and visited only by a select group drawn mainly from the immediate local base camp community. As a result, most sacred on the river have only been visited by an extremely limited subsection of the wider Iugan Khanty population. Visits to all the sites follow general themes, involving arrival, the lighting of the fire, purifications, offerings of gifts, occasional animal sacrifices, feasting, and the eventual symbolic closure of the site until the next visit (Jordan 2003; 2011a, c). The exact performance of these local rituals follows the same broad format year after year and informants commonly report that they are "passed down from ancestors, from generation to generation." However, there is substantial variation in the way that rituals are conducted at different sites—informants are aware of these local conventions and repeatedly explain that "everywhere things are done differently." For example, each site has its own unique 'choreography' that guides the structure, order and content of the rituals.

With most sites housing male deities, there is a strongly gendered theme to the conduct of the ritual: in most cases, women are not allowed to walk up to and look or climb into the structure and look at the deities. The placing of the fire often marks a symbolic line that they must not cross; gifts are smoked over the fire to purify them before they are passed inside. Nonlocal women (i.e., originally from other parts of the river and not born in the local community) must also "close their faces" (i.e., pull their head scarves over their faces) to prevent them seeing what goes on or looking at the deity. In some cases, women are not even allowed to step ashore at the sacred site and must participate in the rituals from the other bank. This does not mean that the female members of the community are not active participants in preparing the food and gifts and clothing, or consuming what's on offer, just that do not generally approach the immediate area of the shrine. The formal role of "guardian" is also held by men, so many of the traditions, practices, and procedures are passed down between males from within the same local patrilineage (Jordan 2003:135–81, 208–16).

Variability in Core Design Features

The sacred nature of these built places ensures that the ways in which the structures are built, used, and abandoned is subject to much greater social sanction and the weight of local tradition than the more pragmatic way in which raised storage platforms appear to be designed and constructed. Most importantly, the structures are understood as divine "houses" that are provided by the human collective, yet occupied and owned by the deities—these spirits are believed to be the individuals from an earlier "heroic age" who settled the land prior to humans and who continue to influence local health and general welfare; they also control general hunting and fishing success. Building and maintaining these structures is therefore about tending spiritual relationships with deities and with the land (Jordan 2003:135–81).

As essentially sacred structures, there appear to be few design constraints or functional requirements other than to provide a roof and shelter for the carved idols that dwell within, as well as to form a built space that serves as a communal focus for leaving gifts and offerings. Despite these common themes and practices, the shrines are built in some strikingly different variants:

- *Raised Platforms.* Some take the form of stilted platforms, occasionally built on the tops of sawn-off trees whose roots are still in the ground; others are built on top of posts like the raised storage platforms (figures 3.10, 3.11).

- *Sheds.* Other shrines take the form of small surface-built structures with very unusual construction styles not seen in any other kinds of buildings—these sheds are large enough to house the idols but in some cases are far too small for humans to stand up inside—when leaving offerings or tending the deities people must crawl in, bow, and circle around with some difficulty (figure 3.11).

- *Larger Barns.* Finally, some shrines on the Salym River are large barnlike buildings housing large idols (Vizgalov 2000:264–65).

There are other local variations, for example, on the Bolshoi Iugan the shrine entrances are symbolically closed with doors, planks, or lengths of cloth. In contrast, on the Malyi Iugan, the entrances are always left open between visits. Each deity—or group of deities—housed at a local shrine is also believed to have his or her own "character," skills, and personal habits and preferences. Perhaps for these reasons the buildings show great variability across sacred sites.

Propagation of Building Traditions

The building and use of these sacred structures forms a major statement in the relationship between humans and the spirit world, such that a shrine falling into disrepair expresses neglect of the deity and a failure

FIGURE 3.11 Examples of large and small shrines.

Some general examples of variability in shrine construction. *Top:* Example of a shrine built on the lower Bolshoi Iugan River that houses one of the most important deities in the region. This is one of the largest raised shrines recorded; it has six supporting legs. Photograph: Peter Jordan, August 2003. *Bottom:* Example of two smaller shrines built on the ground at a sacred site at the very top of the Bolshoi Iugan River. There is just enough space for one person to enter inside and perform the ritual duties. PHOTOGRAPH: Peter Jordan, July 2004.

by the community to fulfill basic obligations. As a result, shrines are kept in good order during the visits, and where signs of rot set in, the elders decide to rebuild the structure, a job undertaken by men drawn from the local patrilineage. However, making radical changes to the basic design of the structure might also risk retribution or compromise luck, and efforts are made to follow the original style when constructing new buildings.

New buildings are occasionally erected in situ, with the old boards and timbers carried to one side, though more often the old building will be left to collapse and rot back into the forest floor (part of a wider tradition of allowing things to "die their own death" out in the forest). A new structure is then built a short distance away, often in the auspicious direction of the east and the sunrise. As a result, at visits to newly built shrines, it is sometimes possible to see older structures in various states of decay, demonstrating a basic continuity in the building's design over several generations. Even when rebuilt in situ, one reconstruction event (Jordan 2003:208–12) demonstrated that the new building was an exact replica of the older one, which was dismantled and the beams and logs laid to one side to rot back into the forest. The entire procedure was directed by the oldest male in the community, assisted by his elderly brother, with the entire procedure, from the felling of the trees to the splitting of the boards to the rehousing of the dolls, supervised by them and carried out by their sons who formed the basic work group—all were drawn from the local patrilineage. Similar rebuilding practices were reported across the entire Iugan Khanty community.

The local propagation of design traits appears to be impacted by a unique constellation of social and symbolic factors—these include the patrilocal kinship and land tenure system, the secret nature of the sites, and the ritualized nature of rebuilding under the close guidance of older males from within the local patrilineage. What is less clear from these descriptive accounts is whether these factors result in the formation of locally coherent building styles over time, perhaps expressed via distinctive shrine "microstyles" within each patrilineage. This is where a more quantitative approach can be a useful.

Analysis of Variability in Shrines

Trait-based surveys were conducted on twenty-two shrine structures (note 7): most sacred sites had only one built structure housing the local idols, though one complex included three structures at one site, and

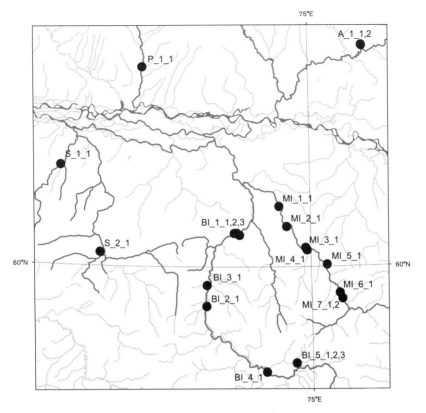

FIGURE 3.12 Location map of shrines.

Location map of shrines surveyed during ethnoarchaeological fieldwork (1998, 2003, 2004, 2005) on the Iugan, Iugan, Agan, Pim, and Trom"egan Rivers. Additional examples of Vakh, Vasiugan, and Salym Rivers have been drawn from the ethnographic literature (these locations are more approximate).

another important deity had structures at three separate locations and was ritually "migrated" around these sites at different seasons. Most of the twenty-two shrines were located within the Iugan basin (eight from the Malyi Iugan and nine from the Bolshoi Iugan), with comparative examples drawn from visits to other Eastern Khanty Rivers (Agan = 2; Pim = 1) and from the ethnographic literature (Salym = 2) (see Vizgalov 2000: 261, 264–65; figure 3.12).

Network-based analyses identified substantial differences in local shrine styles (figure 3.13) that were pulled out into different areas of the plot. The structure of the plot reflects the basic distinction between stilted shrines, which are on the upper right of the plot, and the ground-built

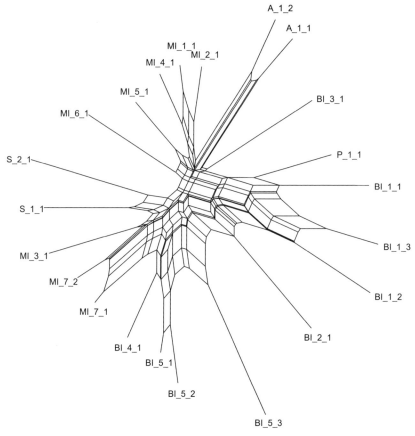

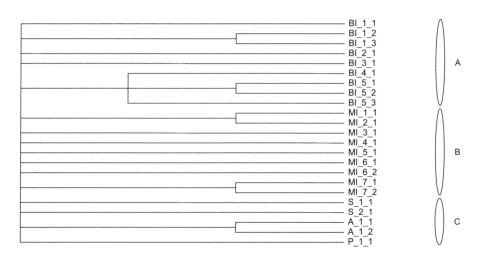

FIGURE 3.13 Shrines' network and tree

Top: Splitstree NeighborNet network illustrating potential branching and blending relationships among Khanty shrine-building traditions. The plots includes examples of shrines from the Bolshoi and Malyi Iugan Rivers (codes starting BI_ and MI_), and also from the Agan, Salym, and Pim Rivers (codes starting A_, P_ and S_ and see locations in figure 3.12). *Bottom:* Phylogenetic tree (created by maximum parsimony) of shrines built by Eastern Khanty communities. This follows the same coding system. Groupings A and B are the Bolshoi and Malyi Iugan rivers; C are other rivers.

structures, which are on the lower left (figure 3.13). However, there is no clear geographic clustering, and each patrilineage appears to be replicating its own highly distinct shrine-making tradition (note 8). The data were also subject to tree-based analyses to test the degree of branching signal in the data set (figure 3.13), and although there were some resolved clades in the tree, the RI score was 0.31 and indicated that processes other than branching had been operating.

Following these results, the trait-based data set and associated photo archive and fieldwork notes were subjected to a closer comparison in order to understand the source of these patterns. Two themes emerged: first, many of the traits associated with construction methods were being combined in highly variable ways (e.g., use of planks versus logs, roof boards versus birch bark sheeting); second, these traits were essentially being used interchangeably across the three basic shrine designs (surface-built sheds, large barns, and raised shrines). This appears to indicate that the primary architectural design of each local shrine was inherently conservative and reflected a more coherent design "recipe" which was being reproduced with considerable fidelity within different patrilineages. In contrast, the more "independent" and perhaps even "free-floating" traits used in the minor construction details of these different types of shrine was much more open to improvisation and creative recombination. Specifically, it appeared to be the latter set of traits that were generating the hybridization signals identified in the NeighborNet plot (figure 3.15); they may also have contributed to the low RI score as well.

Conclusion

Propagation of the traits used in shrine construction appears to be affected to some extent by a deliberate local conservatism in this architectural tradition, possibly motivated by a desire to maintain appropriate ritual conventions at the scale of the patrilineage. Locally coherent microstyles do appear to have formed within each patrilineage, especially with regard to the primary design features of these buildings. In contrast, specific combinations of minor construction methods and materials appear to have been much more open to innovation, with different sets of traits deployed in different combinations to build the same overall "type" of shrine (e.g., sheds versus raised platforms versus the larger barns). Importantly, it seems to be the basic architectural style that forms the primary expression of community commitment to meeting their spiritual obligations. In contrast, the more ephemeral construction traits seem to carry much less symbolic importance—all the local men are already "fluent" in using a wide range of building techniques and materials, and in the end, rebuilding a shrine with either a birch bark roof or a plank-built roof appear to form equally acceptable gestures of veneration and respect.

HUNTERS' SKIS

Functional Demands on Ski Design

Since early prehistory, broad wooden skis have been widely used across the forest zone of northern Eurasia for winter travel (Levin and Potapov 1961:79; Lukina 1985). The term *ski* is somewhat misleading: rather than the narrow downhill skiing variant, these are more akin to wide wooden snowshoes and are used for walking over deep snow in relatively flat landscapes. Consisting of two long thin planks, the front ends of these winter "walking" skis are sharpened and bent upward, with the foot fixed to the ski by bindings. The undersides are covered in fur to aid forward traction and also to muffle the sounds of movements over the snow crusts when hunting moose and other animals.

During the long winters in Northwest Siberia, hunters subject their skis to intensive seasonal usage, traveling tens of kilometer every day to stalk game and check trap lines; skis were also used by members of the entire household when they skied out to their remoter hunting territories, hauling cargo sledges, as well as during the frequent migrations between the isolated short-term bush camps (figure 3.2). These relentless demands placed tight functional requirements on all ski designs, especially those used by hunters: in particular, their skis need to be light and also reliable; broken skis or bindings might leave a hunter stranded in deep snow many kilometers from home or cost precious days of hunting until repairs are made. The skis also needed to be as silent as possible, because rasping movements over snow crusts, or crunching snow that becomes trapped under a heel of the hunting as he "walks" along in the ski could easily scare off animals that might have been stalked for hours. Finally, the skis needed to use materials that were readily available locally.

These intense practical requirements make the study of Khanty ski designs particularly interesting: basic ski and binding designs may well have been learned from parents in childhood and adolescence, but as the new hunter grows up and becomes more autonomous, able to hunt alone for weeks on end, there are new and relentless motivations to subject his inherited ski designs to intense scrutiny, evaluate their performance, and perhaps experiment with his own invented traits or by trying out new techniques that he may have observed among other hunters from wider social networks. All these factors potentially affect variability and cumulative developments in general ski-making traditions.

This case study focuses primarily on identifying and explaining the fascinating processes of cumulative innovation that have affected Iugan Khanty ski and binding designs during the past century, using data from the rich ethnographic record as well as from recent fieldwork (1998–2005): skis remain in widespread use and are still an essential technology in winter hunting. This case study starts by (1) looking at variability in modern Iugan Khanty skis (see "typical" example in figure 3.14) and then examines (2) some of the major changes in local ski design over the past hundred years and explores why these might have come about. Finally, (3) attempts are made to link these local patterns of variability in ski and binding design within the Iugan River basin to wider patterns across other Eastern Khanty river basins, as well as to variability in skis design across Siberia.

Propagation of Modern Ski Designs on the Iugan River

On the Iugan River both men and women share different stages of the ski production sequence: men cut and shape the wooden components, while women prepare glue and cut and sew the underskins and cloth covers. In this way, every hunter makes his own skis with assistance from his wife: the wooden parts are usually made in the summer, when the desired lengths of wood are split off from a felled log. These planks are gradually shaped with an axe and planning knife until the desired form and thickness have been achieved. Usually the front is sharpened, though the rear is cut away in a more angular fashion. For strength, the section under the foot and along the upper middle length of the ski is made slightly thicker and tapers off towards the sides. The flat ski "blank" form is then steamed and bent up at the front before being fixed in a special frame that enables the bend to "hold" while the timber dries out (figure 3.15). Next, two sets of holes are drilled either site of the foot, and wooden D-rings are inserted—these consist of short loops of wild cherry branch that have already been cut and bent into shape, and form the anchors for the bindings.

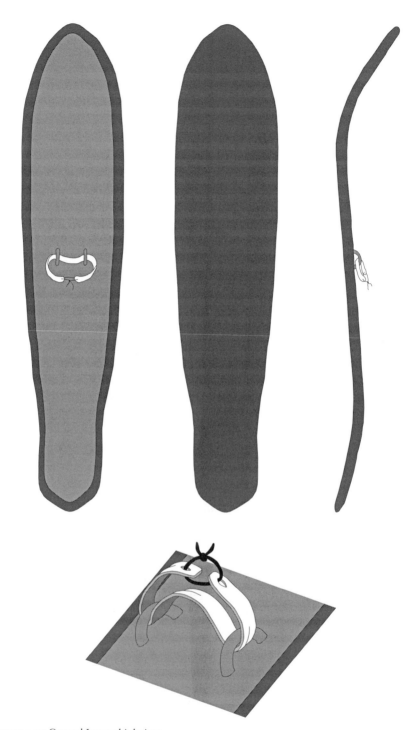

FIGURE 3.14 General Iugan ski designs.

General illustration of the basic ski design found among the Iugan River Khanty. This was first recorded in the late nineteenth century and persists through to the present. The distinctive D-ring binding consists of wild cherry wood, with a leather strap that fits over the foot. The cloth cover is not shown in this example, nor is the heel lace that fastens around the back of the foot and holds it in the binding. SOURCE: redrawn from Levin and Potapov 1961:102.

FIGURE 3.15 Skis in production + finished skis + death of skis in forest.

The life history of Khanty skis. *Top left:* The early stages of ski production at a base camp on the lower Malyi Iugan River. PHOTOGRAPH: Peter Jordan, September 2005. *Bottom:* A finished pair of skis from the middle Malyi Iugan River. They are stored in frames over the summer to retain the important upward bend at the front. PHOTOGRAPH: Peter Jordan, September 2005. *Top right:* An old pair of worn-out "male" skis hung out in the forest to "die their own death" near a path leading out of a base camp on the middle reaches of the Malyi Iugan. Clearly visible are the D-ring bindings and the cloth cover fitted to the ski with nails and an external rubber washer. The upward bend has started to fail, and the owner has attempt to extend the use life of the skis by fitting extra braces sometime prior to their final discard. PHOTOGRAPH: Peter Jordan, September 2005.

Women prepare the underskins and cut and sew them into the required shapes, and they also slowly simmer the glue from fish skins or animal horns or hoofs until it reaches the desired consistency. When the ski is ready, layers of glue are painted onto the skins and underside of the ski and then are slowly pressed into place, so that the skins hook onto the nose of the ski and fold up around the sides. Extra stitches run over the top of the ski and hold the sides of the skins in place until the glue has set. Next, the skis are also subjected to repeated cycles of heating in the steam bath *(bania)* and then freezing out in the snow to ensure that the glue holds. Finally, the leather binding straps are attached to the wooden D-ring and a cloth cover is fixed to the ski around the bindings; this has a drawstring top and knots just under the hunter's knee, protecting the bindings from clogging up with snow (figures 3.14 and 3.15). When skiing, hunters wear long boots made from moose fur; these are slotted under the leather cross straps and are held in place with a lace that runs behind the heel.

During the busy winter season hunters will wear these skis for many hours each day. The wood in a new pair of skis should last several years, and when the underfur wears thin it can be replaced, though a more serious problem is eventual "failure" in the bend in the wood at the front of the ski. In some cases a new splint is attached to the top of the ski, but this adds extra weight and eventually the worn-out skis are eventually discarded (figure 3.15).

Khanty women also used skis during the long winter migrations out to the remote hunting territories; their skis were made from the same general materials but were pointed at both ends so that they could be easily distinguished from male skis. Also, they tended not to have cloth covers because men usually skied in front to break the trail, and during the frequent stops women would be more active around the camp site, preparing skins, food, and firewood, which required them to take the skis on and off more frequently. In contrast, hunters would lace up their skis in the early morning and keep them on until they returned at dusk.

Ski making is intimately embedded in the patrilocal kinship system, and men are required to make skis for their entire household. Therefore, a woman marrying into the lineage was not allowed to bring her old skis with her and had to have new ones made by her husband, part of a wider set of marital prescriptions that ensured that a new bride was symbolically severed from her older lineage and that she was also subject to a new code of conduct in her new household (Lapina 1998). In requiring raw materials to be taken from the trees and game of the surrounding forests, ski making was also linked to cosmological concepts in which "gifts" from the forest had been provided by spirit masters and had to be treated with respect (Jordan 2003, 2006, 2011c); also, in creating a cultural object from these forest materials, the maker also injects some of his own personal "essence" into the skis; burning or destroying old skis was thought very harmful and unlucky for his existence. Instead, worn-out skis were returned to the forest and hung from trees to "die their own death." Old skis, many choked with thick lichen, are a common sight along pathways leading out of base camps and are also found in remoter areas of forest (figure 3.15).

Inheritance and Adjustment in Ski Design Traits

Fieldwork focused on collecting comprehensive trait-based data on modern male hunting skis. Over three summer field seasons (2003–4–5), locally made skis were systematically documented along the full length of the Bolshoi and Malyi Iugan Rivers, and ski makers were interviewed at length about the manufacture and use of skis, as well as how they had learned the skills and traits employed in particular sets of examples (figure 3.16).

Nearly all male informants initially indicated that they had acquired their basic ski-making traditions from their biological parents via vertical transmission or sometimes more generally from "ancestors." Most said that they observed their fathers making skis in childhood and started to experiment with making their own, often succeeding at the first attempt. It was reported that ski making was more challenging than related crafts like sledge manufacture because it consisted of a single piece of wood that needed to shaped and bent in a way that held the angle over its use life. In contrast, sledges are made up of many easy-to-make component parts that can be refitted (see following).

However, as the interviews and conversations unfolded, it was clear that this was only the first stage in a two-step process of cultural inheritance, in which learning from parents was followed by a lifetime of subsequent performance-related adjustment in ski designs. Some had undertaken their own purposive trial-and-error innovation on top of what they had initially been taught (guided variation); others had looked around, observed useful traits invented or employed by other ski makers, and switched to deploying or integrating those into their own skis (i.e., directly biased transmission). In general, subtle variability was noted in all aspects of ski and binding design, but the greatest variation was related to the use of the cloth foot covers (see following).

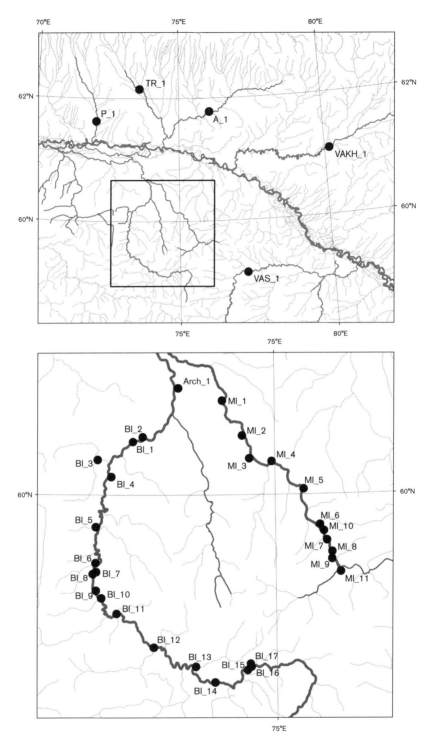

FIGURE 3.16 Location map of skis: Iugan River.

Location map of skis recorded during ethnoarchaeological fieldwork (1998, 1999, 2003, 2004, 2005) on the Iugan and Agan Rivers. Additional examples from the Pim, Trom"egan, Vakh, and Vasiugan Rivers are derived from the ethnographic literature (these locations are more approximate).

Investigating Variability in Modern Ski Designs

Starting the survey at the base camps at the very top of the Bolshoi Iugan (figure 3.16), all skis initially appeared to follow an identical and highly coherent design template: they invariably consisted of two cedar-wood planks, with the undersides covered with moose fur from the front shins of the animal. These had been stuck into place with moose glue. The bindings were made up of four holes drilled through the plank, on either side of the foot position, into which two D-rings of bent wild cherry wood were inserted (figures 3.14, 3.15). A wide leather strap ran through these and up over the foot. The ends of this strap were fastened together with a long leather lace that knotted over the top and also ran around the back of the heel and was laced up to hold the foot in place as the hunter skied forward.

Greater variability crept in with the more "ephemeral" details of ski design, especially relating to the use of the protective foot cloths (figure 3.17, examples a–e). For example, many men had permanently fixed the foot cloth to the upper side of the ski; some had nailed down the bottom edge of the cloth through a leather or rubberized-canvas washer that ran around the inside hem of the material, making the join invisible from the outside; others had nailed the cloth through a washer on the outside of the cloth, so that nails and washer were visible (figure 3.17 examples a, b). Most of these choices appeared to be pragmatic one-off experiments (guided variation) and had little effect on the basic function this attachment, which was to protect the foot and binding from snow. Likewise, other one-off "innovations" were noted: one man had painted commercial glaze on his skis; some had replaced leather straps with nylon strips. Others had left out the heel laces and had instead put a strip of wood or fixed cord on the surface of the ski between the D-rings, so that the foot had traction and would not slip backward. Finally, several different materials—ranging from rubber to felt and birch bark—were used to create a "foot plate" between the D-rings that provided both insulation and traction. There was no evidence that any of these novel traits had been copied by other ski makers.

None of these more ephemeral choices in ski design appeared to have made a major difference to the overall performance of the ski when in use, and there was little general consensus about which—if any—of these latter variants were any better than the other. However, two novel features had appeared and may have improved the performance and

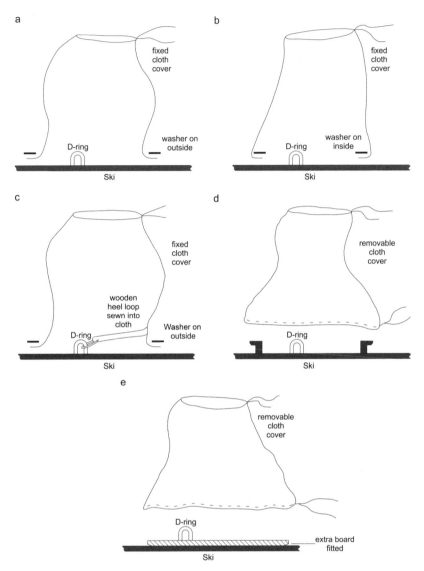

FIGURE 3.17 Variability in cloth ski covers: Iugan Khanty.

Schematic illustration of variability in ski designs recorded along the Iugan River. All skis on this river exhibit the same basic D-ring binding design (see figure 3.14). In contrast, there is much greater variability in traits associated with attachment of the newer cloth covers. For further details, see main text.

utility of skis, but had not yet seen widespread uptake among the wider population:

- One older man on the middle reaches of the Bolshoi Iugan had invented a further addition to the foot cloth: this was a long wooden loop that attached at both ends to the D-ring and also ran around the heel of the foot, where it was sewn into the inside of the foot cloth (figure 3.17, example c). As the hunter walked in the skis, his heels rose and fell, pulling the cloth tight and causing this extra wooden heel loop to flip out any snow that was starting to collect in the bunched-up material at the back of the foot—this also ensured that skiing remained silent. In traveling along the river, younger hunters from other lineages on the Bolshoi Iugan had seen this man's innovation and chosen to copy it (i.e., directly biased transmission), so that it had slowly started to become a *social tradition* rather than a one-off experiment by one individual. Transmitted from an older generation to nonrelated individuals of a younger generation via oblique transmission, this new trait was eventually observed at skis made at the top, middle, and lower reaches of the Bolshoi Iugan, but not yet on the Malyi Iugan.

- Across the wider basin, several men appeared to have independently devised detachable versions of the cloth cover—this involved lacing the cloth around a grooved wooden or metal ring that was fixed to the ski around the foot (figure 3.17, examples d, e). After hunting, these cloths could be removed and dried separately above the stove. If the cloths were fixed to the ski it was difficult to dry them, because placing the skis near the fire could affect the glue, possibly causing the fur to peel off during later use.

The relative lengths and breadths of the skis also varied according to the maker. During interviews, many informants explained that these proportions were ergonomically defined so that the ski width was an outstretched "finger-and-thumb span plus two fingers" (that is, c. 25 cm), and the length was either "to the eyebrows" or equal to "a person's height." Many said these proportions had been taught by their fathers and that they were a useful balance between the skis being too narrow, which would cause them to sink in soft snow, and excessively wide, which would make them heavy and liable to carry extra snow, making

movement and turning difficult. In fact, one man's skis were notable—
and in fact a local novelty—for being so wide, and the broad tracks they
left were likened by others to those left by a motorized snowmobile
(figure 3.18).

The rear of the ski is also cut away to subtly different forms, even
within the more general "male" form of skis. One reason for cutting off
these corners is to aid turning, which involves stepping, with the front
ends of the two skis apart and the rear ends brought together. In addition, the distinctive angling of the rear cuts also generates a "signature"
trail for each owner (and see Lukina 1985:22). This means that the
maker can recognize his own tracks when stalking back on game; identifying which skis have been where in the snows can also signal whether
intruders have been into particular hunting areas, and in some cases,
potentially signal the identity of that intruder.

As the survey moved into the Malyi Iugan (figure 3.16), a much
greater degree of experimentation and variability was noted. Although
use of the basic D-ring bindings remained universal across all base
camps (figure 3.14), there was greater experimentation with different
types of wood. Hunters had experimented with birch, spruce, and aspen:
some argued that aspen and birch were good because they "held the
bend better"; in contrast the bends in cedar skis often failed. One man
was using fish-based glue, which others criticized this for being too
heavy, but he defended the choice because he argued that it dried more
quickly than moose glue; two other hunters used imported chemical
glues. As on the Bolshoi Iugan, fur from the front shins of moose was
universally employed to cover the underside of the skis, although other
fur types were discussed: otter fur was excellent but not locally available; horse fur performed well but had to be obtained through special
contacts because no horses were kept on the river whereas everyone
hunted the local moose; one man had tried horse fur but said it was not
that good because it was very heavy and tended to develop holes in cold
weather. On balance, fur from moose shins was widely available and
performed well, and was universally used across the entire Iugan River
basin.

Multiple variations in the attachment of the cloth covers to the skis
were also noted. One particularly interesting local variation involved
fixing a large wooden foot board on top of the ski, into which the
D-rings were also inserted (figure 3.17 example e; figure 3.19 left). This
formed a raised lip around which a detachable cloth cover could be
fixed: one informant had copied this via vertical transmission from his

FIGURE 3.18 Modern ski examples.

Examples of modern Iugan Khanty skis with fixed *(right)* and detachable *(left)* cloth covers around the foot and bindings (upper Bolshoi Iugan River). The ski on the left is cut to the "female" pattern (sharply pointed front and also rear), and the ski on the right is an extremely large example of skis cut to the "male" pattern (pointed front, but with more angled rear section). Also visible on the left pair of skis is the insulating "foot plate" made of birch bark. For further details, see main text. PHOTOGRAPH: Peter Jordan, July 2004.

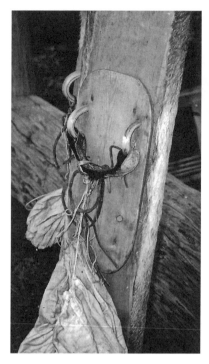

FIGURE 3.19 Examples of unusual ski traits.

Some examples of unusual ski design traits found only on the Malyi Iugan River. *Left:* An additional wooden foot plate is fixed to the ski, forming a rim for a removable cloth cover to be fitted. Photograph: Peter Jordan, July 2004. *Right:* This hunter from the upper Malyi Iugan River had replaced the usual leather heel laces with straps and buckles that he said performed better in heavy frost because they could be easily fastened up and released with gloved hands. PHOTOGRAPH: Peter Jordan, July 2004.

father, and it had also spread horizontally via more informal contacts between nonrelated members of the same generation via directly biased transmission to another younger hunter lower on the river. In one very old example, the raised lip was integral to the ski, and it had all been carved from one piece of wood, though this trait appeared not to have ever been subject to any wider uptake.

Another remarkable ski variant was displayed by a widow who had taken up hunting only after her husband had drowned in an accident: she had sawn off the central sections of an old pair of her husband's skis, which included the bindings, and then nailed this directly onto a crudely fashioned new set of skis. The protective cloth had then been nailed around the rim of this attachment to protect the foot from snow.

Finally, one hunter had started to use wide commercially obtained leather heel straps and buckles, which he said were faster to use in the heavy winter frost than the usual thin heel laces that were prevalent elsewhere. However, there were no signs that this innovation was catching on elsewhere (figure 3.19 right).

Tracing Historical Changes in Iugan River Ski Designs

Looking further back in time to the end of the nineteenth century, two very different kinds of ski and binding designs are recorded on the Iugan River by the Swedish ethnographer Martin (1897); the current dominance of D-ring ski bindings on the Iugan River is therefore a relatively new phenomenon (figure 3.14), as is the practice of using cloth covers to protect the foot and binding from snow (figures 3.15, 3.17). This raises interesting questions about deeper histories of ski innovation within this particular dialect community.

The first ski recorded by Martin is an unusual "platform" style ski. This style of ski has now died out entirely and the only examples are found in the folk museum in the main village of Ugut (figure 3.20). Elders born in the mid-1930s said they had never seen these archaic platform skis in use, so they must have been abandoned in the earlier twentieth century, at the same time as the use of protective cloth around the foot was being adopted on skis with the D-ring bindings. These older platform skis, skillfully carved from a single piece of wood, have a distinctive raised section on which the foot rests and into which a unique hooped binding of bent wood is fitted. In most examples, this raised section consists of a narrow fin running lengthwise along the ski, which then flares out at the top, providing a wide platform for the foot. When the skier walks through fresh snow this platform raises the foot well above the level of the snow, enabling the fin to "slice" through snow and deflect it to either side. By keeping the feet well above the snow surface, the ski bindings do not become clogged; moreover, these skis remain silent when stalking game, because snow is less likely to gather under the heel and crunch as the hunter walks forward.

The second ski type recorded in Martin's late nineteenth-century survey is essentially the same as skis made today on the Iugan River, with the same basic D-ring binding. This indicates a century of basic continuity in ski design, although these older variants do not possess the protective cloth covers around the foot (see the example in figure 3.14). Thus, in the late nineteenth century, the bindings on these kinds of skis were

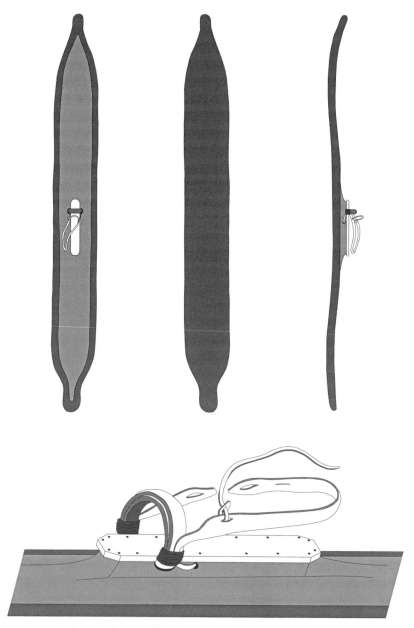

FIGURE 3.20 Archaic platform skis.

Example of the archaic "platform" skis. These have an entirely different binding design and also features a raised "fin" of wood on which the foot rests. These skis required great dexterity to use but were silent because the raised fin cut through the snow and prevented it from collecting under the hunter's heel and crunching as he moved. This design was widely present among the Iugan Khanty in the late nineteenth century but had entirely died out by the early twentieth century. SOURCE: redrawn from Levin and Potapov 1961:103.

essentially open to the elements. Hunters across the wider region wore warm fur boots over which the bindings fitted (see, e.g., numerous pictures from Sirelius 1983:225, 247). However, while the boots kept the feet warm, the open design of the bindings meant that snow could get in, and it often gathered under the foot of the skier, especially under the heel, which was raised and lowered as the hunter "walked" forward in the skis.

The same kinds of fur boots are still in use today. However, the cloth covers around the foot are definitely a very recent innovation in Northwestern Siberia, appearing first among the Mansi, who live to the west of the Eastern Khanty, and gradually spreading via directly biased transmission across Khanty communities (Levin and Potapov 1961:79; Lukina 1985:22–23), probably in the early twentieth century as elders on the Iugan born in 1932 (and interviewed in 2003) said they'd never seen skis without these protective foot cloths.

What makes Martin's late nineteenth-century ethnographic survey so interesting is that it documents the existence of two alternative technological choices (Lemonnier 1993): the archaic platform skis (figure 3.20) broadly solved the same set of practical problems as the new cloth covers on the modern Iugan skis (figures 3.15 and 3.17). However, while both designs existed a coherent cultural traditions in the late nineteenth century, only one of these two traditions survived. Understanding exactly why one of these ski traditions died out contributes some useful insights into the factors that can affect cultural propagation.

Trait-Based Analysis of Coherence in Khanty Ski-Making Traditions

Given this rich and highly dynamic history of ski-making among the Iugan Khanty and adjacent populations, several interesting questions start to emerge:

1. At what social scale do coherent ski-making traditions emerge within the Iugan River basin?

2. In which aspects of the modern ski design is there greatest coherence?

3. How distinctive are the designs of the archaic platform skis versus modern Iugan skis?

4. Which features of modern ski design contain the strongest historical signal?

5. At what social scales is there coherence in ski designs among the different Eastern Khanty groups?

6. At what social scales is there coherence in ski designs across other parts of Siberia?

Addressing these questions involves collection of suitable trait-based datasets and inference of basic patterns of coherence using methods described in chapter 2. Using the same methods across all the chapters provides a useful framework for comparative discussions of results in in chapter 6.

Ski-Making Data Sets. Most data were collected during ethnoarchaeological fieldwork (2003–5) and recorded the basic operational sequence in modern ski production; traits pertaining to details of the binding design; the types of wood, glue, and fur used for the main ski; other features, such as a "sole" placed under the foot for warmth and traction, made of rubber, wood, or birch bark; and details of the cloth sack around the foot. Further data was collected on older ski-making designs recorded at the end of the nineteenth century (Martin 1897), as well as ski-making traditions recorded on other Eastern Khanty rivers (figure 3.16) and from across Siberia (Levin and Potapov 1961: 79–105).

Analysis of Key Questions

1. *At what social scale do coherent ski making traditions emerge within the Iugan River basin?*

Modern Iugan River ski-making designs, recorded across the basin (figure 3.16), including details of the bindings and the cloth covers (forty-one traits, fifty skis), were analyzed with network- and tree-based analyses (see chapter 2; note 9; see figure 3.21) to examine general patterns of coherence in this craft tradition. The boxing in some parts of the NeighborNet plot indicates conflict in the data set, and although some distinct ski designs are pulled out in different directions, these appear to be the result of local innovations; skis from many different patrilineages are arranged almost randomly around the plot. Certainly, there is no evidence that coherent traditions have formed and are being transmitted at the scale of the patrilineages, or within different sections of the river, or even within the main Malyi and Bolshoi Iugan branches. The very low RI score of 0.10 confirms that there is a very little overall coherence in the data set at any social scale, and on balance, these results appear to indicate the independent emergence of essentially unique design features across different parts of the Iugan basin.

2. *In which aspects of the overall modern ski design is there greatest coherence?*

Given these patterns of localized innovation, which features of contemporary ski design are most affected? Close cross-referencing of the NeighborNet plot (figure 3.21) against the lists of individual traits in the original data set indicated that almost all contemporary Iugan skis actually exhibit strong underlying coherence in their basic design features—these traits include the wooden D-ring binding, toe strap, and heel lace, cedarwood base, and the use of moose fur and glue (figure 3.14). These basic traits were the ones that informants explicitly said they had learned via vertical transmission from parents, or more generally, from our "ancestors." For example, of the total fifty pairs of skis documented along the entire Iugan River, forty-nine consisted of flat planks bent upwards, all fifty had D-rings and forty-seven of these shared exactly the same leather straps; forty-three used cedar; forty-seven used moose glue, and all fifty had protective cloth covers around the binding.

Beyond this strong underlying coherence in the basic features of modern ski design, there were some interesting variations on the Malyi Iugan River. For example, there was frequent experimentation with different kinds of wood, mainly due to personal trial-and-error experimentation (guided variation). Some hunters had also started to make the wooden footplate a more integral part of the main ski, and there were some signs that this was becoming established and passed on vertically from fathers to sons and also diffusing on a limited scale via directly biased transmission (figure 3.17 example e; figure 3.19, left).

In contrast to the largely standardized sets of traits used in the relatively coherent basic ski and binding designs, the ways in which the new cloth covers were being attached to the skis was highly variable (see figure 3.17). In other words, there was high coherence and heritable continuity in the main design traits from the late nineteenth-century examples through to the early twenty-first century, especially in relation to the D-ring bindings. However, the traits associated with the new cloth covers had not yet become a coherent tradition; they were more akin to a collection of ephemeral and rapidly changing traits that had only recently become associated with these more coherent and stable aspects of the well-established Iugan ski design with its distinctive D-ring bindings (figure 3.14).

For example, all fifty pairs of skis on the Iugan River had cloth covers. However, in twenty-nine pairs the cloth was permanently fixed to the wooden base with a circular washer that fitted *outside* the cloth, but in twelve pairs of skis the washer was situated *inside* the cloth (see figure 3.17, examples a, b). All these examples used a wide variety of different materials for the washers. Within this subset, seven pairs of skis had an extra wooden heel ring sewn into the cloth so that snow was ejected from the folds of cloth as the hunter walked forward, raising his heels (figure 3.17, example c). In addition, nine of the fifty pairs of skis had detachable cloth covers, but five entirely different methods were used to fasten this cloth to the ski, ranging from wooden and aluminium rings fitted directly to the ski to the use of raised boards under the foot (figure 3.22: example of ring in d; example of board in e). Judging by the interviews, most of this general variability in the attachment of the cloth covers appeared to be a result of independent and often fairly pragmatic experimentation (guided variation) at very different locations within the basin. Only the use of wooden heel ring seemed to have caught on and become transmitted among a few individuals living at different points along the Bolshoi Iugan River via directly biased transmission.

Thus, these results indicate a twin pattern in the propagation of traits within the modern Iugan ski designs. This consists of a highly coherent basic design recipe for the core Iugan ski and D-ring binding design (i.e., figure 3.14), which according to informants had mainly been passed vertically via a system of high-fidelity copying from fathers to sons. This coherent set of traits had already achieved a widespread general distribution on the river by the nineteenth century and then achieved total domination after the "death" of the archaic platform ski tradition (figure 3.20; see previous).

In contrast—and surrounding this stable and coherent core design— were a set of newer traits associated with the cloth covers. These were highly unstable, and also highly diffusible, but had yet to settle into a more coherent tradition (figure 3.17, examples a–e). Most of this variability appears to result from an ongoing process of personal experimentation. In fact, with all other traits exhibiting high coherence across the basin, it appears that these traits associated with the cloth covers are generating much of the hybridization signal noted previously in the network- and tree-based analyses (figures 3.21 and 3.28). There was also no general consensus among informants about the relative efficacy of the different methods for attaching the cloth—all traits seemed to provide equal solutions to the same general requirements. In sum, the overall modern ski design has become highly standardized, but these more recent features of the ski-making tradition are still undergoing a process of rapid innovation and evaluation, and no standardized "recipe" has yet emerged—in other words, strikingly different patterns of individual trait evolution can be identified even *within* the same overall material culture tradition.

3. *How distinctive are the designs of the archaic platform skis versus modern Iugan skis?*

The data set of the modern Iugan ski-making traditions (including bindings and cloth covers) was expanded to include examples of the older archaic platform skis (figure 3.20), generating an expanded data set of fifty-three examples of skis recorded in terms of fifty-nine distinctive traits. This was investigated using network- and tree-based methods (see chapter 2 and note 10). The transformation in the plot is striking; the modern skis and older platform skis clearly have very different designs; the examples of the archaic skis are pulled out from the center of the plot into very different directions, and they also form a separate branch in the tree diagram (plots not shown). However, the tree-based analysis returned an RI of 0.38, which probably reflects the complex ways in which traits in the modern ski tradition are evolving, especially in relation to the incorporation of the new cloth covers (see previous).

4. *Which features of modern ski design contain the strongest historical signal?*

Given the highly variable methods for fixing the new cloth covers to the skis, the data set of modern and archaic platforms skis were revised to include only traits pertaining to the actual ski bindings—traits associated with the new cloth covers were removed. This basically recreated the historical situation documented by Martin (1897), when these two different ski designs existed as rival variants within the same Iugan River basin population (see previous). This resulted in a revised data set of fifty-three skis with thirty-four traits, which was subject to network- and tree-based analysis (note 11). The tree and network plots (not shown) now indicated much deeper separation between the archaic platform skis and the skis with the D-ring bindings, and the RI was also

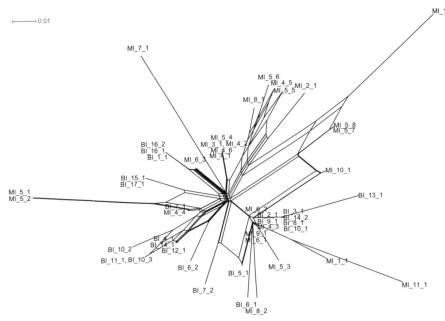

FIGURE 3.21 Modern skis network.

Splitstree NeighborNet network illustrating potential branching and blending
relationships among modern ski designs on the Iugan River. Examples of skis are coded
according to the river (BI = Bolshoi Iugan; MI = Malyi Iugan), base camp, and number
of examples from each location. For example, ski BI_3_1 is ski example number 1 from
location number 3 on the Bolshoi Iugan River. For geographic locations, see figure 3.16.

much higher at 0.86, suggesting the presence of a branching signal in
the data set.

Given that very many of the fifty examples of the modern Iugan skis
share the same D-ring binding technology, there was a high degree of
duplication in the data set. To address this problem and simplify the
plots, examples of skis with the exactly the same sets of traits were
removed. This generated a much smaller data set of nine different skis
and thirty-four traits, which captured the main forms of variability
across the archaic platform skis and also across the newer Iugan skis
with the D-ring bindings. Network- and tree-based analyses showed a
similar bunching of the D-ring ski variants, with the archaic platform
skis pulled out far to the right; the tree also placed all the D-ring variants into a single clade, with the RI score of 0.65 suggesting the presence of a branching signal in ski-making traditions (figure 3.22). Clearly,
both these analyses appear to be identifying patterns of coherence in the

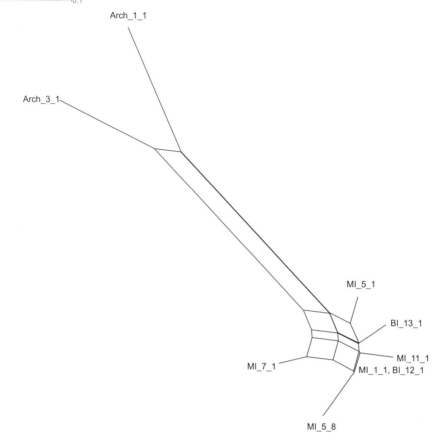

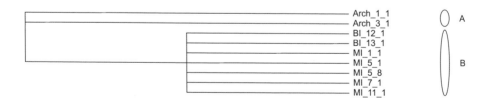

FIGURE 3.22 Archaic and modern Iugan skis network and tree (reduced data).

Top: Splitstree NeighborNet network illustrating potential branching and blending relationships among archaic and modern ski-making traditions on the Iugan River, with examples of duplicate modern skis removed to simplify the plot. The archaic skis are coded with the prefix "Arch_," and skis from the Bolshoi and Malyi Iugan Rivers are coded with BI_ and MI_. For geographic locations, see figure 3.16. *Bottom:* Phylogenetic tree (created by maximum parsimony) of modern and archaic ski-making traditions among the Iugan Khanty. This follows the same coding system. Grouping A is the archaic skis and B is the modern Iugan skis.

specific combinations of traits that make up each of these two very different ski making traditions

If both ski variants were being made and used in the late nineteenth century, and if each tradition exhibits a high degree of internal coherence why did one design persist and the other disappear? The explanation appears to link back to the relative difficulty of mastering the two kinds of skis in relation to their relative advantages in stalking game. However, with the arrival of cheap cloth into the region, the balance between these trade-offs was eventually overturned, leading to the "death" of the archaic platform ski tradition within one or two human generations:

- The modern D-ring walking skis (figure 3.14) are not difficult to master—modern Khanty children become proficient skiers by age six or seven (Lukina 1985: 21), though learning to move silently through the forest, over fallen logs and other obstructions, requires greater practice, as does getting back onto the skis after falling off into the shoulder-deep snow.

- In contrast, the older platform skis (figure 3.20) required much greater dexterity and agility to use, and not all hunters were able to master them (Lukina 1985: 22). Those who could not master them were probably forced to use the alternative D-ring skis. In the platform skis, the great advantage was the raised wooden fin upon which the foot rested; this feature enabled the hunter to slice silently through the snow, whereas the open D-ring more susceptible to clogging. This would require frequent stoppages to clear out the snow, but would also mean that the skis were noisier because the snow gathering under the foot would eventually crunch under the heel as the hunter walked forwards, alerting moose and other game to the hunter's approach. As a result of these unresolved trade-offs between the rival designs, both ski variants were able to coexist on the Iugan River, as documented by Martin (1897), at the end of the nineteenth century.

- The delicate balance between the relative advantages of the two ski variants were radically altered by the arrival of cheap cloth into the region in the 1930s (Levin and Potapov 1961:79; Lukina 1985:22–23). Addition of the new cloth covers prevented snow clogging up the bindings; more importantly, it provided a means for making the easy-to-master D-ring skis more silent. This immediately canceled out all the relative advantages of the archaic platform skis—they remained difficult to master, but their performance during hunting was now no better than the D-ring skis with the new cloth covers.

5. At what social scales is there coherence in ski designs among Eastern Khanty groups?

Clearly, and based on these emerging insights, it would appear to be the combination of traits associated with the modern Iugan D-ring ski bindings—and not the more recent cloth covers – that possesses the strongest signals for internal coherence and deeper historical continuity. But how does this Iugan River ski-making tradition relate to other traditions maintained by adjacent Eastern Khanty groups (figure 3.1)? Are these Iugan River ski binding designs shared by Khanty living on the Pim, Trom"egan, Agan, Vakh, and Vasiugan Rivers, or does each river's population have its own unique tradition? As the fieldwork surveys extended beyond the Iugan River basin, new types of ski binding were quickly encountered (e.g., see figure 3.23, for the Agan River Khanty). The trait-based dataset of ski binding designs was expanded to include examples manufactured by several other Eastern Khanty communities (figure 3.16), and subjected to network- and tree-based analysis (note 12).

Two versions of this data set were analyzed, one that included all fifty examples of Iugan River skis, including duplicate forms, as well as examples of the archaic platform skis, and skis from other Eastern Khanty rivers (sixty-one pairs of skis in total and forty-five cultural traits—plots not shown), and then a smaller, second data set, in which duplicate examples of Iugan skis had been removed (see previous)—this left seventeen examples of distinctive skis and forty-five traits, allowing for simplified plots to be generated (see figure 3.24). The former, complete data set, with many duplicate examples from the Iugan River, had an RI of 0.90, and the latter, smaller data set, with these duplicates removed, had an RI of 0.82, both indicating the presence of coherent local ski-making traditions and, possibly, indicating the evolution of these traditions by branching processes. In the tree plot, the distinctive Iugan River variants form a single clade that maps directly onto local dialect boundaries; a single and distinctive local binding design also appears to exist on the Trom"egan River and on the Vasiugan River, with each local style also mapping directly onto these local dialect boundaries (figure 3.1). In contrast, two distinct kinds of local binding

FIGURE 3.23 Example of Agan skis.
Example of skis recorded on the Agan River. PHOTOGRAPH: Peter Jordan, June 2003.

coexist within the Vakh River basin, and two further distinct variants exist within the Agan River basin, and two more on Pim River basin. Clearly, some apparent coherence in ski design is emerging, in some cases, at the scale of the river basin populations.

These combined results indicate that the Iugan River Khanty have a single highly coherent D-ring ski binding variant, whose distribution maps directly and exclusively onto their river basin and associated dialect boundaries, also correlating with their sense of collective group identity (e.g., Iaun Iakh, "people of the Iugan River"). However, it is

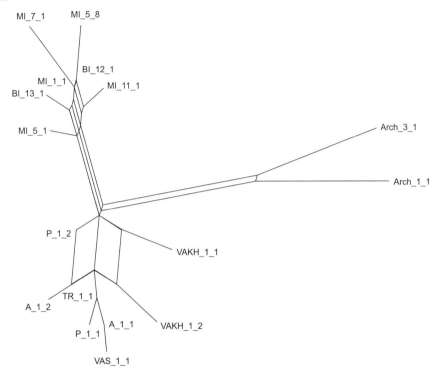

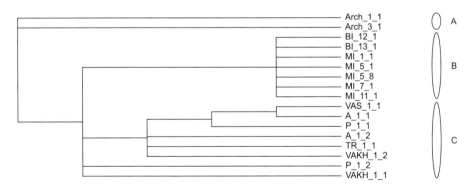

FIGURE 3.24 All Eastern Khanty skis network.

Top: Splitstree NeighborNet network illustrating potential branching and blending relationships among archaic and modern ski-making traditions on the Iugan River, with examples of duplicate skis removed to simplify the plot, and among other Eastern Khanty groups. The archaic skis are coded with the prefix "Arch_," and skis from the Bolshoi and Malyi Iugan Rivers are coded with BI_ and MI_; skis from the Agan, Pim, Trom"egan, Vakh, and Vasiugan Rivers are coded A_, P_, TR_, VAKH_, VAS_. For geographic locations see figure 3.16. *Bottom:* Phylogenetic tree (created by maximum parsimony) of archaic and modern ski-making traditions on the Iugan River and among other Eastern Khanty groups. This follows the same coding system. Grouping A is the archaic skis, B is Iugan skis and C is other Eastern Khanty skis.

highly unlikely that these ski bindings actively "signal" that identity to any kind of audience because they are hidden away under the cloth cover and generally used only by hunters operating in isolation within their own hunting territories where strangers are rarely, if ever, encountered. To link this back to the concept of TRIMs ([transmission isolating mechanisms; see Durham 1992: chapter 1), it is the distinctive geography of the local rivers and seasonal interaction patterns that together appear to be leading to the formation of this coherent tradition at the scale of the Iugan River basin. Interestingly, it is exactly this kind of geographic isolation that has been linked to explain the formation of separate Khanty dialects, as well as other distinctive cultural patterns at the scale of the separate river basins (Shatilov 1931; Tereshkin 1981).

A broadly similar situation appears to exist on the Trom"egan and Vasiugan Rivers, where coherent ski binding designs map directly onto local dialect boundaries, whereas multiple design variants coexist on some other rivers. The reasons for these different distributions are uncertain, because all the same raw materials grow across the region. It could be that on some rivers a single specific ski binding design has converged on to a local "fitness" peak and become highly coherent; in the other rivers, two coherent designs are able to coexist because neither has an inherent advantage over the other.

Finally, the archaic platform ski design is always pulled out as being very different from all the other modern Eastern Khanty ski designs. At the end of the nineteenth century, these archaic platform skis appear to have had a rather wide regional distribution: they appear to have been made and used right along the wider Ob' River basin and some of its tributaries until the early twentieth century. This historical distribution certainly extended as far north as the Northern Khanty on the lower Ob' (Lars-Gunnar Larsson, personal archive), and as far south as the Vasiugan River basin (Sirelius 1983:293); they were also used by adjacent Northwest Siberian groups, including the Mansi and Sel'kup (Federova 2000:304; Lukina 1966:109).

Levin and Potapov (1961:103) term these archaic platform skis *priobskii* type (i.e., "Ob' River" skis) suggesting a general Northwest Siberia distribution along the entire Ob' floodplains prior to the tradition dying out. It can therefore be tentatively concluded that processes by which this ski went "extinct" on the Iugan River also affected the wider West Siberia region—the platform skis died out as soon as cloth covers appeared, leaving various sets of locally coherent open binding designs to persist in the various Eastern Khanty rivers right through to the present.

6. At what social scales is there coherence in ski designs across other parts of Siberia?

Finally, a much larger trans-Siberian trait-based data set of ski bindings was compiled, including the full set of Iugan variants, examples of the archaic platform skis, other Eastern Khanty skis from across North-western Siberia, and additional examples of ski binding designs recorded right across Eastern Siberia and out to the Russian Far East (figures 3.25, 3.26, 3.27). This geographic expansion produced a data set of seventy-one skis and seventy-one traits. In addition, a reduced data set was also generated by again removing duplicate Iugan variants (twenty-seven skis and seventy-one traits). Both data sets were analyzed (note 13). For both data sets, the results indicated substantial coherence in traits on the trees; each data set appears to have had a substantial branching signal (RI of 0.92 for the full data set, and an RI of 0.83 for the reduced data set with the duplicate examples of Iugan skis removed).

For the reduced data set, the NeighborNet plot and many parts of the tree diagram appear to have a clear branching structure. This suggests that that the different sets of traits associated with the archaic platform skis, the Iugan skis, and the range of other Eastern Khanty ski designs each group into a relatively coherent local ski-making tradition. Moreover, there is also some indication that these different traditions may have evolved via a hierarchical branching processes (figure 3.28). However, in areas further to the east of Siberia, and into the Russian Far East, the traits associated with local ski binding designs exhibit some coherence but much less of a hierarchical branching structure. In other words, there appear to be many distinctive local variants, but these differences are not hierarchically organized, and they fit poorly onto a branching tree model.

Linking these overall patterns of cultural coherence in ski binding types in any straightforward or simplistic way onto particular linguistic groups—or even onto distinct geographic areas—is challenging, but in some areas there do appear to be close correlations. For example, the distinctive Iugan Khanty bindings—and those on the Vasiugan and Trom"egan—do appear to map directly onto local river basins, which form both dialect boundaries and a distinctive sense of ethnic identity, but in many other Eastern Khanty river basins two coherent designs coexist within each of the basins.

A broadly similar situation persists across the rest of Siberia (see ski design distribution map in Levin and Potapov 1961: 105): in some areas

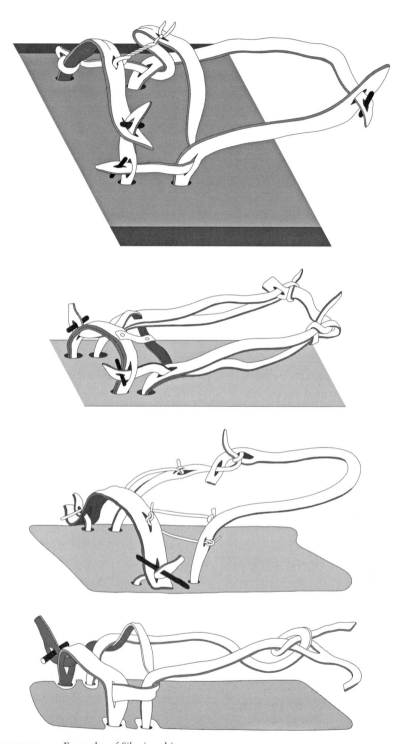

FIGURE 3.25 Examples of Siberian skis 1.

Variability in ski binding designs from across Siberia. *Top*: Northwest variant. *Others,
top to bottom*: Saiano-Altaiskii variants. Source: redrawn from Levin and Potapov
1961:98, 102.

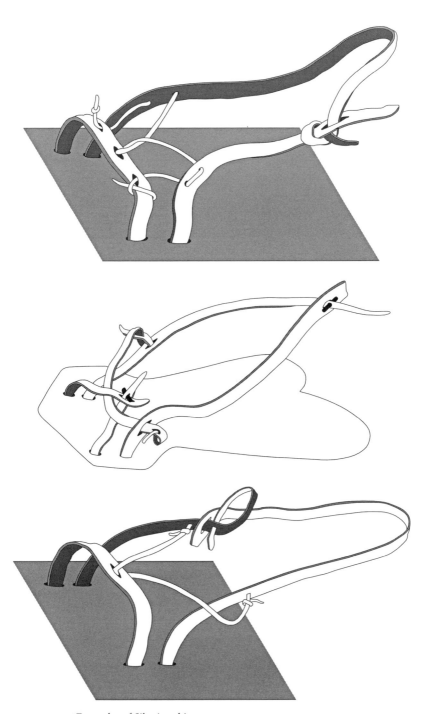

FIGURE 3.26 Examples of Siberian skis 2.

Variability in ski binding designs from across Siberia. *Top to bottom*: East Siberian variants SOURCE: redrawn from Levin and Potapov 1961:100.

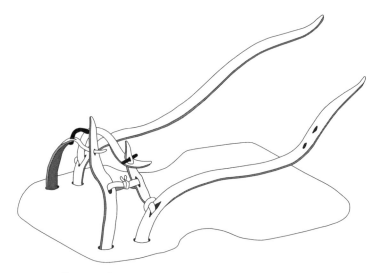

FIGURE 3.26. *(Continued)*

a single type has emerged and spread over large areas; in other regions, distributions of distinctive ski binding traditions often overlap, with several coherent traditions coexisting within the same geographic area. In conclusion then, a wide range of coherent ski binding designs have emerged in many different areas of Siberia, but their relationship to on-the-ground social units and linguistic boundaries is highly variable. Some coherent and distinctive binding designs map directly onto local ethnic and dialect boundaries, as in the case of the Iugan, Vasiugan, and Trom"egan Rivers. However, this may be an exception to the more general tendency, where either one single style dominates over large geographic areas, thereby transcending large numbers of local language groups and ethnic communities, or where multiple binding styles coexist among populations living within in the same general region and often speaking a range of different languages.

Ski Designs: Conclusion

Skis remain a fundamentally important and highly personalized transport technology in Northwest Siberia, and they are still handmade for individual usage, employing resources readily available from local forests. Each pair of skis is placed under enormous functional demands and must be reliable, comfortable, and silent—performance is subject to

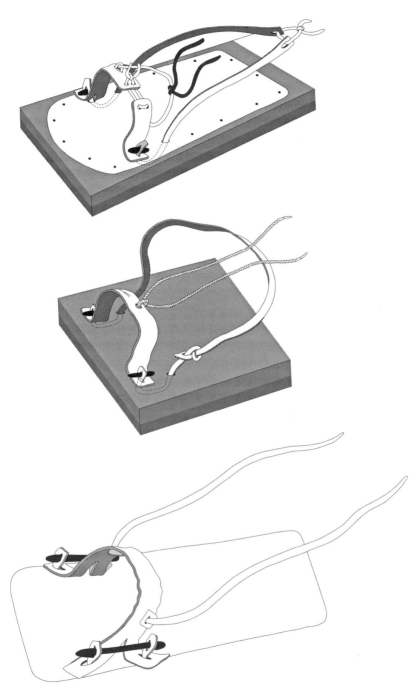

FIGURE 3.27 Examples of Siberian skis 3.

Variability in ski binding designs from across Siberia. *Top and middle*: Amuro-Sakhalinskii variants. *Bottom*: Amurskii variant. SOURCE: redrawn from Levin and Potapov 1961:99, 101.

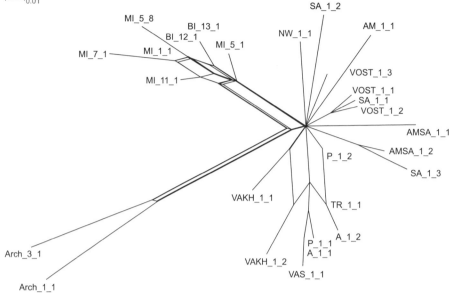

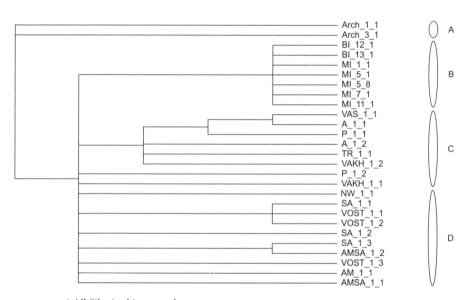

FIGURE 3.28 All Siberia skis network.

Top: Splitstree NeighborNet network illustrating potential branching and blending relationships among an expanded set of ski-making traditions, including examples of archaic and modern skis on the Iugan River (with examples of duplicate skis removed to simplify the plot), examples from other Khanty groups, and also from other regions of Siberia, through to the Russian Far East. The archaic skis are coded with the prefix "Arch_," skis from the Bolshoi and Malyi Iugan Rivers are coded with BI_ and MI_, and skis from the Agan, Pim, Trom"egan, Vakh, and Vasiugan Rivers are coded A_, P_, TR_, VAKH_, VAS_. Additional codes of AM_, AMSA_, SA_, NW, VOST_ equate to Amurskii, Amuro-Sakhalinskii, Saiano-Altaiskii, Northwest, and Eastern variants. For geographic locations of Khanty skis see figure 3.16 and for the other Siberian, see Levin and Potapov 1961:105). *Bottom:* Phylogenetic tree (created by maximum parsimony) built from the same data set of skis. This follows the same coding system. The archaic skis fall into group A; the skis from the Bolshoi and Malyi Iugan form group B. Skis from other Khanty rivers form group C, and examples of skis from other parts of Siberia form group D.

intense scrutiny during intensive use by hunters over the long winters. This case study has primarily focused on understanding propagation of ski design traits within the Iugan River basin (figures 3.12, 3.16) and has examined how skis are made and used and whether ski design traits form a relatively coherent technological tradition with the basin. It has also examined evolution of ski designs across adjacent river basins and has explored some major shifts in ski design over time. Finally, it has explored the distribution of ski binding designs across Siberia.

In general then, local ski designs appear to have been propagated via a two-stage process that starts with vertical transmission of a basic design recipe from parents to sons, via observation, imitation, and direct teaching, and then moves on to a lifelong process during which active hunters engage in continual trial-and-error experimentation (guided variation) with new design features and materials, or sometimes borrow new traits invented by other hunters (directly biased transmission). This cumulative two-step process of inheritance and payoff-based adjustment is driven primarily via functional performance criteria, and there is no evidence that any form of ski is more or less prestigious or subject to any form of social sanction and conformity bias.

These features of the transmission process have affected different aspects of contemporary Iugan River ski design in different ways: the binding design appears to have converged locally on an "adaptive peak," consisting of a highly coherent set of integrated and enduring traits: cedarwood skis, moose skins and glue, and especially the distinctive D-ring binding, all of which appear to be learned as a single "recipe" and are unique to the Iugan Khanty dialect community. In contrast, the new cloth covers are still experiencing ongoing experimentation, and no single or more standardized combination of design traits has yet emerged—in fact, nearly all the recorded variability in contemporary ski designs relates to these new traits that arrived in the region only two or three generations ago.

This cumulative two-stage process of (a) vertical transmission followed by (b) functional "payoff-based adjustment" also appears to explain some of the major evolutions in regional ski designs over the past century. At the end of the nineteenth century, several ski and binding variants existed across Northwest Siberia: the archaic platform skis were ideally suited for hunting but were difficult to master, whereas the other flat skis, which employed open bindings, often clogged up and caused extra noise. Trade-offs among skill, relative performance, and ease of use enabled all these many variants to coexist. However, the arrival of cheap cloth into the region via directly biased transmission in the early twentieth century enabled the overall design of the flat skis to be improved until it eventually out-competed the archaic platform skis, causing their extinction.

The eventual extinction of the archaic platform skis appears to have played out slightly differently across the various Eastern Khanty river basins. Within the Iugan, Vasiugan, and Trom"egan basins (figure 3.1), the binding designs on the flat skis appear to have converged on a single but different kind of solution within each basin. Along other rivers like the Pim, Agan, and Vakh, several coherent ski binding designs emerged and coexisted within each basin, because none appears to have any specific advantage over the others. More generally, this case study illustrates how microscale propagation processes can eventually "scale up" to generate highly coherent material culture traditions. In at least some cases, these distinctive styles can map directly onto dialect boundaries and ethnic groups, but in many other cases, these correlations between language groups and material culture distributions remain enormously complex and highly unpredictable.

FURTHER QUALITATIVE INSIGHTS INTO THE PROPAGATION OF TECHNOLOGICAL TRADITIONS

Two further qualitative case studies generate rich contextual insights into the propagation of traits within technological traditions. The first example is the *dug-out canoe*, whose design remains highly standardized over large areas, and *sledges*, which were also once highly standardized within specific ecological niches but are now currently undergoing complex patterns of modification following the introduction of snowmobiles which in many areas have now largely replaced the use of dogs and domestic reindeer for traction.

Canoes: Coherence and Long-Term Continuity in Technological Traditions

Eastern Khanty Water Craft

In the wetlands of Northwestern Siberia water travel is essential in the summer months, and two kinds of craft evolved among Eastern Khanty communities to fulfill different functional requirements (Kulemzin and Lukina 1977, 1992; Lukina 1985):

- *Large Plank-Built Boats* (Lukina 1985:19–20, 331). These were mainly used for long-distance travel and for the transportation of cargo. Some "covered" versions included a central cabin in which the household slept during travel to the summer fishing grounds on the lower rivers. Production and use of these larger craft declined sharply after the collapse of summer expeditionary fishing in the early 1990s, and as a result of the introduction of faster aluminium-hulled boats and outboard motors in the 1980s. Some people still use these open plank-built boats with outboard motors fitted to the squared-off sterns for local transport of bulk cargoes like fuel drums and also pine cones (see Wiget and Balaeva 2011:231).

- *Small Dug-Out Canoes* (Lukina 1985:18, 330). These light and highly maneuverable craft carry only one person who kneels in the center of the boat and uses a single-bladed paddle. They are widely used for setting fishing nets around the main base camps (figure 3.29), but they can also be loaded onto powered boats and transported quickly to remoter fishing locations, where they can be cached for later use or brought back again. After snow-melt, the canoes provide easy access through the flooded forest to the mosaic of narrow creeks, small lakes, and water bodies that lie behind the main river channel and are targeted for daily fishing. These areas are difficult and costly to access in larger, powered boats because submerged roots and branches damage the propellers—it is much faster to travel by powered boat on the main channel, moor up, and then paddle into the flooded hinterlands and return with the catch. In this way, the older dug-out canoes continue to fill a very specific functional niche and have not been affected by the introduction of other technologies like aluminium speedboat hulls or gasoline motors. They remain in widespread use, and there is some commercial demand for these canoes from local Russian populations who also engage in fishing.

Canoes remain central to Khanty lifeways, both practically and also symbolically. Although the vessels are undecorated, they are associated with travel by the dead to "the other side"—as such, they were widely used as coffins across Western Siberia because of connotations about how souls travel downriver after death to the watery underworld located somewhere in the North (Jordan 2003: 227).

FIGURE 3.29 Canoe pictures.

Khanty dug-out canoes. *Top:* Women checking fishing nets on the middle Bolshoi Iugan, with smudge fire to protect against flies (Photograph: Peter Jordan, August 2003). *Bottom:* Interior view of a dug-out canoe, lower Bolshoi Iugan. The basic design, production stages, and toolkits are virtually identical across both the Iugan River and surrounding tracts of Northwest Siberia, with only minor variations in length, number of thwarts, quality of finish, and thickness of hull. PHOTOGRAPH: Peter Jordan, July 2004.

Russian ethnographers working in the 1970s and 1980s recorded very similar canoe designs over all Eastern Khanty areas (Kulemzin and Lukina 1977, 1992; Lukina 1985:18, 330), and within the Iugan River basin during the past decade, virtually identical canoe designs are maintained via local social learning. Two factors appear to generate this widespread uniformity in design: one is the highly constrained nature of the operational sequence—given the inherent characteristics of locally available wood, there is simply very little scope for deviation or innovation within the standardized design template that has clearly evolved over many generations. The second is that canoes produced by established "ways of doing" fit the highly circumscribed functional niche very closely: these canoes need to be light, agile, and portable; they are not required for bulk transport or motorized travel, because other kinds of craft fulfill these needs much more effectively.

Dug-Out Canoe Operational Sequences

Within the Iugan River basin, canoes are made from aspen trees. These grow tallest and straightest along the banks of the main river, and men continually monitor the forest for suitable trees as they travel, noting potential aspen for later use; when a new canoe is required, they already have a good idea of where to source the required timber. The trees are cut in the spring when the sap is flowing and the wood can be "cut like butter" with the right implements. After felling, the tree is cut to a suitable length and then brought back to the main base camp settlement, where work begins in stripping off the bark. This work is conducted in an open activity area at the front riverbank of the base camp where breezes and smudge fires provide relief from the swarms of biting insects.

The operational sequence and woodworking equipment are highly standardized among practitioners. The toolkits are identical and consist of gouging and smoothing adzes, which are made by local blacksmiths from commercially bought axe heads. After stripping the log to form a cylindrical hull, and shaping the ends to form a sharpened prow and stern, a long deep slot is cut out along the center of the log and the walls are gradually thinned down (see Wiget and Balalaeva 2011: 236). To achieve an even hull thickness, small holes are drilled through the wood in a series of parallel rings located at different points along the canoe's length. Next, dowels are cut to standardized lengths and then inserted from the outside into each of these holes to plug the gaps. The thickness of the inner hull is then carefully reduced along the length of the vessel until it matches the thickness of each of the standardized dowel lengths, ensuring that the finished canoe will be light and strong, but also well balanced, stable, and maneuverable.

Having invested substantial effort into reaching this stage, the craftsmen face the most dangerous and risky step in the production of the canoe. The entire hull is gently heated over a long fire so that the warm sides of the vessel can be slowly bent outward and a series of horizontal wooden thwarts inserted so that the widened hull can maintain its open shape. This requires substantial skill and also good timing and judgment: spread the hull too quickly and it will crack, rendering the project a failure; leave the spreading too late, especially in warmer weather, and the wood will have dried out too far and will split as it is bent.

After successful completion of the bending stage, the inner and outer sides of the vessel are given a final trimming and are then smoothed off and sealed with pitch. The noses of the vessels are either carved into a diamond shape, around which a rope can be tied, or have a small hole drilled through the front of a pointed nose, also enabling a line to be tied—some of the few real choices open to canoe makers; all other steps in the production cycle are highly constrained by the nature of the materials. Slightly longer vessels may have one extra thwart, and there are occasionally minor differences in hull thickness and general finish between craftsmen due to copying error, or personal skill, but in general, all canoes are of the same, highly standardized type, and the traits used in their construction form a highly coherent package of tradition (figure 3.29). For example, extra planks could be fitted along the sides of the canoe to form gunwhales and would increase the volume of the vessel to carry extra passengers (see, e.g., Lukina 2006:105). However, in all the Eastern Khanty communities examined here (figure 3.1), these dug-out canoes need only to be light, fast, and carry one person, so this extra capacity is generally not required—as such, there is little scope and minimal incentive to innovate: the canoes have already evolved to fit the requirements of this highly specialized behavioral niche.

Canoe Production and Social Learning

Within the Iugan basin, production of dug-out canoes is regarded as the most skilled and risky of all the local woodworking crafts. Many other woodworking technologies like ski making, plank-boat building, sledge making, and the construction of shrines and storage platforms are essentially "modular": if one component breaks—either during production or when in use—it can easily be replaced, ensuring that investment in the wider project is not wasted. In contrast, canoes have an extended and highly linear production sequence that demands substantial investment prior to the crucial hull-bending stage; all this effort will be wasted if the hull cracks, and failure at this key stage cannot be reversed. Many informants said that canoe making was very difficult and that only real "masters" could make the lightest and most slender canoes, while "anyone that can hold an axe can make the different parts required for a sledge." Canoe making is thus a widely respected skill, both for these intrinsic reasons and because it provides occasional scope for earning extra income by taking cash orders from other Khanty who have not mastered the craft, or from Russian fishermen living in the main village of Ugut.

Most informants reported that they had learned the basic skills from their fathers (vertical transmission), first by watching, assisting in supervised tasks, and then by trying for themselves. As such, canoe making was a skilled craft, and one that was relatively costly both to teach and also acquire via extended social learning. However, it also became clear that the highly coherent recipe of canoe design could also be transmitted in some very rare cases via oblique routes, perhaps ensuring that the highly standardized design could persist across the wider region.

Only one example of oblique transmission was recorded. The father of one male informant from the lower Bolshoi Iugan had died when he was very young, so the son was not able to learn the skills via vertical transmission from his biological father. During his mid-twenties, however, he became increasingly interested in canoe making, both for his own use and as a means of earning extra income through sale, so he went to visit an older man who was a renowned canoe maker and lived alone, his wife and adolescent children having left him and gone to live on another part of the river. Although this older man was from another patrilineage, he allowed the younger man to stay with him for a few days, watch him closely as he built a new canoe, and also to help out with and imitate him in some minor tasks, perhaps in exchange for the general social company that this teaching arrangement provided. Equipped with these insights, the younger man returned downstream to his own base camp and made an unsuccessful first attempt at his own canoe. A year later he made a successful second attempt, and after that was able to make canoes on a regular basis and to a consistent standard, in effect, completing a process of *oblique transmission* (see example in figure 3.29, bottom).

Discussion: Propagation of Standardized Canoe Designs

Clearly, Eastern Khanty dug-out-canoe designs have become standard-ized across the wider region (Kulemzin and Lukina 1977; 1992; Lukina 1985:18, 330; Lukina 2006:102–4) and qualitative analysis of current canoe making on the Iugan basin generate insights into how this situa-tion might have arisen. Canoe making is a highly skilled practice, requir-ing costly learning, but it appears to have been subject to high-fidelity propagation as a coherent and closely integrated "package" of traits for three main reasons:

1. The operational sequence is highly constrained by the nature of the raw materials—aspen logs can only be shaped, hollowed, and bent outward with thwarts in a limited number of ways.

2. These canoes fit a very specialized niche in Khanty lifeways—they are small, light, and highly portable vessels for transporting individuals to remote and difficult-to-access fishing spots, and they do not need to carry extra passengers or large loads; other vessels fulfil these functions.

3. With only minimal investment in tools, canoes can be produced from widely available forest raw materials for sale and exchange, though there is little scope—or indeed social, commercial, or practical motivation—for innovation or elaboration beyond the standardized design, even though acquisition of these skills is highly desired as a source of income.

Dug-out canoe technology has therefore evolved into a standard format that fits into a highly specialized functional niche. Although the coherent package of canoe-making traits appears to be mainly propagated via verti-cal transmission, from fathers to sons, it is also clear that the highly valued "package" of skills and techniques are also readily portable between unre-lated individuals from different generations (oblique transmission). This ensures that the same standardized design template can be subjected to high-fidelity replication through social learning across the wider popula-tion in ways that cut across social and settlement institutions like patrilin-eages and their base camps, and perhaps also across different river basin communities and their associated dialect boundaries. This ability for this integrated package of traits to disperse easily through extended social net-works may then explain why dug-out canoes—arguably the most prestig-ious and difficult of all the woodworking technologies—exhibit a rather monotonous similarity over large tracts of Northwest Siberia.

Eastern Khanty Sledge Traditions: Continuity and Change

Contrasting Sledge Designs in Western Siberia

Three coherent sledge designs were traditionally used in Western Siberia (Kulemzin and Lukina 1977, 1992; Lukina 1985; Vizgalov 2000), each apparently having evolved via cumulative innovation to fit the requirements of three different ecological niches in the Middle Ob' (figure 3.1) and their associated traditional traction animals of dogs, reindeer, and horses:

- *Reindeer Sledges.* These have a very wide distribution across Northwest Siberia and are used by reindeer pastoralists for rapid travel in treeless tundra landscapes, as well as in the more open forests found on the north side of the Middle Ob.' The sledges' basic design is characterized by a distinctive horizontal front crossbar, although the upper carrying platform is also widely adjusted to carry people, cargo, tent frames, and other loads during seasonal migrations (Kulemzin and Lukina 1977:63; Lukina 1985; figure 3.30). Khanty communities living to the north of the Middle Ob' River (figure 3.1), that is, on the Agan, Trom"egan, Pim, and Vakh Rivers tend to use these kinds of sledge (figure 3.44), and on the Pim, Agan, and Trom"egan, at least, appear to have adopted these sledge designs from Nenets reindeer pastoralist communities who live further to the north. At around the same time, they were also taking on a wider package of innovations associated with the keeping of domestic reindeer (Jordan 2011a:51–2).

- *Horse-Drawn Sledges.* The design consist of thick wooden runners, with short vertical supports that are held together across the width of the sledge by lengths of flexible wild cherry branches. These run around the outer sides of the vertical supports and are lashed together again under the center of the sledge. This base supports a planked wooden box that rises at the back and carries people and cargo; the horse traces are fixed to a central wooden pole that rises vertically out of the front of the sledge. These low, heavy, and sturdily built sledges have their origins in the European part of Russia and were brought to Western Siberia by settlers after the Russian conquest. This type of sledge had an exclusive distribution along the banks of the main Ob' and the lower reaches of the main tributaries; these areas include extensive flood meadows that were mowed to

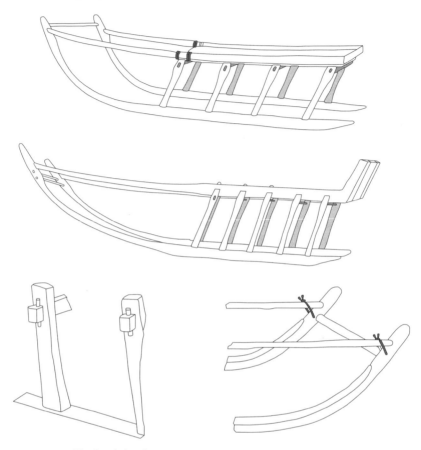

FIGURE 3.30 Tundra sledge design.
The main features of sledge design in the open tundra regions of Northwest Siberia. The size of the decked area is relatively small in relation to the overall length of the sledge, and a horizontal crossbar runs across the front of the sledge between the two runners. SOURCE: redrawn from Levin and Potapov 1961:43, 49.

provide winter fodder for the horses. As a result, these sledges were used by two main groups: Russian incomers who lived in the main administrative centers and practiced animal husbandry and small-scale agriculture, as well as the sedentary communities of Khanty who subsisted primarily by fishing and some local hunting but were also adopting cattle and cottage-gardening in the nineteenth century (see Vizgalov 2000:159). These heavy sledges, and the horses used to pull them, were simply not suited to the dense taiga south of the Middle Ob'.

- *Dog Sledges.* These sledges were widely used by forest hunters living along rivers south of the Middle Ob' (figure 3.1) and were pulled either by dogs or by people on skis via a loop around the chest, or sometimes a combination of the two. As a result, the loads carried were not heavy and the sledges were mainly used for transporting game back to base camps, carrying the minimal kit required by families during its winter fur-hunting migrations, as well as for moving firewood and water around the base camps. These sledges were long, gracile, and extremely light; many of the main struts and legs were carefully shaved down to minimize weight, although one characteristic feature was a rounded "crash bar" across the front of the sledge. This prevented trees from catching into the front of the sledge during travel on the narrow forest trails, and also allowed harnesses to be attached. These sledges were produced to highly standardized designs across the Salym, Iugan, Vasiugan, and beyond (see smaller sledge in figure 3.31) and appear to have evolved slowly to reach an optimal format for use in the dense taiga forests.

Historical Innovation in Iugan Khanty Sledge Design

Located on the south side of the Middle Ob,' the Iugan River basin was initially characterized by exclusive use of dog sledges among the hunter-fisher communities living on the upper rivers, although Russians living in the main administrative village used the horse sledges, as did sedentary Khanty fishing groups living on the Iuganskaia Ob' and main Ob' River (see previous). Occasional visits from Khanty living on the north-side rivers also brought different kinds of reindeer sledges into some of the Lower Iugan base camps (e.g., Martin 1897:85; Vizgalov 2000: 164). Locked into expansive seasonal rounds, upper-river Iugan Khanty would almost certainly definitely have been aware of other "rival" sledge designs but chose to retain their own dog sledge designs for use in their local hunting areas.

Iugan sledge styles eventually began to change. A combination of local forest fires, which destroyed large areas of hunting territory within the Iugan basin, and the ongoing fur boom encouraged many local Khanty to seek out more distant hunting areas during the later nineteenth century and early twentieth century (see Jordan 2011a). In response, Iugan Khanty started to acquire small numbers of transport reindeer from other Khanty communities north of the Middle Ob' and

FIGURE 3.31 Two old Iugan sledges.

Examples of the traditional sledge design found across the Iugan
River. The shorter variant can be pulled by a person on skis, and
the longer variant was usually pulled by domestic reindeer. Both
follow the same basic design, consisting of a long cargo platform,
legs angled to the rear, and a crash bar around the front to
protect against collisions with trees. PHOTOGRAPH: Peter Jordan,
July 2004.

developed their own strategies for keeping them in the difficult conditions of the taiga. Despite these challenges, transport reindeer provided the means to quickly access more distant hunting areas (Jordan 2011a).

Although they took up this transport innovation from outside the basin, they adapted their own preexisting sledge-making traditions to reindeer traction and generally did not adopt the sledge designs from north of the Middle Ob'. The northern reindeer sledges were very poorly suited for the forests south of the Middle Ob'—here the taiga was denser and the trails narrower, but most important, the horizontal crossbar of the classic reindeer sledge would easily snag into passing trees, splitting the sledge in two (figure 3.30). Instead, the Iugan Khanty retained their earlier narrow sledge designs with the round crash bar across the front, merely adding extra legs to increase their length, and attached the reindeer harnesses in the same ways as the dog harnesses (see larger sledge example in figure 3.31).

Although trotting reindeer substantially increased the speed of travel, loads remained relatively light, and the extra strain on the sledge framework was minimal to the extent that many of the struts and supporting legs were still shaved down to reduce weight as much as possible. In essence, sledge design remained exactly the same, despite the adoption of transport reindeer (e.g., compare the dog and reindeer sledges in figure 3.31 that differ in size but are basically built to the same general design).

By the 1960s, however, transport reindeer were widely abandoned for a variety of reasons (Bakhlykov 1996:170) and the last herds had disappeared from the Iugan by the 1980s, primarily because of enforced expeditionary fishing, which left no one back at the upriver base camps to tend the animals and maintain the essential protective smudge fires over the hot, fly-infested summer months (Jordan 2011a). During the winter hunting migrations, hunters and their families went back to hauling their own sledges with the aid of dogs, and so again, the basic sledge design was not altered, maintaining long-term continuity in basic Iugan sledge design for more than a century.

Propagation of Contemporary Sledge Designs in the Iugan Basin

During the later 1980s the first snowmobiles were being adopted by Khanty living in the Iugan basin, part of a wider set of transformations associated with the regional boom in oil and gas development (see Wiget and Balalaeva 2011), and were widely used for pulling cargo sledges. Once again, Iugan Khanty used their existing sledge designs, increasing the size, and bolting Y-shaped metal towing bars into the front runners of the sledges, which then clipped on to the towing hook at the back of the snowmobile, but maintaining the older crash bars to deflect trees when traveling along the forest trails.

By the end of twentieth century and early twenty-first century, all but a few base camps had at least one snowmobile, and in most places there was one, sometimes more, per household. Mechanized traction has transformed travel times, and households are now able to move large loads around at ease, rather than haul minimal equipment and supplies themselves.

If early ethnographic surveys from the nineteenth through to the later twentieth century recorded highly standardized sledge designs across the Iugan River, more recent fieldwork (1998–2005) indicates that the adoption of snowmobiles has triggered a flurry of experimentation and innovation whose cumulative outcomes remain rather unclear.

The older wooden sledge designs consisted of wooden joints slotted and pegged together, with many sections lashed onto this frame with animal sinews; the main legs were angled backward and slightly inwards, with the main cargo placed along a narrow section that ran the length of the sledge (figure 3.31). The large, chunky and solidly built Russian snowmobiles can haul enormous loads at much higher speeds, although many of the circuitous forest trails that link base camps and hunting grounds consist only of packed and deeply rutted snow.

With a large load on board the sledge, for example, two fully laden oil drums (55 US gallons/44 Imperial gallons), haulage by snowmobile generates hammering effects that place an enormous strain on the wooden sledge frame. This strain tends to be concentrated on the front upward bend in the runners, at the base of the vertical legs, and especially along the horizontal crossbars. If any of these parts "fail," for example, the crucial pegs and joint in the cross-strut (see inset detail in figure 3.32, top), then the entire sledge has to either be discarded or stripped down into its component sections, new parts fitted, and then reassembled again—all a major undertaking.

Survey of contemporary sledges throughout the Iugan basin indicated that the same basic combination of design traits had been retained in the new snowmobile-drawn sledges. However, within this evolving tradition, the newer sledge sizes were increasing rapidly in size, electrical wire was being used for lashings instead of animal sinews, and many sledges had strips of sheet metal along the runners to increase strength. In addition, the older and more gracile frames, with the thickness shaved

FIGURE 3.32 Changing sledge traditions.

Evolving Iugan Khanty sledge designs. *Top:* A model of traditional sledge from the lower Bolshoi Iugan, made in the late 1980s. These provided children with an opportunity to learn how to work with all the materials and techniques required for a full-sized sledge. The inset shows the way in which overall weight is reduced by shaving away at the widths of the legs, as well as the method for fitting the cross-struts into the upper legs of the main sledge frame. If this strut or its housing joint fails, the entire sledge has to be taken apart to fit a replacement and then reassembled. PHOTOGRAPH: Frits Steenhuisen, November 2013. *Bottom:* A new kind of hybridized sledge design that has emerged on the Malyi Iugan in recent years in response to the new requirements of skidoo traction. Many elements of the older sledge design have been retained, such as the generous cargo capacity (see figure 3.31), but now with a metal crash bar and towing brace added, and with stronger electrical wire replacing the older leather and sinew bindings. Two other novel traits have been borrowed from the design of Russian horse-drawn sledges: the shorter vertical legs, which may be stronger, as well as the use of cherry wood cross-struts that are wrapped around the legs from the outside and bound together in the center. If they fail, new parts can be fitted without dismantling the entire sledge (PHOTOGRAPH: Peter Jordan, March 1999). *Next page:* The descent with modification of material culture traditions—the integration of cherry-wood struts into the older Iugan sledge design was initially an innovation by an elder on the Malyi Iugan River; it was then passed onto his sons; here, two generations later, one of his grandsons is now making sledges according to this novel design recipe. PHOTOGRAPH: Peter Jordan, September 2005.

FIGURE 3.32. *(Continued)*

away as far as possible to reduce weight, had been replaced by use of much thicker timbers for the legs and cross-struts, all of which mitigated the new stresses associated with heavier loads and the use of snowmobile traction.

Case Study: Social Learning, Experimentation, and Transformation

Sledge making is practiced in all base camps on the Iugan River using the same operational sequence. It is almost universally a male craft, practiced in the warmer spring and summer months, and many informants described how sledge making was quite easy to master because it required production of simple component parts that were then slotted or lashed together to build up the basic frame. In addition, sledge making was "low risk," because failed attempts at manufacturing any one of the individual components could easily be rectified without jeopardizing the entire construction project. This general repertoire of woodworking skills is learned at a very early age, primarily via vertical transmission from father to son, as part of the general process of natural pedagogy described previously. This later shifts to a more extended period of observation, experimentation, and practice within the wider social sphere of the base camp, all of which involve interaction and intervention from older children and other adult male kin. In addition, many children also make model sledges to try out their skills. These are exact replicas or the adult versions, using exactly the same materials, wood types, and construction techniques (see model sledge in figure 3.32, top). A general sense of pride was attached to making a good sledge and ensuring that it was both reliable and attractively and neatly done. It was often said that a sledge reflects the man, and that a shoddily built sledge is the sign of a sloppy man—the poorly made sledges of some individuals were singled out as "only lasting a season."

In earlier times Iugan sledge designs appear to have reached a localized "optimal design" that was subject to high-fidelity copying within the wider Iugan dialect community and also well beyond. The introduction of snowmobile traction within the past generation is transforming this picture. Informants tended to describe processes of guided variation, that is, they had learned the basic style from their fathers—or from the older generation—but were actively experimenting through their own efforts to improve the design, observing the results and sledge performance closely to evaluate the efficacy of the new changes. They were certainly aware of other possible sledge designs—informants were also shown photos of the reindeer sledges from other Khanty areas north of the Ob' (e.g., the Agan River) but mocked them for their lack of cargo capacity and for the open front runners and crossbar that would split the sledge after collisions with trees in the denser Iugan forests (see figure 3.30). They said—in theory—that they could easily make such sledges if they wanted to but that the sledges were poorly suited to local conditions and practical demands.

Although all sledge makers have adopted sturdier sledge frames, one major current debate about innovation is the relative advantage of the older tradition of angled legs, which many said were more "traditional" and therefore more "attractive," versus the more recent use of vertically set legs, which involves easier jointing and enables sledges to be made more quickly. It was simply not clear as to which method was stronger or more durable, and answers were also caught up in wider debate about increasingly expedient technologies that can be made quickly, sold to Russians for cash, or used for a couple of seasons and then abandoned. With new power tools, tree felling and woodworking is much faster, and in contrast, the older, highly crafted sledges took much longer to make and lasted much longer. At present, designs had not settled on a single technological solution.

The complexities of cultural propagation involved in the general quest for improvements in sledge design can be illustrated with a short example from a base camp on the Malyi Iugan. One older informant, born in the mid-1930s, had learned the traditional dog sledge design from his father and had continued to reproduce this kind of sledge until snowmobiles arrived in the 1990s, after which he increased the sizes of the sledges he made but noted that the frames often failed due to the extra stresses.

He then started to experiment by borrowing design traits from the heavily built horse sledges used by Russians and by Khanty living on the main Ob' River, incorporating them into a new kind of "hybridized" sledge design. His inspiration had originally come from his wife's family—she was from one of these sedentary Khanty fishing communities, and in the 1960s the couple had spent a short period living and working there with the in-laws, as is a Khanty custom after marriage. Here he had seen how the horse sledges were made, and he noted the strength of the short, low legs and the use of split wild cherry branches that were wrapped around these legs and formed the crossbraces of the main frame. In contrast, the traditional sledges from the Iugan had much longer legs (figures 3.31, 3.32, top) that were angled backward, and also wooden crossbars that slotted into joints in the upper legs. When adapted for snowmobile haulage, it was these cross-struts that often broke, requiring the whole sledge to be painstakingly disassembled and then reassembled, so that a replacement part could be fitted.

The two advantageous features he saw in the horse sledge design were the low, sturdy legs, and the use of the wraparound wild cherry struts that could be replaced easily without taking the entire sledge apart. Seeking to improve the durability and maintainability of the older Iugan sledge design that he had learned from his father, he incorporated these two new traits into a hybridized sledge design (figure 3.32, middle) that retained many of the advantages of the older Iugan sledges, such as the long cargo capacity running the full length of the sledge, plus the round crashbar at the front to fend off tree impacts, but he lowered the height of the legs, set them vertically, and used wraparound wild cherry branches for the cross-struts.

By the later 1990s, this initial process of directly biased transmission (i.e., learning particular cultural traits from parents, then watching what others do, evaluating the results, and switching to the new model) had become a social tradition that he passed on via vertical transmission to at least two of his three sons, who continued to make both the original and modified Iugan sledge designs on a case-by-case basis (see, e.g., the example in figure 3.32, second image). By 2005 one of his grandsons was also making substantial numbers of this new kind of sledge (figure 3.32, third image), mainly for sale and exchange, because the frame was much simpler and faster to make, as well as being more durable and easier to maintain if the cross-strut broke.

Propagation of this new and innovative combination of different traits within this hybridized ski design had initially remained within his local base camp and patrilineage but had spread no further. However, one of the older man's daughters had married out to another patrilineage living on the Bolshoi Iugan, several days' boat journey away. And just as the original inventor of this new kind of sledge had done after his own marriage, the new couple came to live and work back with her home family for a short time after marriage. Here the son-in-law observed the new sledge design and took the idea back with him from the Malyi Iugan back to the Bolshoi Iugan (figure 3.1), where he started to build sledges to this new hybrid design, as well as sledges to the older design.

As a result of this process—and largely due to kinship institutions and postmarital guesting traditions—two novel design traits—the short vertical legs and the wild cherry crossbars—had been borrowed from the Russian horse-drawn sledges and imported scores of kilometers from the sedentary fishing Khanty communities on the Main Ob' that had adopted this type of sledge, through to the mobile hunting communities on the upper Malyi Iugan, where they had been incorporated via directly biased transmission into a new hybridized form of sledge that had advantages for snowmobile traction and also commercial production. The new sledge design had then been passed via vertical transmission from fathers to sons and grandson, but had also jumped across to the Bolshoi Iugan— via a further process of directly biased transmission, where it was being practiced by his new son-in-law. More generally, then, these new sledge-making traits, both of external origin, have entered into, and now become established within, the wider pool of potential sledge-making traits currently being propagated within the wider Iugan River basin.

Discussion

Historical surveys of sledge making from the nineteenth century to the later twentieth century indicate use of highly standardized dog sledge designs in much of the dense forest area located south of the main Ob' River. In contrast, sedentary Russian and Khanty fishing communities on the main Ob' River had their own distinctive horse-drawn sledges, and northern reindeer pastoralists had developed their own unique sledge forms for the more open forest and tundra areas north of the main Ob' River (see Levin and Potapov 1961:27–31; Lukina 1985:335,337). All three sledge forms were being propagated as highly coherent packages of traits, each within a different ecological zone.

Two recent winter transport innovations went off to affect the Iugan Khanty sledge designs. The first was the adoption of transport reindeer between about C.E. 1850 and C.E. 1920—this had minimal effects on local sledge designs because larger versions of the same sledges could easily be produced. These sledges were still ideal for use in the forest, even if pulled by reindeer, and so the same basic design was propagated.

The second change involved the introduction of snowmobile traction from the 1980s. This disrupted many of the older certainties associated with the performance of the traditional sledge designs, largely because of greater loads, faster travel speeds, and greater associated stressing of the sledge frame. This has triggered an ongoing process of innovation and experimentation that continues to play out over the generations. As part of this process, new traits are now starting to emerge, catch on and become integrated into the older design template. Some new traits, like wild cherry cross-bars and short vertical legs, are borrowed from other rival designs; other, such as the experimentation with thick vertical versus angled legs, are essentially localized innovations within the older sledge design. How this process of experimentation will affect propagation of sledge designs over future generations remains unclear: it could be that vertical legs replace angled legs or that the new hybridized sledges replace the older forms; or it could be that many different variants continue to persist. What is clear from interviews is that all practitioners are creatively seeking out the best ways to reconcile the advantages of snowmobile tractions with the limitations and potentials of the older wooden sledge tradition.

GENERAL DISCUSSION: TECHNOLOGY AND MICROSCALE CULTURAL TRANSMISSION

This chapter has investigated propagation of a range of woodworking traditions in Northwest Siberia and traced the contrasting patterns of coherence that emerge. With rich contextual data extending back more than a century, combined with more recent insights derived from primary ethnoarchaeological fieldwork, it is clear that propagation of each individual material culture tradition is "embedded" very differently in regional social networks, generating some sharply contrasting patterns of material culture variability and change.

In earlier life stages, most social learning appears to involve acquisition of older "design recipes" via vertical transmission from parents to their offspring, usually requiring substantial investments in time. This initial phase of social learning is then generally followed by an extended adjustment stage, during which time individuals engage in extensive experimentation (guided variation), as well as observation, performance-related evaluation, and potential copying (directly biased transmission). In most cases, adoption of new traits involves very minimal investment in acquiring either new skills on the part of the transmittee or engaging in extended teaching on the part of the transmitter. A number of more general insights from the case studies:

- Some of these "design recipes" are very generalized, for example, in the case of the storage platforms: there is only a very general notion of raised cache houses, but these can be built in any number of ways via a highly contingent recombination of a wide number of available traits. In fact, it appears to be very difficult to assess the relative advantage and performance of any of these individual traits or the specific ways in which they are combined—they are so many external considerations and unpredictable factors involved in building a new cache house that pragmatic solutions tend to predominate. The result, in terms of cultural propagation, is a highly rapid recombination of traits that leads to a blur of hybrid forms—these show little overall coherence and no specific relationship to particular social units, language boundaries, or even to geographic proximity.

- In intermediate cases, the weight of highly localized religious traditions encourages deliberate attempts to broadly copy what are perceived as the most important elements of older designs, for example, in the shrines, which are rebuilt in the same basic forms, albeit with innovation in more ephemeral traits associated with building materials and minor construction techniques.

- At the other end of the spectrum, the dug-out canoes occupy such a specialized functional niche, and in addition to this, the materials and technology place further constraints on further innovation, such that a highly coherent tradition has emerged and come to dominate over large geographic areas. In this sense, these very specific designs must be propagated through high-fidelity copying—if there is deviation from these very precisely defined production steps, then either the individual project will fail or the end product will no longer meet the specific local requirements. Although most explicit teaching of this craft is mainly vertical, involving transmission of traits between fathers and their sons, there is also evidence that these kinds of highly coherent packages of traits can also be transmitted between unrelated males from different generations (oblique transmission). However, this adult-to-adult transmission can only proceed if both sides agree—for whatever reason—to invest the time and effort required to make this transmission process a success. The combination of all these factors appears to explain why canoe designs show great similarity over large geographic areas, with this coherence in styles transcending numerous local social, linguistic, and ethnic units.

- All these findings therefore point to a general spectrum that ranges from high coherence through to relative pragmatism in the ways in which traits are combined. This balance can also be traced within individual craft traditions: some elements may follow very precise designs employing a highly integrated set of traits; other features are more open to experimentation and innovation, involving highly variable combinations of traits. One example is the design of shrines, noted previously, which balances deeper continuity and coherence with elements of pragmatism. Another good example is contemporary Iugan ski design, where the D-ring bindings are subject to general coherence at the scale of the dialect community, whereas traits associated with the new cloth covers generate more scope for innovation—no coherent design recipe for the new cloth covers has yet emerged among the wider Iugan population.

- Although coherent production recipes can emerge, they are not fixed and can be rapidly adjusted—and even quickly abandoned—for a range of reasons, and this process generally appears to involve biased transmission within extended social networks. In some cases, external introductions of new traits or technologies is involved—the arrival of cheap cloth gave rise to new cloth ski covers, and led to the abandonment of the entire ski-making tradition in the case of the archaic platform skis; the arrival of snowmobile traction is currently transforming Iugan sledge designs through an ongoing process of cumulative adjustment and innovation, although no single new coherent design recipe has emerged for snowmobile–drawn sledges across the wider population—evidently, the relative advantages and disadvantages of the different combinations of traits are still being assessed.

What therefore emerges from this analysis of how cultural traditions are locally propagated are threads of a general comparative argument about the existence of a continuum between innovation and pragmatism through to cultural conservatism (table 3.1). On one level, the intergenerational propagation of all these traditions involves reproduction of traits and specific trait combinations. But there is also continual and very deliberate adjustment too, especially in the use of traits that make up traditions with the greatest functional requirements and where risks of technological failure are highest. Here, performance of potentially competing traits is subject to close monitoring, and where adoption of new traits offers functional advantages then payoff-based evaluations and biased transmission can quickly outcompete what has been acquired from parents via vertical transmission. Therefore, this chapter highlights the adjustable and highly adaptive nature of human cultural learning. In particular, the importance of biased cultural transmission later in the life-cycle can explain how populations come to possess highly adaptive, locally well-suited, technological complexes that involve integrated sets of engineering insights that the users and manufacturers perhaps themselves don't fully understand. Moreover, biased transmission can also account for why coherent sets of traits associated with highly complex technological adaptations like specific ski, sledge, and boat designs can emerge and persist across extended social networks and over large geographic areas, especially in situations where relative functional performance is both important and relatively easy to evaluate.

CONCLUSION

This chapter has combined ethnoarchaeological fieldwork, ethnohistoric research and cultural transmission theory to investigate the microscale evolution of different material culture traditions among hunter-fisher-gatherer communities in Northwest Siberia. On a methodological level, it demonstrates that targeted research with contemporary populations can generate rich data sets that can be studied with quantitative methods in order to identify general patterning in the propagation of cultural traits. Equally important are the rich and detailed contextual

TABLE 3.1 SUMMARY OF CULTURAL INHERITANCE PATTERNS IN FIVE MATERIAL CULTURE TRADITIONS (EASTERN KHANTY)

Material Culture Tradition	Propagation Processes	Coherence in Design "Recipe"	Scales of Cultural Coherence
Eastern Khanty Storage Platforms (male)	Mainly vertical transmission of generic skills; specific traits used in construction reflect multiple possibilities and contingencies	No overall coherence; highly generalized design recipe requiring only generic woodworking skills.	Highly pragmatic constructions; no coherence so no relationship to social units, dialect boundaries or geographic proximity
Eastern Khanty Shrines (male)	Deliberate attempts to replicate traits used in primary design of older buildings; some conformist transmission at the scale of patrilineages; innovation in building materials and minor construction traits	Some coherence in overall form of building; less coherence in traits associated with minor construction methods and materials	Some evidence that coherence emerges at the scale of the local patrilineages
Contemporary Eastern Khanty Skis (male)	General design recipe transmitted via vertical transmission (bindings, materials); cloth attachment open to greater personal innovation; later potential for adjustment in all design features via personal experimentation and some copying (i.e., horizontal and oblique transmission)	Highly coherent binding designs at scale of river basins; traits associated with newer cloth covers more variable, with less general coherence	Functionally driven coherence in all binding designs: Iugan, Vasiugan. and Trom"agan communities each appear to have converged on a single local binding design, which maps onto local river basin/dialect boundaries; other river basins exhibit coexistence of several coherent variants within basins

Eastern Khanty Canoes (male)	Requires great skill that is relatively costly to acquire and also to pass on to others; predominantly transmitted via vertical transmission; can also be subject to high-fidelity copying between non-kin from different generations (oblique transmission) but only if both parties invest in this process	Functionally-driven standardization of design over large areas; rise of a single coherent style.	Highly coherent design recipe that extends over large areas; no evidence that the scale of coherence has any correlation with specific social or linguistic units
Iugan Khanty Sledges (male)	Older designs transmitted via vertical transmission; these older traits now undergoing intense performance-related evaluation, which includes invention of new traits and the borrowing and integration of new traits drawn from other sledge-making traditions	Strong coherence in older design recipe being eroded by current experimentation and innovation; single, coherent modern style yet to emerge	Older sledge designs highly coherent across the Iugan; unclear what new patterns will emerge

insights into how and also why particular craft traditions evolve. Clearly, each material culture tradition is embedded very differently in local social and learning networks, and contrasting patterns of variability and change emerge, both at the scale of individual traits, as well as the overall craft tradition. Technological traditions therefore evolve along multiple trajectories, ranging from ephemeral collections of traits through to long-term replication of coherent and relatively standardized design recipes.

Microscale cultural evolution is clearly complex, but a useful series of comparative insights and understandings have been produced. However, it remains difficult, and is perhaps impossible, to make specific general predictions about links between particular microscale evolutionary processes and the kinds of larger-scale patterns of cultural coherence that can emerge. In this study, most coherence in craft traditions is related either to functional and performance-related criteria (canoes) or to interaction contained within river basins (for the distinctive Iugan River ski bindings), and at a very local patrilineage scale, to the impact of conservative religious traditions (shrine designs). There is no evidence that coherence is linked to intercommunity violence or xenophobic ideologies (see TRIMs, Durham 1992; chapter 1). However, none of the crafts studied actively express a deeper sense of social cohesion, collective identity, or ethnicity (e.g., in terms of specific clothing or artifacts that advertise membership of, and loyalty to, a specific group). Perhaps for this reason, there is no evidence for the kinds of conformist transmission that might result in social groups possessing standardized assemblages of highly similar material culture. However, the focus on only a limited range of wood-working traditions makes these Siberian conclusions both subjective and historically contingent.

Another important theme framing the insights that can be generated by this chapter is the predominantly male-oriented nature of the woodworking traditions that have been investigated. The wide suite of female crafts such as basketry, box making, and more traditional forms of Khanty clothing and footwear could also provide fertile matter for analysis, but currently lie beyond the scope of the current study (but see Jordan 2009; note 14).

One other important aspect of "gendered technologies" that emerges from this Siberian chapter is the potentially differential ways in which men and women move through social and learning networks over their life histories—this is deeply affected by kinship traditions, postmarital residence rules, and wider social institutions such as territoriality and land-holding systems. These Khanty communities are patrilineal and patrilocal—men tend to stay in the same base camps but women move to new camps after marriage, often long distances away. This may be also affecting the ways in which local male and female traditions are evolving. In fact, the crucial structuring role played by social institutions on the propagation of material culture traditions emerges as a major topic in the next three chapters, and appears to exert a critical influence on the relative social scales at which coherent traditions emerge. In some cases, social institutions also affect the degree of congruence between more coherent and enduring technological traditions and deeper language history.

In conclusion then, this Siberian chapter highlights the enormous complexity and variability inherent in the evolution of material culture traditions within populations, but illustrates that these propagation processes can be successfully explored through an interdisciplinary approach combining fieldwork, cultural transmission theory, and quantitative methods drawn from evolutionary biology. Equipped with these "microscale" insights into the propagation of material culture traditions *within* populations, it is now useful to move up the scale of analysis and investigate the evolution of cultural traits at a macroscale, that is, *across* populations and societies speaking different dialects and languages.

NOTES

Note 1. Seventeenth– to Nineteenth-Century Demography and Marriage Patterns: Iugan River Khanty and Neighboring Populations

Demography

The earliest Russian records of *iasak* fur-taxpayers (not the overall population) living on the Iugan, Iuganskaia Ob', and Balyk Rivers was 116 in 1629, rising to 125 in 1645, followed by 133 in 1680 and 148 in 1706. This might indicate a steady growth in local households or reflect the increasing reach of the tax system into remoter areas (Martynova 1998:140). Later sources record the entire population and indicate that the Iuganskaia Ob' population hovered around 350 from 1782 to 1897, but that populations on the Malyi Iugan went through a major decline, from 352 down to 141, and populations along the Bolshoi Iugan showing a steady rise, from 493 in 1792, to 554 in 1897 (Martynova 1998:140–41). The current Iugan Khanty population numbers just under a thousand (Bakhlykov 1996:6). For demographic information pertaining to other Eastern Khanty rivers, see Martynova (1998).

Regional Marriage Contacts

There were particularly intensive marriage contacts *within* the Iugan basin and also regular marriages with communities on other rivers (Martynova 1998:140–

42). For example, on the Malyi Iugan (figure 3.1), 19 percent of all mid-nine-teenth-century marriages were conducted within that basin, and 28 percent involved partners from the Bolshoi Iugan; 40 percent were from the Iuganskaia Ob' and Balyk, and the rest of partners were drawn from elsewhere, for example, 6 percent with the Trom"egan Khanty. On the Bolshoi Iugan, 30 percent of mar-riages were internal to that basin, 23 percent were with the Malyi Iugan Khanty, 25 percent were with partners from the Iuganskaia Ob' and Balyk Rivers, and the rest involved more distant communities. In general, nearly all marriages across the region involved other Khanty communities, with interethnic marriages (e.g., with Sel'kup or Nenets), amounting to only 0.6 percent of all Eastern Khanty marriages recorded during the seventeenth to nineteenth centuries. Similarly, interactions with Russians were also limited and very infrequent –at the end of the nineteenth century, there were 5,964 Eastern Khanty in the Middle Ob' region but only 140 Russians, living mainly in Surgut and local administrative villages (Lukina 1985:16). Currently, most Iugan Khanty appear to marry within their own com-munity, occasionally with more distant Khanty communities, and also with other occasional incomers to the main village of Ugut (see Wiget and Balalaeva 2011).

Note 2. Ethnoarchaeological Fieldwork

Fieldwork was carried out over an extended period, starting with preliminary visit to the Vasiugan River in 1997, followed by research on the Malyi Iugan in summer 1998 and late winter 1999, which mainly focused on the role of sacred places in Khanty cultural landscapes (Jordan 2003). Work on systematic docu-mentation of technological traditions took place in the summers of 2003, 2004, and 2005 and involved visits to all base camps on the Bolshoi and Malyi Iugan Rivers, as well shorter visits to the Pim, Agan, and Trom"egan to gather com-parative data. All interviews were conducted in Russian.

Note 3. Eastern Khanty Craft Traditions and the Ethnographic Record

There is an extremely rich corpus of historical information on Eastern Khanty craft traditions:

1. Western Siberia has been the focus of ethnographic research that started more than a century ago, generating highly detailed records of local material culture traditions and their geographic distributions at different points in time (see Lukina 1985). Working across Siberia, Soviet ethnographers integrated these localized surveys into conti-nental-scale documentation of "traditional" material culture across the entire region's native peoples (Levin and Potapov 1961). Ener-getic programs of ethnographic research and publication continue to the present day, adding further details to the rich record of Eastern Khanty craft traditions (see, e.g., Lukina 2004, 2006; Perevalova and Karacharov 2006; Vizgalov 2000, and other references in main text).

2. There are also numerous collections in local towns and universities, and these larger collections have been complemented by the recent

growth of local open-air museums on the Iugan, Trom"egan, Agan, and Pim, most of which sprang up in the early 1990s and assembled traditional buildings and other artifacts that had been collected by local enthusiasts since the 1970s.

Note 4. Use of the Same Suite Culture-Evolutionary Methods over Chapters 3–6

This book aims to undertake a systematic comparative analysis of cultural transmission of craft traditions over a range of different scales (micro to macro) and across different geographical and historical settings. For strategic reasons, the same suite of methods described in chapter 2 are applied consistently across chapters 3–5 in order to develop explicit comparison of results in the final chapter 6. However, application of these methods to the data presented in the current chapter is primarily a more prospective exercise in "pattern recognition" in microscale material culture evolution. For example, most of the analyses examine the evolution of material culture within populations, and the chain of closely related dialects spoken by the Eastern Khanty cannot be mapped in terms of a branching language tree, making it impossible to assess the extent to which the deeper history of these material culture traditions potentially has congruence with language history. This kind of question is addressed more fully in chapters 4 and 5. The main goal in this current chapter is to understand how traditions are propagated within populations and the general scales of coherence that can potentially emerge.

Note 5. Eastern Khanty Storage Platforms: Data Sets

A total of 105 separate storage platforms were surveyed across the Middle Ob' zone (figure 3.8). Variability in basic building methods were studied in detail, generating a total of 163 traits, which recorded details of the foundations, flooring, construction of the main cache house, the external shelf projecting from the front, through to the roof designs. This generated a 105 by 163 presence/absence data matrix, with all rows having complete data.

Note 6. Eastern Khanty Storage Platforms: Network- and Tree-Based Analyses

The storage platform data set was converted into a NEXUS file and subjected to preliminary NeighborNet analysis. The plot revealed some striking patterns (figure 3.9): First, each of the storage platforms is pulled out to a considerable distance and, in very different directions, suggesting substantial differences in the styles of each individual platform. Second, the substantial "boxing" at the center of the plot also suggests that there is conflict in the data set and that it poorly fits a branching tree model. Third, some limited branching seems to be forming in certain areas of the plot, suggesting that some distinctive "types" of platforms may be emerging. However, closer analysis of the geographic codings used in the plot indicates that most of these apparent groupings consist of platforms drawn from very different rivers and base camps. One clear exception to this trend is the apparent branching away of some of the Agan River platforms toward the top left, but this grouping also includes a platform from the Malyi Iugan. On balance, this general patterning in the NeighborNet plot points toward a more pragmatic recombination of individual traits within each built structure. Coherent traditions do not seem to be emerging, either at the scale of base camps, nor along the Malyi and Bolshoi branches of the Iugan River, nor at the scale of the other river basins.

To verify these results, the data set was also analyzed in PAUP* 4.0b10 to assess the degree of fit to a branching tree model. A heuristic search was conducted, with two platforms from the remote Vasiugan basin serving as the outgroup. The search returned 267 trees, all with a shared length of 684. A strict consensus tree was generated and bootstrapped at 1,000 replications, generating the single tree (not shown). Only seventeen clades were given more than 50 percent support, mostly in lower-level clades. The overall patterning was very bushlike, with little if any evidence for a hierarchical branching structure, with the very low RI score of 0.16 confirmed these interpretations. Moreover, there was minimal evidence for any kind of geographic clustering of styles, further suggesting that rapid localised innovation had generated these patterns, and not hybridization of styles between adjacent base-camps – each platform appears to be a highly pragmatic recombination of cultural traits drawn from a wide pool of possible alternatives.

Note 7. Khanty Shrines: Data Sets

A total of twenty-two shrines were surveyed across the Middle Ob' zone (figures 3.1, 3.12). Variability in basic building methods were studied in great detail, generating a total of 112 traits. These recorded all the main construction methods and materials, generating a 22 by 105 presence/absence data matrix, with all rows having complete data. These traits recorded only the physical characteristics of the structure itself and did not record details of the ritual events' choreography, which have their own interesting patterns of localized inheritance, nor the details of the idols housed inside—these also vary greatly between sites but tend to swathed in clothing, furs, and other gifts obscuring vision and preventing a more systematic survey.

Note 8. Khanty Shrines: Network- and Tree-Based Analyses

The shrine data set was converted into a NEXUS file and subjected to preliminary NeighborNet analysis. The plot generated some interesting patterns (figure 3.13). First, the general boxing at the center of the plot appears to reflect the general interchangeability of building traits across the different shrines, including the common use of log- and plank-built construction, and their frequent combination with roof boards or birch bark sheets, all of which appeared to reflect a degree of local pragmatism in local construction methods. Second, the plot does appear to have some degree of branching, which reflects a basic fault line between the upper left of the plot and the lower right: this major distinction reflects the basic difference between stilted shrines, which are pulled out to the upper right of the plot, and the ground-built structures, which are pulled down to the lower left. A second fault line pulls the Malyi Iugan shrines out to the lower left and upper central areas of the plot, with the Bolshoi Iugan sites pulled to the bottom, lower right and right. Interestingly, the Salym sites group closer to the Malyi Iugan sites (even though they are geographically closer to the Bolshoi Iugan River). The Pim shrine groups with the three Bolshoi Iugan shrines used by a single regionally important deity—this is interesting because the Pim Khanty also come down to these Iugan sites on regular pilgrimages. In the lower parts of the plot, the shed structures on the Bolshoi Iugan all pull out in the same direction and are all found at different sites on the upper river, while the stilted structures on the Bolshoi Iugan are pulled out to the right, but not in an order that reflects their relative geographic locations, perhaps suggesting that each has a distinctive local microstyle. This kind of highly localized difference in style is even more pronounced among the raised Malyi Iugan shrines, which pull out to the top of the plot, and the shed built shrines that pull out to the bottom left: their order in the plot does not reflect their relative locations on the river, again pointing to the formation of distinct local shrine styles at each of the base camp patrilineages.

The strength of the potential branching signal was further tested in PAUP* 4.0b10, with the Pim shrines selected as the outgroup because they were geographically remotest. A heuristic search returned forty-eight trees, each with a length of 220. A strict consensus tree was generated and then bootstrapped at 1,000 replications, and clades with more than 50 percent support retained, returning a tree with some degree of well-supported branching structure (figure 3.13). Shrines from the Agan River were on a separate clade with 96 percent support, and the shed constructions on the extreme Upper Malyi Iugan also had a separate clade, as did the stilted shrines at the lower end of this river. The four shed-type shrines on the upper Bolshoi Iugan also branched out, with two forming a further subclade, while two of the stilted shrines on the lower river also form a distinct clade. In contrast, shrines on the Salym and on much of the Malyi Iugan were not differentiated and did not form separate clades, possibly reflecting the interchangeability of many of the minor construction traits across these shrines. The bootstrapped consensus tree also had an RI score of 0.31, well below the 0.60 threshold that would indicate that shrine-building traditions had evolved via a relatively straightforward process of phylogenesis.

Note 9. Iugan Khanty Contemporary Ski-Making Traditions: Data Sets, Network- and Tree-Based Analyses

The full data set of contemporary skis recorded across the Iugan River basin (figure 3.16), including cloth covers and bindings (forty-one traits recorded over fifty pairs of skis) was converted into a NEXUS file and subjected to preliminary analysis in NeighborNet to examine general patterning and coherence. The resulting plot (figure 3.21) indicates widespread mixing of traits from the different Iugan River base camps, and also between the main Malyi and Bolshoi Iugan basins, although some styles do seem to be identified as being relatively unique. Analysis in PAUP* 4.0b10 tested the potential strength of a branching signal in the data set, using the first sets of skis from the first base camp on the lower Bolshoi Iugan as the outgroup. A strict consensus tree was bootstrapped at 1,000 repetitions, revealing an overall tree length of 53 and only three clades resolved in an otherwise bushlike pattern (not shown); the RI score of 0.10 was also very low. On balance then, the results suggest that coherent localized ski designs have not generally emerged, neither at the scale of the base camps, nor along the different branches of the Iugan River; nor has there been any substantial hybridization in styles between adjacent base camps—it seems more likely that pragmatic local innovation has generated these general patterns within modern ski designs in the Iugan River basin.

Note 10. Iugan Khanty Skis—Archaic and Contemporary Designs: Data Sets, Network- and Tree-Based Analyses

Examples of three pairs of archaic platform skis were also subject to a trait-based analysis and added to the data set of contemporary Iugan skis (including the cloth covers). This generated an expanded data set of fifty-three skis and fifty-nine design traits, which was converted into a NEXUS file and subjected to preliminary analysis in NeighborNet. The transformation in the plot is striking (not shown): the platform skis and contemporary skis are substantially different and are pulled out into very areas of the plot. The same data set was examined in PAUP* 4.0b10, this time using the platform skis as the outgroup. A strict consensus tree was bootstrapped at 1,000 repetitions, and this returned a tree of length 77, in which the platform skis were on a separate clade with 100 percent support, while the modern skis showed only very little branching signal (not shown). The RI for this tree was slightly higher at 0.38. These results suggest that the two kinds of skis are very different, probably with distinct historical origins.

Note 11. Iugan Khanty Ski Bindings—Archaic and Contemporary Designs: Data Sets, Network- and Tree-Based Analyses

As noted in the text, most innovation in contemporary skis appears to relate to use of the new cloth covers, which remains highly variable. Traits recording these elements of ski design were removed from the data set, generating a revised data set, which covered fifty-three skis but now only thirty-four traits pertaining to the main design of the ski and the bindings only. This was converted into a NEXUS file and examined in NeighborNet. The plot (not shown) also pulled the archaic platform skis sharply out to the right, but the remaining sections of the plot became densely crowded with data labels because the data set now contained many skis with identical sets of design traits, most often those pertaining to the standard design features of cedarwood/moose fur/D-ring bindings, etc. This data set was also analyzed in PAUP* 4.0b10, with the archaic platform skis as the outgroup. A bootstrapped strict consensus tree also revealed the very deep division between the old and contemporary skis. Also, with the traits relating to the cloth covers now removed from the study, there was much greater coherence in the contemporary skis, although some small subgroups formed among skis with the extra foot boards attached. Moreover, the RI rose to 0.86, confirming that a greater degree of branching transmission appeared to be affecting transmission of these ski traits (tree not shown).

To simplify the plots, skis with identical trait descriptions were removed from the data set to generate a reduced subset of nine pairs of skis, each with thirty-three design traits. The NeighborNet plot showed a similar bunching of the D-ring ski variants, with the older platform skis pulled out far to the top left (figure 3.22). In PAUP* 4.0b10, the platform skis were selected as the outgroup, and a heuristic search returned six trees at 30 length, which was converted into a strict consensus tree and bootstrapped. In this tree, all the contemporary D-ring skis now fell into the same clade, which had 100 percent bootstrap support, and branched away from the branch with the older platform skis (figure 3.22). The RI score was 0.65, suggesting the presence of a branching signal.

Note 12. Eastern Khanty Skis: Network- and Tree-Based Analyses: Data Sets, Network- and Tree-Based Analyses

Details of further ski-making traditions from other Eastern Khanty rivers were added to the full data set of Iugan ski bindings and platform skis (see note 11) (recording basic ski design and binding features, but not details relating to the new cloth covers), generating a matrix of sixty-one skis and forty-five design traits. This was converted into a NEXUS file and analyzed in NeighborNet. With multiple examples of identical Iugan ski variants, the plot (not shown) was rather crowded with data labels but identified a basic coherence in Iugan ski designs, with the archaic platform skis and other modern skis from the other rivers branching away. Analysis in PAUP* 4.0b10, again with the older platform skis as the outgroup, generated a well-resolved tree, picking out similar patterns, with a very high RI score of 0.90 (not shown).

To clarify the plots, duplicate examples of skis from the Iugan were again removed from the database, generating a revised matrix of seventeen skis but the same set of forty-five design traits. This was converted into a NEXUS file and analyzed in NeighborNet (figure 3.24); the plot also had a clear branching structure, pulling the platform skis out to the right, the Iugan variants to the top, and other Khanty skis to the bottom. There was a greater degree of apparent hybridization in the latter group, all of which employ variants of a strap-based ski binding system, in contrast to the Iugan Khanty D-ring system. The Vakh skis were pulled out to the lower right, and ski designs from other basins were pulled to the left. In PAUP* 4.0b10, a strict consensus tree bootstrapped with 1,000 replications confirmed the existence of this branching structure in the data set, as did an RI score of 0.82, and also identified the same basic groupings in coherent ski designs (figure 3.24). The distribution of these coherent styles can also be linked to the dialects found in each drainage basin (Tereshkin 1981). For example, the distinctive D-ring binding style is found only on the Iugan River, and therefore maps directly onto the local dialect boundary; a similar situation appears to exist on the Vasiugan and Trom"egan, each of which also has its own distinctive style; on other rivers, two variants appear to coexist within the same dialect community, e.g., on the Vakh and Agan Rivers (figure 3.24).

Note 13. Siberian Skis: Data Sets, Network- and Tree-Based Analyses

The larger data set of Eastern Khanty ski-making traditions (see note 12) was expanded further with addition of examples from other regions of Siberia (data from Levin and Potapov 1961: 79–105). This generated a matrix of seventy-one Siberian ski types and details of seventy-one design traits. This was converted into a NEXUS file and investigated in NeighborNet, which generated a plot with clear groupings (not shown). The large number of Iugan variants clustered to the lower left; platform skis were pulled out to the right, while there was a radiating spread, with little apparent conflict, of coherent ski designs among other Khanty groups and across other regions of Siberia. Analysis in PAUP* 4.0b10 revealed a branching tree (not shown) in which platform skis branched away, as did the Iugan variants, with some minor internal clades to this grouping; most of the other Khanty skis formed a single clade, and there was also some apparent branching structure in the other Siberian variants. The RI score was 0.92 also suggesting a phylogenetic signal in the data set.

Similar results were achieved when the duplicate Iugan ski variants were removed from the data set, which generated a revised matrix of twenty-seven ski types and seventy-one design traits. This was converted into a NEXUS file and examined in NeighborNet. The resulting plot indicated that the platforms skis again formed a coherent tradition, as did the Iugan skis; the other Eastern Khanty ski designs were also pulled out to the lower middle sections of the plot, while the Siberian skis branched away to the left (figure 3.28). Analysis in PAUP* 4.0b10 generated a well-resolved branching tree structure, with an RI score of 0.83, again suggesting the presence of a branching signal (figure 3.28): the platform skis form the first clade, and the Iugan skis a second distinct major clade, while the other Eastern Khanty ski designs also branch away and exhibit some further internal hierarchical branching patterns within this clade. The pattern for the rest of the Siberian skis is less well resolved—many skis appear to form distinct local traditions but there is little evidence for any kind of hierarchical structuring which would suggest evolution by phylogenesis.

Note 14. Comparative Analysis of Gendered Crafts: Potentials for Further Research in Western Siberia

Due to constraints on space, this chapter has only focused on understanding the transmission of a series of interrelated woodworking crafts that are predominantly practiced by Eastern Khanty men. In addition, a series of "female" crafts, including the sewing of traditional clothing and footwear and the making of distinctive highly decorated baskets, are also widespread traditions. Preliminary material culture surveys and the visual exploration of data sets collected to date from the Iugan Khanty and from the wider literature (e.g., Lukina 1985) indicate what appear to be highly standardized design "recipes" for both basketry and female clothing. It is tempting to link this to the local kinship system, which sees women travel to other distant base camps after marriage, possibly taking knowledge of these construction methods with them, which may have eventually standardized designs across the basin. Interestingly, and in sharp contrast to these basic designs, the strips of beaded decoration on the coats and the colorful interlocking zig-zag designs on the basketry all appear to be linked to the personal skill and creativity of the individual practitioner, and are subject to high rates of innovation, to the extent that each "standardized" coat or basket has a unique set of decorations. Formal trait-based analysis of these "female" traditions lies beyond the scope of the current chapter and would require further fieldwork to close gaps in coverage and also gather comparative materials from other Eastern Khanty basins. Quantitative analysis of diversity in the traditional garments, footwear, and bags made by Northern Khanty women living on the Lower Ob' has been completed and generated detailed insights into patterns of transmission among these female crafts (Jordan 2009).

CHAPTER 4

Pacific Northwest Coast

This chapter examines the extent of cultural coherence and deeper historical congruence in the material culture traditions of Coast Salish communities on the Pacific Northwest Coast. Macroscale cultural evolution is examined in three different traditions: housing, canoe making, and basketry/matting. The chapter opens with a general introduction to local environments, subsistence practices, and social institutions, and then examines the evolutionary dynamics of each of the three different traditions in turn (note 1).

Each tradition appears to be embedded differently in local social networks, and this affects the ways in which the cultural traits are propagated. Housing and canoe making appear to form relatively coherent traditions at the scale of the ethnolinguistic communities, and exhibit branching histories, but basketry and matting appear to have been affected by the widespread mixing of traits among local populations and display little local coherence.

The chapter concludes with an attempt to reconstruct general patterns of cultural evolution along this section of the Pacific Northwest Coast. There is some evidence that housing traditions and language history may have been historically congruent, together forming an integrated "core" of cultural traditions. In contrast, canoe-making traditions have their own independent branching history, while variability in basketry and matting traditions appears to be a product of regional ethnogenesis.

THE GULF OF GEORGIA: GEOGRAPHY, ENVIRONMENT, AND PREHISTORY

The Gulf of Georgia, in modern British Colombia, runs between Vancouver Island and mainland North America. Here the basic relief consists of parallel mountain ranges running from Northwest to Southeast—the Rocky Mountain system is the easternmost of these ranges, and the partially submerged island chain, which includes Vancouver Island, forms the highest part of the western range. The gulf itself consists of the southern end of an ancient valley, which was gouged out by glaciers, resulting in a deep-water channel of up to 60 fathoms in depth. More recent glaciations have produced numerous islands and a very broken coastline (Barnett 1955:11; and see figure 4.1). The Gulf is only some 125 miles in length, but this sinuous coastline totals an "ocean frontage" of 1,900 miles and includes many bays and capes, interspaced with islands and offshore reefs. On the mainland side, the land rises sharply into jagged mountain peaks, though many deep inlets allow easy access to the continental interior. The rise in land is less pronounced on the island side. Overall, the complex configuration of land and water make most sea crossings quite short—no more than 25 miles at the widest point of the Gulf—but this requires navigating through a broken mass of inlets, fjords, and islands (Barnett 1955:12).

The warm Japanese current strikes the coast, ensuring that climate remains moderate, with most precipitation falling in November and December during seasonal storms. Variations in precipitation tend to run parallel with the ocean, creating wet and dry belts, and with winds generally from the west, the east of Vancouver Island is drier than the mainland coast mountains (1955:13–14). The warm maritime air is trapped by the mountains, which also prevent dry continental air coming in, and the result is lush rainforest vegetation, including the abundant Douglas fir, though red cedar had the greatest cultural value for ethnographically documented indigenous communities living on the Northwest Coast (Stewart 1984:16, 18).

This unique geography and topography encouraged a subsistence strategy that "makes full use of the facilities and resources of the sea" (Barnett 1955:11); in fact, it is hard to live here without relying on the resources of the sea or rivers, and this trend is exacerbated by the rugged character of the land and its heavy and dense vegetation, which can also make terrestrial journeys difficult, and by the fact that most travel distances are much shorter by water than over the rugged topography.

Archaeology

Extraction and processing of salmon certainly appears to have dominated in the later periods of prehistory and continued into the ethnographic period (Matson 2003a:7), but when did other key aspects of the Coast Salish "ethnographic pattern" start to emerge? Along the Pacific Northwest Coast, most archaeological models suggest a gradual shift from broad-spectrum foraging to more logistically organized strategies with intensified exploitation of some resources, especially salmon. These developments were facilitated by stabilization of sea levels, the development of storage and mass harvesting technologies, and coeval population growth, leading to the formation of "collector" strategies and associated sociopolitical changes (e.g., see Butler and Campbell 2006, with references). These abundant aquatic resources, and the invention of new strategies to exploit them, have long been used to explain the emergence of cultural complexity in the region; these factors also appear to have generated a semi-sedentary settlement pattern, with seasonal aggregations into winter villages (Ames 1994; Ames and Maschner 1999; Barnett 1955; Butler and Campbell 2006:263; Fagan 2000; Maschner 1991; Suttles 1990a).

Certainly, fish resources dominate at most archaeological sites from around the Gulf of Georgia, outnumbering both bird and mammal remains by an order of magnitude (Butler and Campbell 2006:267). Butler and Campbell (2006:273) conclude that although the faunal record illustrates both local variation and also variation in availability, there is "remarkable stability and continuity in overall use of animal resources over 10,000 years" and that "in spite of thousands of years of hunting, fishing and gathering the same animals, resource depression is not evident in . . . .the Northwest Coast.'" In conclusion, salmon was the most abundant and ubiquitous resource and was targeted for over 10,000 years, though these fish populations appear to have been highly resilient because of the salmon life cycle (Butler and Campbell 2006).

The prehistoric culture history of the Northwest Coast is now becoming clearer thanks to decades of archaeological research, and this is generating a better understanding of the sequence of developments that eventually led to the appearance of the main ethnographic patterns that were encountered by Europeans when they started to move into the area (see Matson and Coupland 1995; also Ames and Maschner 1999; Coupland and Mackie 2003; Suttles 1990a, b; etc.). For example, it is clear that the Gulf of Georgia region was already participating in regional exchange networks for many millennia, with widespread obsidian exchange by 6000 B.P. (before present), and nephrite, west coast dentalia, and soapstone by 2500 B.P., all of which indicates a degree of connectivity, though this was most likely just down-the-line long-distance exchange—there is no evidence at this stage that the Gulf of Georgia had emerged as a distinct cultural region (Grier 2003:175–76).

This starts to change, however, as the gulf starts to develop its own intensified and distinctive *intra*regional exchange networks during the Marpole Phase, around 2500–1000 BP (Grier 2003:176). This is also when the core cultural institutions that eventually can be traced into the ethnographic record start to emerge (Matson and Coupland 1995:224–25, 241–42). Certainly, by circa 2200 B.P. the "Developed Northwest Coast Pattern" is well established—this includes winter villages with enormous multifamily plank-built houses, seasonal moves to specialized resource locations, a high dependence on stored fish, usually salmon, supplemented with other resources. Also typical of this period are changes in material culture and social structure, including production of abundant and highly sophisticated artwork, with shared styles over large areas, and indications of ascribed status and emerging social inequality.

Along with these transformations, it becomes possible to identify clearer spatial divisions in the archaeological record, which are thought to anticipate some of the main ethnographic groupings that define later periods. Eventually, the Coast Salish area emerges as a distinct cultural region in terms of its unique natural, archaeological, and ethnographic characteristics (Grier 2003:170; Matson and Coupland 1995:200–42). Much of the cultural distinctiveness, including the shared artifact styles and common kinds of archaeological assemblage—appear to be underpinned by intense *intra*regional social interaction and material exchange networks (Barnett 1955; Grier 2003; Matson and Coupland 1995:211–18; Suttles 1990b:14). These may be linked to the emergence of common cultural "currencies" that serve to index general success, status, and social authority (Ames and Maschner 1999:165–74), and may also indicate the fact that the structure of local sociopolitical systems were becoming more standardized across the wider region (Grier 2003:177). All these cumulative developments appear to feed into a new kind of regional cultural unity that is not evident in earlier periods (Ames and Maschner 1999:165).

THE COAST SALISH: ETHNOGRAPHIC CONTEXT

The Northwest Coast was defined ethnographically as the "Salmon Area" in Wissler's (1917/1938) classification of North American culture areas, and it is clear that local communities took full advantage of locally abundant aquatic resources through specialized seasonal rounds that included mass harvesting and storage technologies (Butler and Cambell 2006:263–65). For example, in the deep fjordlands of the Gulf of Georgia, there were major tidal ranges that often made travel dangerous, but they also exposed islands, banks, and low silt lands at river mouths, with these features especially prominent in the southern reaches of the gulf (Barnett 1955:13). In many places it was possible to place stationary tidal fish traps, which were used across the area, especially in the south; these shallow-water beaches also provided year-round gathering grounds. In addition to fish, there was widespread marine and terrestrial fauna, located on both the islands and mainland, including seals, porpoises, sea lions, and waterfowl, and bear, deer, wolf, and goats (1955:16). Economically, socially, and ritually, the primary hunting animals on the islands were seals, and on the mainland, goats (1955:92).

The staple food across the region remained salmon (Barnett 1955:15), and with many good salmon rivers entering the ocean, all five Pacific species were found here, as well as herring, halibut, eulachon, and other species like cod (1955:15). Salmon was eaten dried out of season and fresh in the season (and see Hill-Tout 1978 Vol. II:50). Because of the unique geography of the region, fish was "superabundant" and "only a few accessories were needed to catch tremendous quantities of salmon" (Barnett 1955:78). This also encouraged a pattern of permanent winter villages, which are discussed in more detail below. The ethnographically documented Coast Salish can be classed as "logistic collectors," moving resources collected at specialized summer processing sites to these winter residential sites (Binford 1980).

Dialect Geography

By the time of European culture contact Coast Salish communities occupied both sides of the Gulf of Georgia and spoke an extended chain of closely related languages and dialects (Thompson and Kincade 1990:33; and see figure 4.1). Salish languages occupy a nearly continuous region from the center of the east side of Vancouver Island, to the area south of the Puget Sound, and eastward from the coast to the Rocky Mountains. There is much greater variability in Salishan languages on the coast; diversity is less in the interior. There are many debates about the exact homeland of Salish languages, but it appears

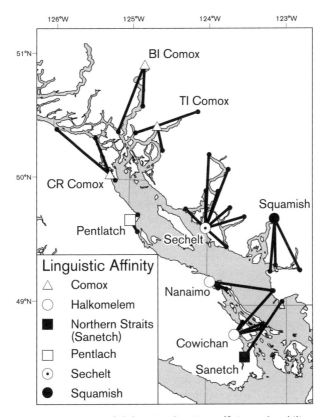

FIGURE 4.1 Coast Salish location, linguistic affinity, and mobility map.

Geographic locations and linguistic affinities of nine Coast Salish ethnolinguistic populations living around the Gulf of Georgia. The black arrows indicate general seasonal mobility patterns: in summer, task groups dispersed to more remote resource extraction points and returned with food supplies; winter months were spent in long-houses located at the main villages (after Barnett 1955:24). For further details, see main text.

that Salishan speakers have inhabited the Northwest Coast for extended periods (Jorgensen 1980:72–75). Suttles (1990a) assigns the Coast Salish to various local culture groupings. For example, the Northern Coast Salish include the Comax, Pentlatch, and Sechelt, and the Central Coast Salish include the Squamish, Nanaimo, Cowichan, and Sanetch (Kennedy and Bouchard 1990:441; Suttles 1990b; and see figure 4.1 and table 4.1).

Settlement, Interaction, and Territoriality

The Coast Salish were excellent sailors. There were few significant geographical factors limiting interactions across the straits, and they could be crossed in summer in an open canoe (Barnett 1955:12–13). Coast Salish main winter villages consisted of large communal long-houses, often set in a row facing out over the water. These were generally located in sheltered sites, near the mouths of rivers, or in bays and inlets, which provided protection from storms and also surprise raids.

Each community also claimed use rights over local resources, and in the busy summer months, people scattered out over the surrounding territory to visit fishing, hunting, and gathering sites (Barnett 1955:18–19). From March to November there was an intense traffic between these remoter camps and the main village. Families undertook extensive resource extraction and processing, returning to the winter villages laden with stores for long months ahead (Barnett 1955:77; figure 4.1). The most intense forms of community interaction took place over the slack winter periods; as the storms and darkness set in, families converged back at the main villages, which formed the main focus of community social life, and engaged in collective festivals and a range of other craft production tasks (Barnett 1955:272).

Social Organization

Coast Salish society is often described as consisting of three rather fixed social classes: worthy, worthless, and slaves (Hill-Tout 1978 Vol. II:31 and Vol. IV:99); or aristocrats, who formed the "real" men and women; and then commoners, and finally slaves (Suttles 1990b:465). However, closer reading of ethnographic sources indicates that these categories were far from rigid, and that the continuous gradations within and between classes provided considerable scope for social advancement but also a perpetual fear of declining social status relative to others (Barnett 1955:247). For example, it was important for a lower-ranking aristocrat to be continually vigilant and to distinguish himself from a self-respecting and industrious common man; moreover, all aristocrats could rapidly lose esteem by failing to be good and extravagant hosts. Overall, it was the maintenance of this esteem that provided all with their relative social rank (1955:248). Slaves, however, were more easily distinguished—they were not treated badly, but were regularly reminded of their marginal position via acts of exclusion. These individuals originated in distant or enemy communities and had often been captured as children. They were expensive to support, and often a general nuisance, but they were kept as indicators of wealth and to advertise the fighting prowess of their masters. Their inferior status blocked them from attempts at self-advancement, and they tended not to work too hard because the products of their labor were owned by their masters (1955:249).

Kinship Institutions and Household Dynamics

For convenience, ethnographers have tended to discuss the Coast Salish in terms of a number of ethnic groups (Barnett 1939; 1955:2–10; and see names listed in figures 4.1, 4.2, and table 4.1). However, these ethnolinguistic terms were not used by the Salish people themselves; they were units of classification employed by outside observers (Barnett 1955:16). For the Salish people, the main residential groups were the family, the collective extended family household, and the main winter village (Suttles 1990b:464).

The immediate nuclear family—of husband, wife, and children—occupied part of the communal long-house, where they had their own stores and cooking fire. Spouses of younger adults and their children tended to eventually bud off and form their own separate family units within the larger, extended family household, all of whom lived in one communal long-house and traced descent from a common ancestor, which provided them with inherited rights to resources and property. In this way, the highest unit of common allegiance was to the extended family, which occupied one large house, with several of these extended family house groups comprising the winter villages (Barnett 1955:241). These families consisted of a family head, his sons and their wives and children, plus his brothers and their wives and children, plus unmarried sisters and sometimes cousins, although they often split away and left to follow their fathers set up new houses (1955:242). In addition to this family core were also parents-in-law, widows, orphans, slaves, and other needy people who provided their labor and loyalty in return for various kinds of general assistance or material reward.

The strength of these extended family groups lay in numbers, and the largest families were the most influential; the core of family and fringe members was bound together by a strong sense of shared descent and ceremonial and economic property rights—for example, the ownership of more distant summer procurement sites and their equipment, to the extent that weak, marginalized, and disaffected people were happy to associate themselves with strong families, who in turn accepted them. Each extended family member was accountable to the other, and so individual interests were backed up by the collective, generating a tendency toward accretion (Barnett 1955:242). The family head could generally trace a direct line of inheritance down from the traditional founder of the extended family and therefore had the strongest claim to the control of material possessions and property rights, although he was more a trustee of common property that a dictator in sole charge of it (1955:244–46).

However, many of these extended families appear to have eventually fragmented into new offshoot families. With blood the main binding factor, the bonds within extended families often tended to weaken as the overall membership grew, either by accretion of new followers or by internal demographic growth. Eventually bonds weakened and failed to serve as motivation for common action; other extended families broke up as the result of fierce rivalries between competing brothers (1955:242). These combined factors appear to have resulted in many winter villages made up of ancestrally related extended families, each forming the collateral outgrowth of an original social nucleus (1955:242–43).

Marriage Contacts and Residence

Highly ritualized marriages were conducted at the elite and more aristocratic social levels; among commoners a simple meal served to mark a new union (Barnett 1955:192). Despite these differences, nearly every man was directly related to his patrilineal house group (Barnett 1939:268) and therefore to his village head, and this was the same for both commoners as well as nobility (1939:267). After successful negotiations, and the completion of the marriage ceremony, the new couple went back immediately to the man's home (Barnett 1955:185–92), because Coast Salish postmarital residence patterns were overwhelmingly patrilocal (Barnett 1939:259; 1955:242). However, there were some exceptions: poorer men unable to pay enough to wed a higher-status woman would occasionally live and work for a time with the bride's people, where he would, perhaps as a valued craftsman, eventually pay off a marriage gift via donations of his own labor. Also, if a newly married couple were dissatisfied with local conditions, they could also shift residence over to the woman's family—if this took place within the same village it often made little difference, sometimes it was simply a move between long-houses, or even just a shift from one household area to another within a single house. Here, "intimate associations might be altered but scenes and faces would remain generally the same"; however, a much more serious adjustment was involved when the mother of the wife came from an alien village because the couple would need to attempt to become established there (1955:193).

In new marriages, the binding importance of blood was initially as strong on the maternal side as it was on the paternal side, but because the new couple generally took up residence with the man's family, this usually tipped the balance. If both the man and the woman came from the same village, the maternal bonds could remain strong, but they would gradually weaken over the generations as core interests were redefined around the patrilineal nucleus of each extended household. If she came from another village, the maternal connections were not necessarily severed, but as the wife saw less and less of her close kin, these relationships tended to alter over time, eventually becoming subsidiary until eventually severed by the dominant patrilineal interests of the local community (Barnett 1955:242).

Many women did marry within villages, but marriage between nearby winter villages was also very common; in fact, in certain areas exchange of brides beyond the local community was highly regarded and an important means of securing potential assistance in times of trouble (Barnett 1939:261), although marriages out of class were rare (Barnett 1955:181). With formal transfers of property upon marriage (1955:182), only wealthier men could practice polygamy and take two or three brides, with the first wife forming the head of the household (Barnett 1939:260). As a result of these practices, a new bride often found herself sharing a house with several other spouses, some perhaps more local, others from far away; with each long- house characterized by multi-family occupancy there was opportunity for much interaction between women drawn from very different communities (Barnett 1955:193).

*Extra*tribal marriages were also preferred for reasons of status, and a man's ambition was to gain as many wives from as many places as possible in order to gain social and political connections outside his immediate territory. In this way, a man with many wives could claim "many homes"; moreover, "it was especially desirable that one should have homes located a great distance from his paternal home, for a man had to be rich and well known to have his suit accepted in a distant village" (Barnett 1955:182). This fed into an "ancient policy of calculated inter-family marriages" (1955:181), with parents making strategic marriage choices (1955:183) for their offspring.

These strategies led to extensive marriage links across tribal and linguistic boundaries. All "these marriage ties involved ritual exchange and promoted trade," and Coast Salish tribes "intermarried with adjacent peoples both within their own region and beyond, regardless of differences in speech and customs" (Suttles 1990b:456). However, because of the kinship and settlement institutions noted previously, it appears that women moved much more frequently after marriage than men, with the scale of postmarital moves ranging from a shift within a single multi-occupancy house or between houses in a village, but also between distant villages and even between other Coast Salish ethnolinguistic populations (see figure 4.1; table 4.1).

Property and Inheritance

Among the Coast Salish, the possession of private property and its social manipulation through established acts of acquisition, distribution, display, and exchange were central to social life (Barnett 1955:250). There was a basic distinction between property held in goods and property expressed in terms of privileges. Property in goods included important procurement sites; resource extraction tools and facilities; houses and their furnishings; canoes; coppers and blankets; personal possessions including clothes and adornment. And "except for minor articles worn by women or used by them in their occupations, all such property was in the hands of men" (1955:250). In contrast, property held in privilege included personal names, rights to certain songs and particular helper spirits; all of these could be owned by both men and women. Finally, the status of slaves was unequivocal: they had either to be raided or bought from a warrior, and they thereby formed another item of wealth (1955:249).

The products of a freeman's labor stayed with him, and he was free to use and display it. Husbands and wives pooled resources and put it toward the common family store. If they separated, the man got this common property. Houses were owned by the several builders and their descendants, and each original builder owned the planks of his part of the long-house. Therefore, when the house was taken apart during seasonal moves, these items of private property were removed as well, which also had longer-term implications, for example, "a case was reported of a quarrel between two Comox brothers which resulted in the literal division of their house on the basis of plank ownership" (Barnett 1955:251).

All ownership was vested in the house chief and with settlements organized along genealogical principles, tracing descent from a single male ancestor (Barnett 1955:18). The dynamics of Salish property inheritance were strictly patrilineal (Barnett 1939:268), and, with post-marital residence predominantly resulting in the movement of women, settlement was also patrilocal (Barnett 1939:259; 1955:242).

Status, Feasting, and Gift Exchange Networks

Feasting and gift exchange were at the core of maintaining inter- and intravillage networks of social interaction, and these events generated the contexts in which prestige and kinship were negotiated and contested. The mere *possession* of material wealth and property did not necessarily bring status (Barnett 1955:253); in fact, any attempt to increase social standing had to be made in front of invited guests from outside a man's own extended family; here they would listen to and perhaps vouch for his claims. In return, he would have to give out gifts like blankets, house boards, skins, tools, weapons, and food. In this way, no new claims could be made without calling the people to witness, and sponsoring such feasts was the only way in which to maintain or advance relative social position, making these gatherings a defining feature of Salish social life (1955:253). However, only specialists or individuals with personal wealth and resources could afford to sponsor the events and "hold the people"; for the poorer "clam diggers," such routes to social advancement were generally blocked (1955:256–57).

Similarly, the *heisut* was an *intra*village gift-giving system in which all had the right to participate if they donated resources. There was no obligation to return these gifts, but in the end everyone did, because all took part in other events held in village. These were very much an "integral part of the social fabric" (Barnett 1955:255) and sometimes involved some additional guests from nearby villages, but only if there were recent marriage ties that served to ensure the likelihood of peaceful treatment. For these more localized events, the main ritual season was the winter period, running from November through to March, when everyone was back at the main villages. This winter way of life contrasted strongly with the intense focus on subsistence activity, trafficking of food resources between sites, and the more dispersed and infrequent social interactions that this required, generating major social rhythms to the annual round (figure 4.1).

According to Barnett (1955:272), there were distinctions between private and public dimensions to religion, with both involving some kind of supernatural intervention. However, private rituals and observations were more solemn, while the public ones were much more about prestige, evolving into massive displays that also served to dramatize and reify privileges and to glean public recognition and gain general acclaim. Coast Salish religious practices could therefore also serve as political vehicles to further the status of the self and the family. These culminated in the proliferation of collective dances and the associated rituals that were held in the winter season (Barnett 1955:273–75). It was as though in winter the dance spirits revealed themselves, and this harmonized well with the general surplus of leisure time, the lack of pressing economic activity, and the general surge of creativity and even boredom that marked the season. Among the Sanetch, Cowichan, and Nanaimo, large dances were held every night from November to April (1955:275).

The *klanak* (potlatch) gatherings sustained and defined the character of longer-range contacts; they were always held in late spring, when the weather was more fit for longer sea journeys. While each Salish dialect had its own term for the various intravillage property redistributions, the term *klanak* was universal among all Coast Salish, suggesting a common regional focus on maintaining such forms of structured interaction between more distant communities. In addition, these *klanak* activities were also very different in character, with a central emphasis on expressing and negotiating power, status, and rank across long-distance social networks in endless and inflating cycles of gifts and counter-gifts. Similar notions of competitive "credit" and obligation to excel in repayment of initial gifts extended along the whole Pacific Northwest Coast (Barnett 1955:259). It is highly likely that these trends were inflated during the later colonial period, transforming the potlatch into huge social events (1955:256).

Conflicts and Raiding

While gift-giving and exchange events created opportunities to forge amicable social relations, common anxieties about relative status, social tensions, and the general mistrust between all the Coast Salish communities led to the ever-present potential for eruption of violence and the pursuit of revenge. At more local scales, for example, there were practical factors dampening the likelihood of outright conflict breaking out, for example, co-residence in a single winter village (Barnett 1955:267). However, internal rivalries between families and even close kin may have driven the localized "fissioning" of communities into local clusters of genealogically related winter villages.

However, at larger social scales, and "beyond [these] village limits, aboriginal contacts tended to be few and mostly of an unfriendly character" (Barnett 1955:267; and see Hill-Tout 1978 Vol. II:49–50; Vol. IV:99; Suttles 1990b:456–57, 465). For example, the Coast Salish engaged in both local and regional warfare, with frequent raids and skirmishes between the Salish communities but also with Kwakiutl, Nootka, and Chilcotin groups from outside the immediate region. As the threat of attack was ever-present, many Coast Salish settlements had some kind of defensive stockade or refuge to defend against the arrival of marauders.

More locally, a primary motivation for raids was the grief felt at local death, which generated the motive for attacks on other communities, because grief was relieved only by murdering, slave raiding, and plundering (Barnett 1955:267–71). Details of the seasonality and intensity of raiding is sparse, as is whether attacks involved unified communities drawn from one village cluster attacking those from another during the slack winter or early summer, or whether smaller and more dispersed fishing camps were also raided during the busy summer harvest season (figures 4.1 and 4.2). In general, the intensive and more peaceful cultural interactions within the genealogically related winter village clusters appear to contrast sharply with the more occasional, unpredictable, and often violent nature of longer-range interactions (Barnett 1955).

Summary

These two opening sections have aimed to outline some of the key geographic, economic, and social aspects of Coast Salish lifeways within a broader historical context. As "complex" hunter-fisher-gatherers, the Coast Salish lived in clustered winter villages, each consisting of rows of long-houses (Barnett 1955:18, 241), with settlements organized along genealogical principles, and generally tracing descent from a common ancestor (1955:18). The most intense social interaction within each village took place during the "slack" winter periods, which were marked by group festivals (1955:272).

Relations within these village clusters were generally peaceful, but more distant contacts tended to be hostile, or at best characterized by high levels of suspicion, and this general pattern of social interaction may have led to the formation of TRIMs (transmission isolating mechanisms), which may have reduced opportunities for cultural exchanges between different groups (see Durham 1992; chapter 1). In part, these TRIMs may also have been upheld by the highly structured patterns of settlement and seasonal mobility, perhaps eventually generating the relatively homogenous "blocks" of Coast Salish culture that have been described by ethnographers, with each of these groupings centered on locally clustered winter village communities (Barnett 1955:21).

COAST SALISH MATERIAL CULTURE TRADITIONS

Hunting and fishing activities consumed most of the time of both men and women during the summer (Barnett 1955:77). Simultaneously during this busy season, but especially in the slack November to March period, several major crafts were also pursued, including general woodworking, canoe making and the production of basketry and matting. Most individuals engaged in general crafts, but there were also highly respected specialists. Raw materials for many Salish crafts came from the lush rainforests that rose up directly from the shorelines into the mountainous interior. Timber, bark, and root resources were harvested during narrow seasonal windows when the sap was running (see Turner and Hamersley-Chambers 2006:257–59). In particular, the cedar was deeply embedded in Northwest Coast life, and the working of cedar wood, bark, and roots formed the basis of several closely related crafts that also made use of other soft resources like rushes and grass (Stewart 1984). With cedar so central to life on the Northwest Coast, the tree also had deep cultural significance: people believed in its spiritual powers, and many taboos and beliefs were associated with harvesting and working these resources (1984:179–82).

CASE STUDIES: INVESTIGATING THE EVOLUTION OF COAST SALISH TECHNOLOGICAL TRADITIONS

The rest of this chapter examines how craft traditions were propagated within Salish social life and reconstructs how and why specific traditions evolved. Three contrasting material culture traditions are investigated: housing; canoe making, and basketry/matting. This section starts by reviewing the earlier ethnographic work that generated the main data sets and defines the social units (populations) that form the basis of the three case studies.

Earlier Ethnographic Research in the Gulf of Georgia

Barnett (1939, 1955) worked systematically with a number of informants from around the Gulf of Georgia, with the aim of building a full picture of Coast Salish culture at around the time of European contact. European explorers had arrived in the Gulf of Georgia in search of sea otter pelts in the late eighteenth century. After some brief contacts the scarcity of sea otter skins meant that trade with the Salish was profitless and they were left very much to themselves, although there were devastating outbreaks of smallpox and other imported diseases. A major watershed came in C.E. 1843 when the Hudson Bay Company shifted from Fort Vancouver on the Colombia River to Victoria on Vancouver Island. This was when acculturation pressures intensified, although the mainland villages north of Vancouver remained very isolated (Barnett 1955).

Working long after these events, Barnett's informants were men already aged sixty or seventy when interviewed in 1935, and he suggests that the grandfathers of these men could have told ethnographers much about the precontact Coast Salish of the late eighteenth century (Barnett 1955:4). Barnett's fieldwork formed part of the general culture area surveys of the 1930s, and he was primarily interested in defining cultural "units" around the Gulf of Georgia and then systematically recording the presence or absence of cultural traits across these social groups. Undertaking some general statistical analysis, he identified general patterns of cultural similarity and difference among these groups, highlighting an interesting inverse C pattern, with many general similarities between adjacent groups broken sharply by a major cultural gap between the Nanaimo and Pentlach (Barnett 1939:225). Kroeber (1939b:226) also worked on the "statistical expression of the relationship of tribal cultures" and noted this "remarkable" cultural gap on Vancouver Island—which formed the biggest break between all the cultures around Gulf of Georgia—linking this phenomenon to an "unknown historic cause" (figure 4.1).

Defining Coast Salish Populations: From Winter Villages to Ethnolinguistic Units

Barnett's original ethnographic study focused on twelve "ethnic groups" (1939, 1955:2–10; for more detailed settlement maps see Kennedy and Bouchard 1990; Suttles 1990b). However, as noted previously, these ethnolinguistic units (see figure 4.1 and table 4.1) were essentially external classifications developed by ethnographers and employ terms and concepts that were never used by the local populations themselves (Barnett 1955:16). Instead, local community names refer to winter villages, which consisted of a number of long-houses, each occupied by an extended family unit. Each single winter village had its own name and preserved its social unity and autonomy, and traced descent from common ancestor. In some areas, several winter villages were located very close to one another, and these clustered settlements also expressed genealogical connections.

In most cases then, a number of these winter village clusters falls into each of Barnett's ethnolinguistic groups, and generally, most of the village clusters are located very close to one another as well (1955:19; and see figure 4.1 and table 4.1). For example, the Sanetch ethnolinguistic group contained four winter villages on the Sanetch peninsula, and at one of these village sites there were seven large houses, six of which were arranged in a line, with another located behind. Likewise, the Cowichan ethnolinguistic group was made up of eight winter villages, each consisting of separate long-house clusters; although each winter village had a distinct character, all the villages within the larger group were located close to one another. In one case, the village consisted of a single house owned by a great warrior, with several henchmen and twenty related wives. This was an offshoot settlement from another of the villages but had itself come to form a separate community. This provides a good illustration of the "ordinary process of growth which gave rise to the clustering of villages found here and elsewhere . . . the indications are in favour of growth by fission rather than accreation of foreign elements" (1955:21).

Similarly, at Nanaimo there were five named communities within the ethnolinguistic unit—all had permanent houses on the mouth of the Nanaimo River (Barnett 1955:22). The Sechelt formed a further one of Barnett's units (1955:30); their winter settlements were in Pender Harbour and consisted of seven large houses, with four standing one behind the other, and three running crosswise. There were some remoter and more subservient houses located some way outside this cluster, but all the houses functioned as one social unit. From here the Sechelt scattered for their summer visiting a series of remoter extraction sites (figure 4.1). A number of Squamish villages lined the rivers at the head of Howe Sound (1955:31–32) and followed the same classic Coast Salish pattern of winter village congregations rather than scattered family dwellings.

A total of nine ethnolinguistic groups were selected for the present case studies, and each had a full data set pertaining to local housing and canoe-making traditions: Cowichan; Nanaimo; Pentlach; the Comox, recorded at three places on the upper Gulf of Georgia (Cambell River, Bute Inlet, and Toba Inlet, and equating to CRComox; BIComox;

TABLE 4.1 LINGUISTIC AFFINITIES OF COAST SALISH ETHNOLINGUISTIC GROUPS

Ethnolinguistic Group	Group Code	Language[a]	Branch	Family
Cowichan proper	Cowichan	Halkomelem	Central Salish	Salishan
Nanaimo, a Cowichan division	Nanaimo	Halkomelem	Central Salish	Salishan
Pentlatch	Pentlatch	Pentlatch	Central Salish	Salishan
Comox, formerly at Campbell River and Cape Mudge	CR Comox	Comox	Central Salish	Salishan
Klahuse, viz., Toba Inlet Comox	TI Comox	Comox	Central Salish	Salishan
Homalco, viz., Bute Inlet Comox	BI Comox	Comox	Central Salish	Salishan
Sechelt (Siciatl), viz., Jervis Inlet Comox	Sechelt	Sechelt	Central Salish	Salishan
Squamish	Squamish	Squamish	Central Salish	Salishan
Sanetch	Sanetch	Northern Straits	Central Salish	Salishan

NOTE: After Barnett 1939.
[a]Based on consensus classification of the Native Languages of North America (Goddard 1990).

TIComox), followed by the Sechelt, Squamish, and West Sanetch (see table 4.1 and figure 4.1). For the basketry and matting case study BI Comox were excluded because of missing data, leaving data on eight ethnolinguistic groups suitable for analysis.

Woodworking on the Northwest Coast

Along the Northwest Coast all males knew how to work with wood, and the general knowledge associated with the broader craft was not supernaturally sanctioned; it also appears to have undergone significant fluorescence after culture contact, and greater access to iron tools. Prior to the late eighteenth century, local communities had had some access to drift iron, but it was probably not essential for the practice of skillful carpentry. Traditional toolkits, developed over millennia of experience working with cedar (Stewart 1984:36), enabled the working of soft timbers like cedar. However, great skill and ingenuity was still needed to master the techniques of felling, transport, splitting and cutting planks, joining pieces, steaming, bending, and sanding (Stewart 1984).

Woodworking was a solely male task; although all men had some basic expertise, major projects were undertaken only by master carvers because the finer aspects of the craft required lengthy training (Stewart 1984:29, 113). Skilled practitioners found it profitable to devote considerable time to it, and woodworking provided avenues for self-advancement through specialization and exchange: "Just as a good hunter could achieve prominence and material gain by supplying meat for feasts . . . so the expert woodworker could expect to reap social and material rewards from the products of his industry" (1984:107). Good hunters and craftsmen could eventually start to hold small feasts to raise their personal standing within the group (Barnett 1955:248).

One major reason for this was that inheritable and exchangeable material wealth consisted of "such directly utilizable items as boards, canoes" (Stewart 1984:107). Many wooden items had general currency—canoes provided transport and displayed the wealth and prestige required to sponsor a skilled carver, while boards were also in great demand across the region because they were central features of the architecture of winter houses and the temporary summer shelters; they could be used as shelves, partitions, and even drums (Barnett 1955:276; Stewart 1984:92). Cedar planks were split from logs with yew wedges of different lengths and forms, then trimmed and smoothed down with adzes (Stewart 1984:40–44, 108; and see figure 4.2). In some cases, the skills of a leading carver would be in considerable demand, and he might be invited to live for substantial periods in neighboring villages in order to undertake lengthy projects—in exchange he received accommodation and sponsorship (Stewart 1984:29).

Men specializing in riskier and specialized pursuits like hunting and wood carving sought out supernatural sanction and encouragement in their activities. They needed spirit helpers to excel: "Spirit aid was imperative . . . for the makers of large canoes" (Stewart 1984:77). In contrast, this was thought not to be necessary for "uneventful" crafts like weaving or other female handicrafts; spirit help was only required for technical proficiency in activities that were directly related to expressions of prestige and status (1984:77). Aspiring young Salish wood carvers entered into a lengthy training and were encouraged to work closely with a specialist master, to watch, participate, and observe, and then seek out a personal helper spirit to practice the craft independently—the best carvers received their talents as supernatural gifts or inherited them from ancestors (1984:29). Apprentices also learned directly from the specialists how to make and handle their own range of tools, including mauls, chisels, adzes, drills, grindstones, and sharkskin for polishing (Nabokov and Easton 1989:231). Cedar could be worked

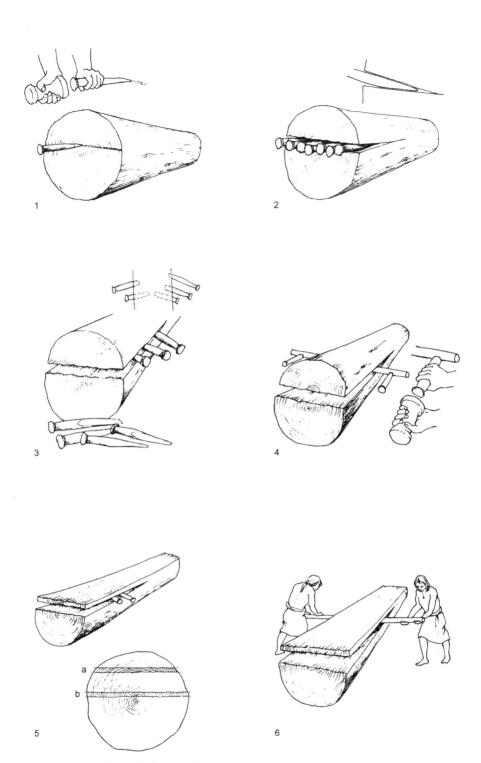

FIGURE 4.2 Plank-splitting techniques.

Methods for splitting off planks. SOURCE: Stewart 1984:41. From *Cedar: Tree of Life to the Northwest Coast Indians* by Hilary Stewart, 1995, Douglas and McIntyre. Reprinted with permission from the publisher.

in many ways using these implements (Stewart 1984:30). All tools were intensely personal items; masters made their own tools to fit their own hands and often created their own techniques and working styles, which they passed on to their apprentices. Learning to carve formed a system of "natural pedagogy" in which masters undertook considerable investment in training new carvers who went on to replicate this highly complex craft tradition, often developing their own methods, toolkits, and techniques (see chapter 1).

PACIFIC NORTHWEST COAST HOUSES

Houses formed the zenith of the woodworking craft on the entire Northwest Coast. Built from massive timber frames with split and adzed planks for walls and roofs, they housed the circa 75,000 people of the 1,200-mile coastline stretching from Alaska down to Oregon (Nabokov and Easton 1989:227) and deeply impressed the first European visitors (Stewart 1984:61). House building was directed by a specialist: he chose the cedars and directed the felling and hauling of logs, with the work often undertaken by slaves (1984:61); he also supervised the work of other craftsmen tasked with completing the boards and posts. A new house represented an enormous input of coordinated labor; for this reason, only wealthy men could afford to build houses, and the size of the new house was an index of the man's ability to pay directly for a workforce and of his capacity to sponsor the associated feasts and ceremonies that were central to raising a new house (1984:61–62). There have been a number of general typologies of Northwest Coast housing (see chapter 2; figure 2.2; Jordan and O'Neill 2010, with references), reflecting the major regional stylistic differences as well as the distinguishing features in housing of smaller tribes (Nabokov and Easton 1989:227). In general, a major distinction can be made between northern areas, where the house walls were permanently fixed vertically into sills, and the southern houses, which consisted of the removable roof and wall boards that served as cladding for permanent timber frames (1984:63). In this chapter, the focus is on Coast Salish housing traditions, which formed some of the latter southern variants.

Coast Salish House-Building Traditions

Ethnographic descriptions of Coast Salish house-building traditions around the Gulf of Georgia form the basis of the current case study (e.g., Barnett 1939, 1955; Hill-Tout 1978; Jorgenson 1980:152; Kennedy and Bouchard 1990:446; Matson 2003b; Nabokov and Easton 1989:236; Stewart 1984; Suttles 1991). Here the Coast Salish lived in long, undecorated houses. Red cedar was the most common wood for these structures, and the houses were often found along curving beach fronts in sheltering coves, where the community was safe from storms, winter winds, and surprise attacks (Nabokov and Easton 1989:229). In summer, small task groups radiated out to more distant resource points, but in winter, the houses were permanently occupied again and became sacred places, the scene of winter ceremonials (Nabokov and Easton 1989:233).

Two basic types of house were built in the Coast Salish region, each with substantial variation at more local scales (Barnett 1955:42–55; 1939: 242–44): the single-pitch "shed roof" house and the double-pitch "gable roof" house (Barnett 1955:35). Both were made up of the permanent frames and plank coverings, as described previously, the shed roof sloped to the rear (figure 4.3), while the gable roof, when viewed from the front, split along the middle and then sloped down either side (figure 4.4).

Shed House Designs. The overall design of the shed houses was simpler (Barnett 1955:36; and see discussion in Matson 2003b). In its most basic format, the structure consisted of four posts set in the ground at the corners, with the back posts shorter than the front (figure 4.3). Two parallel timbers were fitted on top, running from the tall posts at the front of the house through to the lower posts at the rear. The front posts were about 18 feet high, with the rear posts about 10 feet high, and the gap between them about 40 or 50 feet. Pole rafters were then fitted in, so that the roof had a slight incline, sloping away to the rear. These sections of the framework were permanent fixtures and remained in situ (Matson 2003b:77–78). Onto this framework was fixed the plank wall cladding, which was lashed onto the side in horizontal courses that were clamped between the roof support posts and external poles. Cedar withes were used under each course of planking to draw the planks together; they were overlapped like shingles to shed the rain, with moss and old fibre used for chinking. The structures were drafty but kept out the snow and rains (Barnett 1955:35–36). The individual wall boards were about 5 feet wide and 6 feet long, with some roof planks 18 feet long (Stewart 1984:67); all these planks were individually owned (Barnett 1955:251). Many shed houses were about 60 or 70 feet long, but

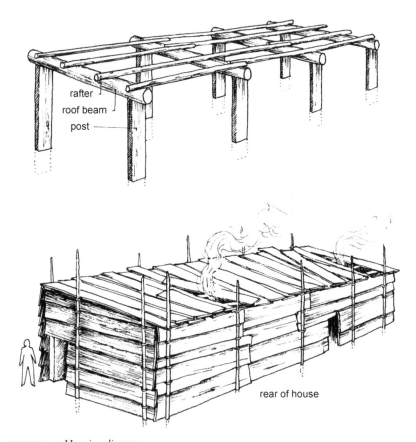

rafter
roof beam
post

rear of house

FIGURE 4.3 Housing diagram.

Construction details of a Coast Salish shed-roof house. Note that the roof and outer wall planks can be removed to leave the main frame in situ, a common practice among some groups during the summer months (see main text). SOURCE: Stewart 1984:64. From *Cedar: Tree of Life to the Northwest Coast Indians* by Hilary Stewart, 1995, Douglas and McIntyre. Reprinted with permission from the publisher.

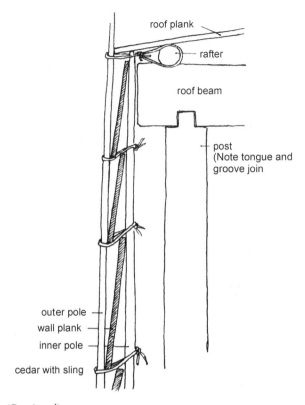

roof plank

rafter

roof beam

post
(Note tongue and
groove join

outer pole
wall plank
inner pole

cedar with sling

FIGURE 4.3. *(Continued)*

the basic framework could be extended by adding extra sets of posts and beams to either side and covering them with planks over a lattice of lighter rafters. Hill-Tout (1978 Vol. II:44) reports that most Salish villages contained one or sometimes two of these extended long-houses. In some of the most populous villages these grew to 600 feet long, but houses of 200 or 300 feet were more common.

Gabled House Designs. In contrast, the main feature of the gabled house (see Barnett 1955:35–36) was the single- or double-ridge pole that ran the length of the house and was supported underneath by crossbeams and vertical posts (figure 4.4). Four additional posts stood at the house corners and supported two stout beams that ran the length of the house, parallel to the ridge pole. Rafters were then set at intervals, connecting the ridge pole to the two parallel beams. A further set of

FIGURE 4.4 Housing section.
Details of Coast Salish gable-roof houses (redrawn from Barnett 1955:44–45). *Top:* Pentlatch; *bottom:* (CR) Comox (see table 4.1 and figure 4.1).

poles was laid on top of these rafters and ran from the front of the house to the rear, parallel to the ridge pole and beams. Finally, on top of these were laid the interlocking cedar roof planks. At the apex of the roof there was no closure; a crack ran the length of the house and served as a smoke hole, or a plank could be pushed aside by a pole from beneath to let in air and light and let out smoke.

Origins and Social Significance of House Designs

Notably, the construction sequence for each of these two kinds of structure was very different. The shed had no tie beam along the front of the house, nor one along the back, analogous to the ones supporting the gabled houses' ridge pole (e.g., compare figures 4.3 and 4.4). This meant that the basic shape of the two house types was set at right angles to one another—when faced from the front the shed inclined to the back, but the roof of the gable houses dropped down from the apex to the left and right (Barnett 1955:36–37). Also, the doors were in different places, located on the side in the shed but centrally, under the apex of the gabled houses (1955:37; Nabokov and Easton 1989:235). However, Barnett explains carefully that the gabled houses were not made up of two shed houses set front to front to form the gables—they were structurally different designs entirely, and most likely the traditions also had different historical origins (1955:35, 37). The distinction between the two types was also largely social, except along the Sechelt and Squamish—the gable roofs were higher status and indicated wealth (1955:35, 37) and see 1955:42–55; 1939:242–44, for detailed discussion of local styles and variations). In contrast, less important families lived in shed-roofed houses.

Modular Design and Annual Cycles of Reconstruction

Coast Salish houses were "modular" and could be extended outward indefinitely by adding new posts and boards as new families came into the household. As Nabokov and Easton (1989:233) explain, Coast Salish shed houses were "commonly hundreds of feet long . . . [and] . . . were actually a sequence of post-and-beam modules that were added on whenever new households, related through the father's line, married into the family." It was usual for leaders to occupy the largest central units, with relative status calculated by distance from the centre; in this way, the house could grow out laterally in both directions, some eventually expanding into extraordinary linear structures (Stewart 1984:65). These served as enormous multifamily households, such that the tasks of seasonal construction, occupation, and dismantling had to be coordinated over this larger social group.

One particularly interesting practice among the Nanaimo, Cowichan, and Sanetch living on Vancouver Island was their annual dismantling of the winter houses, removing the house boards in the spring and carrying them out to summer camps, lashed onto canoes, where they served as coverings for temporary shelters. This left the winter house sites consisting of "abandoned frames" (Stewart 1984:68). Visiting in spring, British naval caption George Vancouver, mistook these open structures as the ruins of deserted native villages (Barnett 1955:40;

Nabokov and Easton 1989:235). In contrast, the mainland Coast Salish groups and the CR Comox tended to build bark shelters at their summer camps, leaving their main homes in place; they did transport planks around for temporary shelter, though these were stripped from the temporary fishing shelters and not the main homes (Barnett 1955:40). Finally, the rows of beams and posts marked the maximum size of the dwelling and not the actual size inhabited in any one year (Matson 2003b:77–78). The important insight arising from these ethnographic accounts is that many Salish families routinely broke up and dismantled their communal long-houses and used the components as portable field kits to build seasonal shelters for small task groups. By necessity, this appears to have resulted in a collectively practiced and socially coordinated tradition of families annually dismantling and then rebuilding the main winter long-houses; even among the groups that did not actually remove exterior planking, the interior volume of long-houses was being constantly adjusted by the local community to reflect changes in the number of seasonal occupants.

Life inside Salish Houses

Salish long-houses were occupied by extended families (Barnett 1955:37), for example, among the Squamish, Barnett's informant had lived in a house occupied by his grandfather, father, and his two uncles and their families each in one corner of a big room; however, this "was but one unit of a much larger structure, for it was inseparably joined to five units just like it. The whole structure comprised the village . . . and externally the observer might take it to be one long house, 120 feet long and 60 feet wide, whereas in reality it was composed of six distinct units more properly called houses, each about twenty feet wide and sixty feet deep" (Barnett 1955:52).

Inside the houses, platforms or benches set on posts ran along the walls and formed areas for sleeping, working, and storage (1955:37), with at least one hearth under each set of rafters (Matson 2003b:80). Each hearth and rafter defined the space of a household compartment: family cubicles were formed by hanging matting or even planks, but the fronts were always left open. In winter, logs burned day and night. Each family unit within the extended house had a fire, and as the number of units increased so did the number of fires—these units were distinct social and economic entities in the native consciousness, and although they were "housed under one roof and related by blood and common interests, the units were nevertheless potentially autonomous and behaved as such. They did not draw their food from a common stock, nor were members of a unit obliged to distribute their individual catches among other units, although sharing was a very common thing" (Barnett 1955:59). The partitions between units could be cleared away for dances and the platforms used as stages (Barnett 1955:45), perhaps adding to the ongoing debates about the presence and permanency of the compartments and hanging matting screens used to divide them (e.g., Nabokov and Easton 1989:235 and Hill-Tout 1978: Vol. II:44).

Finally, it is interesting to note that after a person died the corpse remained in the house while paid undertakers prepared it for disposal (Barnett 1955:216). The house was later exorcised by the burning of branches and by performing incantations to clean it up (1955:219). Although the bed and clothes in which the corpse had rested were burned, the older house continued to be occupied (Barnett 1939:262–63) and was not subject to abandonment taboos; only the TI Comox deserted the house, but this was a temporary act. In this way, many generations lived on in the same houses year after year, perhaps adding only new boards and beams and hearths, but not altering the basic design of the overall structure.

Summary

Together, these local housing traditions consisted of design features (or cultural traits) that were inherited and combined differently in the various parts of the Gulf of Georgia. In addition, several other cultural traits set these local housing traditions apart (Barnett 1955:37; Nabokov and Easton 1989:233). To the north, the floors inside the houses were excavated, although south of the CR Comox on the island, and below Sechelt on the mainland, the floors were not excavated, with the ground just leveled out and packed hard (1955:37). Other features both inside and outside the houses varied substantially, for example, the location of the hearths inside houses and the organization of drying racks and the external display racks. Some houses were associated with totem poles; others had crests painted on the outside or had mythical figures carved into the support posts (Barnett 1939, 1955). Barnett concludes that there was substantial local differentiation in styles (1955:55). For example, the dwellings of the Comox and Pentlach "clearly stood apart from those of other groups in most respects. They were like the rest, but always with certain elaborations and additions"; their houses were often regarded as being superior technologically and aesthetically—they took more labor to excavate floors and erect internal compartments in their housing traditions (1955:55–56). Also, most of the big houses among the Cowichan and Sanetch were sheds; among the Sechelt the sheds and gables are equal in number. North of here on both sides of the gulf the gable roof was in the ascendency socially and numerically (1955:56).

Coherence and Historical Congruence in Coast Salish
Housing Traditions

Barnett (1939:242–44) undertook a systematic trait-based analysis of long-house construction methods along the Coast Salish, recording variability at the scale of the ethnolinguistic communities described previously (table 4.1). An edited version of this data set was subjected to culture-evolutionary analysis using the methods described in chapter 2 (note 2). Network- and tree-based analyses of this housing data set (see figure 4.5, note 3) indicated the emergence of relatively coherent local house-building styles, and that these had evolved through branching processes—the RI statistic of 0.56 was only just below the 0.60 threshold and again tentatively suggests evolution of coherent local housing traditions through the branching process of phylogenesis.

Co-transmission analyses tested whether these coherent housing styles exhibited any congruence with Salish language history. The nine ethnolinguistic communities under investigation speak a chain of closely related languages and dialects; all fall into the Salishan language family and form the Central Salishan branch; in turn, each community speaks a distinct language in this group or may speak related different dialects of the same language (see table 4.1). These historical descent relationships can be represented in different ways, generating different language trees (figure 4.6): the first tree is based on analysis of cognates shared across the various local languages and dialects and has a much stronger branching signal, perhaps because it records patterns of descent in two hundred core items of lexicon, which may be more resistant to borrowing between communities (see Jorgensen 1980:75, with original data from Swadesh 1950). The second tree is based on qualitative assessment of historical descent relationship among the Salishan languages, taking account of evidence for horizontal borrowing as well as branching of core linguistic features (Goddard 1996). As a result, the

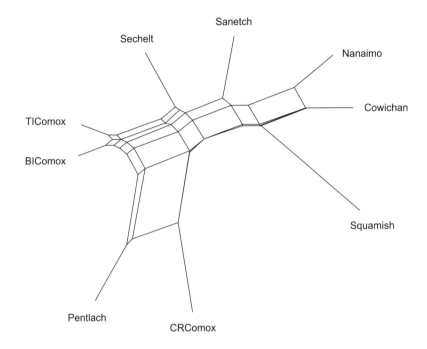

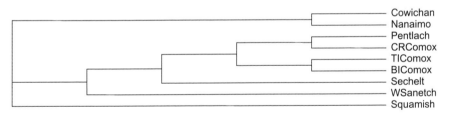

FIGURE 4.5 Housing network and housing tree.

Top: Splitstree NeighborNet network illustrating potential branching and blending relationships among the housing traditions of different Coast Salish populations living around the Gulf of Georgia. Based on the presence/absence of sixty-five housing traits across nine ethnolinguistic populations (see table 4.1 and figure 4.1 for geographic locations). *Bottom:* Phylogenetic tree (created by maximum parsimony) of Coast Salish housing traditions.

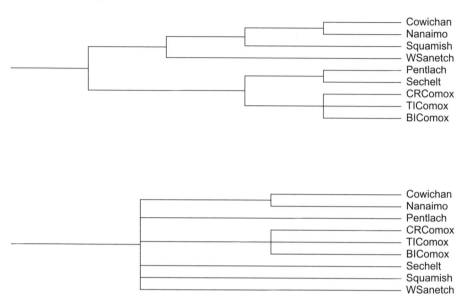

FIGURE 4.6 Language tree cognates and general language tree.

Top: Coast Salish language tree based on the number of shared cognates. *Bottom:* General Coast Salish language tree (based on Goddard 1996). For further details, see main text.

tree has a weaker branching signal, and many nodes remain less well resolved.

The co-transmission tests indicated that housing traditions and language history (whether based on analysis of cognates and in terms of general descent relationships or not) had not tracked each other with perfect fidelity through time. In addition, there appeared to be no general historical association between housing traditions and the tree based on language cognates. However, the tests did identify a higher degree of co-transmission between housing and the general language history than would have been expected by chance alone. This provides tentative evidence for historical congruence in local housing traditions and general language history (and note 4 for more details).

These results were evaluated further using matrix-based analyses of housing variability and its relationship to language diversity and a range of distance measures (see chapter 2; appendix for the full statistics; note 5). The strongest pairwise correlations were with C-distance measures, which accounted for 34 percent of variability in housing styles. The strongest partial correlations involved general language history and the C-distances: language alone accounted for 12 percent of variability and C-distances alone also accounted for a further 12 percent, with 23 percent made up of the combined effects of language and C-distances, accounting in total for 47 percent of the variation in Salish housing styles.

Discussion: Coherence and Congruence in Salish Housing Traditions

On balance, Salish long-house architecture appears to have fallen into a series of highly coherent local styles. These coherent lineages of housing tradition appear to have evolved via branching processes and in broad congruence with general language history, forming a ring of similarity around the Gulf of Georgia, which was broken by the cultural "fault line" running between the Nanaimo and Pentlach (see previous discussion and Barnett 1939:225; Kroeber 1939b:226). These results provide some evidence for the existence of a unified set of core traditions made up of general language history and housing traditions that had evolved together via shared branching processes.

Understanding why these specific patterns emerged requires renewed attention to the ways in which collections of housing traits were being propagated within communities living in the region. These buildings represented large and socially coordinated arenas that often required annual cycles of collective construction and dismantling by the entire extended-family household. The modular nature of the buildings, including the basic frames and house boards, and the fact that the capacity of the household could be expanded or contracted depending on the size of the populations mean that participation in the household could be likened to participation in a language discourse—there would have been strong pressures to maintain collective coordination of the tradition, which would have exerted a strong and also localized conformist bias in the replication of long-house styles (see chapter 1).

In addition, as social institutions and kinship units, the long-houses existed well beyond the life span of most individuals, and each new generation would have had to participate in the older collective traditions of inhabiting and reproducing these built spaces, reducing scope for personal innovation, and probably ensuring high-fidelity replication of the distinctive styles within local populations. Finally, these trends toward the formation of distinct local lineages of architectural tradition would have been reinforced by the fact that Salish society was highly patrilocal and patrilineal—houses were built and owned by males, and these skills and styles were acquired and practiced mostly within the local patrilineal community. In contrast, low-status slaves were the only males traveling long distances between ethnolinguistic communities and would have been unlikely to influence local housing styles after they arrived in a new community. All these factors would have encouraged strong heritable continuity in the propagation of many housing traits at the scale of local ethnolinguistic populations.

At the same time, there is also some evidence of the sharing of traits and thus a degree of hybridization in housing styles around stretches of the coast—in particular the adoption of higher-status gabled roof designs in northern areas. This tendency toward horizontal cultural borrowing between groups may have been linked to the effect of prestige bias among the social elite. The cyclical nature of intra- and inter-community feasting (described previously) would have made wealthy community leaders vigilant about potential challenges to status, either from within the long-house, between long-houses, and also between winter villages and more distant communities. Able to marshal the material resources and social networks that were essential to establishing a new long-house, they would have been quick to seek out and adopt styles that set them apart from rivals and confirmed their aspirations for higher status.

COAST SALISH CANOE-MAKING TRADITIONS

Canoes formed an essential transport technology, and its general production sequence and contexts of use are described in detail by Stewart (1984:48–60). All along the Northwest Coast canoes were made from a single log that was hollowed and shaped with special tools. Use of the dug-out canoe was at the very center of life for these marine-oriented hunter-fisher-gatherers, and developed here to a high degree of sophistication, conferring speed and agility and equipping task groups and war parties with substantial carrying capacities. Without sea-going canoes few villages could have prospered, and the intricate contours of the coasts and islands provided much easier opportunities for rapid movement than did travel along the mountainous shores and the tangled undergrowth of the local rainforests (Stewart 1984:48).

Canoes were also major symbols of wealth; local designs expressed the ever-present demands of vanity and ostentation. Among the Coast Salish, canoe making was a specialist craft that demanded enormous skill and judgment (Barnett 1939:239; Kennedy and Bouchard

1990:446–47) and was practiced mainly by men, with their wives taking part in some key stages in the production process. Accomplished canoe makers were in enormous demand and received sponsorship from wealthy patrons; as a result, the canoe-making craft formed an avenue for economic and social advancement. For example, the largest house group at Sechelt, though not the most aristocratic one, was "important and prosperous because its members devoted themselves to canoe making. They made canoes for everyone at Sechelt" (Barnett 1955:107).

The lengthy canoe production sequence has been described in detail by Barnett (1955:52–57). All the rough work was conducted where the tree had been felled; this was generally near the water edge, but may have been a long way from the village because of the need to find suitable trees (Barnett 1955:109–10). After felling, the log was split with wedges and the outside of the half-log shaped; next, the heart wood was roughly excavated either by charring or by splitting out short sections (figure 4.7). Then, using a method similar to Khanty canoe-making techniques described in chapter 3, a series of tiny holes was drilled from the surface into the wood, serving as a gauge to measure the finer shape and general balance of the hull (figure 4.8).

When the overall hull shape was completed, the friends and relatives of the maker helped tow it back to the beach near the canoe maker's house, and it was here that final shaping took place (Barnett 1955:110; figure 4.8). If time was short, an unfinished canoe could be filled with water, covered and left to be worked on over the winter; it was not a strictly seasonal craft, but most men took advantage of good weather and the fresh condition of the wood to work on canoes over the summer.

As with Khanty dug-outs (chapter 3), one of the most important— and risky—production stages was the spreading out of the hull (Barnett 1955; Hill-Tout 1978:Vol. II—55–56). Among the Salish, this was done by the maker and his wife; no other people were allowed to be there. The canoe hull was filled with water that was then brought to boil with hot rocks—the spreading took enormous skill to ensure that the hull was thin and even. As the hull opened out thwarts were inserted and sewed to the gunwhales with cedar withes; these often served as seats in the larger canoes (figure 4.8). While the steaming was taking place the outer hull was scorched to make it smooth and impervious to weathering. Smoothing was completed with an adze and chisel, and for final polishing dogfish skins and scouring rush were used (Barnett 1955:111).

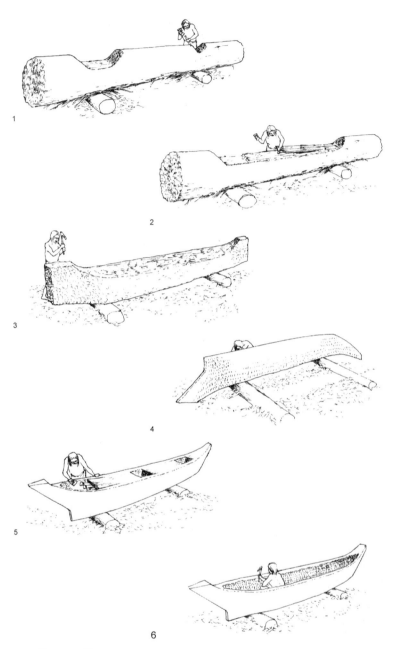

FIGURE 4.7 Canoe making 1.

Early general stages in carving a Northwest Coast dug-out canoe: (1) Removing bark and chiselling out sections at each end; (2) Using wedges and hand maul to split off wood between cuts; (3) Using a large bladed adze to roughly shape the craft and narrow both ends; (4) Canoe turned over and sap wood removed with adze, then hull, bow, and stern adzed into shape; (5) Center hollowed out by chiseling deep holes, then splitting out wood between with wedges and maul; (6) Using smaller-bladed adze to contour insides of canoe and thin hull sides. SOURCE: Stewart 1984:54–55. From *Cedar: Tree of Life to the Northwest Coast Indians* by Hilary Stewart, 1995, Douglas and McIntyre. Reprinted with permission from the publisher.

FIGURE 4.8 Canoe making 2.

Final stages in carving a Northwest Coast dug-out canoe: (7) Canoe maker shapes out hull and then drills a series of holes. Measured pegs then inserted from outside. Inside hull then carved away until pegs reached, and then vertical grooves cut between them. Wood between grooves then split out, leaving slender hull of even thickness; (8) When shaping, completed hull is filled with fresh water, which was heated with stones from fire. Boiling water splashed over hull interior; (9) Exterior then scorched with lighted torch, adding heat and hardening wood. Cedar sides eventually soften, enabling gunwhales to be spread open and wooden thwarts inserted; (10) Stern and bow pieces added and fixed in place with pegs, adding height and graceful lines to canoe; (11) Finished canoe sanded smooth with dogfish skin and rubbed with dogfish oil for preservation. Additional fittings and decorations added.
SOURCE: Stewart 1984: 55. From *Cedar: Tree of Life to the Northwest Coast Indians* by Hilary Stewart, 1995, Douglas and McIntyre. Reprinted with permission from the publisher.

Finally, the surface was rubbed with either fish oil or fish eggs crushed and mixed with charcoal. Occasionally shell was inlaid along the gunwhales, though incised figures along the sides and prow were rare (Barnett 1955:112).

The finished canoes were fitted out with other equipment, which varied from group to group (Barnett 1955:115–16; Jorgenson 1980:151). For example, a false floor was added to protect the crew from the bilge water that collected in the canoe's bottom, strips of cedar were sewn or dowelled along the gunwhales to protect it, and a V-shaped trench was cut into the inside of the prow for storage of harpoons or masts. Sails—thought to be of indigenous invention and not adopted from Europeans—were also added; they consisted of square matting, sometimes thin planks, or even branches placed against the mast to catch the winds (Barnett 1955:115–16). Bailers also varied, most being made of cedar bark, though the Cowichan and Nanaimo used large wooden ladles for this purpose (1955:116).

Working on the canoe had tremendous spiritual significance and was one of the reasons that much of the production work was carried out in isolated places. It was thought that working alone and out of sight the craftsman received mystic help: "Sometimes, as he approached the spot in the early morning, he would hear—if properly sanctioned in his occupation—the rhythmic chop-chop of a supernatural assistant working on his canoe" (Barnett 1955:110). Canoe makers had personal songs that they recounted at key stages in the production sequence, for example, during felling, splitting, excavating, and steaming—failure to perform these songs jeopardized the work and could cause splitting or other problems. The canoe maker's supernatural connections and songs were kept secret, and others were forbidden from watching him work—it was a "serious personal offense" for anyone to do so. Other proscriptions were also in place during work on a canoe. For example, the canoe maker "must, above all, remain continent, at least prior to undertaking critical steps in the work"—these taboos also extended to his wife (1955:110).

Though the general production sequence was the same across the region, several distinct types of canoe were produced by the Coast Salish (figure 4.9). The Salish canoes consisted of single pieces of wood, with no extra sections added. The largest vessels were 35 feet long and 7 feet wide, with capacity for twelve to twenty paddlers (Barnett 1955:112). Two main types were made, and these had quite limited geographic distributions, though the Comox made and used both types. They looked the same but had important differences: the slimmer ver-

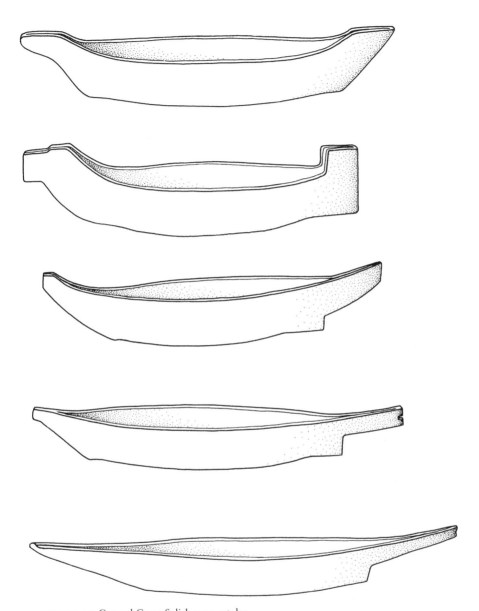

FIGURE 4.9 General Coast Salish canoe styles.

Some examples of general variability in dug-out canoe designs among Coast Salish communities living around the Gulf of Georgia (redrawn from examples originally published in Barnett 1955:112–15). *From top to bottom:* Southeastern type (made by the Squamish), manka, hwektakla (or Northern Type), nakwil, yichelt.

sion was called *yichelt* and was used by communities on Vancouver Island; the second was the *nakwil* and was used along the mainland, as far south as the Fraser River (1955:112–13). A further "Nootka-type" canoe was known across the region but only produced by the Sanetch and Comox, and a further "northern type" canoe had recently been adopted and was being made locally by the Pentlach, Comox, and Sechelt. Finally, the Squamish also made "shovel-nosed" canoes, which were unique to their area. In considering the distribution of these different canoe styles, Barnett (1955:126) identifies a similar structuring to that found in many other forms of material culture: there are two main stylistic boundaries: one between north and south, and the other between island and mainland groups.

The substantial local differences in basic canoe styles were also matched by equal levels of variation in canoe-making toolkits and associated production techniques (Barnett 1955:109; 1939:238–39). For example, horn, yew, or whalebone wedges employed in different areas of the gulf, and the elbow adz was not found south of the Pentlach. In contrast, the Sechelt and others used only a straight adz. This toolkit variability does not appear to have had functional causes. Instead, many central aspects of the canoe-making tradition appear to have formed a corpus of restricted knowledge: "Anyone could make a canoe, but the tools and tricks of the trade were jealously guarded secrets" (Barnett 1955:110). This factor perhaps led to the formation of distinct local traditions.

In conclusion, the repertoire of skills, toolkits, vessel styles, and boat fittings associated with the canoe-making craft formed a coherent yet highly secretive technological tradition that was propagated via a system of natural pedagogy, ensuring both faithful replication—but also cumulative adjustment—of a body of cultural information from one generation to the next. Transmission of these complex skills and knowledge required substantial investment of time, effort, and also valuable social capital by male carvers in the training of their apprentices. Perhaps because of this, transmission tended to follow family lines, either vertically from father to sons, or between generations of males residing in specialist canoe-making long-houses.

Coherence and Congruence in Salish Canoe-Making Traditions

Barnett (1939:238–40) provides a detailed trait-based record of the full canoe-making operational sequence, including toolkits, vessels, and

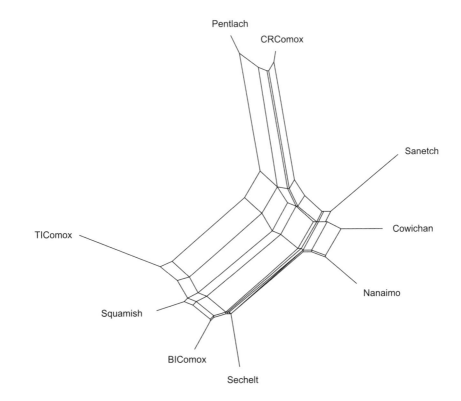

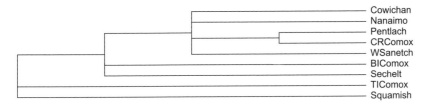

FIGURE 4.10 Canoe network and canoe tree.

Top: Splitstree NeighborNet network illustrating potential branching and blending relationships among the canoe-making traditions of different Coast Salish populations living around the Gulf of Georgia. Based on presence/absence of sixty canoe-making traits across nine ethnolinguistic populations (see table 4.1 and figure 4.1 for geographic locations). *Bottom:* Phylogenetic tree (created by maximum parsimony) of Coast Salish canoe-making traditions.

fittings (note 6). This data set was subjected to a range of culture-evolutionary analyses in order to examine coherence and historical congruence with language (see chapter 2). Network- and tree-based analyses (see figure 4.10 and note 7) indicated a clear branching signal in the data set, with an RI statistic of 0.62, indicating strong heritable continuity in local canoe-making traditions and the evolution of these traditions via a branching process of phylogenesis.

Tests for potential co-transmission between canoe-making traditions and language (both cognates and general language history; see figure 4.6) indicated that although this technological tradition had evolved via branching processes, its history of transmission was entirely independent from that of language, and there was no evidence for congruence (see note 8).

Matrix-based analyses tested the strength of more general correlations among variability in canoe-making traditions, geography, and language (see note 9). Pairwise correlations with language were very weak (see appendix), and the strongest correlation with distance was 18 percent for ring distances around the Gulf of Georgia. The strongest partial correlations involved language cognates and ring-distances and indicated that 3 percent of canoe-making variability was accounted for by language alone, and another 21 percent by ring-distances, these factors accounting for 24 percent of overall variability.

Discussion: Coherence and Congruence in Salish Canoe-Making Traditions

These results indicate that Salish canoe-making traditions exhibit substantial local coherence at the scale of the different Coast Salish ethnolinguistic communities, and that these lineages had primarily evolved via branching processes, leading to a general ring of similarity in local styles around the Gulf of Georgia. However, there was no apparent congruence between canoe-making traditions and language history. Clearly, propagation of the traits that made up canoe-making traditions was embedded very differently in Salish society, though these traits still formed a coherent domain of culture (Boyd et al. 1997:365). The branching patterns of descent can probably be explained by the highly secretive nature of the craft and the trend of inheritance between fathers and sons, and also between generations living within the same long-house.

Why, then, was canoe making not co-transmitted with language, as appears to have been the case with the housing styles? One factor may have been the highly valued nature of the craft and its facilitation of social advancement—expert carvers were often invited into distant villages to complete large and prestigious projects in return for long-term sponsorship and accommodation, as detailed previously. Carvers seeking self-advancement could potentially spend long periods in distant communities, where continued sponsorship and accumulating wealth may eventually have enabled them to take up permanent residence, after which they could raise families and train new generations of carvers. In this way, although canoe-making skills formed a coherent corpus of secretive knowledge that was passed mainly vertically from father to sons, it also formed a coherent package of traits that could have been readily portable *across* dialect boundaries, generating branching patterns of descent in the overall craft tradition but also causing it to have an entirely independent descent history that had little apparent congruence with language.

COAST SALISH BASKETRY AND MATTING TRADITIONS

On the Northwest Coast, plant fiber-craft technologies were embedded differently in local society, and this appears to have affected the ways in which these traditions were propagated. Working with the inner bark of cedar and with other plant fibers was closely associated with female labor (Stewart 1984:113), although men did make some special baskets for carrying harpoon points and lanyards and for storing other tools (1984:131). If men enjoyed working with wood because of the status that was derived from design and creativity, then "women of the Northwest Coast enjoyed the prestige and praise that came from their skill in basketry—which was ... exclusively a woman's art" (1984:128). All women made baskets, but there were also some specialists who focused on this craft and spent less time on other household tasks.

These plant-based crafts were learned via natural pedagogy in childhood, either vertically from mothers, as well as from grandmothers or older female relatives, with some general variation in basic methods, techniques, and materials (Barnett 1955:128; Jorgensen 1980:150; Stewart 1984). Basketry played a vital role in Coast Salish camps and houses and was widely used for storage and transport. Matting was employed as an all-purpose fabric for general padding of surfaces used for sitting and sleeping, and for covering temporary summer shelters. Matting also covered the interior house walls and could be hung from the ceiling to form private spaces for families.

Around the Gulf of Georgia, however, the "art of basketry weaving was not so nearly well developed among the Salish as were other manufactures utilizing fibers and wood," and "taken as a whole, they had but a few types of basketry containers and still fewer techniques for making them" (Barnett 1955:122; and see Barnett 1939:249–50; Kennedy and Bouchard 1990:446). Use was also limited to carrying and storage, and baskets were not used for boiling water or for cooking, as they were further to the south (see chapter 5). The most basic and also characteristic basket of the Coast Salish region was a carrying basketry *(yahai)*—this was a four-sided open-work container made of wrapped twine and featuring rounded corners, with sides that curved inward to a constricted mouth (Barnett 1955:122–23).

Other basketry methods practiced in the region, for example, coiling (figure 4.11), were argued to be of foreign origin and "intrusive" into Salish territory (Barnett 1955:124). At the time of Barnett's research, coiling was said to be new on Vancouver Island and was associated by informants with the mainland communities, although the Sanetch still didn't practice this technique (Barnett 1939:287). Evidence from waterlogged archaeological sites confirms these insights and indicates that all prehistoric basketry in the area was woven (i.e., twined/plaited) and that there had never been any coiled sewed baskets in the precontact Coast Salish area (Bernick 2003:233; Matson and Coupland 2005:220). It appears that during the colonial-contact era Coast Salish communities began to adopt coiled basketry techniques via contacts with the continental interior—this made the Coast Salish a unique group on the Northwest Coast because they alone practiced coiled basketry (figure 4.12), whereas all other groups used only twining (Bernick 2003:234).

Coast Salish matting included twined frayed red-cedar bark mats: these were made by all northern groups on both sides of the Gulf of Georgia, including the Sechelt (Barnett 1955:121). Checker-work mats made from cedar bark had an even more limited distribution and formed a definite northern tradition and on Vancouver Island did not extend south of the Pentlach; in contrast, rush matting was found much more widely (1955:122).

In conclusion, Barnett (1955:127) emphasizes that matting and especially the basketry craft were highly dynamic and rapidly changing at the time of his research, making it difficult to fully reconstruct a detailed sense of the precontact traditions. In particular, he argues, with so much borrowing, innovation, and experimentation taking place it is difficult to define what is local and what is a more recent foreign import. Nonetheless,

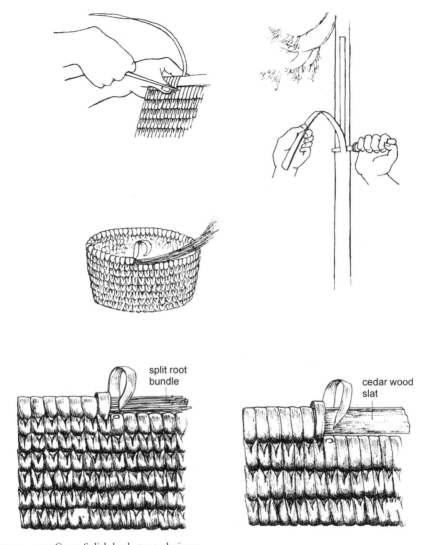

FIGURE 4.11 Coast Salish basketry techniques.

Examples of some basketry construction methods among the Coast Salish. *Clockwise from top right:* Thin slats of wood from cedar saplings widely used in coiled basketry. *Bottom right:* Thin slat of cedar wood coiled around to form sides of basket; rows sewn together with split cedar root. *Bottom left:* Bundles of split cedar root could also be used for this purpose and were coiled around to form sides of basket, with upper row sewn to one below with split cedar root. *Mid left:* Further details of coiled basket with split root bundles serving as the weft. *Top left:* Basket weaver perforates split root bundle (or cedar slat) with awl to allow root strand to pass through. SOURCE: Stewart 1984:173. From *Cedar: Tree of Life to the Northwest Coast Indians* by Hilary Stewart, 1995, Douglas and McIntyre. Reprinted with permission from the publisher.

FIGURE 4.12 Coast Salish basketry examples.

Some finished examples of Coast Salish basketry designs. *Top:* Split cedar root carrying basket with bundle foundation. Leather handles and hinged lid. Diameter 31.7 cm. *Middle:* Watertight basket—split cedar root woven in coiled technique. Diameter 35.5 cm. *Bottom:* Basket of split cedar root, with outside entirely covered with bear-grass and horsetail root imbrication. Diameter 25.2 cm. SOURCE: Stewart 1984:174, 176. From *Cedar: Tree of Life to the Northwest Coast Indians* by Hilary Stewart, 1995, Douglas and McIntyre. Reprinted with permission from the publisher.

there do appear to have been geographic differences (1955:127) that follow similar cultural patterns in several other material culture traditions. For example, Barnett highlights some general stylistic boundaries between the basketry of northern and southern communities and also between islanders and mainlanders, with local informants highly attuned to these regional variations (1955:126–27).

Barnett's trait-based data set of matting practices (1939:242) and basketry traditions (1939:249–50; and see note 10) enable a range of culture-evolutionary analyses to be performed (see chapter 2). Network- and tree-based analyses (see figure 4.13) indicated that there was little evidence for cultural coherence in the data set—clearly, these traditions appear not to have evolved via a branching process of phylogenesis. For example, the RI statistic of 0.50 indicated that processes other than phylogenesis had been operative (note 11). Tests for co-transmission with language were not performed. Matrix-based analyses (see appendix) indicated that the strongest pairwise correlations were with language cognates (18 percent) and proximity (13 percent), while partial correlations indicated that 6 percent of variability in the craft was due to language cognates alone, with a further 1 percent due to proximity alone, and 12 percent resulting from their combined effects, meaning that an overall 19 percent of variability was accounted for (note 12).

Discussion: Coherence and Congruence in Salish Basketry and Matting Traditions

Basketry and matting traditions appear to have been evolving very differently from housing and canoe-making traditions. In particular, their propagation appears to have been characterized by intense innovation and a widespread mixing of traits from different sources, which would have eroded the formation of coherent traditions at the scale of the ethnolinguistic communities and led to a general blending of styles around the Gulf of Georgia.

Several interlocking factors appear to have structured the distinctive ways in which basketry and matting traditions were propagated. One of the most obvious factors is that basketry and matting were almost exclusively female crafts. As a result, the craft was embedded differently into regional kinship institutions and settlement patterns. Here, women were moving around much more frequently—and over greater distances— than men. In some cases, postmarital residence moves by women would have involved a small shift between household compartments in the

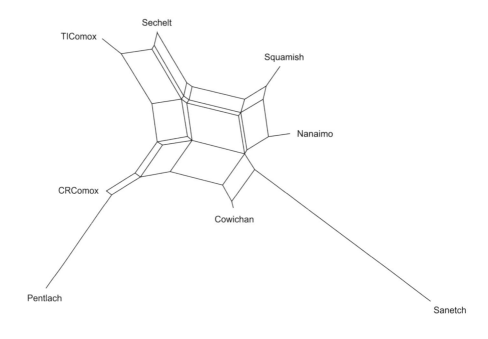

FIGURE 4.13 Basketry net and tree.

Top: Splitstree NeighborNet network illustrating potential branching and blending relationships among the basketry/matting traditions of different Coast Salish populations living around the Gulf of Georgia. Based on presence/absence of forty basketry/matting traits across eight ethnolinguistic populations (see table 4.1 and figure 4.1 for geographic locations). *Bottom:* Phylogenetic tree (created by maximum parsimony) of Coast Salish basketry and matting traditions.

same long house and may also have involved moves between different houses in the same winter village or between adjacent winter villages within the same dialect community. In addition to this, men appear to have been seeking out wives from as far afield as possible, and there may have been a regular long-distance flow of women between more distant communities and even across dialect boundaries.

Although it is clear that general basketry and matting skills appear to have been predominantly transmitted vertically from mothers to daughters, and also from grandmothers and older female relatives (see previous), it is also clear that many women would have spent much of their adult lives married into a different patrilineage and perhaps also occupying a new house or more distant village. Here, in these open, multifamily long houses, they would have met women of different ages and from a wide range of backgrounds, each bringing knowledge of different sets of traits to be observed, imitated, and creatively recombined. Younger girls growing up in these long houses would have been exposed to diversity from a very early age and would have taken knowledge of it to new places after their own marriages. The result appears to have been a cumulative mixing of traits as the wider tradition was being propagated, eroding any potential for coherent local traditions ever to form (see Boyd et al. 1997:367).

Several other factors may have reinforced this trend toward ethnogenesis in basketry and matting styles. Basketry—in contrast to the building of long houses—is a very individual and portable craft and appears not to have been affected by any strong conformity bias or linked to activities requiring collective social coordination, as in house building: it would have been easy to acquire new traits from other women marrying into the patrilineage, or even more casually when meeting women from other communities at some of the remoter summer fishing spots. Finally, at the time of Barnett's (1939, 1955) fieldwork, the basketry craft was already undergoing major transformations associated with colonial culture contact, with the intrusion of new styles and practices such as coiling that were replacing an older exclusive reliance on twined basketry. These factors may have intensified intercommunity contacts and borrowings, increasing the general trend toward regional hybridization noted previously.

HISTORICAL CONGRUENCE ACROSS MULTIPLE CULTURAL TRADITIONS

Although housing, canoes, and basketry/matting traditions were all being practiced across the wider region, these three sets of analyses indicate that each was evolving in strikingly different ways. The manner in which traits making up some traditions were propagated encouraged the formation of coherent cultural entities whose branching history could be reconstructed; traits within other traditions were evolving via a very different process of ethnogenesis.

It is now possible to turn to the final topic of potential historical congruence between traditions: had the three different craft traditions been co-transmitted with one another? Cophylogenetic tests for potential historical congruence were performed on the canoe-making traditions and housing styles that were both evolving via branching processes, but the results indicated that each of these material culture traditions craft had an entirely different descent history (see note 13). Clearly, each of the three traditions had an independent descent history. Only the housing traditions exhibited some apparent congruence with language history (see previous).

Which of Boyd et al.'s (1997:364–66; and see chapter 1, figure 1.3) models therefore best characterizes general patterns of cultural evolution among the Coast Salish? It is clear that in all three traditions there had been at least some mixing of traits between the different ethnolinguistic groups, especially in relation to Coast Salish basketry/matting traditions. Model 1 (cultures as species) can therefore be discounted. At the other end of the continuum, Coast Salish canoe making and housing traits do exhibit some local coherence, enabling the branching histories of these traditions to be reconstructed and Model 4 (cultures as collections of ephemeral entities) to be rejected.

This leaves two intermediate hypotheses: cultures with hierarchically integrated systems (Model 2) and cultures as assemblages of many coherent units (Model 3). On balance, canoe making is probably best understood as a coherent unit with its own independent history of branching descent; housing traditions could also be described in these terms. However, the tentative evidence for congruence between housing traditions and general language history (see previous discussion; note 4; and see figure 4.6) may suggest that these cultural traditions may have formed a loosely integrated set of "core traditions."

If this latter argument can be accepted, the nine Coast Salish cultures examined here could be interpreted as hierarchically integrated systems (Model 2) consisting of the core traditions of housing and language, surrounded by canoe making, which forms a peripheral but coherent unit of culture with its own independent history, and then the basketry/matting traditions, which are perhaps best understood as "ephemeral entities" because of the widespread borrowing and blending of traits from different sources. However, if the tentative case for historical congruence between housing traditions and general language history is rejected, then cultures as assemblages of many coherent units (Model 3) would serve as a better summary of how these multiple cultural traditions have evolved around the Gulf of Georgia.

CONCLUSIONS

This chapter has investigated evidence for coherence and historical congruence in three Coast Salish material culture traditions. Each tradition has different gender associations and appears to have been embedded differently in local social institutions and wider interaction networks, affecting the ways in which each tradition is propagated. At a regional scale, Coast Salish traditions appear to be evolving as hierarchically integrated systems consisting of the core traditions of language and housing. These appear to have been insulated by the effects of cultural borrowing between groups and by the highly structured patterns of kinship and seasonal mobility, combined with the ever-present dangers of violence when traveling beyond the limits of the local community, all of which may together have functioned as TRIMs (Durham 1992; chapter 2). Canoe making forms another coherent unit but has its own independent history. These more coherent traditions are surrounded by a ready mixing and recombination of basketry/matting traits across the region. The apparent links among propagation, coherence, and congruence of these different material culture traditions are summarized in table 4.2; they appear to highlight the importance of gender associations, wider social institutions, and the extent to which the crafts are individual or collective social traditions.

These insights are valuable and directly address many of the key debates about material culture evolution reviewed in chapter 1, but looking further ahead, it is also clear that they are historically contingent on the very many factors that are so specific to this ethnographic setting. For example, all nine Coast Salish communities speak a chain of closely related dialects and languages from the same Salishan family; all share broadly the same social institutions, including stratification, patrilineal and patrilocal kinship, as well as very similar patterns in winter settlement, seasonal mobility, and broader ceremonial life.

How might higher linguistic diversity, greater variability in social institutions, and different patterns of seasonal mobility affect the propagation, coherence, and historical congruence in these and similar kinds of material culture traditions? These are important questions and are examined in the next chapter, providing more explicitly cross-cultural

TABLE 4.2 SUMMARY OF CULTURAL INHERITANCE PATTERNS IN THREE "GENDERED" MATERIAL CULTURE TRADITIONS (COAST SALISH)

Tradition	Coherence and Historical Congruence	Factors Affecting Local Propagation
Houses (male /collective)	Traits form coherent local traditions at scale of ethnolinguistic communities; branching history; some evidence for congruence with general language history. General chain of similarity in long-house styles around Gulf of Georgia, broken by cultural "fault line" on Vancouver Island.	Patrilocal and patrilineal kinship system; houses built and owned by local men; these are collective structures inhabited and seasonally (re)built by the local household community—this ensures strong conformist bias and results in substantial coherence and strong heritable continuity in local housing traditions.
Canoes (male /secret)	Traits form coherent local traditions at scale of ethnolinguistic communities; branching history; no evidence for congruence with language history—these traditions have an entirely independent history. General chain of similarity in canoe styles around Gulf of Georgia.	Coherent but "secretive" craft practiced by male specialists working in isolated locations; strong vertical transmission between fathers and sons (and within specialist canoe-making families); sponsorship by wealthy elites enables practitioners to move between communities for self-advancement—coherent package of traits therefore portable between ethnolinguistic groups, undermining general congruence between canoe-making traditions and language history.
Basketry /Matting (female /individual)	Traits unable to form coherent local traditions; history of blending between ethnolinguistic communities, especially between those in close proximity.	Female craft; evidence for some vertical transmission between mothers and daughters; practitioners move after marriage, carrying knowledge of traits with them and then mix with other women from different backgrounds; no evidence for conformist bias in this individual craft; regional ethnogenesis in styles.

and comparative insights into the potential evolutionary dynamics of different material culture traditions.

NOTES

Note 1. Earlier Culture-Evolutionary Studies in the Gulf of Georgia

This chapter substantially develops and expands an earlier pilot study of Coast Salish material culture conducted by Jordan and Mace (2008). This original study employed only PAUP* 4.0b10, correspondence analyses, and Mantel tests to examine cultural transmission in two very general data sets (2008:42): (1) built structures (including plank housing, but also a wide range of other structures); and (2) woven textiles. In both cases missing data were assigned a zero in the data matrices. In the current study only plank housing traits—a subset of the larger "built structure" data set—are examined, as well as the newly developed data sets of canoe-making traditions and basketry/matting. In the current study, any rows with missing data have been removed; in addition, the range of questions and analytical methods has been expanded to include NeighborNet and also tests for co-transmission using COMPONENT 2.0 and Kishino-Hasegawa tests (see chapter 2). Finally, this chapter also includes a much more detailed investigation of social contexts and operational sequences associated with the different crafts, and thereby generates a series of much more holistic insights into the main factors structuring the evolution of material culture traditions among the Coast Salish.

Note 2. Coast Salish Plank Houses: Data Sets

Barnett's (1939:242–44) data set was carefully edited to remove rows with any missing information, generating a full binary data matrix consisting of sixty-five traits (each marked as a definite present or absent) for the nine ethnolinguistic groups (table 4.1). These traits recorded: basic house forms; construction details; internal features and fittings (e.g., fire positions, storage features, excavated floors); information about the entrances; details about some external features (e.g., exterior posts, totem poles). It is important to note that this matrix is not a "typology" of divergent house types (e.g., describing typical shed-roofed versus gable-roofed houses) but records the entire "pool" of house-building traits that are listed as being present in each of the communities—these traits would have been combined differently in each of the local house-building traditions.

Note 3. Coast Salish Plank Houses: Network- and Tree-Based Analyses

Investigation of coherence in Salish long-house traditions began with a NeighborNet analysis because it was unclear, a priori, whether there was a branching signal in the data set. The 9 × 65 binary data matrix was converted into a NEXUS file and a plot generated. The plot for plank houses has substantial boxing at the center and indicates that there had been a degree of hybridization in styles between the Salish groups. At the same time, many groups are pulled away alone, or in combination with other groups, suggesting a branching signal (figure 4.5). The plot also appears to reflect the relative geographic locations of the ethnolinguistic groups and pulls the housing styles of northern groups to lower left and the more southerly groups to the upper right. For example, Squamish pull away alone to the bottom right; Nanaimo and Cowichan appear to share many traits but pull away together to the upper right; Sanetch pulls away alone to the top right. In contrast, Pentlatch and CR Comox also appear to share many housing traits and pull away to the lower left; TI and BI Comox appear to share traits but pull away to the left; Sechelt pulls away alone to the top. In sum, these preliminary results indicate limited hybridization between local housing styles, but also a substantial branching signal.

The strength of the branching signal was examined more closely in PAUP* 4.0b10. A heuristic search was performed on the same binary data set, with Squamish selected as the outgroup on the grounds that although they had some cultural affiliations with the Sechelt their main winter dwellings were remote from the sea and their culture does not fit well with the wider Gulf of Georgia region. In other words, they shared the same social structure as other Coast Salish groups, but much of their subsistence-related material culture shows an "upriver" and not an "oceanic" adaptation (Barnett 1955:33). The search returned a single tree that was converted into a strict consensus tree and bootstrapped with 1,000 replications to test the support for each branch, with only branches with more than 50 percent support retained (figure 4.5). The resulting tree had six clades and indicates a progressive branching away of the local ethnolinguistic communities' housing traditions: Squamish form the outgroup; Cowichan and Nanaimo form an entirely separate clade; next Sanetch branch away, followed by the Sechelt. The four northern groups then branch away and form two distinct clades: the islanders Pentlatch and CR Comox and the mainlanders BI and TI Comox. The RI statistic for the tree was 0.56, just below the cusp of the 0.60 measure that indicates an unequivocal signal for evolution via a branching process of phylogenesis.

On the basis of these combined results it was tentatively concluded that Salish long house traits had formed relatively coherent traditions at the scale of the nine ethnolinguistic groups, and that these traditions had evolved—at least to some extent—by a branching process of phylogenesis.

Note 4. Coast Salish Plank Houses: Co-Transmission Analyses

As explained in chapter 2, the identification of a substantial branching signal in the housing data opens the way for further testing to identify the degree to which plank housing styles had been co-transmitted with language. Two language trees were employed in the tests, one based on shared cognates (see figure 4.8; and see Jorgensen 1980:75, with original data from Swadesh [1950]), and the other based on a more general language history (see figure 4.6). The cognates tree was built as follows: a 9 ×9 matrix was created listing the names of the nine ethnolinguistic groups (table 4.1) along the top and left side; next, the number cognates shared between each group were entered into the matrix, generating a full table of language similarities between the groups. These measures were converted into a dendrogram in SPSS, then a tree of the same structure was created manually in McClade (Maddison and Maddison 2000) and entered into PAUP* 4.0b10 (see figure 4.6, top). The second tree (figure 4.6, bottom) was also built manually and was based on the general history of Salish languages (see Goddard 1990; table 4.1).

To test for possible co-transmission Kishino-Hasegawa tests were performed using these two language trees to constrain the search for a new best-fit housing tree (see chapter 2). In both cases, the original best-fit tree for plank housing and the new best-fit tree constrained by language cognates and general language history were significantly different. On the basis of these results, it was concluded that plank-housing traditions and language history did not exhibit close historical congruence and had not tracked each other with perfect fidelity through time.

Further tests were then conducted in COMPONENT 2.0 to assess more general similarities between the plank housing tree and the two language trees (see chapter 2). A set of 1,000 randomly generated trees with nine taxa were generated. The triplets measures of difference between these random trees ranged from 12 through to 82, with standard deviation of 9.497 and a mean of 56.2. This establishes a know range of difference between randomly generated trees. When the housing tree and the tree derived from language cognates were investigated, twenty triplets were found to be resolved differently. This score falls within the range of triplets scores for the 1,000 randomly generated trees and indicates that similarities between housing styles and language cognates were no more similar than would have been expected by chance alone. In contrast, only two triplets were resolved differently between the housing and general language tree—this falls outside the range of triplets measures for the 1,000 random trees and indicates that there has been some general congruence between housing traditions and overall language history. These results therefore suggest the existence of some general historical congruence between the tree built from language traits housing and the general language tree. However, these results should also be interpreted with caution because the cognate tree has many more resolved nodes and contains a much stronger branching signal than the general language tree, which has fewer resolved nodes.

Note 5. Coast Salish Plank Houses: Matrix-Based Analyses

Following the pilot study of Jordan and Mace (2008:45–46), several measures of geographic and language distance were generated, each reflecting local opportunities for interaction and contact over land and via sea travel, as well as different ways of measuring intergroup locations and language similarity. These measures were converted into matrices as follows, and formed the basis of Mantel tests (Mantel 1967; and see chapter 2):

- *Salish Plank House Styles*. The binary data set described in note 2 was converted into a 9 × 9 similarity matrix using SPSS and the Jaccard measure (Shennan 1997).
- *Proximity*. Linear point to point "as the crow flies" distances were measured from Barnett's (1955) base map of tribal locations (and see figure 4.1).

- *Sea Distances.* Shortest "as the canoe sails" sea distances were also measured from Barnett's (1955) base map (and see figure 4.1).

- *Ring Distances.* Barnett's (1955) map of seasonal exploitation areas suggests Salish communities' primary seasonal migrations (and see figure 4.1) were along the coast rather than across the straits, and patterns of movement and community-to-community interactions may have generated a "ring" of cultural exchanges around the edges of the gulf rather than directly across it. These ring distances were measured by calculating the least number of communities between each ethnolinguistic group and the others when moving around the coastline, generating a full distance matrix. For example, Sanetch are three groups along the coast from Pentlach (moving clockwise) and four groups from BI Comox (moving anti-clockwise around the Gulf of Georgia).

- *C-Distances.* Both Barnett (1939:224–25) and Kroeber (1939b) note the "remarkable" break in the similarity of social and material culture of Salish communities on the northern and southern ends of Vancouver Island, between the Pentlach and the Nanaimo (see figure 4.1)—this generates a pattern of cultural similarities around the Gulf of Georgia that can best be envisaged as a reversed C-shape. A matrix of C-distances was calculated in a similar way to the ring distances (see previous), except that in this case, it was not possible to cross the cultural "gap." For example, the Sanetch are still four communities away from BI Comox, but the gap between Nanaimo and Pentlach means that the Sanetch are now six communities away from Pentlatch because they have to go anti-clockwise around the gulf.

- *Language Cognates.* This matrix was calculated using two hundred items of "core" Salish vocabulary drawn from Jorgensen (1980:75), with the original data from Swadesh (1950). Data for Cowichan were not available, so it was assumed that they shared eighty items of core vocabulary with the Nanaimo, because both spoke dialects of the same language. The Nanaimo figures were also used to measure language similarities between Cowichan and the other Salish groups. Among the Comox dialects a figure of seventy shared items was used.

- *General Language.* This matrix was based on current linguistic consensus about the historical relationships between the Gulf of Georgia languages and dialects (Goddard 1996), taking account of evidence for historical borrowing as well as vertical branching descent (see table 4.1). Groups were assigned 95 percent similarity in the matrix if they spoke a dialect of the same language (e.g., Nanaimo and Cowichan speak dialects of Halkomelem language and so scored 95 percent; the speakers of Comox languages also scored 95 percent). If groups spoke different Salish languages they were allocated 50 percent.

Using these matrices, pairwise Mantel tests were employed (see appendix) to measure the degree of correlation between geography and Salish housing styles. The strongest pairwise correlations were with C-distance measures, which accounted for 34 percent of variability in housing styles, while others correlations were much weaker (proximity: 10 percent; sea distances: 10 percent; ring distances: 16 percent). The language cognates had the stronger correlations with housing at 35 percent, with only a 19 percent correlation with general language. From the base map (figure 4.1), it is clear that Salish groups located close to one another also tended to speak similar languages, and partial correlations were performed in order to tease apart the individual and combined effects of language and geography on housing styles. These tests focused on the language cognates matrix and the C-distances because these had the strongest pairwise correlations out of all the measures. Language cognates alone accounted for 12 percent of variability and C-distances alone also accounted for a further 12 percent, with 23 percent made up of the combined effects of Language cognates and C-distances, all accounting in total for 47 percent of the variation in Salish housing styles.

Note 6. Salish Canoe Making: An Expanded Data Set

Barnett's (1939:238–40) records of Salish canoe-making traditions were carefully edited to remove any lines with missing data, generating a full presence/absence matrix consisting of sixty cultural traits over the nine ethnolinguistic groups (table 4.1). With so many aspects of boat-making a highly personalized corpus of "secret" knowledge that was generally inherited vertically from fathers to sons, or at least, within generations of the same family, the canoe data set was expanded to include details of the production sequence, including the toolkits used (i.e., wedges, mauls, hammers, and adzes), through to construction methods and canoe forms, and finally to associated equipment and boat fittings.

Note 7. Salish Canoe-Making: Network- and Tree-Based Analyses

The data were converted into a NEXUS file and analyzed in NeighborNet (4.10). The plot has boxed sections indicative of conflict and hybridization, but at the same time, there are clear branching structures in the data set, pulling out three main clusters: in the upper sections of the plot, Pentlach and CR Comox appear to share many canoe traits and pull out alone; the lower Vancouver Island groups of Sanetch, Cowichan, and Nanaimo also pull out to the right; the four northern groups pull out to the lower left. In this plot, mainland groups are all pulled downward and to the left, while the island groups are split away toward the top and to the right of the plot.

Next, the canoe data were analyzed in PAUP* 4.0b10 to assess the strength of this branching signal. A heuristic search was performed, with Squamish again set as the outgroup. This generated three trees that were converted into a strict consensus tree—this was bootstrapped at 1,000 replications, and only branches with more than 50 percent support were retained. This generated a final tree consisting of a large number of resolved clades (figure 4.10): rooted with Squamish, all groups other than the TI Comox branch away on a large clade. Within this large clade all the island groups branch away again, leaving the mainland BI Comox and Sechelt behind. Within this island clade Pentlach and CR Comox form a further, final clade. These patterns appear to indicate that canoe-making traditions were highly coherent at the scale of the ethnolinguistic populations and that they may have evolved via a branching process of phylogenesis, a conclusion supported by the RI statistic of o.62.

Note 8. Coast Salish Canoes: Co-Transmission Analyses

The presence of the branching signal opened the way for testing whether canoe traditions exhibited historical congruence with Salish languages. Using Kishino-Hasegawa tests, a search for new best-fit tree for canoes was constrained first with the cognate-based language tree, and second by the general language tree (figures 4.6). In both cases, the new trees generated by the constrained searches were significantly different from the original best-fit canoe tree, indicating that there had not been perfect congruence between the tree built from canoe traits and the trees recording language history. More general historical associations were measured in COMPONENT 2.0. The triplets scores between 1,000 randomly generated trees ranged between 12 and 82. Triplets measures taken between the original canoe tree and the tree for cognates were 48, and with the general language history tree were 16. This indicates that there was no greater similarity between the tree built from canoe-making traits and the trees of language history than would be expected by chance alone—in short, canoe-making traditions and language appear to have had entirely separate histories in this region, with no evidence for historical congruence.

Note 9. Coast Salish Plank Houses: Matrix-Based Analyses

General correlations among canoe-making traditions, geography, and language were assessed with Mantel (1967) tests. These employed the same sets of language and distance matrices that were used in the housing study, plus a new matrix recording similarity in canoe-making traditions between the ethnolinguistic groups (see note 5, previous). Pairwise correlations with both language measures were weak, just 1 percent for cognates and even less for general language (see appendix). Correlations with geography were somewhat higher, with 7 percent of variability accounted for by proximity, 2 percent by sea distances, 18 percent for ring distances, and 6 percent for C-distances. Partial correlations were then performed using the strongest pairwise correlations—cognates and ring distances. The results suggested that 3 percent were accounted for by cognates alone, plus a further 21 percent explained by the independent effects of ring distances, with no combined effects, generating 24 percent of canoe-making variation accounted for.

Note 10. Basketry and Matting: Data Set

Barnett's (1939) survey records regional-scale variability in both local bark and rushmatting (1939:242) and basketry techniques (1939:249–50), which include the use of twining, coiling, twilling, or checker-work methods and the production of a range of basic forms and types, for example, water baskets, carrying baskets, storage baskets, and general rush bags, plus details of the range of raw materials employed. Lines with any missing data were removed, generating a list of forty traits. Information on BI Comox traditions was missing entirely, so this group were not included in the study. This generated a list of forty traits that were recorded in presence/absence format across the remaining eight ethnolinguistic groups.

Note 11. Basketry and Matting: Network- and Tree-Based Analyses

The data matrix was converted into NEXUS format and analyzed in Neighbor-Net in order to assess whether there were any branching signals in the data set (see chapter 2). The resulting plot (figure 4.13) broadly maps the communities' relative geographic locations: southern groups are pulled away to the right and lower right sections of the plot, while northern groups pull out to the left and upper left portions of the plot. For many groups the branch lengths are very short, indicating little overall difference in local basketry/matting traditions; only Pentlach and Sanech appear to have substantially different traditions because these groups are pulled out much further. In addition, there are large boxed sections at the center of the plot, indicating high levels of hybridization and a relatively weak signal for branching transmission.

The data set were also analyzed in PAUP* 4.0b10 (figure 4.13), with Squamish again assigned as the outgroup. A heuristic search returned four trees that were converted into a strict consensus tree and bootstrapped at 1,000 repetitions, with only clades with more than 50 percent support retained. This generated a tree with only two resolved clades, one including groups in the north of the island, Pentlach and CR Comox, and another including groups living in the north of the mainland, TI Comox and Sechelt (see figure 4.1). The RI statistic was also only 0.50, indicating that processes other than branching transmission had generated variability in local basketry and matting styles. On the basis of these results it was concluded that this craft exhibited little coherence at the scale of the ethnolinguistic populations and had probably been affected by rapid innovation and intense hybridization. This lack of evidence for a branching signal in the basketry/matting data also meant that tests for co-transmission (historical congruence) with language history were not worth performing.

Note 12. Basketry and Matting: Matrix-Based Analyses

Mantel tests measured general correlations between the same distance and geography matrices used previously, plus a new matrix for basketry and matting (see appendix). For language, the strongest pairwise correlations were with cognates, which accounted for 18 percent of variability, while general language accounted for only 9 percent. For geography, proximity had the strongest correlation with matting and basketry at 13 percent, while correlations with the distance measures were much weaker (sea distances: 7 percent; ring distances: 9 percent; C-distances: 6 percent). Partial correlations used the strongest pairwise correlation measures for geography and language and indicated that 6 percent of variability in basketry and matting was accounted for by cognates alone, with a further 1 percent accounted for by proximity alone, with 12 percent resulting from their combined effects, giving an overall 19 percent of variability accounted for.

Note 13. Coast Salish Plank-Houses, Canoes, and Language:
Co-Transmission Analyses

In order to test for co-transmission between multiple craft lineages and language (see chapter 2), the strict consensus trees for housing and canoes (figures 4.5 and 4.10; and see previous), plus the two language trees (figure 4.6) were all loaded into COMPONENT 2.0. Triplets measures for 1,000 randomly trees ranged between 12 and 82. The trees for housing and canoe-making traditions had thirty-nine triplets resolved differently, which was within this range, indicating that the two trees shared no more similarity that would be expected by chance alone, and that the two crafts had entirely different branching histories. For this reason, a Kishino-Hasegawa test, which identifies perfect co-transmission, was not carried out. In addition, a Mantel test indicated a very low pairwise correlation between the matrix of housing and canoe-making of only 4 percent (see appendix), further suggesting that the two crafts had very different histories of transmission. Finally—and as noted previously—canoe-making traditions appear to exhibit no historical congruence with Salish language (either measured as cognates or in terms of more general language history, figure 4.6), while housing traditions may exhibit some degree of historical congruence with general language history (but not with the tree based on cognates—see previous and figure 4.6).

CHAPTER 5

Northern California

This chapter builds on the preceding case study and also examines general coherence and deeper historical congruence in material culture traditions, but aims develop a series of more comparative insights into the ways in which social institutions serve to structure local propagation of cultural traits in areas of higher linguistic diversity.

Macroscale cultural evolution is examined in three different material culture traditions that are practised by large numbers of different ethnolinguistic communities: basketry, housing, and ceremonial dress. However, the evolution of each of these traditions is examined in two contrasting parts of California, the Northwest and the interior Northeast, each region differentiated by very different systems of kinship, territoriality, and ceremonialism. These contrasting social institutions appear to structure propagation of the material culture traditions in very different ways, generating divergent patterns of evolution.

The chapter opens with a general ethnographic description of the wider region and then examines the main cultural differences between the Northwest and Northeast areas of California. The evolution of material culture within each local regional setting is then analyzed in turn. The results indicate that each of the three traditions is being propagated differently. In addition, there are also major contrasts in the ways in which even broadly similar traditions are evolving within each of the two regions. For example, very similar basketry and also ceremonial dress traits are shared widely across much of the Northwest region, while the greater territoriality in the Northeast leads to greater local coherence in these traditions, and also greater historical congruence with language, perhaps due to the operation of TRIMs (Durham 1992; chapter 1) in these communities. Differential propagation of housing traits also leads to contrasting patterns of evolution in the two regions.

The final section attempts to draw out some deeper insights into the ways in which variability in social institutions structures local patterns of material culture evolution. The insights from this chapter pave the way for a general cross-cultural discussion that forms the content of the final concluding chapter.

NORTHERN CALIFORNIA: THE REGIONAL SETTING

Northern California is an ideal setting for this kind of comparative analysis: the lifeways, languages, and material culture traditions of its hunter-fisher-gatherer communities has been systematically documented (Driver 1939; Kroeber 1939c; Voegelin 1942; and see Heizer 1978; Jorgenson 1980, with references). This detailed body of ethnographic data provides rich opportunities to study how propagation of broadly similar kinds of technological tradition are embedded in strongly contrasting social institutions. In addition, the region's high levels of linguistic diversity also make it possible to examine patterns of historical congruence in cultural traditions among groups speaking an enormously different range of languages (see note 1).

Environment and Adaptation

The Northwest California environment is highly diverse, with high rainfall, abundant redwood and pine-fir timberland, and local concentrations of small game and acorn groves, and some of the richest fishing rivers in California, including the Klamath, Trinity, and Eel Rivers (figure 5.1). In contrast, Northeast California is mainly moderate- to high-elevation mountain country. The region includes several major drainages, including the upper Klamath basin, and its major Trinity River tributary, which wind through the Klamath Mountains, and also the Sacramento River drainage, which forms the upper northerly reaches of the Great Central Valley and cuts through the Cascade Range of mountains from the high Modoc Plateau. Most of the area was timberland, consisting of pine, Douglas fir, or juniper. The Sacramento valley also included gallery forest rich in acorns, and the main river and some of its

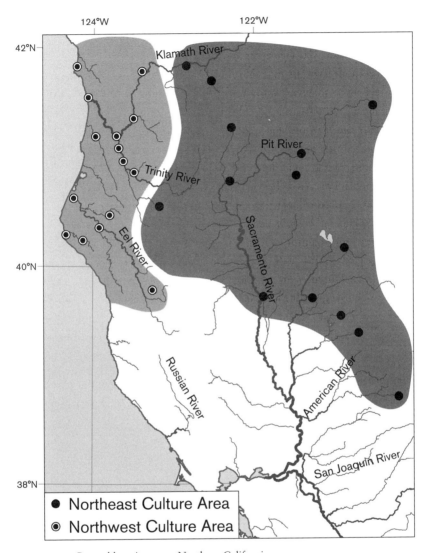

FIGURE 5.1 General location map: Northern California.

Geographic locations of the major salmon rivers in Northern California and the twenty-nine ethnolinguistic populations examined in this chapter. These populations have been grouped into a Northwest Culture Area and a Northeast Culture Area. For further details, see main text.

larger tributaries also produced abundant salmon (Baumhoff 1978:19; and see Bettinger and Wohlgemuth 2006; Hildebrandt and Carpenter 2006:284).

At contact, Northern California was densely populated with communities sharing a common economic focus on hunting, fishing and gathering in the region's rich and varied ecosystem. The larger rivers were rich in fish, especially salmon, there was good ungulate hunting, and a wide range of wild plant resources, primarily acorns and edible roots (Fagan 2003; figure 5.1). The balance between the different branches of the economy varied locally, for example, salmon were of great economic importance on the Klamath and its major tributaries, as well as on the Sacramento River, while hunting was of greater importance higher in the drainages and in the uplands (Baumhoff 1978:16; Heizer 1978; Jørgensen 1980; Kroeber 1925). Processing and storage technologies transformed these seasonally available resources into year-round staples, especially acorns (Bettinger and Wohlgemuth 2006:274–77; 280–82). The intensive use of acorns appears to have started already around 2,500–3,000 years ago, and was followed by exploitation of other seeds about 1,200–1,000 years ago. During the ethnographic period, the acorn economy enabled some of the highest localized population concentrations ever recorded for hunter-gatherers, although at a cost of spectacular investments of female labour, amounting to around five hours of work per day to feed a family of just four (Bettinger and Wohlgemuth 2006:276–77; Fagan 2003:130–46).

Cultural and Linguistic Diversity

The rich Californian environment also attracted many different populations to the region, generating enormous linguistic diversity (Baumhoff 1978: Kroeber 1925; Shipley 1978). Current consensus suggests that there were a series of repeated migrations, each bringing new families of languages into the area. Centuries of cultural interactions eventually resulted in a number of linguistic isolates, for example, the Chimariko language, which was surrounded by more recently arrived languages (Shipley 1978; Silver 1978). Na-Dene languages, whose ultimate origins lie far to the north, are thought to the most recent arrivals and tend to cluster in Northwest California and Oregon.

Across Northern California, the diversity in language was also reflected in high levels of cultural diversity, albeit around a common focus on exploitation of salmon, deer and acorns (Heizer 1978; Jorgenson 1980:

Kroeber 1925). This ethnographic variability has been classified in different ways, often via economic criteria (e.g., see Hildebrandt and Carpenter 2006:285–99). For example, Kroeber and Barrett (1960:1) argued that the Yurok, Karok and Hupa, who lived on the lower Klamath, Trinity, and Salmon Rivers, were the exemplars of a northwest Californian "climax" cultural formation (Kroeber 1925:105). As Jorgenson notes (1980:262), these groups exhibited a unique and independent form of coastal and riverine life in the wet forests and oak woodland environments of Northwest California, with few directly discernable influences from the coastal groups living further to the north (Jorgenson 1980:92; Kroeber 1925). Surrounding these cultures were other groups, including the Tolowa, Chilula, and Wiyot, all of whom shared many features of the Northwest "climax" cultures (Heizer 1978).

Based on different subsistence practices, Kroeber and Barrett (1960) divided local groups into "riverine" and "littoral" peoples. Crowded along the rich salmon grounds were the "riverine" Yurok, Hupa, and Karok, and to some extent, the Chilula. In contrast, the Tolowa, Coast Yurok, and Wiyot lived along the along beaches, rocks and headlands of the immediate shoreline. As "littoral" tribes they practised a range of specialized fishing methods. Transport across the region was easy, and there was frequent interactions between these coastal and riverine peoples, generating broad cultural commonalities across the area.

Kroeber and Barrett's (1960) classification also extends further to the South and East of the region. Forming a kind of cultural "buffer" zone between the Northwestern littoral/riverine groups, on the one hand, and the cultures of the interior Californian drainages on the other, were several communities exhibiting what were regarded as "lesser" features of the Northwest California culture area, combined with increasingly strong cultural influences from Central California. These intermediate groups included the Mattole, Nongatl, Lassik, Sinkyone, Wailaki, and Cahto who lived to the south of the Klamath River, as well as the Chimariko, hill-dwelling Northern Wintu and some Shasta groups of the interior.

Finally, much further to the East and Southeast, occupying the upper Klamath and the barren high plateaux, and extending into the upper Eastern Sacramento valley, were other foraging communities with a culture more akin to Central California. The Achomawi, Atsugewi, and additional groups of Shasta and Wintu occupied the north, while the Maidu and Nisenan inhabited the upper eastern reaches of the Sacramento River and one of its main tributaries the Eel River.

Settlement and Mobility

A major consequence of the varied ecology, elevation, and drainage was the uneven distribution and concentration of resources over the landscape. Local hunter-gatherer communities adjusted their subsistence and mobility regimes accordingly, with groups on the main rivers residing in more permanent village and generally more reliant on fishing, while others, often upstream, were much more mobile and relied more heavily on hunting and on gathered resources. This meant that while overall population density in the region was relatively low, there was "extreme crowding" along the best fishing rivers like the Klamath and Trinity Rivers (Baumhoff 1978:19). On the Sacramento drainage, however, the exploitation of fish was of "major" rather than "paramount" importance (1978:16). In this way, the neat tribal "areas" depicted in many ethnographies of the region (e.g., Heizer 1978:ix) mask more complex local patterns of residential and logistical mobility between base camps and outlying areas.

REGIONAL VARIATION IN NORTHERN CALIFORNIA SOCIAL INSTITUTIONS

It is also important to note that beyond these general patterns, ethnographers have also emphasized the tremendous local variation in the relative balance of the underlying salmon-deer-acorn economy, and also in the apparently arbitrary ways in which populations appear to have adapted to their local environments through a wide range of social and institutions and ceremonial complexes (Jorgenson 1980:130). Although all the tribes in California obtained some food resources via trade with neighbors or via negotiated access to the resources used by other groups, the land was certainly not subject to free and open general access.

In fact, a recurrent feature of landscapes in northern California was the dense, predictable and eminently *defendable* resources (Kelly 1995; Smith 2001; and see chapter 1), and these gave rise to complex local ownership regimes and the fractionation of property rites (Jorgenson 1980:136). While the ways in which these property rights were articulated varied widely, a basic distinction can be drawn between systems based on *private* ownership that prevailed along the main rivers of the Northwest, and those based on a more communal or "tribelet" model of territoriality, that prevailed in other parts of the region. These two regimes, in turn, appear to find further expression in the distinctive ceremonial complexes that were recorded in Northern California, first, the

"World Renewal Ceremonies" of the Northwest, and second, the Big Time festivals recorded in areas occupied by tribelets.

Private Ownership and "World Renewal" Rites (Northwest "Climax" Area)

In this area the local rivers were so rich in fish that there was probably an overabundance of resources. The wealth of the rivers and their key fishing sites (weirs and rapids suitable for A-net fishing) were combined with a unique series of property rights upheld by the force of intercommunity law (Kroeber and Barrett 1960:3). In short, ownership was at the *private* household level, and richest fishing and hunting sites were not owned communally by a larger social unit. For example, fishing rights were primarily held on an *individual* level, or jointly by several people who rotated usage. These rights amounted to personal property of "real and recognized value" and they could be sold, inherited, traded or bought for standard units of currency, for example, one good fishing site might be worth 3 strings of dentalia money (Kroeber and Barrett 1960:3).

A number of ethnographers have also commented on the unique "political" landscapes that emerged along these crowded rivers (Fagan 2003:242), generally describing them as an "anarchic" world where there were more resources than anyone could process, store or use, and where the only route to increased status and self-advancement was not through basic subsistence activities, but through haggling, negotiation, and in particular, through transactions in "treasures." These valued items included shells, woodpecker scalps and especially the large obsidian bifaces that traded over long distances from sources in the interior (see below; and see Fagan 2003:157–68). One of the major opportunities for transacting and accumulating this status-defining wealth was through negotiation of bride-price.

In contrast, treasures accumulated by wealthy individuals could only be displayed at major ritual events but never actually exchanged at them. In the "climax" areas of Northwest California such ceremonials formed a unique and coordinated constellation of activities, where the "straggling and anarchistic Karok, Yurok and Hupa hamlets shared common obligations to propitiate salmon, acorns and deer, to enrich the world and make it whole, and to foster good health" (Jorgenson 1980:263). These large, collective ceremonies were inherently inclusive and the "world-renewal theme . . . was an obligation of people from many communities and many language groups, people who competed for ownership and control over resources" (Jorgenson 1980:263). In this way, the Karoks, Yuroks, Wiyots, Hupas, Tolowas, Chilulas—all speaking different and often unrelated languages—created a "tight ceremonial world that underscored their common purposes rather than their differences" (1980:263: figure 5.2). Interestingly, however, this highly inclusive ceremonialism actually served to mask the highly individualistic nature of their more routine social and economic institutions (1980:264).

Collective Ownership, Boundary Defence and Big Times (Tribelet Areas)

Outside these areas of Northwest climax culture the most important resource sites were not owned privately, but held and defended collectively by tribelets, which formed discrete social units (Kroeber 1932:258; Jorgenson 1980:131–37, 143). These property rightswere also reflected in the ritual sphere, where the "development of tribelets as boundary-defending units was most simply demonstrated in ceremonial events known as Big Times (1980: 265). These rituals included members of the local tribelet community, as well as guests that were deliberately invited in from surrounding tribelets. Being a guest at such events was a rather intimidating experience as many often felt scared and threatened by the power of the local shamans that ran the events, and so looked to the local chief as a source of spiritual protection. As a result, the dynamics central to the holding of Big Time events emphasized inter-tribelet differences, yet also provided an opportunity for sustaining formalized contacts between neighbouring communities. Relative group distinctions and loyalties were reinforced, and also served to redefine the precise land-holding rights of each tribelet group, rendering them beyond challenge. Consequently, the holding of these ceremonial events with potential enemies and interlopers provided a forum for year-to-year negotiation of access and control of resources to be mediated in ways that avoided the higher costs of raiding and outright warfare that might otherwise escalate.

RESEARCH QUESTIONS: SOCIAL INSTITUTIONS, CULTURAL COHERENCE, AND HISTORICAL CONGRUENCE

This broad summary of the cultural and linguistic geography of northern California (figure 5.1) has outlined some of the fundamental differences in local hunter-fisher-gatherer social institutions—in particular, these relate to the highly variable nature of property rights, ceremonial complexes, and territoriality. These institutions would have formed the basic behavioral frameworks within which the routine propagation of material culture traditions would have been embedded.

How would these contrasting institutions have structured the local propagation of these traditions, what kinds of cultural coherence would have emerged, and to what extent would there be historical congruence between material culture traditions and language? For example, Jorgenson makes the explicit point that areas of concentrated, highly productive, and reliable resources would encourage the formation of sharp language divisions among forager communities (Jorgenson 1980:60). Smith (2001:106) has also argued that the salmon streams, shellfish beds, and acorn groves of California are "precisely where we would expect dense and localized populations to evolve considerable linguistic and perhaps cultural diversity" (Smith 2001:108). However, the exact extent to which linguistic diversity was matched by corresponding variability in local technological traditions requires further research.

The question is examined in two case studies, one focusing on groups living within the Northwest Culture Area, and the second investigating the Northeast Culture Area (figure 5.1), with each of these regions defined by a very different range of social institutions. To aid the development of these insights, three sets of analogous traditions are investigated across the two areas: basketry, housing, and ceremonial dress.

CASE STUDY 1: INVESTIGATING MATERIAL CULTURE
DIVERSITY IN NORTHWEST CALIFORNIA

Northwest California: Ethnographic Setting

This first Northwest case study includes the "climax" cultures of Northwest California, as well as the Na-Dene linguistic enclave located further to the south (see figure 5.2). The former includes the Yurok, Karok, and Hupa of the crowded Klamath River, plus several adjacent groups sharing broadly similar variants of this culture. The latter consists of communities speaking Na-Dene languages.

Climax Cultures of Northwest California

The rich salmon rivers of the Northwest have been attracting human settlement for many millennia (Fagan 2003:217–43). By the ethnographic

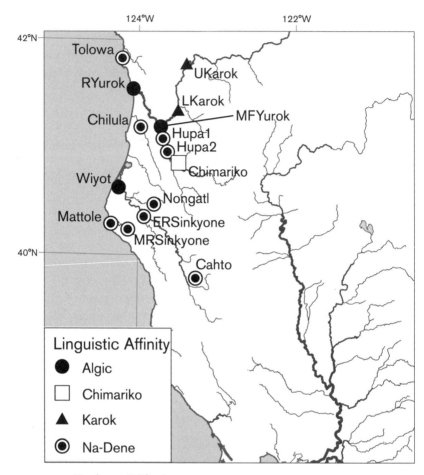

FIGURE 5.2 Northwest California map.

Geographic locations and linguistic affinities of fifteen ethnolinguistic populations living in Northwest California (after Drucker 1939, and see table 5.1).

period, the region was densely settled by a wide range of communities speaking several different languages (figure 5.2). At the very northern edge of coastal California were the Tolowa, who resided along the shoreline and on the Smith River, and spoke a Na-Dene language (Kroeber 1925:121). In the rainy winters they occupied permanent plank-built houses along the coast and trekked inland for hunting game and acorns (Gould 1978:128–30).

Further down the coast, and living on the canyons and gorges of the Klamath River were the Yurok. Here the "superabundance" of fish enabled year-round sedentism in straggling villages (Pilling 1978:137). Although the Yurok had access to almost unlimited fish resources at the mouth of the Klamath River, they resisted exploiting these to the full, perhaps out of fear of reprisals from groups upstream (Baumhoff 1978:19). Yurok society was heavily stratified, and members of elite groups had named house sites and "relished travel and other language skills" (Pilling 1978:141). They had the free and easy relations with all neighbors and shared much material culture, despite the language differences. The region's rivers served as highways with unlimited visiting and intertribal traffic. Nevertheless, the Yurok world appears to have been limited to a 180-mile circle, which was about 12 days travel by canoe, and there was little knowledge of what lay beyond (Waterman 1920 (2003)1993:186).

Upstream from the Yurok were the Karok (figure 5.3), who shared the same distinctive riverine culture, and with whom the Yurok had strong marital ties (Bright 1978:180). As Kroeber detailed, the Karok were "a group so similar to the Yurok in everything but speech," indeed, this extends to their being "indistinguishable in appearance and customs, except for certain minutiae" (Kroeber 1925:97–98). The Na-Dene-speaking Hupa also lived upriver from the Yurok, and in cultural terms, they were equals of both the Yurok and Karok. Importantly, The Hupa differed from other Na-Dene speakers (to the south, see following) in having much higher population density along the banks of the (wider) Trinity River (a major tributary river to the Klamath), which was navigable most of the year (Kroeber 1925:128). The main Hupa exchange partners were the Yurok, and they regularly traded acorns downriver. The family, inhabiting a dwelling house, was the main social unit, although several patrilineally related households sometimes formed a larger informal unit (W. J. Wallace 1978:168).

The Chilula, who also spoke a Na-Dene language, had some southern cultural influences. They relied on the poorer fish resources of the Redwood Creek drainage, so hunting and gathering played a more important role in the local economy (W. J. Wallace 1978:177). They were also "close friends," with the Hupa, but there was little contact with other groups in the area, including the Wiyot (Elsasser 1978c) and Nongatl, although they met the Tolowa at "Yurok dances" (Kroeber 1925:132). The Hupa and Chilula spoke very similar languages, and there is evidence that they recognized a broader language-based kinship with other Na-Dene groups like the Tolowa, whom they called "downstream Hupa speakers," though the languages may not have been mutually intelligible (Golla 1996: 365).

FIGURE 5.3 Ethnographic pictures from Northwest California.

Top: Example of a Karok man ("Little Ike") using a plunge net to fish for salmon in the Klamath River at the end of the nineteenth century. Reproduced courtesy of National Anthropological Archives, National Museum of Natural History, Smithsonian Institution (NAA INV 01138200). There was a "superabundance" of fish in the lower reaches of the river. *Middle:* Wealthy Tolowa man Sam Lopez wearing a red-headed woodpecker scalp headdress and strings of dentalium beads. Reproduced courtesy of National Anthropological Archives, National Museum of Natural History, Smithsonian Institution (NAA Photo Lot 59 (inv. 03393100)). He is holding a traditional painted bow, as well as a large obsidian blade, which was a sign of wealth. Such "treasures" were displayed during World Renewal dances but generally exchanged only in bride-price transactions. *Opposite:* A young Karok woman (probably Phoebe Maddux) making a twined basket at the end of the nineteenth century. Reproduced courtesy of National Anthropological Archives, National Museum of Natural History, Smithsonian Institution (NAA INV 01129300).

FIGURE 5.3 *(Continued)*

The numerically small Chimariko, were linguistic isolates, and formed the "poor" upstream neighbors of the Hupa, occupying a narrow stretch of canyon on the Trinity River (a major tributary of the Klamath). Despite the presence of some marriage contacts, there were recorded hostilities between these groups (Kroeber 1925:109–11). Along the shoreline to the east lived the shore-dwelling Wiyot (Kroeber 1925:117), who exploited the resources of the local marshes, lakes, and streams of the low-lying coastal strip (Elsasser 1978c).

Settlement and Property. Along the steep canyons and high ridges of the Northwest there only narrow strips of land suitable for settlement. As a result, these riverine populations tended to live in long straggling hamlets, where they wielded large A-frame lifting nets, plunge nets and built fish weirs that enabled them extract, process and store large surpluses (figure 5.3, top). These fishing sites were owned privately by individual houses and could be bought, rented and sold for standard currencies, leading to a fractionalisation of property rights (Jorgenson 1980:162–63). In surrounding areas away from the best fishing sites the tendency towards individual or family rights was diminished but did not disappear entirely (Kroeber and Barrett 1960:4). Men also owned gathering sites (i.e. oak trees) and improved hunting area within range of house (Jorgenson 1980:135).

Kroeber and Barrett's (1960:3) analyses also comment on the widespread geographic scattering of household property rights and also suggest the likely mechanisms generating these patterns: "such geographic scattering of ownership was the cumulative result of intermarriage of families, inheritance, payments for wives, wergild, injuries and occasional purchases" (1960:3). Moreover, with so many straggling hamlets packed into the same tight stretches of valley, this fractionation of property rights without political consolidation made settlement boundaries hard to define among the "anarchic" and individualistic families in this densely populated area (Jorgenson 1980:163).

Fish resources were predictable and generally abundant, and so household bartering was motivated by the desire to accumulate goods for increased prestige since they did not need more for survival (Jorgenson 1980:146). Concerns over relative status were widespread—these were anxious, crowded societies with superabundant subsistence resources yet limited supplies of status and prestige. Everything had a price and wealth came to play a "crucial role" in social relations, such that with property rights based around the rights of the individual, and richer men were able to aggregate a group of followers that were indebted to them (Bright 1978:180–81; Kroeber 1925:2, 40; figure 5.3, middle). For example, "all anthropologists who have worked with the Tolowa agree that the principle of acquiring wealth to gain prestige was essential to the whole operation of Tolowa society" (Gould 1978:131), and even in the poorer fishing areas, societies like the Chimariko were based on social status that arose from the acquisition of wealth, like dentalium beads (Kroeber 1925:109–11).

In Northwest California, kinship was primarily patrilineal and patrilocal descent, everything had a price and could be purchased (or compensated for) through use of set currencies and "treasures"—sovereign households were the ultimate property-owning units, and triblets never formed. The extensive trail and river networks of Northern California facilitated long-distance down-the-line trade in many different sorts of exotic items like obsidian, shell-beads, woodpecker scalps and feathers, and these provided the "treasures" and standardised "currencies" with which payments were made and wealth and status acquired (figure 5.3, middle).

Acquiring Property, Connections and Wealth: Marriage and Bride Price. Along the rich coastal strip of Western North America exogamous marriages were desired as an important mechanism for creating formal relationships between autonomous and competing groups that had minimal political organization. In Northwestern California, with its highly developed private property regime, postmarital residence was patrilocal and was linked to unequal bride-groom gift exchanges that were in favour of the bride's family who received "bride price" along with "bride service" where the man lived and worked with her family for a limited period (Jorgenson 1980: 169). These marriage contacts brought significant advantages if pursued strategically, for example, they resulted in valuable political connections and access to a network of scattered property rights, including acorn groves and fishing sites. Consequently, *long-distance* marriages were considered to be "evidence of enterprise and good spirit," whereas marriages closer to home were thought to be "slothful and lacking spirit" (Waterman 1920 (2003):223–4). Among the Tolowa, and other groups, richer men could have more than one wife (W.J. Wallace 1978a). In contrast, poorer men could engage in half-marriages, with residence at the wife's village upon an initial partial payment of bride price, until he could eventually complete the payment and move back to his own community (Gould 1978:131).

In fact, one of the major opportunities for transacting and accumulating status-defining wealth was the lengthy negotiation and payment of bride-price. A number of factors were involved. First, items of material wealth could be used to purchase brides (Figure 5.3, middle). Second, women were economically important in that they made major labor inputs to the household economy, processing acorns and fish; also, they could also produce daughters to be "traded" for bride price later. Prosperous men could eventually obtain several wives, thereby increasing their ability to generate further wealth (Gould 1978:132–3).

This unbalanced gift exchange at marriage generated some unforeseen outcomes. With status defined by differentials in *relative* local wealth, there are repeated accounts of men seeking to secure brides from *distant regions,* so that they could avoid—at all costs—paying their treasures to neighbouring households, which would serve to "close" down the local status gap. In contrast, by obtaining a bride from a more distant village, for example, "a wealthy man avoided paying bride-wealth to affinal kin within his own village. Since there were few wealthy men in any one village, such a man would almost certainly have to marry a woman from a family poorer than his own, thus narrowing the economic gulf between himself and his in-laws (which could undermine his prestige as a wealthy man in his own village)" (Gould 1978:132). As a result of all these factors, men usually aimed to marry "outside" (Kroeber 1925:3). For example, the Yurok "married whom and where they pleased" (ibid. 1925:42), indeed one Yurok polygamist who died around 1859 had wives from Tolowa, Karok, Hupa, and Wiyot communities (Pilling 1978:137). But in contrast to the long-distance postmarital moves undertaken by women, , men tended to stay locally after marriage.

World Renewals and Wealth Display. If marriage negotiations provided an opportunity to acquire wealth, then it was the communal rituals that formed the most important events at which individuals could display their accumulated treasures and signal status. Neither individuals nor households sponsored these "World Renewal" ceremonials; this was done collectively, and so no single person or household was the particular focus of attention in the event. The village holding the feast and dances did not act as specific hosts, even though they were directed by the wealthiest men there. Instead, all households in the community *voluntarily* contributed resources out of a shared desire to "make the world good each year'—there was no duress.

"World Renewal" is a blanket term for several obligations (Kroeber and Gifford 1949:2–3), which included the ritual (re)construction or repair of the sacred timber structure used for the dance; this also served a symbolic model for the rebuilding of the cosmos. New fire was kindled and salmon and acorns were ritually consumed. Each ceremonial was a highly localized event, held in a specific location. This was marked by a special built structure, either a dwelling house, or a hybrid house/sweat house. The symbolic act of repairing or rebuilding this structure at a particular place in the landscape was crucial to each local event. This was a tight ritual world encompassing the Klamath and Trinity Rivers with similar ceremony held at different geographic settings and at different times (figure 5.2; and see maps in Kroeber and Gifford 1949:2).

The public part of the rituals consisted of two world renewal dances, the Jumping Dance and the White Deerskin dance, which lasted between 5 and 10 days (Kroeber 1925:53–62,134–5; Powers 1978:78–9). These dances include regalia that were strictly formalized, but were not sacred, and this involved the display of the most valuable treasures, which were worn and carried in these two dances, for example, head bands of woodpecker scalps, deerskins, especially white ones, which were regarded as treasures, and which together with dentalium consisted the wealth of the tribe (Kroeber and Gifford 1949:4). Also, the flaked knives of obsidian or jasper, some of which were 15 inches long and 3 inch wide, were not properly knives but more like jewellery that was carried aloft at dances sometimes wrapped in skin or cloth to prevent lacerations (Powers 1978:79: figure 5.3, middle). The events gradually built up over several days and at or near the end the most famous treasures were displayed. Rich men handed over their treasures for the dancers to carry and show to the assembled crowds (Kroeber 1925:55; Jorgenson 1980:146).

These dances were actually sponsored by wealthy men (figure 5.3), and enabled them to show their riches off to the wider regional community: "the two dances gave the owners of the regalia their chief opportunity for public ostentation of treasures: they have accordingly been character-ized as "wealth displaying." In contrast, the dancers were little more than "manikins displaying these treasures." In this way, it was rich men who equipped these dance teams of parties or sets, and wealthy friends and contacts also participated from a distance by making reciprocal contribu-tions of dance treasures as they participated as honoured contributors "visiting fifty miles and more away from home" (Kroeber and Gifford 1949:4). In fact, this public display was everything, because it legitimated their status in the wider regional society, and so the spectacle served to "render their possessors illustrious in the eyes of all men" (Powers 1978:79). Women watched but never danced. Importantly, the treasures on display were not only those of the local town hosting the event, but of the whole river, or major stretches of it (Kroeber 1925:54).

However, these treasures were *never exchanged* at the events; the wealthy men did not part with their treasures. Thus, these prestige items were displayed primarily to enhance the positions of the owners and their immediate families. However, this meant that rich men could not display wealth at two places at same time, and so dance rituals were care-fully coordinated (1925:102). This seems to have generated a regional timetable of World Renewal events that enabled the wealthy to compete for, and project, status to a much wider social network, a fact than stands in opposition to their relatively sedentary lives along the narrow river valleys. Interestingly, the otherwise "anarchistic" communities of North-west California ran a set regional program of dances and feasts spaced out over an annual festive cycle, with guests drawn in from far-flung locations for each occasion. Through participation in this ritual program, individuals (and their families) across Northwest California were cer-tainly ranked according to wealth and status, but giveaway potlaches did not occur (Jorgensen 1980: 147; and see chapter 4).

The social scales of the World Renewal events were extensive. For example, at the September World Renewals held by the Karok there was widespread participation, with deputations from the Yurok and Hupa and others; they come in "fleets of canoes, or on foot in joyous throngs along the trails beside the river" (Powers 1978: 28). At the Hupa dances, Yurok and Karok and Hupa and others take part, all recognising each other as equals, and making sure they always sent "deputations to each others' dances" (1978:78). In the core Northwest Californian areas events were carefully co-ordinated so as not to overlap, and there was wide-spread cross-community invitations and participations: "Wiyot, Tolowa, and Chilula people from the coast, and Shastan people from the interior, attended these ceremonies" (Jorgenson 1980: 263). These were enormous events and they integrated communities across the entire region:

> There were about 2500 Yurok; 2000 Karok; 1000 or 1500 Hupa. . . . Some 2000 or 2500 additional Wiyot, Tolowa and Chilula may have participated as occasional dance spectators and contributors of regalia or treasures. This means that the total clientele of the system consisted of fewer than 10,000 individuals—probably around 6000 to 8000. These in turn would comprise 1500 or 2000 adult males; or an average of 120–150 men responsible for the maintenance of each rite. This number is small enough to give almost every man a sense of participation: occasionally in the esoteric ritual, either personally or vicariously through a kinsman; more often as at least a minor contributor of regalia or entertainer of visitors. (Kroeber and Gifford 1949:5)

Through participation in these collective events, the entire region was integrated into a prescribed cycle of ritual activities each marking the first salmon, the acorn harvest, and the plentitude of deer. In these events, the focus was on the good of the general community, the prosperity of individuals and the bountifulness of nature. As a result, the Karoks, Yuroks, Wiyots, Hupas, Tolowas, and Chilulas, all speaking unrelated languages (figure 5.2), created a tight ceremonial world that underscored their common purposes rather than their differences" (Jorgenson 1980:263).

Interestingly, this collective and inclusive ceremonialism actually stood in sharp contrast to their highly individualistic social and economic orders: "World renewal stressed common purposes among many property owners from many localities and speaking many languages" (Jorgenson 1980:264). In summary, communities of the Northwest "shared common obligations to propitiate salmon, acorns and deer, to enrich the world and make it whole, and to foster good health" (1980:263). These world renewal ceremonies were inclusive and the "world-renewal theme . . . was an obligation of people from many communities and many language groups, people who competed for ownership and control over resources" (1980:263).

Na-Dene Enclave for Northwest California

To the south of the broader Northwest California region was a large "enclave" of Na-Dene language speakers, consisting of the Nongatl, Sinkyone, Mattole and Cahto (Baumhoff 1958; Elsasser 1978b; figure 5.2). Although often described as being impoverished marginal communities to the more elaborate "climax" cultures of the Northwest (see above), these groups exhibited many distinctive features, including *tribelet* social organization and Big Times ceremonial complexes (Baumhoff 1958; Elsasser 1978b:191, 202–3; Baumhoff 1958). These were areas of abundant grassland and mountains, with oak and pine-fir forest, and in some areas, chaparral-type vegetation. Fishing was important, with Sinkyone and Mattole primarily reliant on salmon, and Cahto integrating fishing with hunting and gathering. The Sinkyone and Mattole lived on the Mattole River; Sinkyone communities also lived along the upper Eel River, while the Cahto lived on the Eel River (figure 5.2). The Cahto were the most southerly Na-Dene speakers on the Pacific Coast, and Kroeber (1925:154; see also Myers 1978) argued that they were already representatives of another culture, that of north-central California, perhaps due to their being enclosed on three sides by Yukian tribelets (Myers 1978:244).

Although settlements were located along major water courses and the household was the basic social unit, there was not the same degree of emphasis on wealth acquisition as further to the north (Baumhoff 1958: 158; Elsasser 1978b), though bride price remained important (Elsasser 1978b:196). Residence appears to have been largely patrilocal (Myers 1978:245), perhaps with a greater degree of variability in postmarital residence than further north; polygamy was also rare (Baumhoff 1958: 158).

Importantly, in this Na-Dene enclave, society was organized into local "tribelets," which "acted as a homogenous unit in matters of land ownership, reaction to trespass, war and major ceremonies" (Elsasser 1978b:191). Each tribelet possessed a small territory, usually defined by a drainage; this area included a main "town" after which the group was named, as well as some minor settlements and outlying seasonal camps. Leadership was vested in a chief whose authority was recognised by all (Kroeber 1932; and see Baumhoff 1958 for further settlement details; and see Jorgenson 1980:143).

Tribelets also sponsored the Big Times, which were led by a chief and shaman and lasted for several days. Invites were circulated to other tribal leaders, though guests brought their own food, so that there was no asymmetry in gifting and hospitality (Jorgenson 1980: 264). In addition, the events were fewer and much simpler than further north, and lacked much of the more elaborate dance paraphernalia of the Northwest, though other customs and equipment for the events appear to have been adopted from other communities further south; in fact, the Cahto dances and ceremonial customs were very much like the Yuki (Kroeber 1925:148–49; 156). As with many areas of California, the tribelet-based territorial institutions generated highly restricted social worlds in which long-range travel was difficult and even dangerous (Kroeber 1925:145). This contrasted sharply with the more open social networks in areas further to the north where "world renewal" events were celebrated (see previous).

Defining Ethnolinguistic Communities in Northwest California

Ethnographers working in California have used a number of terms to describe local social groups. At the largest scale, a series of "tribes"have been systematically defined, and provides a useful geographic framework for arranging general ethnograhic descriptions since many are also based on language classifications (see Heizer 1978:ix). However, indigenous societies were organized at much smaller social and political scales, and it was these networks that tied together the real fabric of day-to-day existence.

In the present study, the term "ethnolinguistic group" is employed as the primary social "unit" of analysis in the Northwest Culture Area (see figure 5.2 and table 5.1) and equates to the term "population" commonly used in macroscale culture-evolutionary analyses (see chapter 2). These groups are generally much smaller in scale than the "tribes" mapped in Heizer (1978:ix), and each ethnolinguistic group would have been made up of smaller constituent social units. For example, both the Martin's Ferry Yurok and the Requa Yuroket—or the Upper Karok and Lower Karok—can be defined here as *separate* ethnolinguistic groups, but both groups would have been internally made up of the independent households that formed straggling hamlets along the main salmon rivers (Jorgenson 1980:163). Likewise, the Sinkyone can also be subdivided into two smaller ethnolinguistic populations, and each of these would have consisted of a number of small tribelets (table 5.1). For the purpose of the present study, a total of 15 ethnolinguistic groups were selected from Driver's (1939) systematic Culture Element Distribution survey of the Northwest California Culture Area (see table 5.1; figure 5.2).

As noted previously, the language diversity in Northwestern California is particularly high, a result of waves of colonisation by new populations drawn to the region by its rich resources. Languages from Karok, Algic, and Na-Dene families were spoken in the area, in addition to Chimariko, which was a linguistic isolate. Chimariko may be one of the last surviving example of the very earliest languages spoken in the region, while the various Na-Dene languages are accepted to be recent arrivals into the area, and have origins much further to the north (Shipley 1978:81–82). This complex linguistic history can be represented as a well-resolved tree diagram (see below) based on recent consensus classifications of Goddard (1996:4–8).

TABLE 5.1   LINGUISTIC AFFINITIES OF NORTHWEST CALIFORNIAN
ETHNOLINGUISTIC POPULATIONS

Ethnolinguistic Groups	Code	Language	Family
Tolowa	Tolowa	Tolowa	Na-Dene
Chimariko	Chimariko	Chimariko	Isolate
Upper Karok	UKarok	Karok	Karok
Lower Karok	LKarok	Karok	Karok
Martin's Ferry Yurok	MFYurok	Yurok	Algic
Requa Yurok	RYurok	Yurok	Algic
Eel River Wiyot	Wiyot	Wiyot	Algic
Hupa	Hupa1	Hupa	Na-Dene
Hupa	Hupa2	Hupa	Na-Dene
Chilula	Chilula	Chilula	Na-Dene
Nongatl of van Deuzen River	Nongatl	Nongatl	Na-Dene
Mattole	Mattole	Mattole	Na-Dene
Sinkyone (of South Fork of Eel River)	ERSinkyone	Sinkyone	Na-Dene
Sinkyone (of Upper Mattole River)	MRSinkyone	Sinkyone	Na-Dene
Cahto	Cahto	Cahto	Na-Dene

NOTE: After Driver 1939 (and Kroeber 1939a).

Analysis of Northwest Basketry Traditions

In discussing general Californian basketry traditions Kroeber identifies distinct complexes that are practised together (figure 5.4), and that if one part of the complex is abandoned then so is the rest, a phenomenon that "cannot be linked to botanical causes" but only to culture-historical ones (1925: 819). For example, northernmost Californian basketry is entirely twined, and coiling was unknown here (Kroeber 1925:90; figure 5.7). However, coiled basketry was made further to the south, and an important border of styles runs across northern California. For example, in the Northwest, the Yurok twined basketry and that of their neighbors was of the finest ware (figure 5.5). This general twining tradition extended out to the East, and down as far as the Na-Dene enclave as well, where "all basketry followed fairly closely that of Klamath River peoples" (Elsasser 1978b:200), and was "of a wholly northern kind" although the "technique is much less finished than among the Yurok and the ornamentation simpler" (Kroeber 1925:147). Sinkyone baskets were also of a northern type and were entirely twined (Kroeber 1925:146). In contrast, Cahto baskets were very similar to the Yuki baskets of Central California (ibid. 1925:150), but the Cahto, argues Kroeber (1925:154) are already representatives of another culture, that of north-central California, perhaps

Twining Techniques and Nomenclature Used in California Baskets

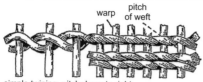

warp | pitch of weft

simple twining, pitch down to right

twining with overlay on one strand, view of exterior; interior is plain

simple twining, pitch down to left

twining with half twist in overlay strand, view of exterior; interior is reserse pattern

three-strand twining, view of exterioir

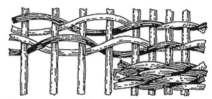

diagonal (twilled) twining

wrapped twining (functional)

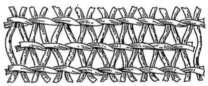

diagonal (twilled) twining, zigzag warp

lattice twining

wicker

Coiling Techniques and Nomenclature Used in California Baskets

interlocked coilnig stitch, one rod foundation, stacked

uninterlocked coiling stitch, two rod and bundle foundation, bunched

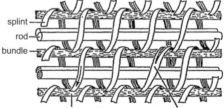

splint
rod
bundle

work surface: sewing awl is thrust through bundle from this side

split stitch

typical stacked foundation

typical bunched foundation

FIGURE 5.4 General basketry techniques.

Summary of main techniques used in Californian basketry. SOURCE: Elsasser 1978a:626, reproduced courtesy of Department of Anthropology, National Museum of Natural History, Smithsonian Institution.

FIGURE 5.5 General Northwest basketry examples.

Some examples of twined basketry styles in Northwest California. *Top row:* Yurok cooking basket (width: 16 cm). Reproduced courtesy of Department of Anthropology, Smithsonian Institution (E411652–0). *Second row down:* Yurok cooking basket (width 18.5 cm). SOURCE: Reproduced courtesy of Department of Anthropology, National Museum of Natural History, Smithsonian Institution (E411612–0). *Third row down:* Yurok cooking basket (width 12.5 cm). SOURCE: Reproduced courtesy of Department of Anthropology, National Museum of Natural History, Smithsonian Institution (E411614–0). *Bottom row:* Yurok cooking basket (width 19 cm). SOURCE: Reproduced courtesy of Department of Anthropology, National Museum of Natural History, Smithsonian Institution (E411687).

due to their being enclosed on three sides by speakers of Yukian languages (Myers 1978:244). Indeed, "Cahto baskets are scarcely distinguishable from those of Yuki manufacture" (Kroeber 1925:155).

Driver (1939: 333–34) undertook a systematic trait-based analysis of basketry traditions in Northwest California, recording variability at the scale of the 15 ethnolinguistic communities described previously (table 5.1; figure 5.2). An edited version of this data set was subjected to culture-evolutionary analysis using the full range of methods described in chapter 2 (see appendix; note 2). While the complex linguistic diversity of the region can be mapped onto a tree diagram (Goddard 1996; figure 5.6), Network and tree-based analyses of basketry data set (figure 5.6; note 3) indicated very little coherence in the basketry traits at the scale of the ethnolinguistic populations—in fact, there appeared to have been intense mixing of traits between these communities and their associated language boundaries, especially within the Klamath River area. These results were supported by a low RI statistic of 0.30. With no evidence for local cultural coherence in basketry traditions, nor for a branching history, tests for historical congruence with language history were not performed. These insights were evaluated further using matrix-based analysis of basketry variability in relation to language and geography (note 4). Proximity had the strongest pairwise correlation (39 percent), while pairwise correlations with language were very weak (less than 1 percent). Partial correlations generated similar results: language alone accounted for 2 percent of variation, while the sole effects of proximity were 42 percent, with no combined effects (see appendix).

On the basis of these results, it was clear that basketry traditions across Northwest California had been affected by a ready mixing of traits, resulting in intensive hybridization among neighbouring ethnolinguistic groups speaking both related but often unrelated languages, especially in the Klamath River area. Here, broadly the same twining traditions (figure 5.5) prevailed over large geographic areas, irrespective of which languages were spoken locally. The only real distinction in local traditions was the practice of coiled basketry (figure 5.4), which was found only in the extreme south of the Na-Dene enclave, with these traits adopted from neighbouring groups (see previous).

Interestingly, basketry was predominantly a female craft (Elsasser 1978a; Heizer 1978; E. Wallace 1978) and appears to have propagated via "vertical transmission" from mothers to daughters (figure 5.3). However, women moved frequently after marriage, and their participation in collective ceremonial events also generated regular contacts with

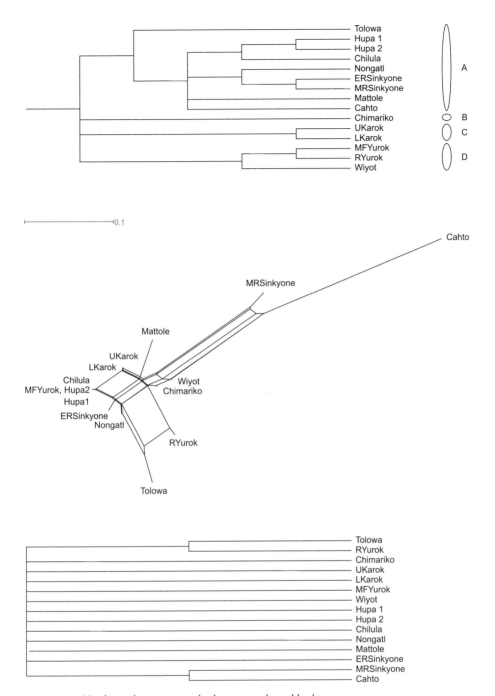

FIGURE 5.6 Northwest language tree, baskets network, and baskets tree.

Top: General language tree for Northwest California (based on Goddard 1996). Groupings A, B, C, and D indicate affinity to the Na-Dene, Chimariko (linguistic isolate), Karok and Algic language families (and see table 5.1). *Middle:* Splitstree NeighborNet network illustrating potential branching and blending relationships among the basketry traditions of fifteen different populations in Northwest California. Based on presence/absence of forty seven basketry traits across fifteen ethnolinguistic populations (see table 5.1 and figures 5.1 and 5.2 for geographic locations and linguistic affinities). *Bottom:* Phylogenetic tree (created by maximum parsimony) of basketry traditions in Northwest California.

other females from across the region (see previous), especially in the Klamath River area (see previous) (Jorgenson 1980:263; Kroeber and Gifford 1949:5; Powers 1978:28). These factors—and especially the distinctive post-marital residence moves made by women—appear to best account for this intense hybridization of basketry styles.

Analysis of Northwest House Traditions

Several types of housing were built in Northwest California. The frame house of the Yurok, Hupa, and Tolowa (figure 5.7; Kroeber 1925:78–80), formed a definite type whose affinity with the larger plank house of the North Pacific coast is sufficiently evident (1925:809). The Karok dwelt in similar rectangular plank houses; the Hupa, like many fishing cultures, also had permanent houses here of a rectangular three-pitch roof structure, including an internal plank-lined pit (W.J. Wallace 1978:167), while the Chimariko had more of an abridged imitation of the style (Kroeber 1925:11; Silver 1978).

Beyond the rectangular plank houses of the Klamath River area, a series of graded changes in architecture start to take place. For example, the plank houses become smaller and are more roughly made, and then bark starts to replace the planks, until eventually the form becomes conical, (Baumhoff 1958:236; Kroeber 1925:809; and see Nabokov and Easton 1989:286–321 for California, and 1989:287–93 for the Northwest). Consequently, the round and conical permanent winter houses of the southern Na-Dene "enclave" stood in stark contrast to the elaborate rectangular plank houses of the Klamath and Smith River peoples, and were dwellings of a "central Californian type" (Kroeber 1925:146) (see example of conical house frame in figure 5.8).

In all areas, was men who owned the house and its site (Jorgenson 1980:135), although currently, there is only limited ethnographic information on the *microscale* transmission of housing traits. It seems likely that younger men would have acquired woodworking skills vertically from fathers and then deployed these skills to construct houses similar to those built by other members of the local community. In the Klamath River area it also seems likely that local housing styles would be subject to some form of prestige bias as builders of new houses sought to compete with, and out-do, their neighbors: established types of housing perceived in any way to be indicative of greater wealth and success may have been the target of repeated copying by other male members of the local community, perhaps generating strong heritability within local tra-

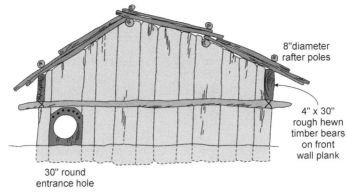

8"diameter rafter poles

4" x 30" rough hewn timber bears on front wall plank

30" round entrance hole

Front Elevation

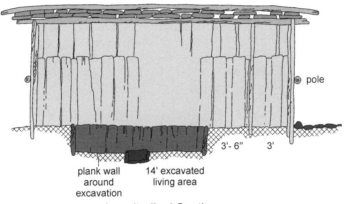

pole

3'- 6"   3'

plank wall around excavation

14' excavated living area

Longitudinal Section

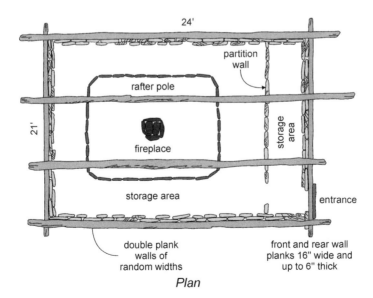

24'

partition wall

rafter pole

21'

storage area

fireplace

storage area

entrance

double plank walls of random widths

front and rear wall planks 16" wide and up to 6" thick

Plan

FIGURE 5.7 Northwest plank house example.

Schematic diagram of a Yurok plank house. This architectural style was common in the northern part of the Northwest Culture Area, especially on the lower Klamath River (figures 5.1 and 5.2). Source: redrawn from Nabokov and Easton 1989:291.

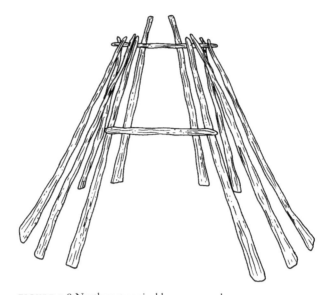

FIGURE 5.8 Northwest conical house example.

General example of the kind of interior framework used in conical houses built in some of the southern parts of Northwest California region (figures 5.1 and 5.2). These were often covered in bark slabs. SOURCE: redrawn from Nabokov and Easton 1989:305.

ditions, and also distinctive microstyles, at the scale of the ethnolinguistic groups.

Driver's (1939: 317–20) systematic systematic survey of house-construction methods was edited into a trait-based data set (note 5) and investigated using the range of methods outlined in chapter 2. Network- and tree-based analyses (figure 5.9) indicated very strong cultural coherence at the scale of the ethnolinguistic groups, and also a strong branching signal, which was confirmed by an RI statistic of 0.90—the clearest evidence that these traits had evolved via branching processes appeared

FIGURE 5.9 (*Opposite*) Northwest housing network and housing tree.

Top: Splitstree NeighborNet network illustrating potential branching and blending relationships among the housing traditions of different populations in Northwest California. Based on presence/absence of fifty-six housing traits across fifteen ethnolinguistic populations (see table 5.1 and figures 5.1 and 5.2 for geographic locations and linguistic affinities). *Bottom:* Phylogenetic tree (created by maximum parsimony) of housing traditions in Northwest California. Ethnolinguistic populations in group A fall into the area of World Renewal ceremonies, while group B includes populations that hold Big Time events.

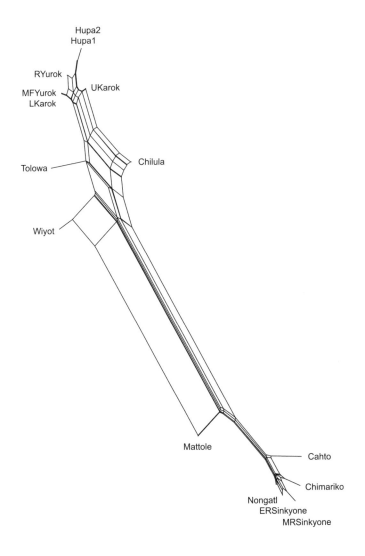

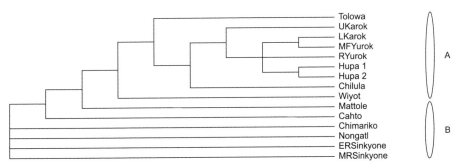

to be among the plank-house traditions of the Klamath River area (note 6). However, tests for historical congruence between these housing traditions and language history (using the language tree in figure 5.6) indicated that each had separate histories in the region (note 7). Matrix-based correlations among housing, language, and geography indicated that the strongest pairwise results were with proximity (27 percent) and not language (only 2 percent). Partial correlations attributed only 1 percent of variability to the independent effects of language, but 26 percent to proximity, with the combined effects of language and proximity adding only a further 1 percent (see appendix; note 8).

On balance, these combined results indicate that housing traits had formed coherent entities at the scale of the ethnolinguistic groups, and that these entities had evolved via branching processes, especially among neighbouring groups in the multilingual Klamath River area (figure 5.2), although there was no apparent congruence between the histories of these housing traditions and language.

Analysis of Northwest Ceremonial Dress

The salient features of Northwest ceremonial life have been discussed previously. Driver undertook a survey of the garments and regalia used at these local ceremonial events (Driver 1939:331–33; and see figure 5.10). There is little direct evidence of how these styles were acquired and transmitted, though it seems likely that both men and women were involved in the acquisition of raw materials and the preparation of the actual garments and decorations. Some degree of conformity bias in the garments and regalia used in the collective and highly inclusive ceremonial complexes of Klamath River area does also seem highly likely as rich men from a wide range of geographic and linguistic backgrounds would have sponsored teams to perform the same sets of standardised dances, and also to display the same kinds of commonly acknowledged currencies (see figure 5.3). In the Na-Dene tribelet areas, where Big Times were held, this kind of conformity bias seems less likely, and more localized microstyles may therefore have emerged.

An edited version of Driver's (1939:331–33) data set (note 9) was subjected to network- and tree-based analyses (note 10). This suggested that ceremonial dress traits recorded among the groups celebrating "World Renewal" in the Klamath River were all rather similar, while those of the groups living outside this area exhibited more localized coherence at the sale of the ethnolinguistic communities (figure 5.11).

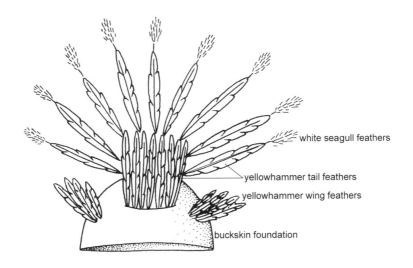

white seagull feathers

yellowhammer tail feathers

yellowhammer wing feathers

buckskin foundation

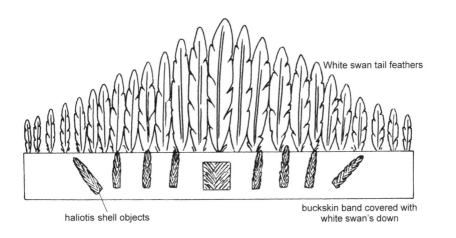

White swan tail feathers

haliotis shell objects

buckskin band covered with white swan's down

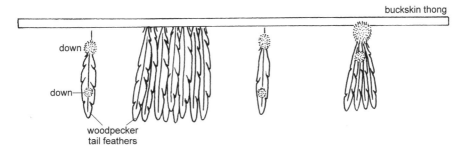

buckskin thong

down

down

woodpecker tail feathers

FIGURE 5.10 Northwest ceremonial dress examples.

Some general examples of ceremonial dress items used in Northwest California. Source: redrawn from Driver 1939:395.

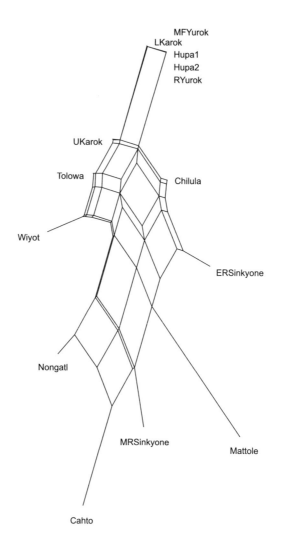

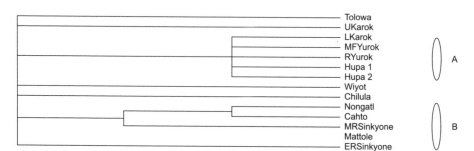

FIGURE 5.11 Northwest ceremonial dress network and ceremonial dress tree.

Top: Splitstree NeighborNet network illustrating potential branching and blending relationships among the ceremonial dress traditions of different populations in Northwest California. Based on presence/absence of thirty-two ceremonial dress traits across fourteen ethnolinguistic populations (see table 5.1 and figures 5.1 and 5.2 for geographic locations and linguistic affinities). *Bottom:* Phylogenetic tree (created by maximum parsimony) of ceremonial dress traditions in Northwest California. Ethnolinguistic populations in group A form the epicenter of the collective World Renewal Ceremonies, while the Big Time events are more important for populations in group B.

However, the overall RI score was 0.51 and indicated that processes other than branching had been operative. Tests for congruence (note 11) indicated that there was no evidence for language and ceremonial dress traditions having had a shared history. General correlations between language and geography were also investigated (note 12): pair wise correlations with language were weak (<1 percent), but stronger for proximity (27 percent), while pairwise correlations indicated that 4 percent of variability was accounted for by language alone, and 31 percent by proximity alone, with no combined effects (see appendix).

These combined results appear to indicate that ceremonial dress traits have been propagated very differently in different parts of the Northwest region. For example, there appeared to have been substantial mixing of traits within the multilingual epicenter of the World Renewal rituals in the Klamath River area, but the emergence of greater local coherence at the scale of the local ethnolinguistic groups, and a stronger branching signal, in the Na-Dene enclave located to the south, where Big Times ceremonials were held. Overall, proximity appeared to have had the greatest effect on general similarity in cultural traits between groups, with very low correlations with language. Finally, there was no evidence for historical congruence between these ceremonial dress traditions and language (figure 5.6).

Summary: Coherence and Historical Congruence in Northwest California Cultural Traditions

Given these three sets of results, which of Boyd et al.'s (1997:364–66; and see chapters 1 and 2) four models best characterises macroscale evolution in the material culture traditions of Northwest California (figure 1.3)? First, it is clear that the material culture and languages of the fifteen ethnolinguistic communities have not evolved as isolated "single entities" (1997:365), and that there has been substantial exchange of cultural traits between them, especially in the case of basketry—the "cultures as species" model can therefore be rejected (Model 1). But at the same time, there is evidence of substantial coherence in local traditions, especially in the case of housing traits, for which branching histories can be reconstructed. Thus, the "cultures as collections of ephemeral entities" (Model 4) can also be rejected (1997:366).

Turning now to the two intermediate models (Models 2 and 3), the general lack of evidence for historical congruence between any of the three material culture traditions, or with language history, would appear to indicate that there are no real "core" traditions, but instead, that some coherent cultural entities do emerge and can be subjected to phylogenetic analysis, but only as independent units (note 13). Thus, local cultures are *not* evolving as "hierarchically integrated systems" that include an integrated set of "core traditions" (Boyd et al. 1997:365), but as "assemblages of many coherent units" (1997:365)—these units include housing traditions and ceremonial dress, while basketry appears to exhibit little coherence at the scale of the ethnolinguistic groups, and is perhaps best understood as a more "peripheral element" whose traits are subjected to mixing across the wider region (1997:365). Model 2 therefore best summarizes the evolution of these cultural traditions in the Northwest Culture Area (figure 1.3).

As with the preceding study of Coast Salish material culture (chapter 4), these three contrasting sets of results from Northwest California are important in demonstrating that traits within each of the three material culture traditions are being propagated very differently across the fifteen ethnolinguistic communities. In other words, each specific tradition is embedded in a different way in local interaction networks and social institutions, resulting in each tradition evolving according to its own historical dynamics. But how and why are these differences in local propagation generating such distinctive patterns in cultural coherence and historical congruence?

Table 5.2 works through some of these potential interconnections. As with the Coast Salish case study in the preceding chapter, these results also highlight the importance of gender associations, the wider social institutions within which propagation of traits is embedded, and the extent to which the crafts are individual or more collective social traditions. In fact, one of the most striking patterns is the distinction between the female craft of basketry (linked to long-range mobility of women in relation to bride-price negotiations) and housing, a craft propagated by men (who tend to remain in their local community).

The evolutionary trends in ceremonial dress traditions tend to cross-cut some of these distinctions—the more "collectivist" World Renewal ritual complexes appears to lead to the sharing of similar traits between different ethnolinguistic populations, but the more "separatist" Big Times, which provide a means for managing the heightened concerns over defense of local territorial boundaries (which, in turn, may be acting as TRIMs (Durham 1992; chapter 1), appear to be associated with greater coherence in local styles, and greater cultural differences between these local populations.

Interestingly, these Northwest California results also provide a striking contrast to Northeast California, where very different social institu-

TABLE 5.2 SUMMARY OF CULTURAL INHERITANCE PATTERNS IN THREE "GENDERED" MATERIAL CULTURE TRADITIONS (NORTHWEST CALIFORNIA)

Tradition	Coherence and Historical Congruence	Factors Affecting Local Propagation
Basketry (female/ individual)	Traits unable to form coherent local traditions; history of blending between ethnolinguistic communities, especially between those in closer proximity	Female craft; evidence for some vertical transmission between mothers and daughters; practitioners often move long distances after marriage and carry knowledge of traits with them; an individual craft and no evidence for local conformist bias; regional ethnogenesis in styles
Houses (male /individual?)	Traits form coherent local traditions at scale of ethnolinguistic communities; branching history; no evidence for historical congruence with language	Patrilocal and patrilineal kinship system; houses built and owned by men who tend to stay within the local community
Ceremonial Dress (both genders/ collective)	Contrasting patterns: (1) Klamath River area—traits unable to form coherent local traditions; history of mixing between adjacent ethnolinguistic communities; (2) Na Dene enclave—traits form more coherent local traditions at scale of ethnolinguistic communities; no historical congruence with language (both areas)	Contrasting settings: (1) Klamath River area—traits propagated within World Renewal events as a widely shared cultural tradition; (2) Na Dene enclave—traits propagated on a more local basis within Big Time events that serve as boundary defense mechanisms in tribelet areas

tions prevailed. Material culture evolution in this second region forms the focus of the next comparative case study, which examines broadly similar material culture traditions (basketry; houses; ceremonial dress) in order to generate comparative insights.

CASE STUDY 2: INVESTIGATING MATERIAL CULTURE DIVERSITY IN NORTHEAST CALIFORNIA

Interior Northeast California: Ethnographic Setting

The Northeast was also characterized by high linguistic diversity, but this time with the different language stocks arranged into large geographic

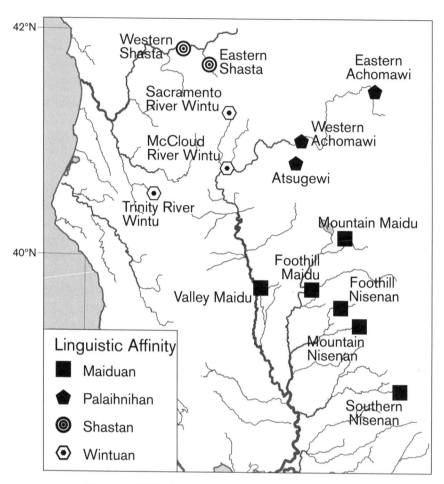

FIGURE 5.12 Northeast California map.
Geographic locations and linguistic affinities of fourteen ethnolinguistic populations living in Northeast California (after Voegelin 1939 [1942]; and see table 5.3).

"blocks" (figure 5.12; table 5.3). Communities living in the interior shared the same broad salmon-deer-acorn adaptation as in the Northwest, though there was less of a primary reliance on fish, which resulted in a more even balance between these different branches of the economy. However, seasonal settlements were still typically located long the best fishing rivers, but there was less of the intense crowding as seen in the Northwest, and along the Klamath River especially (see Fagan 2003:268–94).

For example, the Shasta, Achomawi, and Atsugewi of the far Northeast were predominantly "stream people" and tended to dwell in narrow tracts of drier land interspaced with the extensive bare lava fields. Direct maintenance of cultural borders were less important here as the land became barren beyond these isolated streams, and so there were fewer trips into these empty hinterlands (Garth 1978; Kroeber 1925:305; Olmstead and Stewart 1978). In general then, this part of the Northeast was a much poorer resource area, with fewer salmon streams and acorn oak groves. Deer, rabbits, seeds and roots made up for some of this resource shortfall, and the general culture also tended to be much less elaborate than in the Northwest Culture Area (Heizer and Elsasser 1978:36–7).

Further to the south, the extended Sacramento drainage (figure 5.1 and 5.12), which actually extends right up into Northeast California, also formed a highly variable environment, but one that, overall, had more abundant resources, being rather rich in salmon, acorns, deer, elk and birds, and so in contrast to the previous areas there was never really a problem with food shortages here (Heizer and Elsasser 1978:37–8). Communities here were tightly organized into *tribelets*—these were unique independent political organizations, consisting of a group owning a territory, knowing themselves as a group and acting as a group (Heizer and Elsasser 1978:41). Actually, each tribelet could be made up of several smaller settlements (Kroeber 1925: 396), often consisting of three or four communities living around a central hamlet (Jorgenson 1980:163), with other distinct tribelets located on all sides. For example, among the Wintu the settlements were often quite compact with houses—often semi-subterranean earth houses—plus a main dance house that was larger than the rest (Jorgenson 1980:162). Each tribelet had a chief, and they lived in clustered villages of 250 people located close by one another, so overall there was high population density (Chase-Dunn and Hall 1997:126–27). More generally, tribelets had between 100 and 500 people, and these formed the primary social and political unit (Chase-Dunn and Hall 1997:126–27).

Jorgenson has argued that tribelets emerged as result of newer groups moving into and laying claim to resource areas, which resulted in older social lineages coalescing into tribelets for collective boundary defence (Jorgenson 1980:181–82). Whatever the historical origins of the tribelet system, it had a profound structuring effect of people's ability to travel and interact. With many communities packed into the richer resource areas, strangers arriving unannounced were under immediate suspicion and could suffer lethal violence (Kroeber 1925:308), to the extent that most interior people lived in very small-scale social worlds, with little knowledge, or desire to travel to, regions beyond a few kilometers from their immediate home (Kroeber 1925:395). In this sociopolitical setting individuals were permanently linked into a matrix of kin groups that were embedded in the larger tribelet units, making movement between kin groups and remoter tribelets extremely difficult (Jorgenson 1980:138).

Within these social groupings, two primary patterns of marriage can be identified. First, *most* men married only one wife, and she tended to be from a nearby village and generally from within the same linguistic group, with partners chosen at gatherings of closely adjacent settlements groups (Chase-Dunn and Hall 1997:136). In contrast, higher status families sought to create strategic alliances with more distant tribelets through careful choice of marriage partners: "marriage was an important mechanism in creating formal relations among competitive groups" which otherwise had minimal political organization (Jorgenson 1980:166). As a result, it was only the few headmen that tended to marry women from more distant villages or tribelets; such leaders were also more likely to marry women from different linguistic groups. As multilingualism opened up further contacts and political opportunities, any chance to learn new tribal languages through acquisition of additional wives was highly valued by headmen.

These strategic goals generated a kind of regional elite, all of whom were linked via long-range marriage ties (Chase-Dunn and Hall 1997:127–28,136). But for by far the rest of society the dominant pattern was highly localized marriages and interaction patterns that were grounded firmly within the tribelet. Together, these two factors created social worlds that were "a curious combination of intense cultural localism, in which groups strongly emphasized the superiority of their ways over those of their immediate neighbors, along with larger regional networks, based on linguistic and material ties," a kind of hybrid local/cosmopolitan network based on tribelet territoriality but also headman polygony (Chase-Dunn and Hall 1997:122).

Through these social networks also flowed a vigorous trade in prestige goods, including obsidian and clam shell beads that linked groups via intensive interactions, even though more routine aspects of food production were organized at a household scale (Chase-Dunn and Hall 1997:143). Again, it can be concluded that most raw material and food procurement as well as conflicts over land had "a relatively small spatial scale, with most important interactions occurring within an eighty-kilometer radius of any starting point" and that "more distant interactions were indirect" although "some goods did move very long distances" (1997: 145).

Big Time ceremonials were central feature of inter-tribelet interaction and exchange. A headman would send out runners to neighbouring tribelets and as the leaders arrived they were announced, followed by feasting, dances, and religious ceremonies (Chase-Dunn and Hall 1997:132). The structure of Big Times expressed fundamental distinctions between hosts and guests, stressed continuity of relations among members of the same tribelet, and thereby re-established the collective rights of each groups to exploit their own bounded territories to the exclusion of others (Jorgensen 1980:265). In this way, the events defined and celebrated tribelets as boundary-protecting groups (Jorgensen 1980:264–46) and not the ritual unity of *independent* households scattered over a wide region, as in the World Renewals of Northwest California (see previous).

How did this Northeast social setting—so very different to the "anarchic" Klamath River—affect the propagation of different material culture traditions? In order to explore the dynamic interplay between these social institutions, and the propagation of an analogous set of craft traditions, local basketry, ceremonial dress, and housing traditions were analyzed so that the results could be compared and contrasted with those from the Northwest region.

Defining Ethnolinguistic Communities in Northeast California

Working with Voegelin's (1942) *Culture Element Survey* of Northeast California, fourteen ethnolinguistic populations were selected for this case study, each with detailed data pertaining to their basketry, housing, and ceremonial dress (table 5.4). These groups lived along the rivers and in the uplands of the far northeast, and also around the upper reaches of the Sacramento Valley (figure 5.12); each population would have been made up of a number of constituent tribelets, which in turn would have consisted of smaller hamlets and villages (Kroeber 1925:396; Jorgenson 1980:163).

The Northeast languages fell into four main families—Shatsan, Palainihan, Wintuan, and Maiduan—each forming "blocks" of related languages. Historical relationships among these diverse language families can represented in the form of a well-resolved tree diagram, and reflects current consensus among linguistics (Goddard 1996:4–8; see following). At the same time, this model of language history does not attempt to group the families into larger language stocks. For example, it has been suggested that the Palaihnihan and Shastan families formed part of

316 I Chapter 5

TABLE 5.3   LINGUISTIC AFFINITIES OF NORTHEAST CALIFORNIAN
ETHNOLINGUISTIC POPULATIONS

Ethnolinguistic Groups	Code	Language	Family
Eastern Shasta of Shasta Valley	Shasta 1	Shasta	Shastan
Western Shasta of Klamath and Rogue Rivers	Shasta 2	Shasta	Shastan
Atsugewi (Hat Creek)	Atsugewi	Atsugewi	Palaihnihan
Western Achomawi	Achomawi 1	Achomawi	Palaihnihan
Eastern Achomawi (Hammawi)	Achomawi 2	Achomawi	Palaihnihan
Trinity River (or Hayfork) Wintu	Wintu 1	Wintu	Wintuan
McCloud River Wintu	Wintu 2	Wintu	Wintuan
(Upper) Sacramento River Wintu	Wintu 3	Wintu	Wintuan
Mountain Maidu (Indian Valley)	Maidu 1	Maidu	Maiduan
Foothill Maidu (Dogwood, Cherokee, Yankee Hill)	Maidu 2	Maidu	Maiduan
Valley Maidu (vicinity of Chico)	Maidu 3	Maidu	Maiduan
Foothill Nisenan (Stanfield Hill or Yuba River)	Nisenan 1	Nisenan	Maiduan
Mountain Nisenan (Northerly)	Nisenan 2	Nisenan	Maiduan
Southern Nisenan (of mountains)	Nisenan 3	Nisenan	Maiduan

NOTE: After Voegelin 1942 (and Kroeber 1939a).

the larger Hokan stock, which was made up of the oldest indigenous languages, though many of these have since been surrounded by new languages arriving into the area. Similarly, Maiduan and Wintuan languages have been tentatively placed into a larger Pentutian grouping and are argued to represent later arrivals. However, as many of these higher-order groupings remain no more than working hypotheses, only the more conservative classifications have been retained here (table 5.4; see following).

Northeast Basketry

Basketry was central for the extraction, transport, processing, and cooking of a wide range of foodstuffs, especially acorns. Despite these common patterns of use there was remarkable variation in forms, manufacturing techniques and decorations, often among closely neighboring groups (Elsasser 1978a:626; figure 5.4; figure 5.13). For example, the Wintu lay at the southern end of the Northwest twining traditions, but were also situated at the northern end of Central California coiled basketry traditions (Du Bois 1935:131). As with the Northwest, baskets

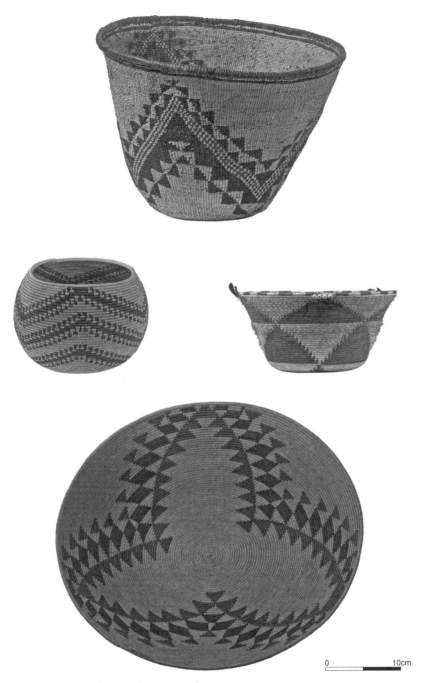

0   10cm

FIGURE 5.13 Northeast basketry examples.

Some examples of basketry made in Northeast California. *Top*: Atsugewi twined basket. SOURCE: Reproduced courtesy of Department of Anthropology, National Museum of Natural History, Smithsonian Institution (E360497)). *Middle left, middle right, bottom*: Maidu coiled baskets. SOURCE: Reproduced courtesy of Department of Anthropology, National Museum of Natural History, Smithsonian Institution (E328035/E131104/ E313252).

here were also made by women (Du Bois 1935:23; Voegelin 1942:63;) and generally used by women (E. Wallace 1978) and skills and relevant cultural traits all—at least during the earlier stages of learning— appear to have been propagated via vertical transmission between mothers and their daughters.

Voegelin's (1942:77–79) basketry survey was edited (note 14) and then analyzed with network- and tree-based methods (see chapter 2; note 15). The results indicated, first, that the basketry traits were grouped into coherent entities at the scale of the ethnolinguistic communities, and second, that the these traditions had evolved by branching processes (figure 5.14), as evidenced by a high RI statistic of 0.77. Tests for historical congruence between the basketry tree and the language tree were therefore conducted (figure 5.14), and indicated that basketry had tracked language history with close, but not perfect fidelity, through time (note 16). Matrix-based correlations added further detail to these interpretations (note 17). Pairwise correlations indicated that 39 percent of basketry variability was accounted for by language and 65 percent by proximity (see appendix). Partial correlations indicated that language alone accounted for 5 percent, geography alone accounted for 30 percent, with their combined effects accounting for 35 percent, together leaving only 30 percent of basketry variability unexplained.

In conclusion, these combined results indicate that Northeast basketry appears to have formed highly coherent local traditions that had evolved via branching processes, and that these traditions also exhibit some apparent congruence with language history. However, the Mantel results suggest that these results require careful interpretation as overall similarity in local basketry traditions has considerable correlations with geography, and that the spatial distribution of the fourteen ethnolinguistic groups and their associated language families also creates strong underlying correlations between geography and linguistic similarity (figure 5.18). These appears to be reflected in the presence of very

---

FIGURE 5.14 (*Opposite*) Northeast language tree, and baskets network, and baskets tree. *Top:* General language tree for Northeast California (based on Goddard 1996). Groupings A, B, C, and D indicate affinity to the Shastan, Palaihnihan, Wintuan, and Maiduan language families (and see table 5.3). *Middle:* Splitstree NeighborNet network illustrating potential branching and blending relationships among the basketry traditions of different populations in Northeast California. Based on presence/absence of seventy-two basketry traits across fourteen ethnolinguistic populations (see table 5.3 and figures 5.1 and 5.12 for geographic locations and linguistic affinities). *Bottom:* Phylogenetic tree (created by maximum parsimony) of basketry traditions in Northeast California.

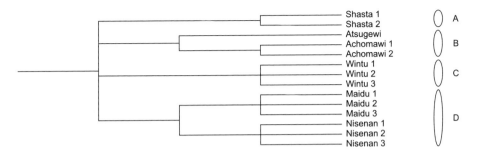

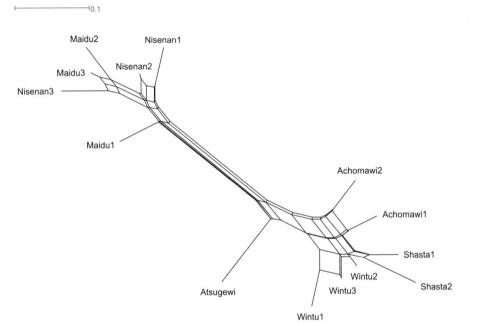

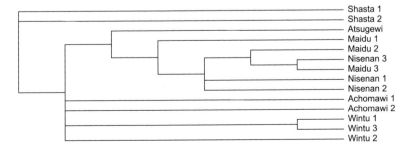

similar "blocks" of culture marked out in different areas by close associations between similar basketry designs and shared linguistic affinity.

Northeast Housing

The range of vernacular architecture in Northeast California included conical huts, lean-to's, domed shelters, and earth lodges, and there was much interchangeability in forms, construction methods, and even overlapping functions, making classification of distinct types difficult (Kroeber 1925:809). The focus here is on earth lodges that were built by all 14 ethnolinguistic groups in the Northeast (Voegelin 1942:64; table 5.4). These were semi-subterranean constructions, and were often sizable, circular structures twenty to forty feet in diameter, whose floors were as much as five feet below ground level. After excavation of this floor pit a pole and log framework was erected, and then various coverings of plank, bark, pole, bough, thatch, or matting were placed on top and were sealed by heavy layer of earth over some or all of the roof surface (see examples in figures 5.15).

Earth-lodge functions ranged from sweat houses, to winter shelters for multiple families, through to assembly houses (and see Nabokov and Easton 1989:294–97); they were built primarily by men, who did most of the heavy construction work, while women sometimes carried away the excavated soil, gathered the covering materials and prepared the thatching (Du Bois 1935:23; Garth 1953:144; Voegelin 1942:63; E. Wallace 1978:684). It is not clear how housing styles were transmitted though earth lodges appear to have been built on an occasional basis, with inputs of labor from a number of individuals, predominantly men. As a result, these large structures would have been built collectively but on a single occasion, possibly via a fairly pragmatic deployment of different techniques, methods and materials. This pattern contrasts with the Salish plank houses (chapter 4), that were "modular" in design, enabling repeated cycles of coordinated reconstruction, and also expansion and contraction, depending on the size of the resident household.

Voegelin's (1942:64–65) survey of Northeast earth lodges was edited into a character matrix (see appendix; note 18). Network- and tree-based analyses (note 19) indicated little overall coherence in local building traditions, and also the absence of any branching signal, but also little geographic ordering in the plots of trees (figure 5.16). The RI statistic was only 0.21 indicating that processes *other* than branching generated variability in local styles. With the lack of a clear branching signal, congruence

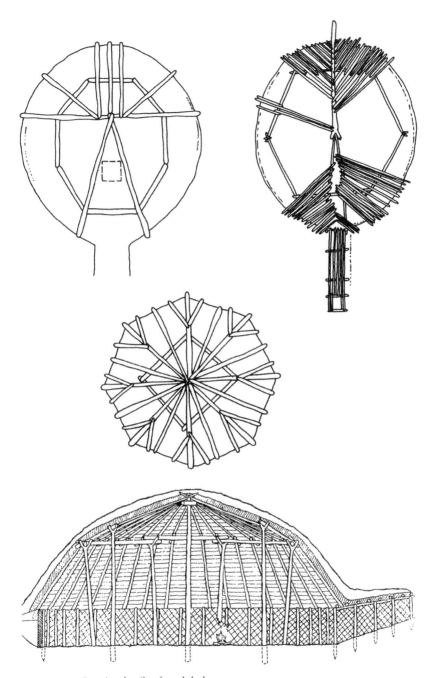

FIGURE 5.15 Interior details of earth lodges.

Some general interior features of Californian semi-subterranean earth lodges. *Top row and center*: Variability in floor plans and roof framing techniques. SOURCE: redrawn from examples published in Nabokov and Easton 1989:295. *Bottom*: Cross-section of an earth lodge. SOURCE: Nabokov and Easton 1989:295, 6, reproduced with permission from Oxford University Press and University of California Press; ORIGINAL SOURCE: McKern 1923:163.

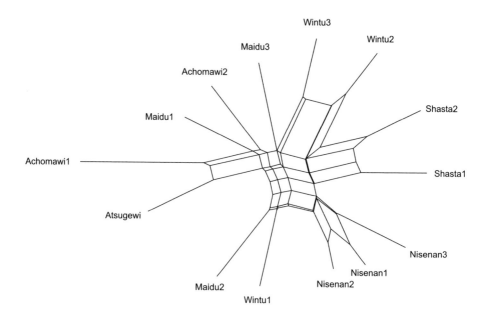

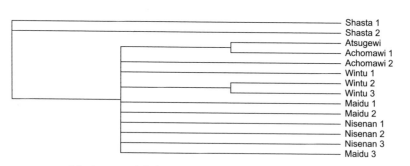

FIGURE 5.16 Northeast earth lodge network and earth lodge tree.

Top: Splitstree NeighborNet network illustrating potential branching and blending relationships among the earth lodge traditions of different populations in Northwest California. Based on presence/absence of seventy-four earth lodge traits across fourteen ethnolinguistic populations (see table 5.3 and figures 5.1 and 5.12 for geographic locations and linguistic affinities). *Bottom:* Phylogenetic tree (created by maximum parsimony) of earth lodge traditions in Northeast California.

with language history analyses were not performed. Matrix-based correlations (see appendix; note 20) indicated pairwise correlations of 14 percent with language and 16 percent with proximity. Partial correlations indicated that 3 percent of variability could be attributed to language alone, 5 percent to proximity alone, and a further 11 percent by their combined effects, leaving a full 81 percent of earth-lodge variability unaccounted for.

These combined results indicate no localized coherence in the traits used to build these earth houses, but also the weak correlations between overall similarity and geographic proximity rule out the ready mixing of traits through hybridization of styles between adjacent populations. Overall then, these results suggest high rates of local innovation in these building traditions. This rapid turnover of traits erodes both deeper historical signals from being preserved, but also the erases effects of borrowing and exchange of traits between adjacent populations. Thus, these local earth-lodge traditions appear to form rather ephemeral collections of traits that are combined differently in different kinds of rather pragmatic constructions, perhaps in a manner broadly akin to the propagation of traits associated with Khanty storage platforms, as examined in chapter 3.

Northeast Ceremonial Dress

In Northeast California Culture Area (figure 5.1; 5.12) there appear to have been substantial local differences in the ceremonial dress worn at Big Time events. Although there is little evidence as to how the ceremonial dress traits were actually propagated, it is clear that the garments and regalia combined materials from a wide range of sources, and that their production would have involved both men and women. With the Big Times collectively organized social events bringing together different communities in a common discourse of ritual, it also seems likely that a degree of local *conformity bias* would have been present, perhaps ensuring heritable continuity in traditions. Also, as these events were also a widely shared social institution for negotiation of boundaries, substantial areas united by regular participation in a common "ritual discourse" may have started to emerge through conformity bias. In turn, this could have lead to shared—and hence mutually intelligible—ceremonial dress styles among a number of adjacent ethnolinguistic groups. These common styles may eventually have expanded in scale to include groups making up some of the larger language families.

To test these ideas Voegelin's (1942:89–91) survey of local variations in ceremonial dress was edited into a character matrix (note 21) and subjected to network- and tree-based analysis (see chapter 2). The results indicated two basic patterns (figures 5.17; note 22): the emergence of larger-scale coherence in dress traits that maps onto groups drawn from each of the larger language families (table 5.4; and see general structure of language tree in figure 5.14 in relation to the map in figure 5.12). In contrast, groups from within each of these larger linguistic family groupings tend to share similar sets of ceremonial dress traits, perhaps indicating mixing of these traits between populations speaking closely related languages. The RI statistic of 0.43 confirmed that branching process alone had not accounted for the variability in ceremonial dress traits. Tests for historical congruence indicated that ceremonial dress history (figure 5.17) had broadly tracked language history (figure 5.14) with close but not perfect fidelity, most likely with some of the broader and more coherent dress styles mapping onto the deeper branches of the major language families (note 23). Mantel (1967) tests returned pairwise correlations of 30 percent with language and 51 percent with proximity; partial correlations indicated that only 3 percent was attributable to language alone, 25 percent to geography alone and 27 percent to their combined effects, leaving 45 percent as unexplained variance (note 24).

These results suggest that ceremonial dress exhibited some general coherence, but only at the slightly larger social scale of the main language families, and not at the scale of the individual ethnolinguistic communities. Thus, the deeper branching history of these larger cultural entities could be reconstructed, and had some apparent congruence with the deeper history of the main language groups. However, within each of these units, there appeared to have been a ready mixing of ceremonial dress traits between the immediately adjacent ethnolinguistic groups.

Summary: Coherence and Historical Congruence in Northeast California Cultural Traditions

These results from Northeast California also indicate that different craft traditions have propagated differentially within local social networks: basketry and ceremonial dress traits have greater local coherence, and these traditions appear to have had branching histories. Further tests also identified substantial historical congruence between basketry traditions, ceremonial dress, and also language, although these were general historical associations, and the these different cultural traditions had certainly not tracked one another with perfect fidelity through time (note 24). In contrast, traits propagated within local

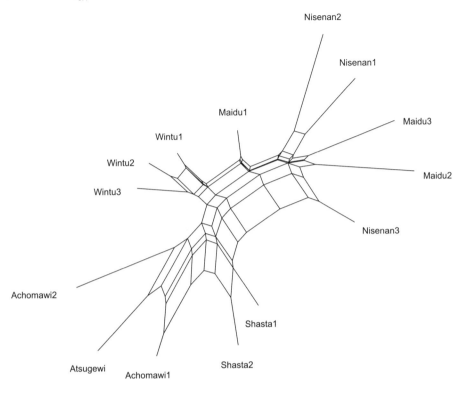

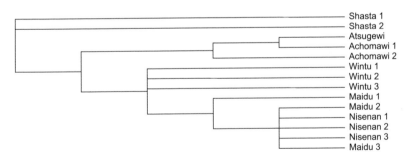

FIGURE 5.17 Northeast ceremonial dress network and ceremonial dress tree.

Top: Splitstree NeighborNet network illustrating potential branching and blending relationships among the ceremonial dress traditions of different populations in Northwest California. Based on presence/absence of fifty-seven ceremonial dress traits across fourteen ethnolinguistic populations (see table 5.3 and figures 5.1 and 5.12 for geographic locations and linguistic affinities). *Bottom:* Phylogenetic tree (created by maximum parsimony) of ceremonial dress traditions in Northeast California.

earth-lodge traditions exhibit minimal coherence, and appear to have been primarily affected by rapid local innovation rather than mixing of traits between adjacent groups.

How can these results be linked back to Boyd et al.'s (1997:364–66; and see chapters 1 and 2) four models? With earth-lodge traits evolving as "ephemeral entities" it is clear that Model 1 can be rejected (cultures as species)—the different cultural traditions in this Northeast Culture Area had not evolved as "single entities" (1997: 365). On the other hand, it has been possible to identify substantial coherence, and branching histories in two separate material culture traditions—basketry and ceremonial dress. Each tradition appears to form a coherent "domain" of culture and so Model 4 (*cultures as collections* of ephemeral entities) can also be rejected (ibid. 1997:366).

Interestingly, the tentative evidence for some degree of historical congruence among some local material culture traditions and language means that Model 3 (assemblages of many coherent units) can also be rejected (Boyd et al. 1997:365). Clearly, there are a number of independent "domains" of culture, although several of these appear to have coalesced into historically congruent set of "core traditions," consisting of language, basketry and ceremonial dress—these point to Model 2 (cultures with hierarchically integrated systems) as being the best summary of cultural evolution within Northeast California (1997:365). But why are such distinctive patterns emerging? What features of local propagation are responsible? Table 5.4 attempts to work through these relationships, and again, highlights the important role played by social institutions in structuring the evolution of material culture traditions.

Although a few higher-status families may have intermarried over longer distances to seal strategic alliances, for most people, life was extremely parochial; straying beyond the local community was dangerous and could provoke lethal retaliation (Kroeber 1925:308;395). This effect was most pronounced in the evolution of basketry traits. In contrast, propagation of ceremonial dress traits was embedded within the Big Times events that involved negotiation of territorial rights *between* neighboring tribelets. Regular participation in this kind of shared ritual discourse may have fostered *conformity bias,* such that ceremonial dress styles needed to be *mutually comprehensible* across *different* communities in order for the events to provide an effective means of maintaining the territorial order. Here, the main historical branching patterns are at the higher-order level of language families (figure 5.14), and not at the scale of the individual ethnolinguistic groups (figure 5.17). Finally, the

TABLE 5.4 SUMMARY OF CULTURAL INHERITANCE PATTERNS IN THREE
"GENDERED" MATERIAL CULTURE TRADITIONS (NORTHEAST CALIFORNIA)

Tradition	Coherence and Historical Congruence	Factors Affecting Local Propagation
Basketry (female /individual)	Traits form coherent local traditions at scale of ethnolinguistic communities; branching history; some evidence for historical congruence with language.	Female craft; evidence for some vertical transmission between mothers and daughters; practitioners do *not* tend to move long distances after marriage; formation of coherent local traditions (local conformist bias?).
Earth Lodges (male/collective)	Traits unable to form coherent local traditions; no evidence for blending between adjacent ethnolinguistic communities; local innovations rates high.	Appear to be pragmatic local constructions by the local community; each earth lodge built differently using novel combinations drawn from a very wide range of available traits.
Ceremonial Dress (both genders /collective)	Traits form coherent traditions, but generally at the scale of the larger language families, less at the scale of the individual ethnolinguistic communities; branching history; some evidence for general historical congruence with language.	Local propagation details unclear; formed part of Big Time traditions that negotiated territorial claims between different tribelets; potential that ceremonial dress formed a coherent and collective tradition, participation in which united styles among locally-adjacent ethnolinguistic groups.

evolution of earth-lodge styles appears to be affected by high innovation and low-fidelity copying—these traits appear to have been subject to pragmatic recombination during each construction event.

Overall then, propagation of material culture traits in the Northeast California Culture Area (figure 5.1, 5.12) appears to have been strongly affected by the tribelet social organization and the highly developed sense of local territoriality, that this institution served to underpin. Together, this reduced interaction between groups, and the maintenance of rather strict territorial regimes may have served as TRIM's (Durham 1992; chapter 1), which served to canalise the propagation of traits, especially with the basketry traditions, and to some extent also for ceremonial dress traits. These insights emerging from Northeast California are summarised in Table 5.4, and provide a useful contrast to the results for the Northwest California case study (table 5.2).

Together, these combined results now generate potential for a comparative and concluding examination of *how* and also *why* the three broadly analogous material culture traditions of basketry, ceremonial dress and housing—are being propagated in such different ways in the two adjacent regions of northern California.

CONCLUSIONS

This chapter has examined the degree of coherence and historical congruence in three contrasting material culture traditions: basketry, housing, and ceremonial dress. Each tradition appears to have evolved differently. In addition, the chapter has compared and contrasted how these three traditions evolve in *two* geographically adjacent regions, where each region is characterized by very different sets of social institutions. These institutions appear to have structured the propagation of local material culture traditions in very different ways. As a result, contrasting evolutionary patterns can not only be identified in *each* of the three technologies, but also in the ways in which each tradition has evolved within the two adjacent regions of Northwest and Northeast California.

The overarching aim in this exercise has been to shed more empirical light on how different kinds of social institution serve to structure the propagation of local cultural traditions, and to link the impact of these specific factors back to the kinds of broader culture evolutionary patterns that emerge, namely Boyd et al.'s four culture evolutionary models (1997:364-6). Some striking insights have emerged, and these are summarized in table 5.5. In order to draw out the greatest of these contrasts, only the Klamath River area of the Northwest (figure 5.2) is compared with the interior Northeast (figure 5.12).

In the Klamath River region of the Northwest, basketry and ceremonial dress exhibit intensive mixing of traits between adjacent ethnolinguistic groups—for ceremonial dress it is caused by regional participation in communal festivals; but for basketry, this same pattern is caused by postmarital residence rules and the concerns with wealth and relative local status that motivate local bride-price negotiations and the quest to seek out wives from more distant communities. Together these results form an interesting example of the *same* basic cultural patterns being formed by very *different* process of local propagation. In contrast, the

TABLE 5.5 IMPACTS OF SOCIAL INSTITUTIONS ON PROPAGATION, COHERENCE, AND HISTORICAL CONGRUENCE IN THREE MATERIAL CULTURE TRADITIONS IN NORTHWEST (KLAMATH RIVER REGION) AND NORTHEAST (INTERIOR) CALIFORNIA *(see figure 5.1)*

	Klamath River Region[a] (*Northwest California*)	Northeast California (*Interior*)
1. Contrasts in Primary Social Institutions		
Territoriality	Private ownership only (household scale); no collective territoriality.	Collective ownership and defence of specific territories by local tribelets.
Ceremonial Complexes	Active participation in collective World Renewal events unites members of all ethnolinguistic groups; provides forum for display of wealth-defining treasures.	Participation in localised Big Times maintains sharp territorial boundaries between adjacent tribelets.
Kinship, Postmarital Residence Patterns, Wealth and Status Accumulation	Patrilocal and patrilineal; extensive long-distance female mobility as partners from distant communities strongly favored in bride-price negotiations.	Patrilocal and patrilineal; geographically restricted postmarital movements; parochial life-worlds and generally localized marriages; only elites engage in longer-range marriages.
Wealth and Status Negotiation	Relative wealth and status measured in accumulated treasures (acquired through bride price negotiations).	Wealth and status acquired through hard work.

Material Culture Tradition	Gender Association	Klamath River Region[a] (*Northwest California*)	Northeast California (*Interior*)
2. Likely Impact of Social Institutions on Propagation of Material Culture Traditions			
Basketry	Female	Ready mixing of traits between ethnolinguistic groups; regional ethnogenesis of traditions.	Very limited mixing of traits between groups; greater heritable continuity of traits within ethnolinguistic groups; coherent traditions emerge; deeper historical congruence with language.

(continued)

TABLE 5.5 *Continued*

Material Culture Tradition	Gender Association	Klamath River Region[a] (*Northwest California*)	Northeast California (*Interior*)
Houses/Earth Lodges	Male	Reduced mixing of traits between groups; heritable continuity of traits *within* groups; coherent traditions emerge; no historical congruence with language.	High rates of local innovation; coherent traditions not forming.
Ceremonial Dress	Mixed	Ready mixing of traits between ethnolinguistic groups; regional ethnogenesis of traditions.	Mixing of traits between adjacent groups (who probably participate in similar kinds of Big Time traditions); coherent traditions do emerge, but only at scale of larger language families; some general congruence with language history.
General Model of Cultural Evolution (Boyd et al. 1997)		Model 3 (assemblages of many coherent units): some coherent cultural packages form, but each has an independent branching history (housing, language).	Model 2 (cultures with hierarchically integrated systems): several coherent cultural traditions form; these also appear to be broadly integrated into a "cultural core" (basketry, ceremonial dress, language).

[a]The Na-Dene enclave in the Northwest has not been included in this summary order to draw out some of the contrasting ways in which social institutions appear to structure the evolution of different material culture traditions.

same kinship rules that result in high female geographic mobility also serve to "lock" men into more localized communities, and this factor most probably results in the formation of the more coherent local housing traditions in the Klamath area.

In the interior Northeast, the same range of social institutions intersects with the propagation of three analogous material culture traditions, but the outcomes are very different. Here, the tribelet land-holding system is associated with intercommunity suspicion and violence, active defense of territorial boundaries, and much lower levels of intermarriage among groups. These factors may result in the emergence of TRIMS, and in turn are associated with increased local coherence in basketry and ceremonial dress traditions, and also in greater historical congruence between these traditions and language history: all appear to be integrated into an enduring set of core traditions that are propagated from generation to generation *within* each local group, yet sealed from outside influences by the effects of TRIMs noted previously.

In conclusion then, the insights from this chapter build directly on the results from chapter 4 on the Coast Salish. Here in Northern California, it is also clear that each different material culture tradition has its own evolutionary dynamic, and that these appear to relate primarily to the local social institutions in which propagation of each of these local traditions is differentially embedded. However, the more comparative and interregional analysis conducted in this chapter makes the additional point that as these primary social institutions vary between regions, so to do the evolutionary dynamics of broadly similar kinds of material culture. In other words, basketry and ceremonial dress traditions are being propagated right across northern California, but are evolving very differently due to major contrasts in local social institutions, especially those that relate to territoriality in the Northeast, but also to the unique ways in which local wealth and status are negotiated and displayed in parts of the Northwest.

Interestingly, Jorgenson argued that there were often close links between the local economies and associated redistribution systems—in many areas these formed distinct complexes, each of which was tightly embedded in native understandings and practice (Jorgenson 1980:138). In the Northwest and Northeast Culture Area (figure 5.1), some of the fundamental differences between these local "complexes" are also expressed in the nature of primary social institutions. From the results of these case studies, it is now also clear that these social institutions also structure local propagation of material culture traditions, with variability in institutions feeding into very different patterns of material culture diversity as well.

More generally then, and looking back over the accumulating insights from the last three chapters, it is possible to start identifying some recurrent themes that build into a general comparative argument about the complex links between microscale cultural propagation and macroscale coherence and historical congruence. For example, there appears to be a general continuum between innovation and pragmatism, through to cultural conservatism and coordination in different material culture traditions due to their inherent nature of production, but also clearly because of the different structuring roles played by various social institutions. These higher-order insights into the three overarching themes of propagation, coherence and congruence in material culture traditions are developed further in the final concluding chapter.

NOTES

Note 1. Earlier Culture-Evolutionary Studies in Northern California

This chapter expands and develops several earlier pilot-studies conducted in the region but adopts an explicitly comparative perspective in order to explain why local patterns of cultural diversification in the same three craft traditions are so different in the two adjacent areas of Northern California. In addition to deploying the full range of analytical methods presented in chapter 2, the chapter also includes a much deeper analysis of local social, political and ceremonial institutions in an attempt to understand the operation of local transmission processes. Very preliminary analysis of cultural transmission patterns in basketry in Northwest, Northeast, and Pomo areas of California was presented in Jordan and Shennan (2005). A further pilot-study of housing and basketry in the Northwest (Jordan 2007) attempted to identify whether the recent arrival of Na-Dene speakers into the areas was visible in regional material culture variability; the current study employs a revised Northwest housing and language data set, and also includes new data on ceremonial dress. In the Northeast, a more comprehensive study of material culture variability was presented by Jordan and Shennan (2009); the current study employs stricter editing criteria to Voegelin's (1942) data sets—any rows with missing data removed entirely. This led to the loss of fifteen basketry traits, eleven earth lodge traits, and twenty-one ceremonial dress traits. However, despite the removal of these traits, the basic results remain the same. In addition, the comparative analysis undertaken here between the Northeast and the Northwest also explains why such distinctive patterns of transmission emerged in the two adjacent regions. In sum, the current chapter builds on—but also substantially expands—the scope of all these earlier pilot-studies, and generates a more comprehensive exploration of the links between material culture evolution and hunter-gatherer social institutions across Northern California.

Note 2. Northwest Basketry: Data Sets

Driver (1939: 333–4) undertook a systematic trait-based analysis of basketry traditions in Northwest California, recording variability at the scale of ethnolinguistic communities. This survey was carefully edited to remove rows with any missing information, generating a full data matrix of 47 basketry traits for fifteen ethnolinguistic groups (see table 5.1; figure 5.2). These traits recorded the presence (or definite absence) of basic construction methods, as well as the forms and decorations of different beaters, trays, boiling,-carrying- and storage baskets. Thus, the data matrix records the entire "pool" of basket-making traits recorded as being present in each of the ethnolinguistic communities; these traits would have been combined differently in each of the local basketry-making traditions.

Note 3. Northwest Basketry: Network- and Tree-Based Analyses

Investigation of basketry transmission patterns began with a NeighborNet analysis as it was unclear, a priori, whether there had been substantial degree of branching in the data set. The data matrix was converted into a NEXUS file and a plot generated (figure 5.6). The boxing at the centre of this plot suggested the presence of major conflicts within the data set, probably indicating hybridization of basketry traditions between different ethnolinguistic populations. Most of these communities were bunched together at the center of the plot, although two main outliers were pulled away to the top right of the plot: Cahto and MR Sinkyone, both of whom are located in the extreme geographic south of the region (figure 5.2). The basketry of RYurok and Tolowa also appeared to have some differences to other basketry, and both groups were pulled away to the bottom right.

The basketry data set was then analysed in PAUP* 4.0b10. A heuristic search performed, with the linguistic isolate Chimariko used the out-group. A single strict consensus tree was calculated and bootstrapped at 1,000 repetitions, with only branches with greater than 50 percent support retained. This generated a tree with only two resolved clades; these included Tolowa and RYurok in the far north and MR Sinkyone and Cahto in the south (figure 5.6). The RI statistic of 0.30 indicated that processes other than branching had generated variability in basketry, most likely hybridization, which appears to have been most intense in the Klamath River area (figure 5.2).

Note 4. Northwest Basketry: Matrix-Based Analyses

Mantel tests (Mantel 1967; and see chapter 2 and appendix 1) employed the following matrices:

- *Basketry Styles.* The presence/absence basketry data set was converted into a 15 ×15 similarity matrix using SPSS and the Jaccard measure (Shennan 1997).
- *Proximity.* Linear point-to-point distances were measured from Driver's (1939) base map of tribal locations (and see figure 5.2) and entered into a 15 ×15 matrix.
- *Language.* Current consensus on language history in Northwest California is derived from Goddard (1996; and see table 5.1; figure 5.5). These descent relationships were converted into 15 ×15 linguistic

similarity matrix using the following method: groups speaking the same language were assigned 95 percent similarity; languages from the same family 50 percent; languages from unrelated families 5 percent.

Note 5. Northwest Houses: Data Set

Driver's (1939:317–20) systematic survey of housing traditions in Northwest California was edited to remove rows with missing information. This generated a matrix of fifty-six housing traits, each recorded as being definitely present (or absent) for each of the fifteen ethnolinguistic groups (table 5.1). This full list of design traits therefore represents the entire "pool" of house-building traits, and includes the details of house forms, construction methods, internal features and fittings, details of the entrances, and some external features; these individual traits would have been combined differently in each of the local house-building traditions.

Note 6. Northwest Houses: Network- and Tree-Based Analyses

The data set was analysed in NeighborNet to examine general patterns of variability in local housing styles. The plot provides some very interesting results (figure 5.9). Two main sub-groups are identified: first, the circular bark-built houses of southern groups were pulled out to the bottom right of the plot, though there appears to be little to differentiate these into more local styles. Second, northern groups producing plank-built houses are pulled out to the upper left of the plot, and there appears to be a sequential branching away of at least some of these traditions, for example, among the Tolowa and Wiyot and Chilula, and to a lesser extent the Yurok, Karok, and Hupa groups.

The housing data set was loaded into PAUP* 4.0b10 and a heuristic search performed, using the linguistic isolates Chimariko, as the out-group. A strict consensus tree was calculated, and subjected to bootstrapping at 1,000 repetitions, with only clades with greater than 50 percent support retained. This generated a well-structured tree with nine clades, which had an RI score of 0.90, indicating very high levels of branching transmission (figure 5.9). The branching pattern appears to be most pronounced in the evolution of local plank-housing traditions of the northern groups living in and around the Klamath River (Group A), with very little evidence for branching processes in the housing styles of southern groups including the Chimariko, Nongatl, ERSinkyone, and MR Sinkyone (Group B).

Note 7. Northwest Houses: Co-Transmission Analyses

A Kishino-Hasegawa test was performed, with the search constrained by the Northwest language tree (figure 5.6; and see chapter 2). However, the new best fit tree for housing, which had been constrained by language history, was significantly different to the original best fit tree at $p < 0.05$, indicating that there had not been perfect branching co-transmission between housing and language. More general historical associations between housing and language were investigated in COMPONENT 2.0. However, the measure of 194 triplets resolved differently between the housing tree and language tree fell inside the range of triplets measures between 1,000 randomly generated trees, which was 152–406. On the basis of these results, it was concluded that local housing traditions had evolved via ranching processes, but had no congruence with language history.

Note 8. Northwest Houses: Matrix-Based Analyses

Mantel tests employed the same proximity and language matrices described above, plus a new 15 ×15 matrix for housing styles, which calculated in the same way as the matrix for basketry (and see appendix).

Note 9. Northwest Ceremonial Dress: Data Set

Driver's survey of ceremonial dress styles in Northwest California (1939:331–33) was edited to remove rows with missing information; unfortunately there was insufficient data on the Chimariko, and so this group was dropped from the analysis, generating a matrix of thirty-two cultural traits that were recorded as being definitely present (or absent) in each of the remaining fourteen ethnolinguistic groups (table 5.1). These traits record a wide range of garments and regalia and equate to the wider "pool" of traits that would have been combined differently in each of the local ceremonial dress traditions (see figure 5.10).

Note 10. Northwest Ceremonial Dress: Network- and Tree-Based Analyses

The data set was converted into a NEXUS file and analysed in NeighborNet in order to explore for general signals in ceremonial dress traditions (figure 5.11). The plot contained some interesting patterns, with groups from in and around the Klamath River (e.g., the Hupa, Karok, and Yurok), possessing what appeared to be very similar traditions that were hardly differentiated. In contrast, other groups (especially communities from the southern Na-Dene enclave) appeared to have a greater degree of local differentiation in their ceremonial dress styles. The tree diagram also indicated the presence of a branching signal in the dataset (Group A includes the "epicentre"' of the World Renewal ceremonies on the Klamath River; Group B includes areas that maintain Big Time events). However, the RI was only 0.51.

Note 11. Northwest California Ceremonial Dress and Language: Co-Transmission Analyses

Potential co-transmission of ceremonial dress and language (see chapter 2) was investigated with a Kishino-Hasegawa test, which indicated that the new best-fit tree constrained by language history was significantly different (at p <0.05) to the original best-fit tree, and therefore, that the hypothesis of perfect co-transmission could be rejected. The best-fit tree for ceremonial dress (figure 5.11) and language history (figure 5.6) were also examined in COMPONENT 2.0. In this test, however, the tree for languages was modified to reflect the fact that Chimariko had been excluded from the study due to missing data, and a new set of

1,000 random trees was also generated. When these trees for language and ceremonial dress were compared, it was clear that the triplets score of 133 fell inside the range of differences between the 1,000 randomly-generated trees, whose range was 112–331. These combined results indicate that ceremonial dress traditions had not been co-transmitted with language, and that they had an entirely independent history.

Note 12. Northwest Ceremonial Dress: Matrix-Based Analyses

Correlations between ceremonial dress, language and geography were investigated with Mantel tests (see appendix). The language and proximity matrices (described previously) were modified to reflect the fact that Chimariko had been excluded due to absent data, and a new 14 ×14 matrix for ceremonial dress was calculated using the same methods used for the basketry and housing data sets.

Note 13. Northwest California: Multiple Traditions and Co-Transmission Analyses

Tests to identify potential co-transmission among basketry, housing, and ceremonial dress were not performed. First, the basketry data set does not contain a signal for branching history, and although a branching signal was identified in the data sets for housing and ceremonial dress, in both cases it was clear that this did not relate to language history (see previous). Second, tests to identify potential co-transmission between housing and ceremonial dress could not be performed because the data sets (and subsequent trees) were of different sizes—the housing data set included fifteen ethnolinguistic groups whereas the ceremonial dress data set covered only fourteen of these groups (data on Chimariko were missing—see note 9 above). However, it seems highly unlikely that they had been co-transmitted as the trees mapping their branching histories are strikingly different. For example, in the housing tree (figure 5.9), the strongest branching signal is among the Karok, Hupa, and Yurok, while other groups in the region exhibit a more hybridized signal. In contrast, the tree for ceremonial dress (figure 5.11) indicates hybridization between the Karok, Hupa, and Yurok, with a greater branching signal among the other groups. Finally, Mantel correlations between basketry and houses were very low; ceremonial dress data could not be correlated due to the missing data (see appendix). Overall, these combined results suggest that these three material culture traditions—and also language traditions—all have their own entirely independent histories in the Northwest Culture Area (figure 5.2; and see table 5.2).

Note 14. Northeast Basketry: Data Set

Voegelin's (1942:77–79) basketry survey was edited to remove rows with missing data, generating a list of seventy-two traits recorded as being definitely present (or absent) across fourteen ethnolinguistic groups (table 5.3). These traits recorded basic coiling and twining methods (e.g., figure 5.4), decorative techniques, as well as the range of basket types made by each group, including seed beaters, trays, boiling baskets, burden baskets and storage baskets.

Note 15. Northeast Basketry: Network- and Tree-Based Analyses

The data set was converted into NEXUS format and analyzed in NeighborNet to examine the strength of a branching signal. The plot showed substantial differentiation, with relatively long branch lengths, and only limited internal boxing (figure 5.14; chapter 2): Maidu and Nisenan (all speakers of Maiduan languages) were pulled out to the upper left, while the other groups were pulled away to the bottom right, each group branching away in sequence.

The data were then loaded into PAUP* 4.0b10 and a heuristic search performed, with the Shasta groups as the outgroup on the basis that they speak a language with no known relatives in the study area (table 5.3). A strict consensus tree was generated, and subject to bootstrapping at 1,000 repetitions, with only branches with over 50 percent support retained. This returned a well-structured tree with a progressive branching of many clades (figure 5.14). An RI score of 0.77 confirmed that relatively coherent local traditions had evolved via branching process: all groups branch away from the Shasta, with a further major branch between the Wintu and Achumawi on the one hand, and the Maidu, Nisenan, and Atsugewi, on the other. Basketry of the Maidu and Nisenan groups, in particular, appear to show high levels of local coherence and evolution via branching processes.

Note 16. Northeast Basketry: Co-Transmission Analyses

Potential co-transmission of basketry and language was assessed with a Kishino-Hasegawa test. The language tree for this test (figure 5.14) was translated into a constraint tree using MacClade 4.03 (Maddison and Maddison 2000; and see; chapter 2). However, the results indicated that the original best fit tree for basketry (figure 5.14) was significantly different at $p < 0.05$ to the new best fit tree for basketry constrained by language history, and that perfect co-transmission had not taken place. However, when the original basketry tree and the language tree (figure 5.14) were compared in COMPONENT 2.0, the results indicated that local basketry traditions had tracked language history with close, but not perfect, fidelity through time—the range of triplets scores between 1,000 randomly-generated trees was 105–323, while the number of triplets resolved differently in the basketry and language trees was only twenty-two.

Note 17. Northeast Basketry: Matrix-Based Analyses

Mantel tests investigated general correlations between basketry, language and geography (see appendix), with the matrices constructed as follows:

- *Basketry Styles.* The presence/absence data set was converted into a 14 by 14 similarity matrix using SPSS and the Jaccard measure (Shennan 1997).
- *Proximity.* Linear point-to-point distances were measured from Voegelin's (1942) base map of tribal locations (and see figure 5.12), and entered into a 14 ×14 matrix.
- *Language.* Current consensus on language history in Northwest California is derived from Goddard (1996; and see table 5.3; figure

5.14). These historical relationships were converted into 14 ×14 linguistic similarity matrix using the following method: groups speaking dialects of the same language were assigned 95 percent similarity; languages from the same family 50 percent; languages from unrelated families 5 percent.

Note 18. Northeast Houses: Data Set

Voegelin's (1942:64–65) data on earth lodges was edited to remove any rows with missing data, generating a full data matrix of seventy-four characters for the fourteen ethnolinguistic groups (table 5.3). These traits record the presence (or definite absence) of different roof-construction methods, ground plans and floor excavation details, the materials used for covering the roof, details of entrances, fireplaces, smoke holes, and internal fittings and features. Thus, the data matrix records the entire pool of possible earth lodge construction techniques employed by different ethnolinguistic communities; these traits would have been combined differently in each of the local earth lodge traditions. Voegelin is also careful to note that none of these construction practices or materials are explained by ecological or environmental factors and that all have their origins in cultural-historical factors (1942:64–65).

Note 19. Northeast Housing: Network- and Tree-Based Analyses

The data set was converted into a NEXUS file and analyzed in NeighborNet to test for possible branching signals. The plot has relatively short branch lengths and a substantial degree of boxing at the center; moreover the different groups appear to be pulled out to equal lengths but in different directions (figure 5.16), making the plot difficult to interpret—each local earth lodge tradition appears to be equally different from the others.

The data set was then loaded into PAUP* 4.0b10 and subjected to a heuristic search with the two Shasta groups placed in the out-group. A strict consensus tree was generated and bootstrapped at 1,000 replications, and only branches with over 50 percent support were retained. The resulting tree (figure 5.16) has very little branching structure—the Shasta groups branch away but then there is very little internal differentiation, with only two further clades, one grouping the Wintu 2 and Wintu 3, and another grouping the Atsugewi and Achomawi 1. The low RI statistic of 0.21 indicated that processes other than branching transmission had predominated. Co-transmission tests were not performed due to this apparent absence of a branching signal.

Note 20. Northeast Housing: Matrix-Based Analyses

Mantel tests examined more general correlations between earth lodges, language, and geography (see appendix). Analyses employed the same language and proximity matrices described previously in note 17, plus a further matrix of earth lodge similarity, which was generated by the same approach.

Note 21. Northeast Ceremonial Dress: Data Set

Voegelin's (1942:89–91) survey of ceremonial dress was edited to remove rows with missing data, generating a list of fifty-seven traits recorded as being definitely present (or absent) across fourteen ethnolinguistic groups (table 5.3). These traits covered the complex range of garments and adornments used in the region, including yellowhammer quills and feathers and woodpecker-scalps, all of which were incorporated into belts, braces, bands, necklaces, and bandoliers, and also into visors, head nets, feather head-dresses, and plumes.

Note 22. Northeast Ceremonial Dress: Network- and Tree-Based Analyses

The data set was converted into a NEXUS file and subjected to preliminary analysis in NeighborNet. The boxing in the plot suggested a degree of conflict in the data set, but also some branching structure was also apparent: Atsugewi and Achomawi groups were pulled away to the bottom left of the plot; Maidu and Nisenan groups were pulled to the top right; the Shasta groups were pulled out to the bottom of the plot; Wintu groups were pulled out to the top and to the left (figure 5.17).

The data set was then investigated in PAUP 4.ob10 and subjected to a heuristic search, with the two Shasta communities forming as the outgroup. A strict consensus tree was generated and bootstrapped at 1,000 replications, and only clades with over 50 percent support were retained. This produced a well-resolved tree, with a clear branching structure (figure 5.17). First, the Shasta branch away from all other groups, and in a second major split, the Palaihnihan speakers branch away, with the Atsugewi and Achomawi 1 forming a further clade. This leaves all the Wintuan and Maiduan speakers on a single clade: the Wintu appear to have broadly similar traditions, while all the Maidu and Nisenan speakers branch away again. Within this latter branch, the Maidu 1 form a further separate clade, while all the remaining Maidu and Nisenan groups branch into a final clade. This branching pattern appears to separate out the region's major language-family groupings into different branches, but also suggests some hybridization within each of these language-family groupings. Overall, the relatively low RI score of 0.43 indicates that process other than branching have generated variability in the data set, and may reflect a combined signal for (a) higher-level branching of ceremonial dress styles into the larger language families, combined with (b) more localized hybridization among ethnolinguistic populations speaking these related languages.

Note 23. Northeast Ceremonial Dress: Co-Transmission Analyses

Co-transmission between ceremonial dress and language was investigated with a Kishino-Hasegawa test, which failed to identify perfect co-transmission, although triplets testing in COMPONENT 2.0 identified that ceremonial dress and language did appear to exhibit some historical congruence. The triplets scores for 1,000 randomly generated trees ranged between 105–323 but only eleven triplets resolved differently in the trees for ceremonial dress (figure 5.17) and the tree for language history (figure 5.14).

Note 24. Northeast Ceremonial Dress: Matrix-Based Analyses

Mantel tests investigated general correlations among ceremonial dress, language, and geography (see appendix). The tests employed the same language and proximity matrices described previously. A similarity matrix for similarity in ceremonial dress was also calculated using the same methods outlined in note 17.

Note 25. Northeast California Basketry, Ceremonial Dress, and Language: Co-Transmission Analyses

To test for possible historical congruence among several craft traditions (see chapter 2) the trees for language (figure 5.14), basketry (figure 5.14) and ceremonial dress (figure 5.17) were loaded into COMPONENT 2.0 in order to calculate triplets scores between them. The earth lodge data set was not included as no branching signal had been identified (see note 19, above). The number of triplets resolved differently in the basketry and language tree was twenty-two, and the number of triplets resolved differently in the ceremonial dress and language tree was eleven. In addition, the number of triplets resolved differently in the basketry and language trees was thirty-four. All these scores fall outside the range of triplets scores for 1,000 randomly-generated trees, which was 105 to 323. This suggests that basketry, ceremonial dress and language traditions exhibit some degree of congruence, and have a broadly shared history in Northeast California.

Kishino-Hasegawa tests were also performed in order to test for perfect co-transmission between these traditions. As already noted, the search for new best-fit trees in basketry and ceremonial dress was constrained by the language tree (figure 5.14). However, in both cases, the new best-fit trees were significantly different at $p > 0.05$ indicating that neither exhibited perfect historical congruence with the language tree. One further test assessed the degree of co-transmission between basketry and ceremonial dress, with the search for a new best-fit basketry tree constrained by tree for ceremonial dress (figure 5.17). Again, the new best-fit tree was significantly different at $p > 0.05$, indicating that perfect co-transmission between basketry and ceremonial dress traditions had not taken place.

On balance, these results suggest that language, basketry and ceremonial dress traditions do exhibit a broadly congruent branching history in the region, but that these different traditions had not tracked one another with *perfect* fidelity through time. Finally, Mantel tests support these general conclusions; they examined general correlations between the three material culture traditions (see appendix), with the strongest correlations between basketry and ceremonial dress (49%).

CHAPTER 6

Conclusions

This book has outlined a new approach to studying the origins of variability and change in material culture, which is one of the primary research questions in archaeology and also anthropology. In fact, the overwhelming reliance on technology and material culture in all spheres of activity—ranging from subsistence, travel, shelter and general community life—remains one of the central feature of all human existence. The key argument presented in this book is that these diverse forms of material culture are best understood as expressions of *social tradition*. Production of each object, artifact, or built structure is the result of a distinctive operational sequence, which consists of the specific choices made at each stage in its manufacture. For analytical purposes, these choices can be defined as cultural traits, with specific combinations of these cultural traits constituting distinctive material culture traditions.

Technological traditions can therefore be understood as a complex system of cultural inheritance, with information passed on between individuals through the sophisticated human capacity for high-fidelity social learning. This transmission system enables particular combinations of cultural information to persist from one generation to the next in lineages of deeper heritable continuity. Change in these bodies of cultural information is, of course, also possible, and this change can proceed at different speeds. In living out their daily lives, individuals make constant decisions within their daily routines and cultural practices about which traits are to be retained, added, or discarded; the effects of these individual decisions are important, because they have cumulative effects within the population. This sum of individual decisions can result in very rapid cultural adjustments within a single generation, through to the persistence of deeper, slowly changing historical traditions that extend in recognisable forms over extended time periods.

Language was cited as good example of this kind of complex cultural inheritance system. People aren't born with language; they acquire it in infancy from biological parents, primary carers and other members of the older generation, and later on from peers and other social contacts; they can also make their own adjustments and improvisations, but they cannot stray too far, or too quickly, or they will be unable to communicate effectively with the rest of the group. Languages are therefore inherited cultural traditions that are highly dynamic, and do change constantly, but they cannot change overnight, and only from an established base line, and so tend to maintain at least some degree of historical continuity. This strong tendency toward coherence and heritable continuity in such communicative traditions means that the deeper patterns of inheritance that make up language histories can often be reconstructed with the right kinds of tools and approaches.

This book argues that *material culture* traditions can be viewed in some broadly similar terms. Developing new ways to understand exactly *how* these material culture traditions are reproduced, and *why* these processes generate continuity and change, are the central goals of this investigation.

In chapter 1 it was argued that viewing technology as a social tradition highlights the importance of cultural information being replicated over time through teaching, imitation, and other forms of social learning. This approach to the study of cultural transmission has broad analogies with the ways in which evolutionary biologists have investigated the inheritance of genetic information as part of a modern evolutionary framework of "descent with modification."

These analogies work on different levels: they provide new ways of thinking about the reproduction of cultural knowledge, but at other levels, they generate a new framework for empirical research, because the sophisticated quantitative methodology developed in the biological sciences can be adapted and retooled to study the history of material culture traditions. Very little coordinated comparative and contextual research has been directed at understanding exactly how and why such technological traditions evolve at different scales and across different cultural contexts. Three overarching research themes pertaining to the evolution of technology therefore run through the book: *propagation, coherence,* and *congruence.* This approach enables anthropologists and archaeologists to revisit long-standing questions about the history of different material culture traditions, how and why specific histories might intersect, and the extent to which they might map onto language histories.

In order to maintain a broadly comparative approach to these three research themes, a common methodology (chapter 2) was applied to three different case studies, all of which shared an overarching focus on hunter-gatherer populations (chapters 3, 4, 5). These case studies were also designed to investigate technology and material culture traditions at contrasting social scales, ranging from households and patrilineages, through to larger ethnolinguistic groups:

- Chapter 3 (Northwest Siberia) focused primarily on understanding the *propagation* of material culture traditions within dialect communities, but also examined the extent to which more enduring patterns of *coherence* emerge.

- Chapter 4 (Pacific Northwest Coast) shifted focus to examine cultural *coherence* and deeper historical *congruence* of material culture traditions across communities speaking different dialects, but in seeking to explain these historical patterns, explored the contrasting ways in which sets of cultural traits are *propagated* among different genders and task groups.

- Chapter 5 (Northern California) also investigated *coherence* and deeper historical *congruence* in different material culture traditions but focused on contrasting distributions of traits across populations speaking different languages, linking these patterns back to the divergent ways in which the traditions are locally propagated.

With these comparative foundations in place, this goal of this final chapter is to bring together the results of the different case studies within a broader, cross-cultural analysis that attempts to draw out some of the major factors that affect patterns of continuity and change in material culture traditions at different social scales. The chapter ends with a final, forward-looking discussion that attempts link these specific research findings, and the longer-range potentials of the general approach, to wider traditions of enquiry that span archaeology and anthropology.

DEVELOPING CROSS-CULTURAL INSIGHTS INTO
THE EVOLUTION OF MATERIAL CULTURE TRADITIONS
Propagation of Cultural Traditions

This theme primarily addresses how material culture traditions are replicated by individuals *within* populations. At the center of these general mechanisms of cultural reproduction are individuals and their decision-making processes: who and where do they gain cultural information from and at what stage in their lives; how and why do they choose to adopt, invent, retain, or reject cultural traits as they propagate existing technological traditions? Much previous research and discussion about cultural inheritance has tended to focus on the dynamics of social learning in childhood, which tends to emphasize the importance of vertical transmission (i.e., from parents to their offspring). In contrast, the Siberian case study focused instead on investigating the physical details of specific craft traditions, and examined decisions made throughout individuals' lifespans: when had particular design features been learnt, where, and from whom?

The fieldwork results indicated that propagation of different craft traditions was caught up in a two-stage cultural transmission process, which broadly mapped onto the different life stages of individuals, whose biographies were then played out in local kinship and interaction networks. In the first stage, basic woodworking skills and also many specific design recipes were acquired during childhood and early adolescence, often from parents investing substantial time in teaching and demonstration (vertical transmission), but also through novices observing older male relatives. Most of this early interaction and social learning also took place within the setting of the local patrilineage base camp.

This early phase of intense social learning was followed by a second stage of lifelong observations, experimentation, and careful payoff-based evaluation of different design traits by adult practitioners keen to improve performance, especially in technologies like skis, sledges, and canoes which were most directly involved in subsistence-related activities such as hunting, trapping, and fishing. These newer design traits, acquired from the onset of early adulthood, were primarily acquired from a much wider social network—for example, friends, distant relatives, acquaintances—and for the most part, they were easy traits to copy through simple observation and examination and required minimal or no investment in teaching for successful transmission to take place. Generally, their adoption also involved only minor adjustments to older design recipes (e.g., new elements of ski or sledge design), and so many of these new traits could also spread very rapidly across extended social networks, some "leaping" large geographic distances within a few seasons. Here they could rapidly become part of established traditions in these new settings (e.g., the hybrid sledge designs). Only in one case did a novice acquire an entirely new design recipe (canoe making) by sustained investment in teaching by an unrelated member of the older generation, but this was a very rare occurrence.

These insights highlight that the propagation of technological traditions is highly complex, but that vertical transmission of traits in childhood is generally followed by a lifetime of biased transmission. In fact, this two-stage transmission emphasizes the potentially adaptive nature of cultural learning as new and useful ideas can spread quickly across the population well within a generation, but only if they if they are deemed locally useful. This wider dispersal of new design variants is particularly rapid when the take-up of the new trait requires only minimal or even no further investment by the transmitter in teaching the adopter.

This ability to react quickly to new traits and build them into existing designs when they improve functionality appears to explain why foragers come to possess highly adaptive technological complexes that involve integrated sets of performance-related insights that individuals might not be able to accumulate in an entire lifetime of trial-and-error learning and experimentation. Biased cultural transmission is therefore central to these unique technological solutions, and probably also explains the existence of highly standardized variants across large regions (e.g., very similar dug-out canoe designs across much of Siberia) or within similar ecological zones (e.g., the contrasting tundra and taiga sledge designs).

The geographic structure and spatial extent of social networks also appears to influence how far new traits can disperse. These appear to spread first via biased transmission, until they become part of more established and standardized traditions that are propagated via vertical transmission. In the Siberian case study, social interaction tends to be strongly confined to within particular river basins, and it was interesting to note that the distinctive D-ring Iugan River bindings had become established as an locally optimal design variant, but only within a specific river basin community. At the same time, other adjacent communities had reached equally viable design solutions, generating contrasting patterns of regional diversity (e.g., the different ski binding designs noted across Northwest Siberia).

If new traits offer clear advantages, and these improvements can easily be detected by adopters, then the traits can spread widely and even replace other variants. In some cases, entire "packages" of design traits can be abandoned. A good example of this is the disappearance of the archaic platform ski designs after the introduction of cloth covers to rival ski variants. However, if the relative advantages of older and more recent traits is hard to evaluate, and generates "noisy" performance data, the rival variants can coexist for long periods within the same population. This appears to be the case with the adjustment of older dog sledge designs to the heavier demands of snowmobile traction—it is simply not clear whether straight or angled legs offer better performance, so both variants are still routinely produced, though overall, the new sledges being made are now larger and much heavier. Nor is it clear whether the new kinds of crossbar are substantially better suited to modern sledge frames. At present they just appear to offer equally viable alternatives, and so their adoption by the wider population remains largely a matter of personal inclination.

What is clear from the Siberian case study is that all these practical technologies are under intense scrutiny for performance and durability, and that individuals neither follow older traditions without questioning them nor adopt new traits without evaluating them carefully. In fact, these unique features of the human cultural transmission provide a powerful mechanism for payoff-based transmission to outcompete vertical transmission in specific situations; this can exert a rapid, widespread, and cumulative impact on the form and cultural content of subsequent traditions. These kinds of evolutionary dynamics most pronounced among the transport technologies where improvement of performance was a central goal.

However, it is important to note that *none* of these craft traditions were overt signalers of group-based identity. Perhaps as a result of this factor, there was no widespread evidence for frequency dependent bias, that is, people acquiring and reproducing new traits because the majority had already done so. The only evidence for a general desire for conformity was in the design of the local shrines, where people worked together and tended to follow the same combination of traits used by the elders when rebuilding new structures to the same overall design template. Nor was there substantive evidence for prestige bias, that is, people copying traits from high-status individuals, at least in the limited range of craft traditions that were examined. However, this trend may be detected in the rapid spread of new consumer goods among the population (Wiget and Balalaeva 2011:295–96). In general then, these Siberian insights into propagation are highly contextualized, both in terms of the specific cultural setting but also because of the nature of the specific craft traditions that were examined.

The other important theme running through these discussions is the strongly "gendered" nature of these Siberian traditions, and the implications of this factor within local kinship and settlement institutions. All these woodworking traditions are generally associated with male work; society is also structured into patrilineages, and these map closely onto local base camps and associated hunting territories, such that men tend generally not to relocate their home residence unless it is to found a new base camp. In contrast, women move much more widely after marriage, generally settling in the community of their new husband in early adulthood. This is broadly the juncture at which the second stage of cultural inheritance really opens up—individuals are doing much less of what their parents and elders have taught them and are more open to adopting new traits.

This complex intersection between the "gendered" propagation of particular crafts, local kinship institutions, and broader settlement systems becomes more apparent in the later Northwest Coast and California case studies. Here, all the insights point to women acquiring the content of their basic traditions vertically from parents, but then later adjusting their traditions after they have undertaken postmarital relocation. Exactly how far individuals move—and especially whether this move is *within* or *between* ethnolinguistic communities—appears to exert a profound influence on the general evolution of the wider tradition. Shorter, more constrained moves tend to propagate traditions within the original groups, but longer-range moves appear to be one of the primary factors that encourages the wider mixing of traits between ethnolinguistic populations. These complex and contingent intersections between gender, interaction networks, and postmarital residence practices eventually emerge as one of the most important factors underpinning deeper patterns of coherence and historical congruence in material culture traditions.

Coherence in Cultural Traditions

It is clear from all the case studies that the propagation of cultural tradition is a highly contingent historical process. The factors structuring propagation of specific traits are deeply embedded within local contexts and include the nature of the specific technology, local social institutions, and perhaps especially for hunter-gatherers, the ways in which subsistence and settlement regimes are adjusted to the local ecology. The intersection of all these factors makes it difficult to predict exactly how, where, and when more *coherent* bundles of cultural traits will eventually start to emerge, or the extent to which they will go on to exhibit more enduring patterns of heritable continuity. Despite this inherent complexity, the comparative framework running through the design of the case studies enables three important topics to be examined: (1) how *inherently* coherent are material culture traditions; (2) at what *social scale* does this coherence tend to emerge; and (3) what form does the deeper *history* of these coherent cultural entities tend to take?

How Coherent Are Material Culture Traditions?

The case studies examine how different kinds of material culture are produced, highlighting inherent potential for flexibility and change within their particular design features. The combined set of findings point again to the complex and contingent nature of all craft traditions, but they are useful in a more comparative sense because they identify an important continuum between innovation and pragmatism, through to cultural conservatism and coordination in different material culture traditions. These relate, in turn, to their specific social roles, the inherent nature of production, and their overall functionality.

For example, at one end of this continuum, the Khanty storage platforms consist of highly contingent combinations of traits, each example reflecting a suite of practical contingencies at the time of construction. These platforms can be built in any number of different ways, and as long as they broadly meet their basic functional requirements, each unique example forms a viable cultural product. As a result, large numbers of traits are combined and recombined on a rapid, very arbitrary, and highly pragmatic basis, such that individual traits are shared easily across social units and over large geographic areas. Similarly, the traits that make up Northeast California earth lodges also appear to be largely pragmatic local combinations, with little localized coherence.

In contrast, greater coherence is found among some of the other craft traditions, but here the comparative nature of the case studies is important because it highlights that greater coherence can form for a range of very *different* reasons. As examined previously, biased cultural transmission appears to ensure that ski, sledge, and canoe designs have come to form highly coherent design recipes probably because these technologies have highly specific functional and performance requirements, and these define the criteria for retaining older designs or making new adjustments: new traits offering improvements catch on rapidly and become quickly incorporated into the highly standardized designs.

In addition to this, the specific nature of the production sequence—that is, the tools, techniques, and materials—may also favor a single coherent design recipe. The best example of this is the lean and lightweight Siberian dug-out canoe, which basically follows the same design over large geographic areas. At least some of this coherence appears to be derived from the essential nature of aspen trees—there are only a limited number of ways in which a log can be hollowed out, steamed open, and the boat shape held in place by insertion of thwarts. Coherence resulting from general raw material constraints is further reinforced by the highly specific use requirements of these small craft within Northwest Siberia's extensive wetlands and waterways.

The much broader suite of cultural traits associated with Salish canoe-making traditions—ranging from production tools, vessel designs, fixtures, and fittings—also form highly coherent local traditions. However, much of this bundling together of specific traits appears linked to the fact that each local tradition is propagated as a body of secret, ritualized knowledge, rather than to narrow functionality or limits imposed by raw materials. Similar insights emerge in the study of Khanty shrines, which also form essentially arbitrary but locally distinct and relatively coherent traditions that are reproduced by social groups with a rather restricted membership, in this case, males within the patrilineage working under the guidance of local elders. In addition, coherence can also emerge in traditions that require social coordination, and the best example of this appeared to be the Salish long houses that are built and occupied by the extended families of the local patrilineal kin group.

Finally, it is worth highlighting some of the factors that work to undermine the formation of such coherent traditions. One is that some traditions are just inherently pragmatic, and can accommodate use of a wide range of different traits to achieve the same broad goal, as with storage platforms or earth lodges noted previously. But the other important factor is the extent to which individuals tend to stay in the same place across their life history, recreating highly coherent traditions within a single location, or the extent to which they move easily through more extended social networks. Postmarital moves into new communities *again* appear to be one of main processes eroding the formation of local cultural coherence; this can be noted among the basketry tradi-

350 I Chapter 6

tions of the Salish and in Northwest California. In both cases these are female crafts embedded within a patrilocal kinship system. This important insight links into the question of the likely social scales at which coherence forms and the factors generating this.

At What Social Scales Does Coherence Emerge?

Clearly, coherence can potentially form in different material culture traditions, and for a wide range of different reasons. A similar degree of variability can be noted in both pattern and underlying causality in the social scales at which coherent traditions emerge. Siberia provided the most detailed insights into the propagation of material culture traditions *within* populations, and these results indicated that coherence can form at the scale of patrilineages (shrine architecture), dialect communities (some features of ski binding designs), and also over much larger geographic regions (sledges and canoe designs). More generally, these insights highlighted the underlying challenge of equifinality in linking particular kinds of propagation to specific scales of cultural coherence—similar patterns emerge across a wide range of social scales, but often for very different reasons.

Clearer insights emerge at the macroscale, that is, in the analysis of the distribution of cultural traits across different ethnolinguistic communities on the Northwest Coast and in Northern California. Generally, coherence in cultural traditions tended to map onto the boundaries of ethnolinguistic communities whenever a range of factors converged to dampen the movement of people and cultural traits across these boundaries. Among the Coast Salish, these ranged from local housing designs, which formed a socially coordinated male tradition that was reproduced by patrilineal groups living in large winter villages that clustered together, forming the local dialect community, through to canoe-making traditions, which were reproduced by a limited number of specialists within each of these dialect communities.

Similar correlations between coherent traditions and ethnolinguistic groups can be noted for basketry and ceremonial dress in Northeast California, where territoriality was highly developed and movement of people across such boundaries extremely limited. Coherence can also emerge at slightly larger social scales but for slightly different reasons, for example, groups participating in the same ritual complexes share the same coherent set of ceremonial dress traditions, and the World Renewal sites in Northwest California provide a good example of this.

It is also worth noting again that the regular movement of individuals between groups—in almost all cases in chapters 4 and 5, the postmarital movement of *women* into new communities—serves to erode the links between some coherent cultural entities and specific ethnolinguistic groups, as seen in more hybridized "female" basketry traditions among the Coast Salish and in Northwest California groups. Paradoxically, this regular movement of people can also eventually lead to the emergence of new and much larger scales of cultural coherence—eventually, the distinctive basketry traditions of Northwest California form a distinctive and highly standardized technological complex, but one that is reproduced across, and thereby transcends, an extremely diverse range of ethnolinguistic groups, many speaking entirely unrelated languages. A similar pattern emerges at this larger scale among the Coast Salish basketry traditions, which propagate the same, broadly similar sets of traits but across a range of different dialect groups within a wider region.

And to return to the Siberian case study, these large, regional scales of cultural coherence can also be linked to the spread of useful traits between populations, leading to the formation of highly standardized sledge and canoe designs over large geographic areas. This brings discussion back to the theme of equifinality, as these wider Siberian material culture distributions appear to be linked to the spread of successful new design features among extended social networks, rather than to the physical movement of people or the mixing of traditions as these individuals move into new communities, particularly after marriage.

To conclude, coherence in cultural traditions can form at a range of ascending social scales, and for a range of different reasons; in some cases, similar scales of coherence can form in different cultural traditions, but the factors causing this can be quite distinct. Despite these inherent challenges in linking *particular* modes of propagation in any direct of predictable law-like way to *specific* social scales of cultural coherence, the main insight that emerges from all the case studies is that coherent cultural entities can and do regularly form. This leads into the next theme: to what extent can the deeper history of these coherent entities be reconstructed, and what patterns do these histories of tradition take?

What Form Does the Deeper History of These Coherent Entities Tend to Take?

This theme ties into long-running debates about the specific forms of cultural history: are these coherent cultural entities genealogically related, and do such cultural traditions evolve in ways that exhibit branching, treelike properties? As examined in chapters 1 and 2, biologists have asked similar questions about the genealogy of different biological entities and have developed a range of powerful analytical methods for investigating different evolutionary scenarios. These historical reconstructions are based on a model of descent with modification in which new entities arise from the bifurcation of existing ones; the phylogenetic trees that are produced represent hypothetical statements of evolutionary relatedness. In other words, it is not assumed that a particular history should actually have treelike properties; the main question is *how well* a particular tree model depicts that unique history (O'Brien et al. 2013).

Similar questions can be asked about patterns of historical relatedness among coherent cultural entities, and the application of the same analytical approach across the three case study chapters is useful in creating opportunities for a cross-cultural analysis of these results. The following discussion is based on the implications of Retention Index (RI) scores calculated for the tree models built from material culture traits in each of the different case studies (table 6.1). To recap, RI measures of 0.6 or above indicate that phylogenesis has been the dominant process of evolution, that is, descent from a common ancestor, with new entities emerging through bifurcation of existing ones. In contrast, RI measures lower than 0.6 are more difficult to interpret, but they generally indicate the operation of a combination of other processes (Nunn et al. 2010).

Looking over the RI results from the various case studies, the first and most general point to be made is that there is enormous variability in the way that material culture traditions evolve. As discussed in the preceding sections, differences in local propagation of cultural traits means that coherent entities only form among *some* traditions and only at *certain* social scales. The RI statistic then provides a simple tool for undertaking a basic cross-cultural and comparative measure of the extent to which the history of these different entities is, or is not, treelike. This variability is readily apparent in the range of RI measurements in part a of table 6.1.

In Siberia, the only indication of a phylogenetic history are present in the RI figures for Eastern Khanty ski bindings and in general Siberian ski binding designs—in contrast, general ski designs on the Iugan River, as well as shrines and storage platforms, all have RI scores under 0.6. Among the Coast Salish, RI scores for basketry are under 0.6, but for both canoe-making and housing traditions the scores are at or around 0.6. In Northwest California, only housing is above 0.6, and in Northeast California, only basketry is above 0.6. These results are important

Description	Source	NT*	NC*	RI*
1. Material Culture Data Sets	This book			
Case-study 1: Northwest Siberia	Chapter 3			
Modern Iugan Khanty Skis (skis, covers, bindings)		50	45	0.10
Eastern Khanty Ski Bindings		17	45	0.82
All Siberian Ski Bindings		27	71	0.83
Khanty Storage platforms		105	163	0.16
Khanty Shrines		22	112	0.31
Case-study 2: Coast Salish	Chapter 4			
Plank-housing		9	65	0.56
Canoe-making traditions		9	60	0.62
Basketry		8	40	0.50
Case-study 3: Northwest California	Chapter 5			
Basketry		15	47	0.30
Housing		15	56	0.90
Ceremonial Dress		14	32	0.51
Case-study 4: Northeast California	Chapter 5			
Basketry		14	72	0.77
Housing		14	74	0.21
Ceremonial Dress		14	57	0.43
2. Comparative Biological Data Sets	Collard et al. 2006, with references			
Austalasian teal mtDNA		7	1172	0.94
Corbiculate bee behaviour		23	42	0.94
Pelecaniforme bird behaviour		20	37	0.84
Anoles lizards morphology		24	18	0.79
Primate behaviour		38	34	0.73
Strepsirhine primate morphology		29	43	0.72
Fossil hominid morphology		9	48	0.71
New World monkey morphology		20	76	0.70
Ungulate morphology		40	123	0.70
Phalacrocoracid bird mtDNA		24	1141	0.65
Phocid seal morphology		27	196	0.60
Hawaiian fruit fly mtDNA		17	2550	0.50
Hominoid primate cranial morphology		6	96	0.49
Carnivore mtDNA		25	2001	0.47
Mammal mtDNA with emphasis on Malagasy primates		36	1812	0.47
Carnivore mtDNA with emphasis on Malagasy taxa		35	1140	0.47
Mammal mtDNA		31	10806	0.44
Insectivore mtDNA		43	2086	0.44

(Continued)

TABLE 6.1   *Continued*

Description	Source	NT*	NC*	RI*
Lagomorph mtDNA		12	739	0.39
Hominoid primate soft-tissue morphology		5	171	0.38
Anolis lizard mtDNA		55	1456	0.35

*NT = Number of Taxa (i.e., number of biological taxa or, for the cultural data sets, the number of artifact examples documented (chapter 3) or number of ethnolinguistic populations (chapters 4 and 5); NC = number of characters (biological characters or cultural traits); RI = reticulation index scores (see chapter 2).

NOTE: Data on the additional twenty-one biological data sets were originally published by Collard et al. 2006a and 2006b.

on two levels. First they indicate that the evolutionary history of material culture traditions is always highly variable. Second, they indicate that the biological analytical methods applied to these cultural data sets are successfully picking up this range of variability, recognizing both treelike patterns in the data, but also frequent deviance from this pattern.

In other words, and linking into previous discussions, the propagation of material culture traditions through teaching, imitation, and other forms of social learning can *sometimes* lead to the formation of coherent cultural entities, and in some cases, the history of these entities *does* appear to exhibit treelike properties (e.g., Coast Salish canoe making). However, many other material culture traditions do not display this tendency, either because they have little inherent coherence anyway and involve pragmatic recombination of large numbers of different traits (e.g., Khanty storage platforms), or because any deeper historical signals are apparently being swamped by the frequent horizontal borrowing and blending of traits between different ethnolinguistic populations (e.g., Coast Salish basketry).

These new insights are important on a third level because they make fresh empirical contributions to ongoing debates in the wider literature about the extent to which cultural and biological evolution tend to be broadly similar, or perhaps fundamentally different. To recap, some argue that cultural phylogenesis is theoretically possible but needs to be identified empirically on a case-by-case basis using appropriate methods, an approach adopted here. Others have argued that cultural evolution is fundamentally different from biological evolution and involves a faster tempo and different mode—horizontal transmission—all of which serve to create reticulation. This erases all traces of phylogenetic history, leaving only a blur of interrelated forms (ethnogenesis), and rendering attempts to reconstruct the deeper history of any cultural entities a fundamentally flawed exercise (chapter 1).

The use of the RI scores across all this book's case studies provides a direct and robust means of situating these new findings right back into the heart of some of the most important and central debates about how human cultural traditions evolve (chapter 1 and 2). For example, an earlier comparative study by Collard et al. (2006a, b) also employed the RI statistic to examine whether cultural data sets tended to be more reticulate than biological data sets and to test the hypothesis that ethnogenesis would always predominate in cultural evolution whereas phylogenesis predominantly characterizes biological evolution. Table 6.1, part b summarizes the RI scores from Collard et al.'s biological data sets. This study found that the mean, minimum, and maximum RIs pertaining to the biological data sets were 0.61, 0.35, and 0.94, respectively. In addition, Collard et al. (2006b) also looked at twenty-one cultural data sets (not shown in table 6.1) and found that the corresponding RI figures for these data were 0.59, 0.42, and 0.78. On this basis it was argued that not only are the average RIs similar across the biological and cultural data sets, but also that the ranges are comparable. The study concluded that these twenty-one cultural data sets appeared to be no more reticulate than the biological data sets, and that the results failed to support the hypothesis that ethnogenesis is *always* more important in cultural evolution than phylogenesis, but that it varies on a case-by-case basis (2006b:177).

Turning now to the results from chapters 3, 4 and 5, the mean, minimum, and maximum RI scores for these fourteen new material culture data sets was 0.50, 0.10, and 0.90, respectively (see table 6.1, part a). The mean is somewhat *lower* than in Collard et al.'s (2006b) study of twenty-one biological data sets, as is the lowest RI score, and this appears to suggest higher general levels of reticulation in these fourteen new material culture data sets, and that ethnogenesis had generally been more important than phylogenesis. However, several of the individual new RI scores (e.g., for Khanty and Siberian ski bindings; Salish canoes; houses in the Northwest and basketry in Northeast California) fall *above* the mean RI score for both Collard et al.'s twenty-one biological and also the twenty-one cultural data sets. Results from this book's new case studies therefore indicate that in *some* cases, phylogenesis *can* also be an important process in cultural evolution.

At this point it is also important to note that Collard et al.'s biological data sets were made up of discrete taxa and also that the twenty-one cultural data sets also examined *macro*scale cultural evolution *across* populations and societies. In contrast, many of the Khanty data sets from chapter 3 were generated by analysis of microscale propagation of cultural traditions *within* dialect populations; here, the analytical methods were primarily being used in a more "pattern recognition" mode in an attempt to examine how microscale propagation potentially fed through into the emergence of cultural coherence at different social scales. In other words, this inclusion of results pertaining to microscale cultural evolution appears to be affecting the RI scores and bringing both the mean and the minimum scores downward. For example, the lowest overall RI scores (RI = 0.10) are for the modern skis made by the Iugan Khanty dialect community, and this included all the traits associated with skis, their bindings, and the newer cloth covers and often involved recording large numbers of highly similar variants across the wider population. Details of large numbers of local storage platforms, whose basic design elements were enormously variable, were also recoded both within and between different river basin dialect groups (RI = 0.16). In general then, inclusion of RI scores from these essentially *microscale* studies of cultural propagation may lowering the overall mean and minimum RI scores for these fourteen new material culture data sets.

Somewhat different insights emerge when the RI scores from the five *microscale* Siberian case studies are removed. Analysis is now concentrated on the RI scores from the Coast Salish and Northern California case studies—these all examined *macro*scale evolution of cultural traits across different ethnolinguistic populations. The mean, minimum, and maximum RI scores for these nine material culture data sets was 0.53, 0.21, and 0.90, respectively. In fact, this sharper focus on patterns of *macro*scale cultural evolution brings this new set of findings much closer in line with Collard et al.'s (2006b) original study (i.e., the mean, minimum, maximum RI scores for twenty-one cultural data sets = 0.59, 0.42, and 0.78 respectively; for twenty-one biological data sets = 0.61, 0.35, and 0.94 respectively). On balance then, the new material cultural data sets analyzed in chapters 4 and 5 appear to broadly confirm the earlier position outlined by Collard et al. (2006a, b): biological and cultural data sets are not characterized by fundamentally different patterning, and both can contain evidence for both branching and also more reticulate process of evolution. But probably more important for debates about how cultural traditions evolve, it is clear from these new results that the process of ethnogenesis does *not* always dominate; in numerous cases phylogenesis also appears to play an important role in human cultural evolution.

These new results also underline the broader conclusion that if cultural evolution can be characterized by very different patterns, then each culture historical setting needs to be studied on a case-by-case basis by using a combined range of methods that can identify evidence for both branching processes and reticulation rather than asserting a priori that *either* phylogenesis *or* ethnogenesis must always have dominated cultural evolution. In fact, this more empirical case-by-case approach to the study of material culture evolution has been applied throughout this book.

On more contextual levels, this book has also gone deeper into older debates about general patterns in cultural and biological evolution because it has directed renewed cross-cultural analysis at understanding the propagation of cultural traditions within different cultural settings, exploring how these processes feed through into the formation of coherent cultural entities of different kinds and social scales—it is these variable aspects of propagation that explain why cultural phylogenesis may—or may not—predominate in given historical settings. And having confirmed that both branching and blending processes characterize the macroscale evolution of cultural data sets, this book also transcends these earlier debates about ethnogenesis versus phylogenesis by tackling the more exciting theme of *historical congruence,* that is, the extent to which the histories of *different* lineages of cultural tradition might start to become bundled together, a theme examined in the next section.

Historical Congruence among Material Culture Traditions

Preceding discussions have confirmed that some technological traditions are propagated in ways that lead to the emergence of coherent cultural entities, and that, in some cases, the deeper histories of these entities can exhibit branching patterns that make them amenable to phylogenetic reconstruction. These findings lead on to the next question—the extent to which these different cultural lineages might exhibit *similar* histories: Have different technological traditions tracked each other though time, and to what extent does material culture history map onto language history? In other words, humans are unique in being able to replicate a large number of different cultural traditions, potentially with great fidelity—but to what extent is there historical *congruence* between these different cultural traditions?

Investigating the extent of deeper historical congruence between different cultural traditions has been the third overarching theme in this book. To aid comparative analysis of this question, the chapters have examined the same set of models drawn from Boyd et al. (1997), but in different geographic and cultural settings (figure 1.3). These four contrasting models examine macroscale cultural evolution, and range from "cultures as species" (model 1) through to "cultures as collections of ephemeral entities" (model 4). They form a useful framework for integrating insights into propagation, cultural coherence, and deeper historical congruence. In fact, it was argued in chapter 1 that the most likely scenarios formed intermediate positions. For example, in some settings, it might be possible to reconstruct the individual history of coherent cultural entities on a more individual basis using phylogenetic methods (model 3), but in others, several traditions might exhibit a stronger degree of historical congruence, becoming bundled together and co-transmitted as a more integrated cultural "core" (model 2). The methodology outlined in chapter 2 also provided a unified framework for addressing these questions and now provides a solid basis for cross-cultural analysis of the results.

Table 6.2 provides a descriptive summary of the results presented in each of the individual case studies (chapters 3, 4, and 5). It identifies the degree of general coherence in each cultural tradition and the extent to which this history has branching, treelike properties or is being affected by rapid innovation or mixing. Also noted is the association between each technological tradition and gender and the extent of historical congruence between different cultural traditions (including both material culture and language history). Finally, each section of the table provides a general descriptive summary of which of Boyd et al.'s (1997) models best describes the process of cultural evolution in each case study. These combined insights into multiple cultural traditions take debates well beyond older polarized position statements about the extent to which branching (phylogenesis) *versus* blending (ethnogenesis) will always dominate in cultural evolution; instead, they grapple with the historical complexities of cultural evolution across a wide range of different settings and attempt to explain why particular processes of propagation lead to specific patterns of cultural coherence and historical congruence.

The Siberian case study primarily examined microscale propagation of cultural traditions within a single dialect community, and the results are more difficult to link back to a more formal testing of the four macroscale models. The main insight emerging from this chapter is that

TABLE 6.2 INVESTIGATING HISTORICAL CONGRUENCE AMONG MULTIPLE CULTURAL TRADITIONS

Case study/Technological tradition	Coherence and history of tradition	Gender association?	Congruence with language history?	Congruence with other material culture traditions?
Northwestern Siberia (Chapter 3)[a]				
Khanty Storage platforms	Rapid Innovation	Male	No	No
Khanty Shrines	Rapid Innovation/Branching?	Male	No	No
Iugan Khanty Skis (skis, covers, bindings)	Rapid Innovation	Male	Examined diversity *within* a dialect community.	No
Khanty Ski Bindings	Branching?	Male	Appears to be a broad correlation with dialect boundaries	Not clear at present and would require analysis of other datasets.
Siberian Ski Bindings	Branching?	Male	Not clear at present and would require further analysis.	Not clear at present and would require analysis of other datasets.

CONCLUSION: APPROPRIATE MODEL (BOYD ET AL. 1997; FIGURE 1.3)?

Mainly examines how different material culture traditions are propagated, and the extent to which coherent traditions emerge, and at what social scales. Difficult therefore to formally test the models. Main insight is that each material culture tradition can have very different evolutionary dynamics. This is due to the inherent nature of the technology itself, the role it plays in specific activities, and the ways in which each tradition is embedded in local social institutions.

[a] Develops both quantitative and qualitative conclusions

	Coherence and history of tradition	Gender association?	Congruence with language history?	Historical congruence with other material culture traditions?
Coast Salish (Chapter 4)				
Plank-housing	Branching	Male	Yes	No
Canoe-making traditions	Branching	Male	No	No
Basketry	Rapid Innovation/Mixing	Female	–	–

CONCLUSION: APPROPRIATE MODEL (BOYD ET AL. 1997; FIGURE 1.3)?

Appears to be intermediate between Model 2 and 3; housing is a coherent tradition that appears to be evolving via branching processes, and has some historical congruence with language; canoe-making is also a coherent tradition that has evolved via branching processes, but forms separate lineages – together, these two lineages may form a 'cultural core'; surrounded by blending and rapid innovation in basketry traditions, which have little coherence.

TABLE 6.2 *Continued*

	Coherence and history of tradition	Gender association?	Congruence with language history?	Historical congruence with other material culture traditions?
Northwest California (Chapter 5)				
Basketry	Mixing	Female	n/a	—
Housing	Branching	Male	No	No
Ceremonial Dress	Localised Blending /Branching (see: text)	Mixed	No	Probably not (but no data on Chimariko)

CONCLUSION: APPROPRIATE MODEL (BOYD ET AL. 1997; FIGURE 1.3)?

Appears to fit Model 3: housing emerges as a coherent local tradition, but has its own branching history with little congruence with language; ceremonial dress has been subjected to hybridization where collective 'World Renewal' festivals are held, but forms a more coherent tradition elsewhere, though its branching history has no congruence with language; surrounded by basketry traditions that have evolved via strong regional-scale hybridization.

	Coherence and history of tradition	Gender association?	Congruence with language history?	Historical congruence with other material culture traditions?
Northeast California (Chapter 5)				
Basketry	Branching	Female	Yes	Yes (ceremonial dress)
Housing	Rapid Innovation	Male	No	No
Ceremonial Dress	Branching	Mixed	Yes	Yes (basketry)

CONCLUSION: APPROPRIATE MODEL (BOYD ET AL. 1997; FIGURE 1.3)?

Appears to fit Model 2: basketry and ceremonial dress are coherent traditions that have evolved in tandem *via* branching processes, and in congruence with language history – together, these three cultural traditions appear to form a relatively integrated and enduring '*cultural core*'; surrounded by earth-lodge traditions that form ephemeral cultural entities and have evolved via intensive local innovation.

each technological tradition is propagated differently, that only in some cases do more coherent cultural entities emerge, and that these entities tend not to map in a consistent or predictable way onto specific ethno-linguistic entities—in other words, each technological tradition has its own evolutionary dynamics, even at this microscale.

As the scale of analysis shifts to the macroscale case studies in chapters 4 and 5, testing the four models becomes a more straightforward exercise. Here, the focus is on understanding the evolution of traits across distinct ethnolinguistic groups. The Coast Salish insights are striking: basketry traditions do not exhibit coherence at the scale of the ethnolinguistic groups and appear to have been heavily affected by mixing processes; canoes and housing traditions have much greater coherence, and each of these collections of traits appear to have had a branching history. In addition, there are some indications that the history of housing traits exhibits some congruence with local language history, but the canoe traditions have their own independent branching history. These results indicate that this case study falls somewhere between models 2 and 3: housing and language appear to form a culture core; canoe history can be reconstructed but is an independent package of traits; basketry traditions have evolved through the mixing of traits between groups. Contrasting gender roles and the kinship and settlement system appear to be structuring propagation of housing and basketry traditions, but canoe making is a body of secret but highly valued knowledge that generates different evolutionary dynamics.

The Northwest California case study appears to equate to model 3—each cultural tradition is propagated differently and has its own history, some of which exhibit branching properties. Again, gender roles, kinship, settlement systems—and in this region, ceremonial complexes—appear to structure propagation of the traits within each of these different traditions. Basketry has been subjected to mixing processes; housing traits are more coherent and appear to have had a branching history, though this does not follow language history. Ceremonial dress has been subject to mixing processes among the groups that participate in the collective World Renewal events but has a more branching history in other areas.

The history of cultural traditions in Northeast California is different again and appears to equate to model 2: earth lodges form more ephemeral collections of traits, but basketry traditions and ceremonial dress traditions have more coherence at the scale of the ethnolinguistic groups and appear to exhibit branching histories. The highly developed territorial institutions in this region appear to be dampening the flow of people between groups, and this may have resulted in these two traditions being propagated at a more constrained and local scale. Basketry, ceremonial dress and language appear to have had congruent histories.

To summarize, these combined insights into coherence and historical congruence highlight the flawed logic in the older entrenched arguments that asserted that *either* ethnogenesis *or* phylogenesis must always have predominated in general cultural evolution. By looking instead at *individual* cultural traditions it is clear from these results that each tends to have its own unique evolutionary dynamics, and should be studied on a case-by-case basis. But perhaps more important, these results also transcend these more recent debates—by looking instead at the evolution of *multiple* traditions across *different* case studies, it is clear not only that each tradition has its own unique history, but also that the ways in which these different traditions co-evolve is also highly variable. Finally, it is clear that the methodology and general approach succeed in untangling some of the rich and complex histories of local cultural evolution, and that explaining these contingent patterns must include a focus on cultural propagation, scales of coherence, and historical congruence.

GENERAL DISCUSSION

To what extent do these results improve general understandings of the factors that contribute to variability and change in material culture traditions? They certainly highlight the rich, complex, and historically contingent ways in which material culture traditions evolve over intersecting temporal, social, and spatial scales. Clearly, there are many factors at work, and these tend to generate highly variable outcomes, such that material culture traditions can potentially evolve in some strikingly different ways. Human culture *is* complex. And so is the history of cultural traditions. But is it possible to take interpretations beyond such general statements? This has been a carefully structured comparative and contextual analysis of the evolutionary dynamics of material culture traditions, so to what extent can the results be used to calibrate the likely range of variability, usefully highlighting common themes, likely linkages, and primary causality? This book can't answer all these questions, but a useful start can be been made. To review general progress into these comparative insights, it is useful to return to here to some of the core concepts in the anthropology of technology (chapter 1 and 2).

Operational Sequences

The operational sequence *(chaîne opératoire)* is the series of stages involved in the socially embedded production of an object or built structure, and the case studies draw out some interesting contrasts. Some production sequences are relatively short, constrained by the desired end function of the object and also by the basic limitations of the raw materials (e.g., Siberian dug-outs). In the microscale studies, a major contrast then emerges between technologies under strong functional selection such as skis and sledges, which often leads to similar designs over large areas. In contrast, traditions like the storage platforms need to perform a rather general function, but the specific combination of traits used in each construction is rather arbitrary, balancing speed, time, available resources, and pragmatic judgments, and the result is a highly flexible operational sequence and little overall coherence. In many of the macroscale studies, the material culture traditions such as basketry, housing, canoes, and ceremonial dress have very long but essentially arbitrary operational sequences whose specific cultural content could be propagated in any number of different ways, yet still exhibit internal coherence and even historical congruence. Exactly how these traditions evolve is therefore linked much more to when people learn them and why they adjust or maintain them.

Cultural Propagation, Agency, and Human Life Histories

At the heart of cultural evolution is propagation, that is, the replication of these often arbitrary cultural traditions through teaching, imitation, and other forms of social learning. Clearly, material culture traditions are propagated in very different ways and are subject to a wide range of transmission modes and biases. Particularly important in the evolution of material culture traditions appears to be the two-stage process that maps broadly onto human life histories—in the early life stages, vertical transmission appears to predominate, often requiring major investments in teaching, but this is followed by a lifetime of further observation and adjustment. Understanding both these biographic learning stages is especially important for technological traditions as biased cultural transmission can often outcompete vertical transmission.

However, the intersection of these factors make it hard to identify hard-and-fast linkages between different kinds of propagation and subsequent outcomes—coherent long-term traditions can emerge at different scales and for different reasons. In fact in these open social systems of cultural inheritance and transformation, very different sets of processes can eventually lead to similar outcomes, and so the challenge of equifinality continues to hover over these attempts to link microscale propagation to specific macroscale outcomes. But beyond all this complexity, what is clear is that individual and collective decision-making processes are at the epicenter of cultural propagation. In other words, investigating propagation of these traditions is about understanding the contributions of human agency to long-term culture history. So how are decisions made, and where, when, and from whom do individuals acquire cultural information? This requires understanding how people situate themselves within social networks, and also whom they interact with at different life stages.

Gender, Social Institutions, and "Embedded" Technologies

Two further factors therefore appear to be central in structuring larger-scale variability in material culture. One is gender—in these traditional, small-scale societies, many craft traditions have strong but again arbitrary associations with local notions of appropriate male or female work and the gendered division of labor. However, the implications of these gender associations for cultural propagation only start to emerge in relation to the structuring roles played by local social institutions. As a second overarching factor, these social institutions are particularly important in structuring the general life histories of individuals, and therefore, in influencing whom they interact with and where they learn from. In fact, they provide the key mechanism that operates at a kind of "meso-scale", serving to structure how microscale propagation of craft traditions eventually feeds into macroscale evolution of cultural diversity

The unifying focus on hunter-gatherers then provides a common framework for analyzing the localized effects of comparable institutions, which generally relate to mobility, interaction, long-term residence patterns, and perhaps most important, postmarital residence patterns. Each can be examined in some more detail:

- *Kinship and postmarital residence rules.* All three regional case studies are characterized by patrilineal and patrilocal settlement and kinship systems; women appear to be moving more frequently than men after marriage. In many areas this may be encouraging a tendency for "male" craft traditions to evolve via branching processes. This tendency certainly applies to Coast Salish housing and canoes, and for plank houses in the Klamath River area. In contrast, "female" crafts like Northwest Californian basketry, and also Coast Salish basketry and matting, appear to be subjected to greater hybridization, in large part because of the more frequent movement of women into new households and communities after marriage than men.

· *Additional amplifiers/dampeners.* A number of contingent factors can then serve to either amplify or dampen this trend toward gendered technologies evolving in contrasting ways. For example, the unique system of paying bride-price to more distant communities in parts of Northwest California can amplify this trend toward greater long-range female mobility, with a coeval intensification in mixing of traits in female material culture traditions, as evidenced by similar basketry traditions that are shared over large parts of the Klamath River area. In contrast, other institutional factors such as the "tribelet" land-holding regimes in the Northeast can reduce these effects if people are only moving short distances after marriage, and in general, tend to stay within a limited vicinity—this is certainly case with non-elite marriages in Northeast California and may have contributed to the formation of more coherent localized basketry traditions here.

· *Ceremonial complexes.* Local land-holding institutions are closely related to ceremonial complexes in Northern California. It is insightful that the more open and inclusive World Renewal ceremonies in the Northwest result in a shared set of dance equipment and regalia, despite the fact that participants speak many unrelated languages. In contrast, the tribelet-sponsored Big Times, which express territoriality and exclusive ownership, are characterized by more localized coherence in ceremonial dress traditions.

In conclusion, then, chapters 3–5 have essentially "lifted the lid" on the evolutionary dynamics of different craft traditions across a range of hunter-gatherer societies. The detailed results overturn simple predictions about the replication of material culture traits always proceeding according to a limited number of trajectories and succeed in empirically mapping out a continuum of different evolutionary outcomes, as well as the behavioral factors that have produced them. In these local case studies, the nature of each operational sequences is extremely variable and affected by the nature of craft, as well as the way in which propagation of the craft is embedded into local social networks. But at a more general, cross-cultural level, it is clear that beyond all the historical contingency, it is social institutions—and their links to different gendering of traditions and practices—that provide some of the main structuring effects on cultural evolution.

In some cases, these institutions act as TRIMS (transmission isolating mechanisms; Durham 1992; chapter 2), serving to "canalize" the propagation of relatively coherent cultural traditions within the boundaries of specific social units. At other times, they actively promote the long-range mobility of people across a wider region, which in turn contributes to more hybridized patterns among local cultural traditions. In many cases, different patterns emerge for the differently gendered traditions—local institutions function as TRIMs for the crafts of one gender but have exactly the opposite effects for crafts propagated by the other gender. Clearly, the book can't give a definitive answer to every question or definitively resolve all debates, but many recurrent themes, intersections and relationships are now starting to emerge; this adds to an growing sense of clarity and perspective in the ongoing quest for more generalized understandings of how and why human technology evolves at interlocking social and spatial scales, and across different culture-historical settings.

OUTLOOK: APPROACHING HUMAN TECHNOLOGY AS
AN *EVOLVING* SOCIAL TRADITION

This book has argued that variability and change in human technology can be researched and understood from a broadly evolutionary perspective, that is, as an expression of the long-term descent with modification of socially-propagated cultural traditions. It has illustrated its approach with a comparative contextual framework, using a shared methodology and the systematic testing of same models in order to produce insights into the themes of cultural propagation, coherence, and congruence. But what is the deeper relevance of these results—and the general approach—to some of the different streams of scholarship identified in chapter 1? These potentially range from the relatively small but now well-established community of specialist culture-evolutionary researchers, through to the more general archaeological and anthropological researchers for whom this book is primarily targeted, as well as scholars who advocate a more exclusively interpretive perspective of human cultural diversity, and who tend to be inherently skeptical of applying any kind of "evolutionary" concepts to humans and their cultural traditions.

Current Culture-Evolutionary Researchers

Following the earlier foundational work on cultural transmission by Cavalli Sforza and Feldman (1981), Boyd and Richerson (1985), and Durham (1991) simulation work and theory building have proceeded apace, but empirical research has generally lagged behind these developments, in part because the lack of openly available high-resolution cultural data sets, especially with regard to variability in technology over time and space (Shennan 2011:3176). This book makes several original contributions to this field, starting most directly with the publication of all the data sets used in the book's case studies (Jordan, forthcoming a and forthcoming b).

Primarily, the book tackles an important gap in current culture evolutionary research, where phylogenetic studies of material culture are still not that common (Gray et al 2010:3929). Building on the published results of a small number of existing ethnographic case-studies (chapter 1), this research project has undertaken the first extended empirical analysis of how *multiple* technological traditions evolve across a comparative range of historical settings and ascending social scales. In addition, it also demonstrates that dual inheritance theory can be successfully combined with fresh ethnographic *fieldwork,* generating new data sets; it also explores how older ethnographic information can be made amenable to these new kinds of analysis. Finally, in studying propagation, coherence, and congruence across a range of different scales, it starts to identify some common patterns in material culture evolution, including the importance of gender and social institutions (see previous), which can generate sharply contrasting patterns in the evolution of different craft traditions within the same geographic region.

But much more work could also be done. One obvious direction for future research with these and related material culture data sets would be to apply a broader range of analytical methods, including the new generation of probability-based phylogenetic tree building methods (see chapter 2). These involve analyzing the same data set with multiple models to make better sense of measures of fit. In contrast, the maximum parsimony methods used here make strong assumptions about many central aspects of descent. Further analytical work could also start to deploy some of the more sophisticated co-phylogenetic methods now available; these move beyond the more generalized comparison of different tree structures that have been conducted in this book (e.g., see Mathews et al. 2011; Tehrani et al. 2010). Overall then, the methods used in this book are relatively basic and have been used in a more "prospective" mode (O'Brien et al. 2013:46); they were also chosen as being more accessible and therefore more suitable for the general archaeological and anthropological readership for whom this book was primarily written. Other methods could also have been directed at analyzing the data generated by the microscale studies of cultural propagation in chapter 3. Instead, a common set of methods were applied across all the chapters; these were primarily used in a more prospective "pattern recognition" mode, so that results from across all chapters could be built into this concluding chapter. Finally, these three ethnographic case studies raise insights and deeper questions about all kind of general relationships that appear to structure diversification and change in material culture lineages. These implications could be explored further via further simulation studies, where such parameters could be used to provide the known dynamics of an empirical system and then used to predict a range of specific outcomes for a given parameter constellation (Steele et al. 2010:3782).

General Archaeological and Anthropological Scholarship

With its broader focus on technology, cultural traditions, and hunter-gatherers, the book also engages with long-running debates in archaeology and anthropology. It generates new and more integrative ways of thinking about the relationships between process, scale, and pattern, especially in the archaeological study of evolution in *long-term* lineages of cultural tradition, and the ways in which these interact with one another. Framed as an empirical exercise in hunter-gatherer ethnoarchaeology, the book also examines how social action and the reproduction of knowledge and skill are caught up with the negotiation of human identities and the formation of cultural boundaries (David and Kramer 2001; Lane 2014; Stark et al. 2008b). In particular, these case studies feed into wider archaeological debates about the factors generating diversity in material culture and its social significance and provide a series of closely worked ethnoarchaeological insights that link material culture patterning with different learning and institutional factors; they also explore how microscale technological practice generates wider material culture distributions of the scale and coherence that might eventually enter the archaeological record in the form of "archaeological cultures" of different spatial scales and temporal durations.

The perennial debate about the extent to which such archaeological cultures, that is, the persistent patterns in time and space that make up the archaeological record, reflect ethnic identity or map in any automatic or predictable way onto language histories remains an open question (Roberts and Vander Linden 2011; Shennan 1989). However, understandings derived from these new case studies might assist archaeologists working in different regions and time periods to forge their own interpretive paths through a wide range of contextual data on settlement, mobility, exchange, and general interaction. Moreover, some of the more specific ethnoarchaeological insights may also help them identify the kinds of situations in which tightly congruent histories that combine long-term material culture traditions, enduring group identities, and language history may—or may not—potentially start to form. Most of the case studies have examined soft and perishable organic technologies like basketry, clothing, and other wooden crafts, but the conceptual analogies with other more archaeologically "visible" material culture traditions like pottery and lithics should be clear. More generally then, this descent-with-modification approach might also be understood as a retooled and refitted version of culture history, one that uses new approaches and concepts for studying the form and content of extended lineages of material culture tradition, but looking at individual and often gendered traditions in turn, and without being weighed down by an overarching imperative to link all these lineages of tradition to particular ethnic groups or modern national identities (see Roberts and van der Linden 2011 for recent revival of long-standing debates about how best to analyze "archaeological cultures").

Finally, it was noted in chapter 1 that the genes–culture analogies could also be taken a step further. In fact, even making this useful analytical distinction between separate—or parallel—biological and cultural inheritance systems may, in the end, be ultimately flawed. The biological processes of development involve a living human organism within its environment, but this is also precisely the process by which cultural skills and knowledge are also inculcated and embodied (Ingold 2007:16). In other words, human life histories are bound up in an unfolding process regenerating both genetic information and also cultural knowledge. This book has focused specifically on the reproduction of material culture traditions, but much more work could be done to examine how these combined genetic and cultural inheritance mechanisms form a more general "co-evolutionary" system, with a renewed focus on examining the "swirling dance" of genetic information and cultural traditions as they are propagated among individuals, populations, and across multiple generations (Boyd and Richerson 1985; Durham 1990, 1991, 1992; Richerson and Boyd 2005:191–95). As argued in chapter 1, the biological histories of people and the histories of cultural traditions will always be linked to one another, but they are certainly not the same thing (Shennan 2004:25). However, exciting prospects for exploring how they do interact are raised by the new scope for integrating research into both modern and ancient human DNA, with the bioarchaeological study of human populations, the (co)evolution of multiple material culture traditions, all of which could also be integrated better within the new "biographic life-histories" approach now emerging in archaeology (see Weber and Zvelebil 2010). Here, analysis of diet, health, and particularly (male *versus* female) mobility patterns, combined with settlement and subsistence studies, could provide insights into how social institutions might be structuring opportunities for social learning, general interaction, and in turn, the wider intergenerational propagation of cultural traditions and genetic information among individuals, communities, and wider populations.

Clearly then, the explicit *ethnoarchaeological* focus in all three case studies generate new ways for archaeologists to start at least *thinking* through some of these potential connections and interrelationships binding knowledge (re)production, heritable continuity in cultural traditions, and both the social and also biological identities of past populations. And looking to the future, it is clear that many regional specialists, with their abiding interests in explaining cultural variability and change at multiple scales, could draw inspiration from these approaches, and in turn, make major contributions to emerging culture-evolutionary research efforts by using their own in-depth knowledge and local data sets to conduct a new generation of empirical case studies that are so badly needed if the field is to move forward (Prentiss 2013; Whiten 2011:945).

Interpretive Perspectives on Cultural Evolution

Finally, it is worth trying to evaluate some of the implications of the descent-with-modification approach to cultural traditions to some of the more exclusively interpretive approaches in archaeology and anthropology. Many scholars working in this intellectual tradition remain uneasy or even actively antithetical about applying any notions of "evolution" to human culture, often mistakenly assuming that it still refers to either the progressive social evolution of Tylor and Morgan, or to a kind of crushing and deterministic imperative on human behavior imposed by the adaptive constraints of local environments. As examined in chapter 1, modern evolutionary perspectives focus on the theme of social learning and the uniquely developed human capacity for cumulative culture; this means that one primary concern is understanding the propagation and contingent history of cultural traditions at a range of different social and temporal scales. As a result, these new approaches break new ground and serve to take debates about the precise nature of cultural evolution into entirely new directions, and as examined here, can be used to study material culture *not* as a simple index of progress, or as adaptive tools, or even as a kind of automatic and "memetic" process of simple and particulate cultural transfer, but as an expression of the complex unfolding of long-term *social tradition.*

This modern evolutionary perspective therefore builds directly upon—but also largely transcends—most of the foundational achievements and assumptions in interpretive archaeology: that material culture is "meaningfully constituted"; that technological traditions are "embedded" in contingent social relations and identities; that they represent stocks of cultural knowledge that are discovered and reproduced through enskillment and routine social practice; and that the active and creative intervention of human agency in these practices makes long-term culture change possible. It is clear then, that many of these processes of cultural (re)production do in fact have some important positive but also negative analogies with genetic inheritance: "Human beings are the bearers of genes whose specific combination is a product of variation under natural selection. . . . They [can also] . . . be the bearers of cultural traditions that may be passed on by a process of learning in some ways analogous to, but by the same token fundamentally distinct from, the processes of genetic replication" (Ingold 2000:2).

This book has systematically worked through some of these parallels, not by building up abstract and highly theoretical position statements, nor by premature claims of grand synthesis and transdisciplinary conquest, but by working through the application of new theory and method to a series of empirical case studies. In fact, it quickly becomes evident that a descent-with-modification perspective provides a useful means of formulating some deeper and also much more *precise* questions about the nature of human social learning and cultural inheritance—in other words, the role of *human agency* within particular times and particular places. For example, it is clear that cultural knowledge is not passed on ready-made but undergoes a process of a continual process of regeneration through guided rediscovery within the social contexts of interaction between instructors and novices (Ingold 2007:16). But such social traditions also persist over time; they exhibit heritable continuity. Thus, it is one thing to highlight the immediate social and environmental contexts associated with the process of enskillment (Ingold 2000), but it is another to ask how best to examine the more specific ways in which these processes of cultural reproduction *unfold* over time, that is, from year to year, from one generation to the next, and onward into deeper historical and archaeological timescales.

Specifically then, *how* and *why* do individuals and their communities make decisions about what aspects of a given corpus of cultural knowledge should be retained and reproduced and what should be actively abandoned or simply forgotten? And how is this creative process reflected in physicality and materiality of technological traditions? It is this latter question that often distinguishes anthropological interest in the localized and interpersonal reproduction of cultural knowledge from the goal of archaeologists, which is to explore how this socially grounded process generates the material residues that go on to form enduring evidence for long-term cultural histories. Ethnoarchaeological research then seeks to bridge these two concerns (David and Kramer 2001), asking how and why do these day-to-day decisions have cumulative, population-scale outcomes that generate the kinds of large-scale patterning in material culture variability and change that make up the extended archaeological record.

At a deeper intellectual level, then, the book aims to creatively integrate a *qualitative*, historical, and humanities-based traditions of interpretation on the one side, with an analytical, *quantitative*, and model-based approach on the other. There are signs that this intellectual engagement is now starting to generate a fuller understanding of the range of factors that generate human technological diversity. If this kind of approach can be developed further, then a shared focus on understanding the descent with modification of technological and other cultural traditions could serve as a unifying project spanning archaeology and anthropology, one built on shared concerns with understanding all the evolved capacities, local complexities, and historical contingencies of social learning and cultural inheritance that make humans so strikingly different from even closely related primate species (table 1.1). This will be a challenging engagement, and will no doubt produce many difficulties and frustrations on all sides (Ingold 2007:13), but there are positive indications of grounds for at least some degree of future synthesis, especially around the central themes of social learning and the creative reproduction of cultural knowledge. These, in turn, could provide a common focus in the renewed pursuit of a "generous, comparative but nonetheless critical understanding of human being and knowing in the one world we all inhabit" (Ingold 2007:17).

CONCLUSION

This monograph represents the first book-length empirical analysis of material culture traditions using an explicitly descent-with-modification perspective. The central focus on the "socially embedded" nature of technological traditions and knowledge reproduction illustrates how pursuit of microscale insights into social meanings and identities can effectively be integrated with analyses that focus on understanding larger-scale patterns and processes of material culture diversification. In tracking the operation of hunter-gatherer social networks in historically contingent settings, this book also sets out news ways of researching and understanding the operation of *agency* in forager societies at different social scales and over ascending time periods. A focus on the inheritance and practice of technological traditions builds on, and also bridges, the enduring divide between adaptive perspectives and those that emphasize the more localized roles of human action and social meaning. Instead, through each of the case studies, it is possible to start to identify the ways in which the "political" agency of social aspiration, negotiation of wealth, status and marital contracts, and the central role of ceremonial and kinship institutions all serve to create the social conditions in which the content of individual material culture traditions are acquired, practised and transformed.

In turn, by using a descent-with-modification approach, and by explicitly focusing on comparative analysis of evolutionary dynamics across a series of "embedded" technological traditions, it is possible to gain richer and more holistic insights into the social mechanisms that generate cultural diversity in both the past and the present. In this way, identifying and tracking particular trajectories of cultural inheritance provide ethnoarchaeological insights into the broader social significance of material culture as well as its complex relationships with skilled technological practice, social networks, and cultural boundaries.

In summary then, this book concludes that a descent-with-modification framework emerges as the most productive means for uniting different branches of current anthropological and archaeological research, as well as for untangling the complexities of interlocking cultural, linguistic, and (potentially) genetic transmission histories via specific case studies. Thus, a renewed focus on the dynamic histories of cultural inheritance provides the conceptual "glue" to bring together material culture studies, the anthropology of technology, hunter-gatherers research, and many other related fields of general archaeological and anthropological inquiry.

The approach presented here is *integrative*, bringing together interlocking scales and theoretical perspectives, for example, from enskillment and agency/practice theory through to modern culture-evolutionary studies inspired by dual inheritance theorists and the biological sciences, and it is also *empirical*, which is the touchstone of all good theory and research. Moreover, the analytical framework outlined here is also readily *portable* to other case studies, data sets, periods, and regions. And above all, the analyses and approaches presented in this book promise new ways of exploring and understanding the factors that generate the endless richness of human cultural diversity in both the deeper past and in the present. And that has been the overarching intellectual goal of archaeology and anthropology since the earliest inception of these closely related disciplines.

Appendix

Mantel Matrix Correlations

Gulf of Georgia Salish

PART I   PAIRWISE CORRELATIONS

Cultural Assemblage and Linguistic Affinity (cognates)	Plank Houses	Canoes	Baskets /Matting
Mean value	0,655028	0,703611	0,699857
Sums of squares Y	0,267143	0,257199	0,398041
Mean value X1	42,583333	42,583333	41,857143
Sums of squares MX1	9230,75	9230,75	6067,428571
ZY1	1033,398	1082,437	841,298
Sum of products (SP(Y,X1))	29,240417	3,801167	21,065429
Regression coefficient (*b*Y1)	0,003168	0,000412	0,003472
Correlation coefficient (*r*Y1)	0,588834	0,078012	0,428651
Determination of cultural assemblage (Y) variability by language cognates (X1)(%)	0,346726	0,006086	0,183742

Cultural Assemblage and General Linguistic Affinity (Goddard 1996)	Plank Houses	Canoes	Baskets /Matting
Mean value Y	0,655028	0,703611	0,699857
Sums of squares Y	0,267143	0,257199	0,398041

Mean value X1	55	55	53,214286
Sums of squares MX1	7200	7200	3760,714286
ZY1	1315,85	1394,975	1054,95
Sum of products (SP(Y,X1))	18,895	1,825	12,162857
Regression coefficient (bY1)	0,002624	0,000253	0,003234
Correlation coefficient (rY1)	0,430833	0,042409	0,314367
Determination of cultural assemblage (Y) variability by general linguistic affinity (X1)(%)	0,185617	0,001799	0,098826

Cultural Assemblage and Proximity	Plank Houses	Canoes	Baskets /Matting
Mean value Y	0,655028	0,703611	0,699857
Sums of squares Y	0,267143	0,257199	0,398041
Mean value X1	82	82	75,5
Sums of squares MX1	51186	51186	30311
ZY1	1896,531	2046,235	1439,59
Sum of products (SP(Y,X1))	−37,111	−30,825	−39,908
Regression coefficient (bY1)	−0,000725	−0,000602	−0,001317
Correlation coefficient (rY1)	−0,317362	−0,268654	−0,363325
Determination of cultural assemblage (Y) variability by proximity (X1)(%)	0,100719	0,072175	0,132005

Cultural Assemblage and Sea Distances	Plank Houses	Canoes	Baskets /Matting
Mean value Y	0,655028	0,703611	0,699857
Sums of squares Y	0,267143	0,257199	0,398041
Mean value X1	99,527778	99,527778	90,535714
Sums of squares MX1	68544,97222	68544,97222	42884,96429
ZY1	2304,729	2503,034	1739,401
Sum of products (SP(Y,X1))	−42,235528	−18,004611	−34,736857
Regression coefficient (bY1)	−0,000616	−0,000263	−0,00081
Correlation coefficient (rY1)	−0,312118	−0,135601	−0,265873
Determination of cultural assemblage (Y) variability by sea distances (X1)(%)	0,097417	0,018388	0,070688

Cultural Assemblage and Ring Distances	Plank Houses	Canoes	Baskets/ Matting
Mean value Y	0,655028	0,703611	0,699857
Sums of squares Y	0,267143	0,257199	0,398041
Mean value X1	2,5	2,5	2,5
Sums of squares MX1	45	45	35
ZY1	57,551	61,868	47,871
Sum of products (SP(Y,X1))	−1,4015	−1,457	−1,119
Regression coefficient (bY1)	−0,031144	−0,032378	−0,031971
Correlation coefficient (rY1)	−0,404217	−0,428271	−0,2998
Determination of cultural assemblage (Y) variability by ring distances (X1)(%)	0,163392	0,183416	0,08988

Cultural Assemblage and C-Distances	Plank Houses	Canoes	Baskets/ Matting
Mean value Y	0,655028	0,703611	0,699857
Sums of squares Y	0,267143	0,257199	0,398041
Mean value X1	3,5	3,5	3,642857
Sums of squares MX1	147	147	120,428571
ZY1	78,878	87,185	69,718
Sum of products (SP(Y,X1))	−3,6555	−1,47	−1,667429
Regression coefficient (bY1)	−0,024867	−0,01	−0,013846
Correlation coefficient (rY1)	−0,583333	−0,23907	−0,240834
Determination of cultural assemblage (Y) variability by C-distances (X1)(%)	0,340277	0,057154	0,058001

PART 2   PARTIAL CORRELATIONS *(using strongest pairwise correlations)*

Material Culture/Language Measure/Distance Measure	Plank Houses	Canoes	Baskets /Matting
Mean value Y	0,655028	0,703611	0,699857
Sums of squares Y	0,267143	0,257199	0,398041
Mean value X1	42,583333	42,583333	41,857143
Sums of squares MX1	9230,75	9230,75	6067,428571
Mean value X2	3,5	2,5	75,5
Sums of squares MX1	147	45	30311
ZY1	1033,398	1082,437	841,298
ZY2	78,878	61,868	1439,59
Z12	4799	3493	79704
Sum of products (SP(Y,X1))	29,240417	3,801167	21,065429

Sum of products (SP(Y,X2))	–3,6555	–1,457	–39,908
Sum of products (SP(X1,X1))	–566,5	–339,5	–8782
Regression coefficient (bY1)	0,003168	0,000412	0,003472
Regression coefficient (bY2)	–0,024867	–0,032378	–0,001317
Partial regression (bY1_2)	0,00215	–0,001078	0,002697
Partial regression (bY2_1)	–0,016581	–0,040512	–0,000535
Correlation coefficient (rY1)	0,588834	0,078012	0,428651
	$p = 0.000$	$p = 0.000$	$p = 0.001$
Correlation coefficient (rY2)	–0,583333	–0,428271	–0,363325
	$p = 0.005$	$p = 0.000$	$p = 0.000$
Correlation coefficient (r12)	–0,486321	–0,526763	–0,647576
Partial correlation (rY1_2)	0,429959	–0,192139	0,27238
	$p = 0.036$	$p = 0.000$	$p = 0.012$
Partial correlation (rY2_1)	–0,420497	–0,456888	–0,124543
	$p = 0.008$	$p = 0.000$	$p = 0.000$
Effects of			
Language alone (%)	12	3	6
Distance alone (%)	12	21	1
Effects combined			
Raw r^2 for language	0,35	0,01	0,18
Add distance	0,12	0,21	0,01
Total	0,47	0,22	0,19
Total effect (%)	47	22	19
Effect made up of			
Just language (%)	12	3	6
Just distance (%)	12	21	1
Joint effect (%)	23	0	12
Total % effect	47	24	19

PART 3   PAIRWISE TESTS FOR CO-TRANSMISSION OF LANGUAGE AND
TECHNOLOGICAL TRADITIONS

	Plank houses	Canoes	Language	Cognates
Plank houses				
Canoes	4			
Language	18	0		
Cognates	34	1	55	

CHAPTER 5

Section A. NW California

Cultural Assemblage and Linguistic Affinity	Basketry	Houses	Ceremonial Dress
Mean value Y	0,805876	0,50881	0,455011
Sums of squares Y	1,937145	8,775626	6,463785
Mean value X1	24,142857	24,142857	27,087912
Sums of squares MX1	81772,85714	81772,85714	75853,2967
ZY1	2030,095	1409,43	1089,21
Sum of products (SP(Y,X1))	–12,801143	119,597857	–32,392088
Regression coefficient (bY1)	–0,000157	0,001463	–0,000427
Correlation coefficient (rY1)	–0,032163	0,141182	–0,04626
Determination of cultural assemblage (Y) variability by linguistic affinity (X1)(%)	0,001034	0,019932	0,00214

Cultural Assemblage and Proximity	Basketry	Houses	Ceremonial Dress
Mean value Y	0,805876	0,50881	0,455011
Sums of squares Y	1,937145	8,775626	6,463785
Mean value X1	5,600735	5,600735	5,773818
Sums of squares MX1	1016,803648	1016,803648	936,745236
ZY1	446,322015	250,099643	198,407975
Sum of products (SP(Y,X1))	–27,595399	–49,119637	–40,662716
Regression coefficient (bY1)	–0,027139	–0,048308	–0,043409
Correlation coefficient (rY1)	–0,62178	–0,519993	–0,522567
Determination of cultural assemblage (Y) variability by proximity (X1)(%)	0,386611	0,270393	0,273077

Material Culture/Language /Proximity	Basketry	Houses	Ceremonial Dress
Mean value Y	0,805876	0,50881	0,455011
Sums of squares Y	1,937145	8,775626	6,463785
Mean value X1	24,142857	24,142857	27,087912
Sums of squares MX1	81772,85714	81772,85714	75853,2967
Mean value X2	5,600735	5,600735	5,773818

Sums of squares MX1	1016,803648	1016,803648	936,745236
ZY1	2030,095	1409,43	1089,21
ZY2	446,322015	250,099643	198,407975
Z12	12222,705	12222,705	11909,406
Sum of products (SP(Y,X1))	-12,801143	119,597857	-32,392088
Sum of products (SP(Y,X2))	-27,595399	-49,119637	-40,662716
Sum of products (SP(X1,X1))	-1975,158829	-1975,158829	-2323,054341
Regression coefficient (bY1)	-0,000157	0,001463	-0,000427
Regression coefficient (bY2)	-0,027139	-0,048308	-0,043409
Partial regression (bY1_2)	-0,000852	0,00031	-0,001901
Partial regression (bY2_1)	-0,028794	-0,047705	-0,048122
Correlation coefficient (rY1)	-0,032163	0,141182	-0,04626
	$p = 0.000$	$p = 0.000$	$p = 0.001$
Correlation coefficient (rY2)	-0,62178	-0,519993	-0,522567
	$p = 0.000$	$p = 0.000$	$p = 0.000$
Correlation coefficient (r12)	-0,21661	-0,21661	-0,275589
Partial correlation (rY1_2)	-0,218216	0,034233	-0,23216
	$p = 0.003$	$p = 0.012$	$p = 0.000$
Partial correlation (rY2_1)	-0,644371	-0,506386	-0,557478
	$p = 0.000$	$p = 0.021$	$p = 0.004$
Effects of			
Language alone (%)	2	1	4
Proximity alone (%)	42	26	31
Effects combined			
Raw r^2 for language	0,001	0,020	0,002
Add proximity	0,42	0,26	0,31
Total	0,42	0,28	0,31
Total effect (%)	42	28	31
Effect made up of			
Just language (%)	2	1	4
Just proximity (%)	42	26	31
Joint effect (%)	0	1	0
Total % effect	44	28	35

PART 3 PAIRWISE TESTS FOR CO-TRANSMISSION OF LANGUAGE AND
TECHNOLOGICAL TRADITIONS

	Basketry	Houses	Ceremonial Dress	Language
Basketry				
Houses	7			
Ceremonial Dress	n/a	n/a		
Language	0	14	n/a	

NOTE: The matrix for ceremonial traits was a different size so impossible to correlate with basketry or houses.

Section B. NE California

Cultural Assemblage and Linguistic Affinity	Basketry	Earth Lodges	Ceremonial Dress
Mean value Y	0,545849	0,382187	0,32278
Sums of squares Y	3,014211	0,78453	1,638942
Mean value X1	20,824176	20,824176	20,824176
Sums of squares MX1	82513,18681	82513,18681	82513,18681
ZY1	1345,398876	821,085	814,125
Sum of products (SP(Y,X1))	311,014256	96,840989	202,456484
Regression coefficient (bY1)	0,003769	0,001174	0,002454
Correlation coefficient (rY1)	0,623637	0,380621	0,550539
Determination of cultural assemblage (Y) variability by linguistic affinity (X1)(%)	0,388923	0,144872	0,303093

Cultural Assemblage and Proximity	Basketry	Earth Lodges	Ceremonial Dress
Mean value Y	0,545849	0,382187	0,32278
Sums of squares Y	3,014211	0,78453	1,638942
Mean value X1	4,397021	4,397021	4,397021
Sums of squares MX1	435,346656	435,346656	435,346656
ZY1	189,180754	145,61745	110,042689
Sum of products (SP(Y,X1))	−29,229368	−7,306539	−19,111005
Regression coefficient (bY1)	−0,06714	−0,016783	−0,043898
Correlation coefficient (rY1)	−0,806891	−0,395357	−0,715458
Determination of cultural assemblage (Y) variability by proximity (X1)(%)	0,651073	0,156307	0,51188

Material Culture/Language/ Proximity	Basketry	Earth Lodges	Ceremonial Dress
Mean value Y	0,545849	0,382187	0,32278
Sums of squares Y	3,014211	0,78453	1,638942
Mean value X1	20,824176	20,824176	20,824176
Sums of squares MX1	82513,18681	82513,18681	82513,18681
Mean value X2	4,397021	4,397021	4,397021
Sums of squares MX1	435,346656	435,346656	435,346656

ZY1	1345,398876	821,085	814,125
ZY2	189,180754	145,61745	110,042689
Z12	5007,6075	5007,6075	5007,6075
Sum of products (SP(Y,X1))	311,014256	96,840989	202,456484
Sum of products (SP(Y,X2))	-29,229368	-7.306539	-19,111005
Sum of products (SP(X1,X1))	-3324,747066	-3324,747066	-3324,747066
Regression coefficient (bY1)	0,003769	0,001174	0,002454
Regression coefficient (bY2)	-0,06714	-0,016783	-0,043898
Partial regression (bY1_2)	0,001537	0,000718	0,000989
Partial regression (bY2_1)	-0,055403	-0,011296	-0,036344
Correlation coefficient (rY1)	0,623637	0,380621	0,550539
	$p = 0.000$	$p = 0.001$	$p = 0.000$
Correlation coefficient (rY2)	-0,806891	-0,395357	-0,715458
	$p = 0.000$	$p = 0.000$	$p = 0.000$
Correlation coefficient (r12)	-0,554727	-0,554727	-0,554727
Partial correlation (rY1_2)	0,358167	0,211066	0,264329
	$p = 0.000$	$p = 0.002$	$p = 0.000$
Partial correlation (rY2_1)	-0,708694	-0,239426	-0,590363
	$p = 0.005$	$p = 0.026$	$p = 0.012$
Effects of			
Language alone (%)	5	3	3
Proximity alone (%)	30	5	25
Effects combined			
Raw r2 for language	0,4	0,14	0,3
Add proximity	0,3	0,5	0,25
Total	0,7	0,19	0,55
Total effect (%)	70	19	55
Effect made up of			
Just language (%)	5	3	3
Just proximity (%)	30	5	25
Joint effect (%)	35	11	27
Total % effect	70	19	55

PART 3   PAIRWISE TESTS FOR CO-TRANSMISSION OF LANGUAGE AND
TECHNOLOGICAL TRADITIONS

Basketry			
Earth Lodges	9		
Ceremonial Dress	49	13	
Language	39	14	30
	Basketry	Earth Lodges	Ceremonial Dress	Language

References

Ames, K.M. 1994. The Northwest Coast: Complex Hunter-Gatherers, Ecology, and Social Evolution. *Annual Review of Anthropology* 23: 209–29.

Ames, K.M., and H.D.G. Maschner. 1999. *Peoples of the Northwest Coast: Their Archaeology and Prehistory*. London: Thames and Hudson.

Anderson, D.G. 2006. Dwellings, Storage and Summer Site Structure among Siberian Orochen Evenkis: Hunter-Gatherer Vernacular Architecture under Post-Socialist Conditions. *Norwegian Archaeological Review* 39 (1): 1–26.

Apel, J. 2001. *Daggers, Knowledge and Power: The Social Aspects of Flint-Dagger Technology in Scandinavia 2350–1500 cal BC*. Kust till Kust Bok 3. Uppsala: Dept. of Archaeology and Ancient History, Uppsala University.

Bakhlykov, P. 1996. *Iuganskie khanty: Istoriia, byt, kul'tura*. Tiumen: Softdizain.

Barbujani, G. 1995. Reply to Roberts, Moore and Romney. *Current Anthropology* 36: 769–88.

Barnett, H.G. 1939. *Culture Element Distributions: IX Gulf of Georgia Salish*. University of California Anthropological Records 1(5): i–iv, 221–95.

———. 1955. *The Coast Salish of British Columbia*. Eugene: University of Oregon Press.

Bateman, R., and I. Goddard, R.O'Grady, V.A. Funk, R. Mooi, W.J. Kress, and P. Cannell. 1990. Speaking of Forked Tongues: The Feasibility of Reconciling Human Phylogeny and the History of Language. *Current Anthropology* 31:124.

Baumhoff, M.A. 1958. California Athapaskan Groups. *Anthropological Records* 16:5.

———. 1978. Environmental Background. In R.F. Heizer (ed.), *California: Handbook of North American Indians*. Vol. 8. William C. Sturtevant, gen. ed. Washington DC: Smithsonian Institution Press, 16–24.

Bentley, R.A., M.W. Hahn, and S.J. Shennan. 2004. Random Drift and Culture Change. *Proceedings of the Royal Society of London* B 271: 1443–50.

Bentley, R.A., C. Lipo, Maschner H.D.G., and B. Marler. 2008. Darwinian Archaeologies. In R.A. Bentley, H.D.G. Maschner, and C. Chippendale (eds.), *Handbook of Archaeological Theories.* Lanham, MD: Rowman and Littlefield, 109–32.

Bernick, K. 2003. A stitch in Time: Recovering the Antiquity of a Coast Salish Basket Type. In R.G. Matson, G. Coupland, and Q. Mackie (eds.), *Emerging from the Mist: Studies in Northwest Coast Culture History.* Vancouver: University of British Columbia Press, 230–43.

Bettinger, R.L., and J. Eerkens, 1999. Point Typologies, Cultural Transmission, and the Spread of Bow-and-Arrow Technology in the Prehistoric Great Basin. *American Antiquity* 64 (2): 231–42.

Bettinger, R.L., and E. Wohlgemuth, 2006. California Plants. In D.H. Ubelaker (ed.), *Handbook of North American Indians.* Vol. 3. William C. Sturtevant, gen. ed. Washington, DC: Smithsonian Institution Press, 274–83.

Binford, L.R. 1980. Willow Smoke and Dogs' Tails: Hunter Gatherer Settlement Systems and Archaeological Site Formation. *American Antiquity* 45: 4–20.

Borgerhoff Mulder, M., C.L. Nunn, and M.C.Towner, 2006. Cultural Macroevolution and the Transmission of Traits. *Evolutionary Anthropology* 15 (2): 52–64.

Bowern, C. 2010. Historical Linguistics in Australia. *Philosophical Transactions of the Royal Society* 365 (1559): 3845–85.

Boyd, R., and P.J. Richerson, 1985. *Culture and the Evolutionary Process.* Chicago: University of Chicago Press.

———. 2005. *The Origin and Evolution of Cultures.* Oxford: Oxford University Press.

Boyd, R., M. Borgerhoff-Mulder, W.H. Durham, and P.J. Richerson, 1997. Are cultural Phylogenies Possible? In P. Weingart, S.D. Mitchell, P.J. Richerson, and S. Maasen (eds.), *Human by Nature: Between Biology and the Social Sciences.* London: Erlbaum, 355–86.

Bright, W. 1978. Karok. In Robert F. Heizer (ed.): *California: Handbook of North American Indians.* Vol. 8. William C. Sturtevant, gen. ed. Washington, DC: Smithsonian Institution Press, 180–89.

Brooks, D.R., and D.A. McLennan. 1991. *Phylogeny, Ecology and Behavior.* Chicago: University of Chicago Press.

Bryant, D., F. Filimon, and R.D. Gray. 2005. Untangling Our Past: Languages, Trees, Splits and Networks. In R. Mace, C. Holden, and S.J. Shennan (eds.), *The Evolution of Cultural Diversity: A Phylogenetic Approach.* London: University College London Press, 67–85.

Bryant. D., and V. Moulton. 2002. NeighborNet: An Agglomerative Clustering Method for the Construction of Planar Phylogenetic Networks. In: R.Guigo and D. Gusfield (eds.), *Workshop in Bioinformatics (WABI).* Berlin and London: Springer, 375-91.

———. 2004. NeighborNet: An Agglomerative Method for the Construction of Planar Phylogenetic Networks. *Molecular Biology and Evolution* 21 (2): 255–65.

Buchanon, B., and M. Collard. 2007. Investigating the Peopling of North America through Cladistic Analysis of early Paleoindian Projectile Points. *Journal of Archaeological Science* 26: 366–93.

———. 2008. Phenetics, Cladistics, and the Search for the Alaskan Ancestors of the Palaeoindians: A Reassessment of Relationships among the Clovis, Nenana, and Denali Archaeological Complexes. *Journal of Archaeological Science* 35 (2008): 1683–94.

Butler, V.L., and SK. Campbell. 2006. Northwest Coast and Plateau Animals. In D.H. Ubelaker (ed.), *Handbook of North American Indians*. Vol. 3. William C. Sturtevant, gen. ed. Washington: Smithsonian Institution Press, 263–73.

Caldwell, C.A., and A.E. Millen, 2009. Social Learning Mechanisms and Cumulative Cultural Evolution: Is Imitation Necessary? *Psychological Science* 20 (12): 1478–83.

Cameron, H.D. 1987. The Upside-Down Cladogram: Problems in Manuscript Affiliation. In H.M., Hoenigswald and L.F Wiener (eds.), *Biological Metaphor and Cladistic Classification: An Interdisciplinary Perspective*. Philadelphia: University of Pennsylvania Press, 227–42.

Castro, L., and M.A Toro. 2004. The Evolution of Culture: From Primate Social Learning to Human Culture. *Proceedings of the National Academy of Sciences of the United States of America* 101: 10235–40.

Cavalli-Sforza, L.L., and M.W. Feldman. 1981. *Cultural Transmission and Evolution: A Quantitative Approach*. Princeton: Princeton University Press.

Chagnon, N.A., and W. Irons (eds.). 1979. *Evolutionary Biology and Human Social Behavior*. North Scituate, MA: Duxbury.

Chase-Dunn, C., and T.D. Hall. 1997. *Rise and Demise: Comparing World Systems*. Oxford: Westview.

Childe, V.G. 1951. *Social Evolution*. New York: Schuman.

Clark, C., and D.J. Curran, 1986. Outgroup Analysis, Homoplasy, and Global Parsimony: A Response to Maddison, Donoghue, and Maddison. *Systematic Zoology* 35: 422–26.

Cochrane, E.E. 2009. Evolutionary Explanation and the Record of Interest: Using Evolutionary Archaeology and Dual Inheritance Theory to Explain the Archaeological Record. In S.J. Shennan (ed.), *Pattern and Process in Cultural Evolution*. Berkeley: University of California Press, 113–32.

Cochrane, E.E., and C.P. Lipo, 2010. Phylogenetic Analyses of Lapita Decoration Do Not Support Branching Evolution or Regional Population Structure during Colonization of Remote Oceania. *Philosophical Transactions of the Royal Society B* 365: 3889–902.

Collard, M., and S.J. Shennan, 2008. Patterns, Processes and Parsimony: Studying Cultural Evolution with Analytical Techniques from Evolutionary Biology. In M. Stark, B.J. Bowser, and L. Horne (eds.), *Cultural Transmission and Material Culture: Breaking Down Boundaries*. Tucson: University of Arizona Press, 17–33.

Collard, M., S.J. Shennan, B. Buchanan, and R.A. Bentley. 2008. Evolutionary Biological Methods and Cultural Data. In R.A. Bentley, H.D.G. Maschner, and C. Chippendale (eds.), *Handbook of Archaeological Theories*. Lanham MD: Rowman and Littlefield, 203–24.

Collard, M., Shennan, S.J., and J.J. Tehrani. 2006a. Branching Versus Blending in Macro-Scale Cultural Evolution. In C. Lipo et al. (eds.), *Mapping Our Ancestors. Phylogenetic Approaches in Anthropology and Prehistory.* New Brunswick, NJ: Aldine Transaction, 53–56.

———. 2006b. Branching, Blending and the Evolution of Cultural Similarities and Differences among Human Populations. *Evolution and Human Behavior* 27: 169–84.

Collard, M., and J.J. Tehrani. 2005. Phylogenesis Versus Ethnogenesis in Turkmen Cultural Evolution. In R. Mace, C.J. Holden, and S. Shennan (eds.), *The Evolution of Cultural Diversity: A Phylogenetic Approach.* London: University College London Press, 109–13.

Croes, D.R. 2003. Northwest Coast Wet-Site Artifacts: A Key to Understanding Resource Procurement, Storage, Management and Exchange. In R.G. Matson, G. Coupland, and Q. Mackie (eds.), *Emerging from the Mist: Studies in Northwest Coast Culture History.* Vancouver: University of British Columbia Press, 51–75.

Csibra, G., and G. Gergely. 2006. Social Learning and Social Cognition: The Case for Pedagogy. In Y. Munakata and M.H. Johnson (eds.), *Attention and Performance XXI: Processes of Change in Brain and Cognitive Development.* Oxford: Oxford University Press, 249–74.

———. 2011. Natural Pedagogy as Evolutionary Adaptation. *Philosophical Transactions of the Royal Society* B 366: 1149–57.

Danchin, E., S. Blanchet, F. Mery, and R.H. Wagner. 2010. Do Invertebrates Have Culture? *Communicative and Integrative Biology* 3 (4): 303–5.

Darwin, C. 1859. *On the Origin of Species.* London: John Murray.

David, N., and C. Kramer. 2001. *Ethnoarchaeology in Action.* Cambridge: Cambridge University Press.

Dawkins, R. 1976. *The Selfish Gene.* Oxford: Oxford University Press.

Dean, L.G., R.L., Kendal, S.J., Schapiro, B. Thierry, and K. Laland. 2012. Identification of the Social and Cognitive Processes Underlying Human Cumulative Culture. *Science* 335: 1114–18.

Dewar, R.E. 1995. Of Nets and Trees: Untangling the Reticulate and Dendritic in Madagascar Prehistory. *World Archaeology* 26: 301–18.

Dobres, M-A. 2000. *Technology and Social Agency. Outlining a Practice Framework for Archaeology.* Oxford: Blackwell.

Driver, H.E. 1939. Culture Element Distributions: X, Northwest California. *Anthropological Records* 1(6): i–v, 297–43.

Drucker, P.A. 1950. Culture Element Distributions: XXVI, Northwest Coast. *Anthropological Records* 9: i–iv, 157–29.

Du Bois, C. 1935. Wintu Ethnography. *University of California Publications in American Archaeology and Ethnology* 36 (1): 1–148.

Dunin-Gorkavitch, A.A. 1995 [1904]. *Tobol'skii Sever.* Vol. 1. Moscow: Liberia Publishing House.

———. 1996 [1910]. *Tobol'skii Sever.* Vol. 2. Moscow: Liberia Publishing House.

Dunnell, R.C. 1978. Style and Function: A Fundamental Dichotomy. *American Antiquity* 43: 192–20.

———. 1980. Evolutionary Theory and Archaeology. In M.B. Schiffer (ed.), *Advances in Archaeological Method and Theory*. Vol. 3. New York: Academic Press, 35–99.

Durham, W.H. 1979. Toward a Coevolutionary Theory of Human Biology and Culture. In N. Chagnon and W. Irons (eds.), *Evolutionary Biology and Human Social Behavior*. North Scituate, MA: Duxbury, 39–59.

———. 1982. Interactions of Genetic and Cultural Evolution: Models and Examples. *Human Ecology* 10: 289–32.

———. 1990. Advances in Evolutionary Culture Theory. *Annual Review of Anthropology*, 19: 187–210.

———. 1991. *Coevolution: Genes, Culture and Human Diversity*. Stanford CA: Stanford University Press.

———. 1992. Applications of Evolutionary Culture Theory. *Annual Review of Anthropology* 21: 331–55.

Eerkens, J.W. 2000. Practice Makes within 5% of Perfect: Visual Perception, Motor Skills, and Memory in Artifact Variation. *Current Anthropology* 41 (4): 663–68.

Eerkens, J.W., and C.P. Lipo. 2005. Cultural Transmission, Copying Errors, and the Generation of Variation in Material Culture and the Archaeological Record. *Journal of Anthropological Archaeology* 24: 316–34.

———. 2007. Cultural Transmission Theory and the Archaeological Record: Context to Understanding Variation and Temporal Changes in Material Culture. *Journal of Archaeological Research* 15: 239–74.

Ellen, R.F., S.J. Lycett, and S.E. Johns (eds.). 2013. *Understanding Cultural Transmission in Anthropology: A Critical Synthesis*. New York and Oxford: Berghahn.

Elsasser, A.B. 1978a. Basketry. In Robert F. Heizer (ed.), *California: Handbook of North American Indians*. Vol. 8. William C. Sturtevant, gen. ed. Washington, DC: Smithsonian Institution Press, 626–41.

Elsasser, A.B. 1978b. Mattole, Nongatl, Sinkyone, Lassik and Wailaki. In Robert F. Heizer (ed.), *California: Handbook of North American Indians*. Vol. 8. William C. Sturtevant, gen. ed. Washington, DC: Smithsonian Institution Press, 190–204.

Elsasser, A.B 1978c. Wiyot. In Robert F. Heizer, ed. *California: Handbook of North American Indians*. Vol. 8. William C. Sturtevant, gen. ed. Washington, DC: Smithsonian Institution Press, 155–63.

Fagan, B. 2000. *Ancient North America: The Archaeology of a Continent,* 3rd ed. New York: Thames and Hudson.

———. 2003. *Before California: An Archaeologist Looks at Our Earliest Inhabitants*. New York: Rowman and Littlefield.

Farris, J.S. 1982. Outgroups and Parsimony. *Systematic Zoology* 31: 328–34.

———. 1989a. The Retention Index and Homoplasy Excess. *Systematic Zoology* 38: 406–7.

———. 1989b. The Retention Index and the Rescaled Consistency Index. *Cladistics* 5: 417–19.

Fedorova, E.G. 2000. *Rybolovy i okhotniki basseina obi: Problemy formirovaniia kultury khantov i mansi.* Saint Petersburg: Evropeiskii Dom.

Felsenstein, J. 2004. *Inferring Phylogenies.* Sunderland, MA: Sinauer Associates, Inc.

Foley, R., and M.M. Lahr. 2011. The Evolution of the Diversity of Cultures. *Philosophical Transactions of the Royal Society* B 366: 1080–89.

Forey, P.L., C.J. Humphries, I.J., Kitching, R.W., Scotland, D.J. Siebert, and D.M. Williams. 1992. *Cladistics: A Practical Course in Systematics.* Oxford: Claredon Press.

Forsyth, J. 1992. *A History of the Peoples of Siberia: Russia's North Asian Colony, 1581—1990.* Cambridge: Cambridge University Press.

Fragaszy, D.M., and S. Perry. 2003. *The Biology of Traditions: Models and Evidence.* Cambridge: Cambridge University Press.

Fuentes, A. 2009. *Evolution of Human Behaviour.* Oxford: Oxford University Press.

Garth, T.R. 1953. Atsugewi Ethnography. *University of California Publications in American Archaeology and Ethnology* 14 (2): 129–212.

———. 1978. Atsugewi. In R.F. Heizer (ed.), *California: Handbook of North American Indians.* Vol. 8. William C. Sturtevant, gen. ed. Washington, DC: Smithsonian Institution, 236–43.

Giddens, A. 1984. *The Constitution of Society: Outline of the Theory of Structuration.* Cambridge: Polity.

Glavatskaia, E. 2002. *Khanty v sostave russkogo gosudarstva.* In A. Wiget (ed.), *Ocherki istorii traditsionnogo zemlepol'zovanniia khantov (Materialy k Atlasu).* 2nd ed. Ekaterinburg: Tezis, 76–122.

Goddard, I. 1996. Introduction. In I. Goddard (ed.), *Languages. Handbook of North American Indians.* Vol. 17. William C. Sturtevant, gen. ed. Washington, DC: Smithsonian Institution Press, 1–16.

Golla, V. 1996. Sketch of Hupa, an Athapaskan language. In I. Goddard (ed.), *Languages. Handbook of North American Indians.* Vol. 17. William C. Sturtevant, gen. ed. Washington, DC: Smithsonian Institution, 364–89.

Golovnev, A.V. 1993. *Istoricheskaia tipologia khoziaistva narodov Severo-Zapadnoi Sibiri.* Novosibirsk: INU.

Gosselain, O. 1998. Social and Technical Identity in a Clay Crystal Ball. In M. Stark (ed.), *The Archaeology of Social Boundaries.* Washington, DC: Smithsonian Institution Press, 78–106.

Gould, R.A. 1978. Tolowa. In Robert F. Heizer (ed.), *California: Handbook of North American Indians.* Vol. 8. William C. Sturtevant, gen. ed. Washington, DC: Smithsonian Institution Press, 128–36.

Grandcolas, P., and R. Pellens. 2005. Evolving *sensu lato:* All We Need Is Systematics. *Cladistics* 21: 501–5.

Gray, R. D., D. Bryant, and S. J. Greenhill. 2010. On the shape and fabric of human history. *Philosophical Transactions of the Royal Society* B: 3923–33.

Gray, R.D., S.J. Greenhill, and R.M. Ross, 2007. The Pleasures and Perils of Darwinzing Culture (with Phylogenies). *Biological Theory* 2: 360–75.

Greenhill, S.J., and R.D. Gray. 2009. Austronesian Language Phylogenies: Myths and Misconceptions about Bayesian Computational Methods. In A.

Adelaar and A. Pawley (eds.), *Austronesian Historical Linguistics and Culture History: A Festschrift for Robert Blust*. Canberra: Pacific Linguistics, 1–23.

Grier, C., 2003. Dimensions of Regional Interaction in the Prehistoric Gulf. In R.G. Matson, G. Coupland, and Q. Mackie (eds.), *Emerging from the Mist: Studies in Northwest Coast Culture History*. Vancouver: University of British Columbia Press, 170–87.

Guglielmino, C.R., C. Vignotti, B. Hewlett, and L.L. Cavali-Sforza. 1995. Cultural Variation in Africa: Role of Mechanisms of Transmission and Adaptation. *Proceedings of the National Academy of Science* 92: 7585–89.

Harmon, M.J., T.L. Van Pool, R.D. Leonard, C.S. Van Pool, and L.A. Salter. (2006). Reconstructing the Flow of Information across Time and Space: A Phylogenetic Analysis of Ceramic Traditions from Prehispanic Western and Northern Mexico and the American Southwest. In C.P. Lipo, M.J. O'Brien, M. Collard, and S. Shennan (eds.), *Mapping Our Ancestors: Phylogenetic Approaches in Anthropology and Prehistory*. New Brunswick, NJ: Aldine Transaction, 209–29.

Harris, P.L., and K.H. Corriveau 2011. Young Children's Selective Trust in Informants. *Philosophical Transactions of the Royal Society* B 366: 1179–87.

Heggarty, P., W. Maguire, and A. McMahon. 2010. Splits or waves? Trees or webs? How divergence measures and network analysis can unravel language histories. *Philosophical Transactions of the Royal Society* B 365: 3829–43.

Heizer, Robert. F. (ed.). 1978. *California: Handbook of North American Indians*. Vol. 8. William C. Sturtevant, gen. ed. Washington, DC: Smithsonian Institution Press.

Heizer, R.F., and A.B. Elsasser. 1978. *The Natural World of the California Indians*. Berkeley: University of California Press.

Hennig, W. 1966. *Phylogenetic Systematics*. Urbana: University of Illinois Press.

Henrich, J. 2004. Demography and Cultural Evolution: How Adaptive Cultural Processes Can Produce Maladaptive Losses—the Tasmanian Case. *American Antiquity* 69 (2): 197–214.

Henrich, J., and F.J. Gil-White 2001. The Evolution of Prestige: Freely Conferred Deference as a Mechanism for Enhancing the Benefits of Cultural Transmission. *Evolution and Human Behavior* 22:165–96.

Henrich, J., and R. McElreath. 2003. The Evolution of Cultural Evolution. *Evolutionary Anthropology*. 12:123–35.

———. (2007). Dual Inheritance Theory: The Evolution of Human Cultural Capacities and Cultural Evolution. In R. Dunbar and L. Barrett (eds.), *Oxford Handbook of Evolutionary Psychology* Oxford: Oxford University Press, 555–70.

Herbich, I., and M. Dietler. 2008. The Long Arm of the Mother-in-Law: Learning, Postmarital Resocialization of Women, and Material Culture Style. In M. Stark, B. Bowser, and L. Horne (eds.), *Cultural Transmission and Material Culture Breaking Down Boundaries*. Tucson: University of Arizona Press, 223-44.

Hewlett, B., H.N. Fouts, A.H. Boyette, and B.L. Hewlett. 2011. Social Learning among Congo Basin Hunter-Gatherers. *Philosophical Transactions of the Royal Society* B 366: 116878.

Hildebrandt, W. R., and K. Carpenter. 2006. California Animals. In D.H. Ubelaker (vol. ed.). 2006. *Handbook of North American Indians*. Vol. 3. William C. Sturtevant, gen. ed. Washington, DC: Smithsonian Institution Press, 284–91.

Hill-Tout, C. 1978. *The Salish People*. Vols. I, II, III, IV. Vancouver: Talonbooks.

Hodder, I. 1982. *Symbols in Action: Ethnoarchaeological Studies of Material Culture*. Cambridge: Cambridge University Press.

———. 1986. *Reading the Past*. Cambridge University Press, Cambridge.

Hoenigswald, H.M., and L.F.Wiener (eds.). *Biological Metaphor and Cladistic Classification*. Philadelphia: University of Pennsylvania Press, 227–42.

Holden, C., and S.J. Shennan. 2005 Introduction to Part 1: How Treelike Is Cultural Evolution? In R. Mace, C. Holden, and S.J. Shennan (eds.), *The Evolution of Cultural Diversity: A Phylogenetic Approach*. London: University College London Press, 13–30.

Hornborg, A. 2005. Ethnogenesis, Regional Integration, and Ecology in Prehistoric Amazonia. *Current Anthropology* 46: 589–620.

Hoppitt, W., and Kevin N. Laland. 2013. *Social Learning: An Introduction to Mechanisms, Methods, and Models*. Princeton: Princeton University Press.

Hosfield, R. 2009. Modes of Transmission and Material Culture Patterns in Craft Skills. In S.J. Shennan (ed.), *Pattern and Process in Cultural Evolution*. Berkeley: University of California Press, 45–60.

Humle, T., and N.E. Newton-Fisher. 2013. Culture in Non-Human Primates. In R. Ellen, S. Lycett, and S. Johns (eds.), *Understanding Cultural Transmission: A Critical Anthropological Synthesis*. Oxford and New York: Berghahn.

Husan, D.H., and D. Bryant. 2004. SplitsTree 4beta10.

———. 2006. Application of Phylogenetic Networks in Evolutionary Studies. *Molecular Biology and Evolution* 23: 254–67.

Huxley, J. (ed.). 1940. *The New Systematics*. Oxford: Clarendon Press.

———. 1942. *Evolution: The Modern Synthesis*. London: Allen and Unwin.

Ingold, T. 2000. *The Perception of the Environment: Essays in Livelihood, Dwelling and Skill*. London: Routledge.

———. 2007. The Trouble with "Evolutionary Biology." *Anthropology Today* 23: 13–17.

Jordan, P. 2001. Cultural Landscapes and Colonial History: Siberian Khanty Settlements of the Sacred, the Living and the dead. *Landscapes* 2 (2): 83–105.

———. 2003. *Material Culture and Sacred Landscape: The Anthropology of the Siberian Khanty*. New York: Rowman and Littlefield.

———. 2006. Analogy. In G. Warren and C. Conneller (eds.), *Reconstructing the British and Irish Mesolithic*. Oxford: Oxbow, 83–100.

———. 2007. Continuity and Change in Different Domains of Culture: An Emerging Approach to Understanding Diversity in Technological Traditions. In T.A Kohler, and S.E. van der Leeuw (eds.), *The Model-Based Archaeology of Socionatural Systems*. Santa Fe, NM: School for Advanced Research Press, 13–39.

————. 2009. Linking Pattern to Process in Cultural Evolution: Explaining Material Culture Diversity among the Northern Khanty of Northwest Siberia. In S.J. Shennan (ed.), *Pattern and Process in Cultural Evolution*. Berkeley: University of California Press, 61–83.

————. 2011a. Seasonal Mobility and Sacred Landscape Geography among Northern Hunter-Gatherers. In D. Anderson (ed.), *The 1926/27 Soviet Polar Census Expeditions: Identity, Ethnography and Demography of Siberian Peoples*. New York and Oxford: Berghahn, 33–66.

————. 2011b. Landscape and Culture in Northern Eurasia: An Introduction. In P. Jordan (ed.), *Landscape and Culture in Northern Eurasia*. London: University College London Institute of Archaeology Publications, 17–45.

————. 2011c. Material Culture Perspectives on the Worldview of Northern Hunter-Gatherers. In Aubrey Cannon (ed.), *Structured Worlds: The Archaeology of Hunter-Gatherer Thought and Action*. Sheffield, UK: Equinox, 11–31.

————. 2014a. Technology as Human Social Tradition: Trait-Based Datasets of Hunter-Gatherer Material Culture (NW Siberia, Northwest Coast, Northern California). [doi:10.5284/1026780 (Archaeological Data Service Archive-1734-1)]

————. 2014b. Technology as Human Social Tradition: Trait-Based Datasets of Hunter-Gatherer Material Culture (NW Siberia, Northwest Coast, Northern California). (Data Paper). Internet Archaeology. Council for British Archaeology.

Jordan, P. and V. Cummings. 2014. Analytical Frames of Reference in Hunter-Gatherer Research. In V. Cummings, P. Jordan, and M. Zvelebil (eds.), *The Oxford Handbook of the Archaeology and Anthropology of Hunter-Gatherers*. Oxford: Oxford University Press, 33–42.

Jordan, P., and A. Filtchenko. 2005. Continuity and Change in Eastern Khanty Language and Worldview. In E. Kasten (ed.), *Rebuilding Identities in Post-Soviet Siberia*. Berlin: Dietrich Reimer, 63–88.

Jordan, P., and T. Mace. 2006. Tracking Culture-Historical Lineages: Can Descent with Modification Be Linked with Association by Descent? In C.P. Lipo, M.J. O'Brien, S.J. Shennan, and M. Collard (eds.), *Mapping Our Ancestors: Phylogenetic Methods in Anthropology and Prehistory*. New Brunswick, NJ: Aldine Transaction, 53–63.

————. 2008. "Gendered" Technology, Kinship and Cultural Transmission among Salish-Speaking Communities on the Pacific Northwest Coast: A Preliminary Investigation. In M. Stark, B. Bowser, and L. Horne (eds.), *Cultural Transmission and Material Culture Breaking Down Boundaries*. Tucson: University of Arizona Press, 34–62.

Jordan, P., and S. O'Neill. 2010. Untangling Cultural Inheritance: Language Diversity and Long-House Architecture on the Pacific Northwest Coast. In J. Steele, P. Jordan, and E. Cochrane (guest eds.), Cultural and Linguistic Diversity: Evolutionary Approaches. Themed Issue. *Philosophical Transactions of the Royal Society* B 365: 3875–88.

Jordan, P., and S.J. Shennan, 2003. Cultural Transmission, Language, and Basketry Traditions amongst the California Indians. *Anthropological Archaeology* 22: 42–74.

———. 2005 Cultural Transmission in Indigenous California. In R. Mace, C.J. Holden, and S. Shennan (eds.), *The Evolution of Cultural Diversity: A Phylogenetic Approach*. London: University College London Press, 165–98.

———. 2009. Diversity in Hunter-Gatherer Technological Traditions: Mapping Trajectories of Cultural "Descent with Modification" in Northeast California. *Journal of Anthropological Archaeology* 28 (3): 342–65.

Jorgensen, J.G. 1980. *Western Indians: Comparative Environments, Languages, and Cultures of 172 Western American Indian Tribes*. San Francisco: W.H. Freeman and Company.

Kelly, K.M. 2002. Population. In J.P. Hart and J.E. Terrell (eds.), *Darwin and Archaeology: A Handbook of Key Concepts*. Westport, CT: Bergen and Garvey, 243–56.

Kelly, R.L. 1995. *The Foraging Spectrum: Diversity in Hunter-Gatherer Lifeways*. Washington, DC: Smithsonian Institution Press.

———. 2013. *The Lifeways of Hunter-Gatherers: The Foraging Spectrum*. Cambridge: Cambridge University Press.

Kennedy, D.I.D., and R.T. Bouchard. 1990. Northern Coast Salish. In W. Suttles (ed.), *Handbook of North American Indians*. Vol. 7. William C. Sturtevant, gen. ed. Washington, DC: Smithsonian Institution Press, 441–52.

Kennedy, M.R., B.R. Holland, R.D. Gray, and H.G. Spencer. 2005. Untangling long Branches: Identifying Conflicting Phylogenetic Signals Using Spectral Analysis, NeighborNet and Consensus Networks. *Systematic Biology* 54: 620–33.

Killick, D. 2004. Social Constructionist Approaches to the Study of Technology. *World Archaeology* 36 (4): 571–78.

Kishino, H., and M. Hasegawa. 1989. Evaluation of Maximum Likelihood Estimate of the Evolutionary Tree Topologies from DNA Sequence Data, and the Branching Order in Hominoidea. *Molecular Evolution* 29: 170–79.

Kitching, I.J., P.L. Forey, C.J. Humphries, and D.M. Williams. 1998. *Cladistics: The Theory and Practice of Parsimony Analysis*. Oxford: Oxford University Press.

Klement'ev, E.I., and N.V. Shlygina. 2003. *Pribaltiisko-Finskie Narody Rossii*. Moscow: Nauka.

Kline, M.A., and R., Boyd, 2010. Population Size Predicts Technological Complexity in Oceania. *Proceedings of the Royal Society* B. doiB (2010) 277, 2559–2564.

Kohler, T.A., S. Van Buskirk, and S. Ruscavage-Barz, 2004. Vessels and Villages: Evidence for Conformist Transmission in Early Village Aggregations on the Pajarito Palteau, New Mexico. *Journal of Anthropological Archaeology* 23: 100–118.

Kroeber, A.L. 1905. Basket Designs of the Indians of Northwestern California. *University of California Publications in American Archaeology and Ethnology* 2 (4):102–64.

———. 1925. *Handbook of the Indians of California*. Smithsonian Institution Bureau of American Ethnology. Bulletin 78. Washington, DC: Government Printing Office.

———. 1932. The Patwin and Their Neighbours. *University of California Publications in American Archaeology and Enthnology* 29: 253–423.

————. 1939a. *Cultural and Natural Areas of Native North America*. Berkeley: University of California Press.

————. 1939b. Statistical Note. In H.G. Barnett, Culture Element Distributions: IX Gulf of Georgia Salish. *University of California Anthropological Records* 1 (5): 226.

————. 1939c. Culture Element Distributions XI: Tribes Surveyed. *University of California Anthropological Records* 1 (7): 435–40.

————. 1948. *Anthropology: race, Language, Culture, Psychology, Pre-history*. New York: Harcourt, Brace.

Kroeber, A. L., and S. A. Barrett, 1960. Fishing among the Indians of Northwestern California. *University of California Anthropological Records* 21:1.

Kroeber, A. L., and F.W. Gifford. 1949. World Renewal: A Cult System of Native Northwest California. *University of California Anthropological Records* 13: 1–155.

Kroeber, A.L. and Kluckhohn, C. 1952. Culture: A Critical Review of Concepts and Definitions. *Papers of the Peabody Museum of American Archaeology and Ethnology* 4: 41–72.

Krützen, M., J. Mann, M.R. Heithaus, R.C. Connor, L. Bejder, and W.B. Sherwin. 2005. Cultural Transmission of Tool Use in Bottlenose Dolphins. *Proceedings of the National Academy of Sciences of the United States of America* 102: 8939–43.

Kulemzin, V.M., and N.V. Lukina. 1977. *Vasiugansko-vakhovskie khanty v kontse XIX—nachale XX vv.* Tomsk: Tomsk University Press.

————. 1992. *Znakom'tes': Khanty*. Novosibirsk: Nauka.

Laland, K.N., et al. 2013. What Animals Other Than Primates Can Tell Us about Cultural Transmission in Humans? In R. Ellen, S.J. Lycett, and S.E. Johns (eds.), *Cultural Transmission in Anthropology: A Critical Synthesis*. New York and Oxford: Berghahn, 55–79.

Lane, P.J. 2014. Hunter-Gatherer-Fishers, Ethnoarchaeology and Analogical Reasoning. In V. Cummings, P. Jordan, and M. Zvelebil (eds.), *The Oxford Handbook of the Archaeology and Anthropology of Hunter-Gatherers*. Oxford: Oxford University Press, 104–50.

Lapina, M.A. 1998. *Etika i etiket khantov*. Tomsk: Tomsk University Press.

Larsen, A.W. 2011. Evolution of Polynesian Bark Cloth and Factors Influencing Cultural Change. *Journal of Anthropological Archaeology* 30: 116–34.

Lee, S., and T. Hasegawa. 2011. Bayesian Phylogenetic Analysis Supports an Agricultural Origin of Japonic Languages. *Proceedings of the Royal Society B*. doi:10.1098/rspb.2011.0518.

Lemmonier, Pierre. (ed.) 1993. *Technological Choices: Transformations in Material Culture since the Neolithic*. London: Routledge.

Leroi-Gourhan, A. 1993. *Gestures and Speech*. Cambridge, MA: MIT Press.

Levin, Maksim G., and L.P. Potapov. 1961. *Istoriko-etnograficheskii atlas Sibiri*. Moscow and Leningrad: Academy of Sciences of the USSR.

Lewis, H.M., and K. Laland. 2012. Transmission Fidelity Is the Key to the Build-Up of Cumulative Culture. *Philosophical Transactions of the Royal Society B* 367: 2171–80.

Lipo C.P., M.E. Madsen, R.C. Dunnell, and T.L. Hunt. 1997. Population Structure, Cultural Transmission and Frequency Seriation. *Journal of Anthropological Archaeology* 16: 301–34.

Lipo, C.P., M.J. O'Brien, S.J. Shennan, and M. Collard. (eds.). 2006. *Mapping Our Ancestors: Phylogenetic Methods in Anthropology and Prehistory*. New Brunswick, NJ: and London: Aldine Transaction.

Lukina, N.V. (1966). *Sredstva peredvezheniia Narymskikh Sel'kupov. Uchenye Zapiski (Tomskii Gosudarstvennyi Universitet)* 60: 108–18.

———. 1985. *Formirovanie material'noi kultury Khantov*. Tomsk: Izdatel'stvo Tomskogo Universiteta.

———. 2004. *Khanty ot vasiugan'i do zapoliar'ia: Istochniki po etnografii. Vol. I: vasiugan*. Tomsk: Tomsk University Press.

———. 2006. *Khanty ot vasiugan'i do zapoliar'ia: istochniki po etnografii. Vol. II, Book 2: sredniaia ob'. Vakh*. Tomsk: Tomsk University Press.

Lycett, S.J. (2007). Why Is There a Lack of Mode 3 Levallois Technologies in East Asia? A Phylogenetic Test of the Movius-Schick Hypothesis. *Journal of Anthropological Archaeology* 26 (4): 541–75.

———. 2008. Acheulean Variation and Selection: Does Handaxe Symmetry Fit Neutral Expectations? *Journal of Archaeological Science* 35: 2640–48.

———. 2009a. Understanding ancient Hominin Dispersals Using Artefactual Data: A Phylogeographic Analysis of Acheulean Handaxes. *PLoS ONE* 4 (10)/e7404: 1–6.

———. 2009b. Are Victoria West Cores "Proto-Levallois"? A Phylogenetic Assessment. *Journal of Human Evolution* 56 (2): 175–91.

———. 2010. The Importance of History in Definitions of "Culture": Implications from Phylogenetic Approaches to the Study of Social Learning in Chimpanzees. *Learning and Behavior* 38 (3): 252–64.

———. 2011. "Most Beautiful and Most Wonderful": Those Endless Stone Tool Forms. *Journal of Evolutionary Psychology* 9 (2): 143–71.

Lycett, S.J., and C.J. Norton. 2010. A Demographic Model for Palaeolithic technological Evolution: The Case of East Asia and the Movius Line. *Quaternary International* 211 (1): 55–65.

Lyman, R.L. 2008. Cultural Transmission in North American Anthropology and Archaeology, ca. 1895–1965. In M.J. O'Brien (ed.), *Cultural Transmission in Archaeology: Issues and Case-Studies*. Washington, DC: Society of American Archaeology, 10–20.

Lyman, R.L., and M.J. O'Brien. 2000. Measuring and Explaining Change in Artifact Variation with Clade Diversity Diagrams. *Journal of Anthropological Archaeology* 19: 39–74.

Lyman, R.L., M.J. O'Brien, and R.C. Dunnell. 1997. *The Rise and Fall of Culture History*. New York and London: Plenum.

Mace, R., and C.J. Holden. 2005. A Phylogenetic Approach to Cultural Evolution. *Trends in Ecology & Evolution* 20: 116–21.

Mace, R., C. Holden, and S.J. Shennan. (eds.). 2005. *The Evolution of Cultural Diversity: A Phylogenetic Approach*. London: University College London Press.

Maddison, D.R., and W.P. Maddison. 2000. *MacClade 4: Analysis of Phylogeny and Character Evolution*. Sunderland, MA: Sinauer.

Mantel, N. 1967. The Detection of Disease Clustering and a Generalized Regression Approach. *Cancer Research* 27: 209–20.

Martin, F.R. 1897. *Siberica: Ein Beitrag zur Kenntnis der Vorgeschichte und Kultur Sibirischer Völker.* Stockholm: Gustaf Chelius in Komission.

Martynova, E.P. 1995. *Obshchectvennoe ustroistvo v XVII-XIX vv.* In N.V. Lukina (ed.), *Istoriia i kul'tura Khantov.* Tomsk: Izdatel'stvo TGU, 77–121.

———. 1998. *Ocherki Istorii i Kul'tury Khantov.* Moscow: Russian Academy of Sciences Publishing House.

Maschner, H.D.G. 1991. Emergence of Cultural Complexity on the Northern Northwest Coast. *Antiquity* 65 (249): 924–34.

Mathews, L.J., J. Tehrani, F.M. Jordan, M. Collard, and C.L. Nunn. 2011. Testing for Divergent Transmission Histories among Cultural Characters: A Study Using Bayesian Phylogenetic Methods and Iranian Tribal Textile Data. April 29. doi: 10.1371/journal.pone.0014810.

Matson, R.G., 2003a. Introduction: The Northwest Coast in Perspective. In R.G. Matson, G. Coupland, and Q. Mackie (eds.), *Emerging from the Mist: Studies in Northwest Coast Culture History.* Vancouver: University of British Columbia Press, 1–11.

———. 2003b. The Coast Salish House: Lessons from Shingle Point, Valdes Island, British Columbia. In R.G. Matson, G. Coupland, and Q. Mackie (eds.), *Emerging from the Mist: Studies in Northwest Coast Culture History.* Vancouver: University of British Columbia Press, 76–104.

Matson, R.G., and G. Coupland. 1995. *The Prehistory of the Northwest Coast.* San Diego: Academic Press.

Mauss, M. 1979. The Notion of Body Techniques. In M. Mauss (ed.), *Sociology and Psychology.* London: Routledge and Keegan Paul, 97–123.

McEachern, S. 1998. Scale, Style and Cultural Variation: Technological Traditions in the Northern Mandara Mountains. In M.T. Stark (ed.), *The Archaeology of Social Boundaries.* Washington, DC: Smithsonian Institution Press, 107–31.

McGrew, W.C., 2004. *The Cultured Chimpanzee: Reflections on Cultural Primatology.* Cambridge: Cambridge University Press.

McMahon, A., and R. McMahon. 2005. *Language Classification by Numbers.* Oxford: Oxford University Press.

Mesoudi, A. 2011. *Cultural Evolution: How Darwinian Theory Can Explain Culture and Synthesize the Social Sciences.* Chicago: University of Chicago Press.

Mesoudi, A., and S.J. Lycett. 2009. Random Copying, Frequency Dependent Copying and Culture Change. *Evolution and Human Behaviour* 30: 41–48.

Mesoudi, A., and M.J. O'Brien. 2009. Placing Archaeology within a Unified Science of Cultural Evolution. In S.J. Shennan (ed.), *Pattern and Process in Cultural Evolution.* Berkeley: University of California Press, 21–32.

Mesoudi, A., A. Whiten, and K.N. Laland. 2004. Is Human Cultural Evolution Darwinian? Evidence Reviewed from the Perspective of *The Origin of Species. Evolution* 58: 1–11.

———. 2006. Towards a Unified Science of Cultural Evolution. *Behavioural and Brain Sciences* 29: 329–83.

Moore, J.H. 1994a. Ethnogenetic Theories of Human Evolution. *National Geographic Research and Exploration* 10: 10–23.

———. 1994b. Putting Anthropology Back Together Again: The Ethnogenetic Critique of Cladistic Theory. *American Anthropology* 96: 925–48.

———. 2001. Ethnogenetic Patterns in Native North America. In J.E. Terrell (ed.), *Archaeology, Language and History: Essays on Culture and Ethnicity*. Westport, CT: Bergin and Garvey, 30–56.

Myers, J.E. 1978. Cahto. In Robert F. Heizer (ed.), *California: Handbook of North American Indians*. Vol. 8. William C. Sturtevant, gen. ed. Washington, DC: Smithsonian Institution Press, 244–48.

Nabokov, P., and R. Easton. 1989. *Native American Architecture*. Oxford: Oxford University Press.

Neiman, F.D. 1995. Stylistic Variation in Evolutionary Perspective: Inferences from Decorative Diversity and Interassemblage Distance in Illinois Woodland ceramic Assemblages. *American Antiquity* 60 (1): 7–36.

Nunn, C.L., C. Arnold, L. Matthews, and M. Borgerhoff Mulder.2010. Simulating Trait Evolution for Cross-Cultural Comparison. *Philosophical Transactions of the Royal Society* B 365 (1559): 3807–19.

O'Brien, M.J. (ed.). 2008. *Cultural Transmission in Archaeology: Issues and Case-Studies*. Washington, DC: Society of American Archaeology.

O'Brien, M.J., M. Collard, B. Buchanon, and M.T. Boulanger. 2013. Trees, Thickets, or Something In Between? Recent Theoretical and Empirical Work in Cultural Phylogeny. *Israel Journal of Ecology and Evolution* 59(2): 45–61.

O'Brien, M.J., J. Darwent, and R.L. Lyman. 2001. Cladistics Is Useful for Reconstructing Archaeological Phylogenies: Palaeoindian Points from the Southeastern United States. *Journal of Archaeological Science* 28: 1115–36.

O'Brien, M.J., and R.L. Lyman. 2000. *Applying Evolutionary Archaeology: A Systematic Approach*. New York: Kluwer Academic/Plenum.

———. 2003a. Style, Function, Transmission; An Introduction. In M.J. O'Brien and R.L. Lyman (eds.), *Style, Function, Transmission*. Salt Lake City: University of Utah Press, 1–32.

———. 2003b. *Cladistics and Archaeology*. Salt Lake City: University of Utah Press.

O'Brien, M.J., R.L. Lyman, M. Collard, C.J. Holden, R.D. Gray, and S.J. Shennan. 2008. Transmission, Phylogenetics, and the Evolution of Cultural Diversity. In M.J. O'Brien (ed.), *Cultural Transmission and Archaeology: Issues and Case-Studies*. Washington, DC: Society for American Archaeology Press, 39–58.

O'Brien, M.J., R.L. Lyman, A. Mesoudi, and T.L. VanPool. 2010. Cultural Traits as Units of Analysis. *Philosophical Transactions of the Royal Society* B 365: 3797–806.

O'Brien, M.J., R.L. Lyman, Y. Saab, E. Saab, J. Darwent, and D.S. Glover. 2002. Two Issues in Archaeological Phylogenetics: Taxon Construction and Outgroup Selection. *Journal of Theoretical Biology* 215 (2–21): 133–50.

Olmstead, D.L., and O.C. Stewart. 1978. Achumawi. In R.F. Heizer (ed.), *California: Handbook of North American Indians*. Vol. 8. William C. Sturtevant, gen. ed. Washington, DC: Smithsonian Institution Press, 225–35.

Page, R. 1993. COMPONENT (version 2.0). London: Natural History Museum.
———. 2003. Introduction. In R. Page (ed.), *Tangled Trees: Phylogeny, Cospeciation and Coevolution*. Chicago: University of Chicago Press, 1–21.

Page, R. (ed.) 2003. *Tangled Trees: Phylogeny, Cospeciation and Coevolution*. Chicago Il: University of Chicago Press.

Page, R., and M. Charleston, 1998. Trees within Trees: Phylogeny and Historical Associations. *Tree* 13: 356–59.

Pagel, M., and R. Mace. 2004. The Cultural Wealth of Nations. *Nature* 428: 275–78.

Perevalova, E.V. 2004. *Severnye Khanty: Etnicheskaia istoriia*. Ekaterinburg: Urals Branch of the Russian Academy of Sciences.

Perevalova, E.V., and K.G. Karacharov. 2006. *Reka Agan i ee obitateli*. Ekaterinburg and Nizhnevartovsk: Urals Branch of the Russian Academy of Sciences (Studiia GRAFO).

Pilling, A.J. 1978. Yurok. In Robert F. Heizer (ed.), *California: Handbook of North American Indians*. Vol. 8. William C. Sturtevant, gen. ed. Washington, DC: Smithsonian Institution Press, 137–54.

Platnick, N.I., and D. Cameron, 1977. Cladistic Methods in Textual, Linguistic, and Phylogenetic Analysis. *Systematic Zoology* 26: 380–85.

Pluciennik, M. 2005. *Social Evolution*. London: Gerald Duckworth and Co.

Powell, A., S. Shennan, and M.G. Thomas. 2009. Late Pleistocene Demography and the Appearance of Modern Human Behavior. *Science* 324: 1298–301.

Powers, S. 1978. *Tribes of California*. Berkeley: University of California Press.

Pred, A. 1990. Context and Bodies in Flux: Some Comments on Space and Time in the Writings of Anthony Giddens. In J. Clark, C. Modgil, and S. Modgil (eds.), *Anthony Giddens: Consensus and Controversy*. London: Falmer, 117–29.

Prentiss, A.M. 2011. Special Issue on Material Cultural Evolution. *Evolution: Education and Outreach* 4: 374–78.

Prentiss, A.M., J.C. Chatters, M.J. Walsh, and R.R. Skelton. 2014. Cultural Macroevolution in the Pacific Northwest: A Phylogenetic Test of the Diversification and Decimation Model. *Journal of Archaeological Science* 41: 29–43.

Rexová, K., D. Frynta, and J. Zrzavý. 2003. Cladistic Analysis of Languages: Indo-European Classification Based on Lexicostatistical Data. *Cladistics* 19: 120–27.

Richerson, P.J., and R. Boyd. 2005. *Not By Genes Alone: How Culture Transformed Human Evolution*. Berkeley: University of California Press.

Ridley, M. 2004. *Evolution*, 3rd ed. Oxford: Blackwell.

Riede, F. 2009. Tangled Trees: Modelling Material Culture Evolution as Host-Parasite Co-speciation. In S.J. Shennan (ed.), *Pattern and Process in Cultural Evolution*. Berkeley: University of California Press, 45–60.

Ringe, D.A., T. Warnow, and A. Taylor. 2002. Indo-European and Computational Cladistics. *Philosophical Transactions of the Royal Society* 100: 58–129.

Rogers, D.S., and P.R. Ehrlich. 2008. Natural Selection and Cultural Rates of Change. *Proceedings of the National Academy of Sciences of the United States of America* 105 (9): 3416–20.

Rogers, D.S., M W. Feldman, and P.R.Ehrlich, 2009. Inferring Population Histories Using Cultural Data. *Proceedings of the Royal Society of London* B 276: 3835–43.

Rogers, E.M. 1962. *Diffusion of Innovations.* New York: Free Press.

Rorabaugh, A.N. 2012. Prestige, Transmission, and Barbed Bone and Antler Points in the Gulf of Georgia, Northwest Coast. *Journal of Contemporary Anthropology* 3 (1): 17–36.

Rowley-Conwy, P., and M. Zvelebil 1989. Saving It For Later: Storage by Prehistoric Hunter-Gatherers in Europe. In P. Halstead and J. O'Shea (eds.), *Bad Year Economics: Cultural Responses to Risk and Uncertainty.* Cambridge: Cambridge University Press, 40–57.

Shatilov, M.B. 1931. *Vakhovskie Ostiaki (Etnograficheskie Ocherki).* Tomsk: Izdanie Tomskogo Kraevogo Muzeia.

Shennan, S.J. 1996. Cultural Transmission and Cultural Change. In R. Preucel and I. Hodder (eds.), *Contemporary Archaeology in Theory.* Oxford: Blackwell, 282–96.

———. 1997 *Quantifying Archaeology.* Edinburgh: Edinburgh University Press.

———. 2000. Population, Culture History, and the Dynamics of Culture Change. *Current Anthropology* 4: 811–35.

———. 2001. Demography and Cultural Innovation: A Model and Its Implications for the Emergence of Modern Human Culture. *Cambridge Archaeological Journal* 11: 5–6.

———. 2002a. *Genes, Memes and Human History: Darwinian Archaeology and Cultural Evolution.* London: Thames and Hudson.

———. 2002b. Learning. In J.P. Hart and J.E. Terrell (eds.), *Darwin and Archaeology: A Handbook of Key Concepts.* Westport, CT: Bergen and Garvey, 183–99.

———. 2004. An Evolutionary Perspective on Agency in Archaeology. In A. Gardner (ed.), *Agency Uncovered.* London: University College London Press.

———. 2006. From Culture History to Cultural Evolution: An Archaeological Perspective on Social Information Transmission. In J.C.K. Wells, S. Strickland, and K. Laland (eds.), *Social Information Transmission and Human Biology.* New York: Taylor and Francis, 173–89.

———. 2008a. Canoes and Cultural Evolution. *Proceedings of the National Academy of Sciences of the United States of America* 105 (9): 3175–76.

———. 2008b. Evolution in Archaeology. *Annual Review of Anthropology* 37: 75–81.

———. 2009a. Pattern and Process in Cultural Evolution: An Introduction. In S.J. Shennan (ed.), *Pattern and Process in Cultural Evolution.* Berkeley: University of California Press, 1–18.

———. (ed.). 2009b. *Pattern and Process in Cultural Evolution.* Berkeley: University of California Press.

———. 2011. Descent with Modification and the Archaeological Record. *Philosophical Transactions of the Royal Society B* 366 1070–1079.

Shennan, S.J., and J. Steele. 1999. Cultural Learning in Hominids: A Behavioural Ecological Approach. In H.O. Box, and K.R. Gibson (eds.), *Mamma-*

lian Social Learning: Comparative and Ecological Perspectives. Cambridge: Cambridge University Press, 367-88.

Shennan, S J., and J.R. Wilkinson. 2001. Ceramic Style Change and Neutral Evolution: A Case Study from Neolithic Europe. American Antiquity 66: 577–93.

Shipley, W. 1978. Native Languages of California. In R.F. Heizer (ed.), California: Handbook of North American Indians. Vol. 8. William C. Sturtevant, gen. ed. Washington, DC: Smithsonian Institution Press, 80–90.

Sillar, B., 2000. Dung by Preference: The Choice of fuel as an Examplar of How Andean Pottery Production Is Embedded within Wider Technical, Social and Economic Practices. Archaeometry 42 (1): 43–60.

Sillar, B., and M. Tite, 2000. The Challenge of "Technological Choices" for Materials Science Approaches in Archaeology. Archaeometry 42 (1): 2–20.

Silver, S. 1978. Chimariko. In R.F. Heizer (ed.), California: Handbook of North American Indians. Vol. 8. William C. Sturtevant, gen. ed. Washington, DC: Smithsonian Institution Press, 205–10.

Sirelius, U.T. 1983. Reise zu den Ostjaken (Expeditions 1898 and 1899–1900). Helsinki: Finnisch-Ugrische Gesellschaft.

Smith, A.B. 1994. Systematics and the Fossil Record: Documenting Evolutionary Patterns. Oxford: Blackwell Science.

Sirina, A.A. 2002. Katangskie Evenki v XX veke: Rasselenie, organizatsiia sredy zhiznedeiatel'nosti. Moscow-Irkutsk: Izdatel'stvo Ottisk.

Smith, E.A. 2000. Three Styles in the Evolutionary Analysis of Human Behavior. In L. Cronk, N. Chagnon, and W. Irons (eds.), Adaptation and Human Behavior: An Anthropological Perspective. New York: Aldine de Gruyter, 27–46.

———. 2001. On the Co-evolution of Cultural, Linguistic and Biological Diversity. In L. Maffi (ed.), On Biocultural Diversity: Linking Language, Knowledge, and the Environment. Washington, DC: Smithsonian Institution Press, 95–117.

Smith, E.A. and B. Winterhalder (eds.). 1992. Evolutionary Ecology and Human Behavior. New York: Aldine de Gruyter.

Stark, M. 1998. Technical Choices and Social Boundaries in Material Culture Patterning: An Introduction. In M.T. Stark (ed.), The Archaeology of Social Boundaries. Washington, DC: Smithsonian Institution Press, 1–11.

Stark, M., B.J. Bowser, and L. Horne (eds.). 2008a. Cultural Transmission and Material Culture: Breaking Down Boundaries. Tucson: University of Arizona Press.

———. 2008b. Why Breaking Down Boundaries Matters for Archaeological Research on Learning and Cultural Transmission: An Introduction. In M. Stark, B.J. Bowser, and L. Horne (eds.), Cultural Transmission and Material Culture: Breaking down Boundaries. Tucson: University of Arizona Press, 1–16.

Steele, J., P. Jordan, and E. Cochrane (guest eds.). 2010. Cultural and Linguistic Diversity: Evolutionary Approaches. Themed Issue. Philosophical Transactions of the Royal Society B 365.

Steward, J. H. 1955. The Theory of Cultural Change: The Methodology of Multilinear Evolution. Urbana: University of Illinois Press.

Stewart, H. 1984. *Cedar: Tree of Life to the Northwest Coast Indians*. Vancouver: Douglas and McIntyre.

Suttles, W. 1990a. Introduction. In W. Suttles (vol. ed.), *Handbook of North American Indians*. Vol. 7. William C. Sturtevant, gen. ed. Washington, DC: Smithsonian Institution Press, 1–15.

———. 1990b. Central Coast Salish. In W. Suttles (vol. ed.), *Handbook of North American Indians*. Vol. 7. William C. Sturtevant, gen. ed. Washington, DC: Smithsonian Institution Press, 453–84.

———. 1991. The Shed-Roof House. In Robin K. Wright (ed.), *A Time of Gathering: Native Heritage in Washington State*. Seattle: University of Washington Press, 212–22.

Swadesh, M. 1950. Salish Internal Relationships. *International Journal of American Linguistics* 16: 157–67.

Swofford, D.L. 1998. *PAUP*: Phylogenetic Analysis Using Parsimony (*and Other Methods)* (version 4). Sunderland, MA: Sinauer.

Tehrani, J.J. 2006. The Role of Ethnography in the Science of Cultural Evolution Comment on Mesoudi, Whiten and Laland. *Behavioural and Brain Sciences* 29: 363–64.

Tehrani, J.J., and M. Collard. 2002. Investigating Cultural Evolution through Biological Phylogenetic Analyses of Turkmen Textiles. *Journal of Anthropological Archaeology* 21: 443–63.

———. 2009a. The Evolution of Material Culture Diversity among Iranian Tribal Populations. In S.J. Shennan (ed.), *Pattern and Process in Cultural Evolution*. Berkeley: University of California Press, 99–111.

———. 2009b. On the Relationship between Inter-Individual Cultural Transmission and Population-Level Cultural Diversity: A Case-Study of Weaving in Iranian Tribal Populations. *Evolution and Human Behaviour* 30: 286–300.

Tehrani, J.J., M. Collard, and S.J.Shennan. 2010. The Cophylogeny of Populations and Cultures: Reconstructing the Evolution of Iranian Tribal Craft Traditions Using Trees and Jungles. *Philosophical Transactions of the Royal Society* 365 (1559): 3865–74.

Tehrani, J.J., and M. Collard. 2013. Do Transmission Isolating Mechanisms (TRIMS) Influence Cultural Evolution? In R. Ellen, S.J. Lycett, and S.E. Johns (eds.), *Cultural Transmission in Anthropology: A Critical Synthesis*. New York and Oxford: Berghahn, 149-64.

Tehrani, J.J., and F. Riede. 2008. Towards an Archaeology of Pedagogy: Learning, Teaching and the Generation of Material Culture Traditions. *World Archaeology* 40 (3): 316–31.

Tëmkin, I., and N. Eldridge. 2007. Phylogenetics and Material Culture Evolution. *Current Anthropology* 48: 146–53.

Tereshkin, N.I. 1981. *Slovar' vostochno-khantyiskikh dialektov*. Leningrad, USSR: Nauka (Leningradskoe Otdelenie).

Terrell, J. 1987. Comment on "History, Phylogeny and Evolution in Polynesia," by P.V. Kirch and R.C. Green. *Current Anthropology* 28: 447–48.

———. 1988. History as a Family Tree, History as an Entangled Bank: Constructing Images and Interpretations of Prehistory in the South Pacific. *Antiquity* 62: 642–57.

———. 2001. Introduction. In J.E.Terrell (ed.), *Archaeology, Language, and History: Essays on Culture and Ethnicity*. Westport, CT: Bergin and Garvey, 1–10.

———. 2004. Review of "Cladistics and Archaeology" by M.J. O'Brien and R.L. Lyman. *Journal of Anthropological Research* 60: 303–5.

Terrell, J.E., T.L. Hunt, and C. Gosden. 1997. The Dimensions of Social Life in the Pacific: Human Diversity and the Myth of the Primitive Isolate. *Current Anthropology* 38: 155–95.

Terrell, J.E., K.M. Kelly, and P. Rainbird, 2001. Foregone Conclusions? In Search of "Papuans" and "Austronesians." *Current Anthropology* 42: 97–124.

Terrell, J.E., and P.J. Stewart 1996. The Paradox of Human Genetics at the End of the Twentieth Century. *Annual Review of Anthropology* 26: 13–33.

Thompson, L.C., and M.D. Kincade, 1990. Language. In W. Suttles (ed.), *Handbook of North American Indians*. Vol. 7. William C. Sturtevant, gen. ed. Washington, DC: Smithsonian Institution Press, 30–51.

Tilley, C., W. Keane, S. Küchler, M. Rowlands, and P. Spyer. (eds.). 2006. *Handbook of Material Culture*. London: Sage.

Tomasello, M., A.C. Kruger, and H.H. Ratner. 1993. Cultural Learning. *Behavioural and Brain Sciences* 16: 495–510.

Trigger, B.G. 2006. *A History of Archaeological Thought*. 2nd ed. Cambridge: Cambridge University Press.

Turner, N.J., and F. Hamersley-Chambers. 2006. Northwest Coast and Plateau Plants. In D.H. Ubelaker (vol. ed.) *Handbook of North American Indians*. Vol. 3. Washington, DC: Smithsonian Institution Press. 251–62.

Turov, M.G. 2008. *Evenki: Osnovyi problemy etnogeneza i etnicheskoi istorii*. Irkutsk: Izdatel'stvo Amtera.

Van Schaik, C.P., M. Ancrenaz, G. Borgen, B. Galdikas, C.D. Knott, I., Singleton, A. Suzuki, S.S. Utami, and M. Merrill. 2003. Orangutan Cultures and the Evolution of Material Culture. *Science* 299: 102–5.

Vizgalov, Iu. P. 2000. *Salymskii Krai*. Ekaterinburg: Tezis.

Voegelin, E. 1942. Culture Element Distributions, XX: Northeast California. *University of California Anthropological Records* 7 (2): vi, 47–252.

Wallace, E. 1978. Sexual Status and Role Differences. In R. F. Heizer (ed.), *California: Handbook of North American Indians*. Vol. 8. William C. Sturtevant, gen. ed. Washington, DC: Smithsonian Institution Press, 683–89.

Wallace, William. J. 1978. Hupa, Chilula and Whilkut. In R. F. Heizer (ed.), *California: Handbook of North American Indians*. Vol. 8. William C. Sturtevant, gen. ed. Washington, DC: Smithsonian Institution Press, 164–79.

Want, S.C., and P.L. Harris. 2002. How Do Children Ape? Applying Concepts from the Study of Non-human Primates to the Developmental Study of "Imitation" in Children. *Developmental Science* 5: 1–13.

Waterman, T.T. 1920. Yurok Geography. *University of California Publications in American Archaeology and Ethnology* XVI: 272 (reprinted 1993).

Watrous, L.E., and Q.D. Wheeler. 1981. The Outgroup Method of Character Analysis. *Systematic Zoology* 30: 1–11.

Welsch, R.L. 1987. Reply to Kirch and Green: "History, Phylogeny and Evolution in Polynesia." *Current Anthropology* 28: 448–50.

Welsch, R.L., and J.E. Terrell. 1994. Reply to Moore and Romney. *American Anthropology* 96: 392–96.

Welsch, R.L., J.E. Terrell, and J.A. Nadolski. 1992. Language and Culture on the North Coast of New Guinea. *American Anthropologist* 94: 568–600.

White, L.A. 1949. *The Science of Culture*. New York: Farrar, Strauss.

———. 1959. *The Evolution of Culture*. New York: McGraw-Hill.

Whiten, A. 2007. Pan African Culture: Memes and Genes in Wild Chimpanzees. *Proceedings of the National Academy of Sciences United States of America* 104: 17559–60.

———. 2010. A Coming of Age for Cultural Panthropology. In E.V. Lonsdorf, S.R. Ross, and T. Matsuzawa (eds.), *The Mind of the Chimpanzee: Ecological and Experimental Perspectives*. Chicago: University of Chicago Press, 87–100.

Whiten, A., E. Flynn, K. Brown, and T. Lee. 2006. Imitation of Hierarchical Action Structure by Young Children. *Developmental Science* 9: 574–82.

Whiten, A., J. Goodall, W.C. McGrew, T. Nishida, V. Reynolds, Y. Sugiyama, C.E.G. Tutin, R.W. Wrangham, and C. Boesch, 1999. Cultures in Chimpanzees. *Nature* 399: 682–85.

Whiten, A., V. Horner, and F.B.M.de Waal. 2005. Conformity to Cultural Norms of Tool Use in Chimpanzees. *Nature* 437: 737–40.

———. 2011. The Scope of Culture in Champanzees, Humans and Ancestral Apes. *Philosophical Transactions of the Royal Society* B 366: 997–1007.

Whiten, A., R.A. Hinde, K.N. Laland, and C.B. Stringer. 2011. Culture Evolves. *Philosophical Transactions of the Royal Society* B 366: 935–1187.

Wiget, A. (ed.). 2002a. *Ocherki istorii traditsionnogo zemlepol'sovania Khantov (materialy k atlasu)*. Ekaterinburg: Tezis.

Wiget, A. 2002b. Ekonomika i traditsionnoe zemlepol'zovanie vostochnykh Khantov. In: Wiget, A. (ed.), *Ocherki istorii traditsionnogo zemlepol'sovania Khantov*. Ekaterinburg: Tezis, 167-222.

Wiget, A., and O. Balalaeva. 2011. *Khanty: People of the Taiga: Surviving the Twentieth Century*. Fairbanks: University of Alaska Press.

Wilson, E.O. 1975. *Sociobiology: The New Synthesis*. Harvard: Belknap Press.

Winterhalder, B. 2001. The Behavioural Ecology of Hunter Gatherers. In C. Panter-Brick, R.H. Layton, and P. Rowley-Conwy(eds.), *Hunter-Gatherers: An Interdisciplinary Perspective*. Cambridge: Cambridge University Press, 12–38.

Winterhalder, B., and E.A. Smith. 2000. Analyzing Adaptive Strategies: Human Behavioral Ecology at Twenty-Five. *Evolutionary Anthropology* 9: 51–110.

Wissler, C.D. 1917. *The Relation of Nature to Man in Aboriginal America*. New York: McMurtie (reprinted 1938).

Index

Achomawi, 281, 312–13, 316

agency, human, 18, 23–24, 30, 31; continuity and change in social traditions and, 371–72, 273; cultural propagation and, 364; in microscale cultural evolution, 34

Atsugewi, 281, 312–13, 316, 317

Barnett, H.G.: on Coast Salish basketry and matting, 260, 263; on Coast Salish canoes, 251, 254–56; on Coast Salish houses, 243, 244–46, 270; on environment and ethnographic background of Coast Salish, 219, 222, 224, 225–27, 228, 229–30, 231, 232–33, 271–72

Barrett, S.A., 281, 289

basketry, Northeast California, 316–18; coherence in propagation of, 318, 324, 327, 329, 331, 337, 360, 365; congruence with language of, 318, 320; co-transmission analyses of, 337; cultural inheritance pattern of, 327; data set for, 336; effect of tribelet organization on, 265; Mantel matrix correlations with language and geography of, 337–38 381–82; network- and tree-based analyses of, 318–20, 336–37; photos of, 317; vertical transmission of designs for, 318, 327

basketry, Northwest California: cultural inheritance patterns of, 311; data sets

for, 332–33; as female craft, 300, 302; hybridization of styles of, 300, 302; Mantel matrix correlations with language and geography of, 333–34 379–80; network- and tree-based analyses of, 300, 301, 333; photos of, 299; no coherence in propagation of, 300, 310, 311, 351, 360; techniques and nomenclature for, 298; traditions of, 297, 300; vertical transmission of designs for, 300, 301

basketry and matting, Coast Salish, 259–62; coiled, 260; cultural inheritance pattern of, 268; data set for, 274; horizontal transmission of designs for, 259, 265, 268; Mantel matrix correlations with language and geography of, 375–78; network- and tree-base analyses of, 263, 264, 275; no coherence in propagation of, 263–65, 268, 275, 359, 361; not subject to conformity bias, 265; operational sequence for, 261; as women's task, 263–64

Bella Coola, 74, 76, 87

biased transmission. *See under* cultural transmission

Big Time festivals, 306, 335; as boundary defense mechanism, 311, 315, 329; difference from World Renewal ceremonies of, 295, 315, 365; ethnolinguistic association of, 304–5, 308;

coevolution of genes and culture, 19, 20, 88, 369–70

coherence: absent in Coast Salish basketry and matting, 263–65, 268, 275, 359, 361; absent in Iugan Khanty storage platforms, 137, 203, 206, 348; absent in Northeast California houses, 320–23, 324, 326, 327, 330, 348, 360; absent in Northwest California basketry, 300, 310, 311, 351, 360; absent in situations of postmarital moves into new communities of, 349–50; among multiple traditions, 42–49; in Coast Salish canoes, 256–59, 266, 268, 273, 350, 359, 361; in Coast Salish houses, 246, 249, 268, 269–70, 349, 350, 359, 361; as contingent historical process, 347–49, 352, 354, 357, 363–64; dependence on social scale of, 36, 59, 350–51, 356; factors that undermine, 40, 349–50, 354; in hypothetical example, 102, 103, 104; identification of highest scale of, 49; in Iugan Khanty canoes, 207, 349; in Iugan Khanty shrines, 149, 206; in Iugan Khanty skis, 166–69, 170, 172, 173–74, 176, 177, 180, 206, 214–15; in Iugan Khanty sledges, 207; lack in inherently pragmatic traditions of, 349, 363; meaning of, 35–36; in Northeast California basketry, 318, 324, 327, 329, 331, 337, 360, 365; in Northeast California ceremonial dress, 324, 326, 327, 330, 331, 360; in Northwest California ceremonial dress, 309, 310, 311, 350, 360, 365; in Northwest California houses, 304, 306, 310, 311, 331, 360; range of in Iugan Khanty technological traditions, 203–5, 206, 208; as research theme, 5, 61; as result of biased transmission of older design recipes, 348–49; as result of raw material constraints in Khanty canoes, 349; situations where it is found, 208, 349; transmission isolating mechanisms (TRIMs) and, 47, 310, 366

Collard, M. et al., 86, 355, 356

communication, to facilitate learning, 10–11

Comox, 228; basketry of, 275; canoes of, 254, 256, 273; houses of, 242, 244, 245–46, 270; linguistic affinities of, 235

COMPONENT 2.0, 90–91, 92: used on Coast Salish data, 271, 274, 276; used on hypothetical example, 103; used on

Northeast California data, 337, 339, 340; used on Northwest California data, 334, 335–36; used on Pacific Northwest Coast data, 93

conformity bias, 33, 39; of ceremonial dress in Northern California, 306, 323, 326; in craft traditions, 50–51

congruence, historical: in Coast Salish traditions, 248–49, 256–58; examined through models of Boyd et al., 358–62; identifying, 42–49, 89–96; in Northeast California traditions, 318, 320, 329–30, 360, 361–62; in Northwest California traditions, 360, 361; in Northwest Coast housing styles, 92–94; as research theme, 61; summary table of findings about, 359–60

consistency index (CI), 86

co-phylogenic analyses, 87–94

copying, 8, 9; children make choices about, 33; error, 22, 26, 30, 65; of Iugan Khanty ski designs, 168, 206; of Iugan Khanty sledge designs, 199; of Northern California house designs, 302, 327; 'rational,' 10; of Siberian canoe designs, 203–4, 207

Corriveau, K.H., 33

co-transmission analyses. See COMPONENT 2.0; Kishino-Hasegawa test

Cowichan, 223, 230, 254; canoes of, 273; houses of, 243, 246, 270; linguistic affinities of, 235, 272; winter villages of, 234

cultural diversity: high levels of, 51; in Northern California, 280–81, 285; related to modes of transmission, 25; as the result of cultural phylogeny, 44–45; science of, 49–50

cultural evolution: advantage of ethnographic studies of, 96–97; analogy with biological evolution of, 18, 19, 43, 49–50, 61, 369–70; archaeology allows investigation of microscale and macroscale of, 51; is cumulative, 8, 12, 31; decision-making forces in, 18, 26–29, 34; defining, 15–19; as descent with modification, 18–19, 53; distinguishing phylogenesis from hybridization in, 82–83; evolution of idea of, 15–17; forces in, 26–31; four models of, 367–68; future research needs of, 45–49; identifying congruence in, 42–49, 89–96; implication of descent with modification approach to, 18–19;

38–39, 41–42, 90–94; horizontal borrowing in, 41; method of comparing macroscale culture-evolutionary models with, 45, 47, 79, 81, 89, 102–4, as special kind of cultural evolution, 38–39, 50; transmission isolating mechanisms for, 44
learning, social: among Northeast California cultures, 318; among Pacific Northwest Coast cultures, 236, 238; among the Iugan Khanty, 122, 124, 155, 189, 198–201; children make choices about whom to copy during, 33; compared with individual, 1, 7, 15; conformity in, 8, 10; costs of, 31–32; cumulative culture and, 12, 13; early stages involves acquisition of older design recipes, 203, 344; as extended process, 11, 31–32; high-fidelity, 42–43, 190; importance of communication in, 10–11; main research questions about, 125–26; mechanisms of, 9–12; process of, 8; ratcheting in, 8, 10; reproduced like genetic information, 61–62, 67–68, 342; scaffolding of, 66; as two-stage process, 31–32, 111, 155, 203, 344–45; what gets passed on during? 13–14, 65–66. *See also* copying; imitation; inheritance; propagation; teaching; transmission
Levin, M.G., 152, 164, 176, 178, 179, 181, 192

Mace, T., 108, 269, 271
Maidu, 281; baskets of, 317, 319, 336–37; ceremonial dress of, 339; linguistic affinities of, 315–16, 318–19
Mansi, 165, 176
Mantel matrix correlations, 94–95; application to a hypothetical example, 102–4; of Coast Salish basketry and matting, 275; of Coast Salish houses, 271–73, 274, 275, 276; correlation tables for, 375–82; earlier application to Northern California basketry of, 95–96; of Northeast California basketry, 337–38; of Northeast California ceremonial dress, 324; of Northwest California basketry, 333–34
Martin, F.R., 163, 165
material culture, 1; defining populations in surveys of, 69–70; ethnoarchaeological studies of, 54–55; evolution of, 50–54; generating data sets to study, 70–71;

investigating variability in, 65–69; as "meaningfully constituted," 96; renewed interest in, 2–3; as a social tradition, 76–77, 341, 371. *See also* cultural traditions
Mattole, 281, 294, 295, 297
memes/memetic transfer, 13, 66, 371
mutation, 21, 22, 26, 30, 37–38

Nabokov, P., 243
Na-Dene, 280, 286, 287, 294–95, 297, 302
Nanaimo, 230, 234, 249, 254; canoes of, 273; cultural "gap" between Pentlach and, 233, 272; houses of, 243, 270; linguistic affinities of, 235, 272
NeighborNet algorithm, 82, 83
NeighborNet networks: for Coast Salish material culture, 247, 257, 264, 269–70, 273, 274–75; for hypothetical example, 102, 103; for Iugan Khanty and Siberian material culture, 139, 148, 166, 167, 170, 171, 175, 177, 182, 211–16; for Northeast California material culture, 322, 325, 336, 338, 339; for Northwest California material culture, 301, 305, 308, 319, 333, 334, 335; for Northwest Coast houses, 82–83
Nenets, 191
Nisenan, 281, 316, 336, 337, 339
Nongatl, 281, 287, 294, 297, 334
Northeast California: Boyd et al. Model 2 fits best for, 326, 330, 360; contrast with Northwest California of, 310–11; co-transmission analyses among craft traditions of, 340; ethnographic setting of, 311–15; ethnolinguistic communities of, 312, 315–16; historical congruence of multiple traditions in, 360, 361–62; propagation, coherence, and historical congruence of material culture traditions in, 329–30; transmission isolating mechanisms (TRIMs) in, 278, 327–28, 331; tribelet organization in, 313, 327. *See also* basketry, Northeast California; ceremonial dress, Northeast California; houses, Northeast California
Northern California: cultural and linguistic diversity in, 280–81; culture-evolution-ary studies in, 332; environment and adaptation in, 278, 280; location map of, 279; ownership in, 282, 283, 284; settlement and mobility in, 282; variation in social institutions of, 281–84